THE 50 GREATEST PLAYERS IN ST. LOUIS CARDINALS HISTORY

Robert W. Cohen

TAYLOR TRADE PUBLISHING

Lanham • Boulder • New York • London

Published by Taylor Trade Publishing
An imprint of The Rowman & Littlefield Publishing Group, Inc.
4501 Forbes Boulevard, Suite 200, Lanham, Maryland 20706
www.rowman.com

Unit A, Whitacre Mews, 26-34 Stannary Street, London SE11 4AB, United Kingdom

Distributed by NATIONAL BOOK NETWORK

British Library Cataloguing in Publication Information Available

The Library of Congress has cataloged the hardcover edition of this book as follows:

Cohen, Robert W.
The 50 greatest players in St. Louis Cardinals history / Robert W. Cohen.
pages cm.
Includes bibliographical references and index.
1. Baseball players—Missouri—St. Louis—Biography. 2. St. Louis Cardinals (Baseball team)—History. I. Title. II. Title: Fifty greatest players in St. Louis Cardinals history.
GV875.S3 C65 2013 2013015309
796.357/640977866—dc23

ISBN 978-1-63076-085-4 (pbk. : alk. paper)
ISBN 978-0-8108-9215-6 (cloth : alk. paper)
ISBN 978-0-8108-9216-3 (ebook)

∞™ The paper used in this publication meets the minimum requirements of American National Standard for Information Sciences—Permanence of Paper for Printed Library Materials, ANSI/NISO Z39.48-1992.

Printed in the United States of America

This book is dedicated to Stan Musial, the greatest Cardinal of them all, whose passing in January 2013 deeply saddened baseball fans everywhere.

CONTENTS

INTRODUCTION

THE CARDINAL LEGACY

Originally founded by St. Louis saloon and beer garden owner Chris Von der Ahe, who dubbed his new team the Brown Stockings (or Browns), the franchise known since 1900 as the St. Louis Cardinals first entered the world of professional baseball in 1882 as a charter member of the newly formed American Association (AA). Established, in part, to offer fans the beer and Sunday baseball forbidden by the older National League (NL), the AA lasted only ten seasons. During that time, however, the Browns developed into one of the circuit's most formidable squads. Led by hard-hitting outfielder Tip O'Neill and staff aces Bob Caruthers and Dave Foutz, the Browns captured four consecutive league championships from 1885 to 1888, before finishing second, third, and second again the next three seasons.

After the AA folded at the conclusion of the 1891 campaign, the NL absorbed the Browns, who struggled for most of the next three decades, even after changing their names to the Cardinals in 1900. The NL franchise situated in the city of St. Louis finished higher than fifth just three times between 1892 and 1920; however, with Branch Rickey running the team and Rogers Hornsby developing into the senior circuit's greatest player, the Cardinals gradually rose to prominence during the 1920s. The innovative Rickey helped the Cardinals pioneer baseball into a new era by building the team's farm system. Meanwhile, Hornsby established himself as the NL's premier hitter by winning six straight batting titles between 1920 and 1925, compiling a mark in excess of .400 on three separate occasions, and capturing two Triple Crowns.

With Hornsby leading the way, the Cardinals won their first NL pennant in 1926, after which they stunned the baseball world by defeating the heavily favored New York Yankees in seven games in the World Series. The Cardinals finished atop the NL standings again in 1928, although the Yankees gained a measure of revenge against them in the Fall Classic by sweeping their NL counterparts in four straight games.

St. Louis captured consecutive pennants in 1930 and 1931, losing to a powerful Philadelphia Athletics team in the 1930 World Series, before upsetting them in the following year's Fall Classic. After a two-year hiatus, a Cardinals club frequently referred to as "The Gas House Gang" for its ability to drive opposing teams crazy with its aggressive style of play returned to the World Series. The Redbirds ended up defeating the Detroit Tigers in a hotly-contested seven-game 1934 World Series behind the stellar pitching of thirty-game winner Dizzy Dean and the timely hitting of slugging outfielder Joe "Ducky" Medwick.

Although the New York Yankees created baseball's greatest dynasty during the 1920s and 1930s, the American public found itself gravitating more toward the Cardinals' Gas House Gang. A gritty, tenacious, battling bunch that wore dirty uniforms and quarreled amongst themselves as much as they fought with the opposition, the Cardinals represented the vast majority of Americans, who had to struggle to survive during the Great Depression. Furthermore, with the Dodgers and Giants still situated in New York, the Cardinals represented Major League Baseball's only link to the Midwest. All cities west of the Mississippi and south of the Mason-Dixon Line broadcasted Cardinals games over the radio, making the Redbirds "America's Team" in many ways.

Although the Cardinals failed to make another appearance in the Fall Classic until 1942, they ended up representing the senior circuit in four of the next five World Series, proving victorious in three of those years. Future Hall of Famers Stan Musial and Enos Slaughter led the Cardinals during their most successful period in franchise history. Unfortunately, the Redbirds maintained their level of dominance for just a brief period of time, coming up short in their bid to return to the World Series seventeen straight times between 1947 and 1963.

However, with the addition of speedster Lou Brock, the emergence of Bob Gibson as a truly great pitcher, and the continued outstanding play of veterans Ken Boyer, Bill White, and Curt Flood, the Cardinals rose to the top of the NL standings again in 1964, after which they helped put an end to the Yankee dynasty by defeating their American League counterparts in seven games in the World Series. The Dodgers represented the senior circuit in the Fall Classic in each of the next two seasons, but the Cardinals reclaimed the top spot in the NL standings in both 1967 and 1968, defeating Boston in seven games in the 1967 World Series, before losing to Detroit in seven games the following year.

The Cardinals subsequently entered their next period of mediocrity, failing to advance to the postseason again until 1982. Nevertheless, they made their return to postseason play a successful one, capturing the NL pennant by sweeping Atlanta in the National League Championship Series before edging out Milwaukee in seven games in the World Series. St. Louis returned to the Fall Classic in 1985 and 1987, only to lose in seven games both times, first to Kansas City, and then to Minnesota.

The Cardinals remained respectable the next decade and a half, earning a postseason berth in four of the next sixteen seasons. But they didn't make it back to the World Series again until 2004, when the Boston Red Sox ended eighty-six years of futility by sweeping them in four straight games in the Fall Classic. Led by slugging first baseman Albert Pujols, the Cardinals earned return trips to the World Series in 2006 and 2011, capturing their tenth and eleventh world championships by defeating Detroit and Texas, respectively.

The Cardinals' eleven World Series victories place them second only to the New York Yankees among major-league teams. Meanwhile, only the Giants and Dodgers, who have captured championship honors in the senior circuit twenty-three and twenty-one times, respectively, have won more than the eighteen NL pennants to which the Cardinals can lay claim.

In addition to the level of success the Cardinals have reached as a team throughout the years, a number of players have attained notable individual honors while wearing a Redbirds uniform. The Cardinals boast nineteen Most Valuable Player (MVP) winners—more than any other NL team. They have also featured three Triple Crown winners and twenty-two batting champions. Meanwhile, thirty-five members of the National Baseball Hall of Fame spent at least one full season playing in St. Louis.

FACTORS USED TO DETERMINE RANKINGS

It should come as no surprise that selecting the fifty greatest players ever to perform for a team with the rich history of the St. Louis Cardinals presented a difficult and daunting task. Even after I narrowed the field down to a mere fifty men, I found myself faced with the challenge of ranking the elite players that remained. Certainly, the names of Stan Musial, Bob Gibson, Lou Brock, Albert Pujols, and Rogers Hornsby would appear at, or near, the top of virtually everyone's list, although the order might vary somewhat from one person to the next. Several other outstanding performers have gained general recognition through the years as being among the greatest players ever to wear a Cardinals uniform. Ozzie Smith, Dizzy Dean, Enos Slaughter, Joe Medwick, and Jim Edmonds head the list of other Cardinal icons. But how does one differentiate between the defensive brilliance of Ozzie Smith and the offensive dominance of Rogers Hornsby, or the pitching greatness of Bob Gibson and the extraordinary hitting ability of Stan Musial? After initially deciding who to include on my list, I then needed to determine what criteria I should use to formulate my final rankings.

The first thing I decided to examine was the level of dominance a player attained during his time in St. Louis. How often did he lead the NL in some major offensive or pitching statistical category? How did he fare in the annual MVP and/or Cy Young voting? How many times did he make the All-Star Team?

I also needed to weigh the level of statistical compilation a player achieved while wearing a Redbirds uniform. Where does a batter rank among the all-time Cardinals in the major offensive categories? How high on the all-time list of Cardinal hurlers does a pitcher rank in wins, ERA, complete games, innings pitched, shutouts, and saves?

Of course, I also needed to consider the era in which the player performed when evaluating his overall numbers. For example, such modern-day starting pitchers as Chris Carpenter and Adam Wainwright are not likely to throw nearly as many complete games or shutouts as Dizzy Dean or Bob Gibson, who anchored the St. Louis starting rotation during the 1930s and 1960s, respectively. And slugging outfielder Jim Edmonds, who played for the Cardinals from 2000 to 2007, was likely to hit more home runs than someone like Ken Boyer, who had most of his finest seasons for the team during the pitching-dominated 1960s.

Other important factors I needed to consider were the overall contributions a player made to the success of the team; the degree to which he improved the fortunes of the ball club during his time in St. Louis; the manner in which he impacted the team, both on and off the field; and the degree to which he added to the Cardinal legacy of winning. While the number of championships the Cardinals won during a particular player's years with the ball club certainly entered into the equation, I chose not to deny a top performer his rightful place on the list if his years in St. Louis happened to coincide with a lack of overall success by the team. As a result, the names of such players as Ted Simmons and Joe Torre will appear in these rankings.

One other thing I should mention is that I only considered a player's performance while playing for the Cardinals when formulating my rankings. That being the case, the names of such great players as Steve Carlton and Orlando Cepeda, both of whom had most of their best years while playing for other teams, may appear lower on this list than one might expect.

And, finally, there is the case of Mark McGwire, who reached legendary status during his relatively short stay in St. Louis, captivating the nation with his pursuit of the single-season home run record in 1998, and thrilling fans everywhere with his mammoth home runs. Although McGwire certainly earned a spot in these rankings with his extraordinary slugging feats, I felt compelled to drop him a few notches since, despite his claims to the contrary, there can be no doubting that he accomplished many of the things he did through the use of performance-enhancing drugs.

Having established the guidelines to be used throughout this book, we are ready to take a look at the fifty greatest players in Cardinals history, starting with number one and working our way down to number fifty.

RANKINGS

1

STAN MUSIAL

Stan Musial, Rogers Hornsby, and Albert Pujols ended up vying for the number one spot in these rankings, with each man establishing himself throughout the course of his career as one of the greatest hitters in baseball history. Musial holds virtually every Cardinals batting record, while Hornsby is considered by some baseball historians to be the greatest right-handed hitter of all-time. Yet, Pujols also earned serious consideration for the top spot by posting monstrous numbers in his eleven years with the Cardinals. In fact, he likely would have supplanted Musial as the team's all-time leader in several offensive categories had he not left St. Louis via free agency at the conclusion of the 2011 campaign. In 4,650 fewer official at bats than Musial, Pujols hit only thirty fewer home runs. He also compiled an on-base plus slugging percentage (OPS) of 1.037, which exceeded "Stan the Man's" mark of .976 by sixty-one percentage points (although Pujols surpassed the league average in that category by only eleven more points than Musial). Another argument that can be waged on Pujols's behalf is that he won three National League (NL) Most Valuable Player (MVP) Awards while playing for the Cardinals. But Musial also earned league MVP honors three times, and his overall numbers surpass the figures compiled by Pujols by a fairly wide margin. In addition to knocking in 622 more runs and scoring 658 more times than Pujols, Stan the Man collected almost 1,600 more hits, amassed 270 more doubles, and accumulated almost 12 times as many triples (177 to 15). Musial also earned a spot on the NL All-Star Team in each of his final twenty seasons, won seven batting titles, and topped the senior circuit in a major offensive statistical category an amazing fifty-two times. Those are figures that even "Prince Albert" cannot approach.

Hornsby provided Musial with the only other serious challenge for the top spot here, reaching a level of dominance during his time in St. Louis that rivaled the one Stan the Man attained during the course of his twenty-two seasons as a Cardinal. Hornsby won six batting titles during his eleven full seasons in a Redbird uniform, captured two Triple Crowns, won a league MVP Award, and topped the senior circuit in a major offensive statistical category a total of forty-five times. Hornsby's .359 batting average as a member of the team surpasses Musial's mark of .331 by twenty-eight points. He also compiled slightly better on-base and slugging percentages than Musial. Of course, it must be remembered that Hornsby had his greatest seasons during the hitting-dominated 1920s.

In the end, however, Musial's total body of work proved to be too much for Hornsby to overcome. Traded by the Cardinals to the Giants at the conclusion of the 1926 campaign, Hornsby spent his last several seasons playing for other teams. As a result, Musial compiled almost twice as many at bats as "The Rajah" in a Redbirds uniform. Doing so enabled Stan the Man to hit almost 300 more home runs, drive in almost 900 more runs, score almost 900 more times, and amass 1,520 more hits than Hornsby as a Cardinal. Although some might wish to make a case for Hornsby being a greater hitter than Musial, he didn't accomplish as much during his time in St. Louis. That being the case, Musial would have to be considered the greatest Cardinals player ever.

The most beloved player in St. Louis Cardinals history, and one of the most popular players ever to don a major-league uniform, Stan Musial earned the respect and admiration of everyone in and around baseball during his twenty-two years in St. Louis. Musial's warm, unpretentious, and easygoing manner made him a favorite of teammates and opponents alike. Meanwhile, with the Cardinals situated farther west than any other major-league team until the Dodgers and Giants moved to California in 1958, Musial's self-effacing nature and greatness as a ballplayer enabled him to become a hero to virtually every young boy who lived beyond the banks of the Mississippi River during the 1940s and 1950s. One of baseball's truly great hitters, Musial held or shared 17 major-league records, 29 NL marks, and 9 All-Star Game records at the time of his retirement in 1963. In addition to his seven batting titles, which place him behind only Ty Cobb, Honus Wagner, and Tony Gwynn on the all-time list, Musial ranked as Major League Baseball's career leader in extra-base hits (1,377) and total bases (6,134) when he left the game. He also held NL career marks in hits (3,630), games played (3,026), doubles (725), and RBIs (1,951).

Born to Polish immigrants in Donora, Pennsylvania, on November 21, 1920, Stanislaw Franciszek Musial had his name formally changed to "Stanley Frank" when he enrolled in school. He began playing semiprofessional ball at the age of fifteen while still attending Donora High School, spending the vast majority of his time on the mound hoping to pursue a career as a pitcher. After signing an amateur free-agent contract with the Cardinals in 1938, the seventeen-year-old Musial found himself being used exclusively as a pitcher his first two years in the minors, before splitting his time between the mound and the outfield in his third season. However, any aspirations Musial had of eventually becoming a big-league pitcher came to an abrupt end during the latter stages of the 1940 campaign when he injured his left shoulder while making a diving catch in the outfield. After subsequently being convinced by his manager to move to the outfield full time, Musial peppered International League pitching throughout much of the following year, before finally being called up by the Cardinals on September 17, 1941.

Musial provided a brief glimpse into his ability to hit a baseball in the final two weeks of the 1941 campaign, posting a .426 batting average in his forty-seven official at bats and hitting his first home run in the major leagues. He became the Cardinals' starting left fielder the following year, batting .315 and scoring eighty-seven runs in his first full season, to help St. Louis capture the world championship. The young outfielder developed into a star in 1943, leading the Cardinals to their second straight NL pennant by topping the circuit in seven different offensive categories, including batting average (.357), hits (220), triples (20), and doubles (48), en route to earning NL MVP honors.

Musial had another outstanding year in 1944. He drove in 94 runs; finished second in the league with 112 runs scored and a .347 batting average; and topped the circuit with 51 doubles, 197 hits, a .440 on-base percentage, and a .549 slugging percentage. The Cardinals captured their third pennant and second world championship in his first three seasons with the team, with Musial finishing fourth in the league MVP voting.

Musial entered the U.S. Navy in January 1945, forcing him to miss the entire 1945 campaign; however, he returned to the Cardinals the following year and picked up right where he had left off. Splitting his time between first base and left field, Musial established new career highs in virtually every offensive category. In addition to hitting 16 home runs and driving in 103 runs, he led the league with 124 runs scored, 228 hits, 20 triples, 50 doubles, a .365 batting average, and a .587 slugging percentage. The Cardinals won their fourth NL pennant in five seasons and subsequently captured their third world championship during that time by defeating Ted Williams and the Boston Red Sox in a classic seven-game World Series highlighted by Enos Slaughter's "Mad Dash" around the bases in the Series finale. The baseball writers named Musial NL MVP for the second time at season's end.

Despite suffering through concurrent bouts with appendicitis and tonsillitis that caused his batting average to drop more than fifty points, to .312, Musial posted solid overall offensive numbers in 1947. Spending the entire year at first base, he hit 19 home runs, drove in 95 runs, and scored 113 others. After having both his appendix and tonsils removed during the off-season, Musial returned to left field in 1948 to have the greatest season of his career. Predominantly a line-drive hitter who compiled huge sums of doubles and triples by driving balls to both gaps his first several years in the league, Stan the Man changed his approach at the plate somewhat in 1948. He retained his unorthodox batting stance, in which he faced the opposing pitcher with his front shoulder, while crouching down low to make the strike zone smaller. He also continued to hold his hands back until the last possible instant so that he could maintain his balance in the batter's box and not commit to the pitcher's offering too soon. But the left-handed-hitting Musial perfected the art of using his famed "corkscrew" stance to turn on inside offerings and drive them into the right-field stands with greater frequency. Developing into more of a power threat, Musial ended up leading the league in nine different offensive categories. Although his career-high 39 home runs left him just one homer shy of capturing the Triple Crown, Musial topped the senior circuit with

131 RBIs, 135 runs scored, 230 hits, 18 triples, 46 doubles, a .376 batting average, a .450 on-base percentage, a .702 slugging percentage, and 429 total bases. By striking out only thirty-four times, he accomplished the rare feat of compiling more home runs than strikeouts. Musial's extraordinary performance earned him league MVP honors for the third time.

A true student of hitting, Musial described some of the techniques he used to become the NL's dominant hitter of his time, saying, "I consciously memorized the speed at which every pitcher in the league threw his fastball, curve, and slider; then, I'd pick up the speed of the ball in the first thirty feet of its flight and knew how it would move once it had crossed the plate."[1] He added, "I learned early to hit the curveball. From the beginning, I was a natural fastball hitter, so they started throwing me curves . . . so many of them that I sharpened up against the breaking ball."[2]

Musial contended that the most important aspects of hitting were relaxation and concentration, writing in his autobiography, *Stan Musial: "The Man's" Own Story*, that, "It's necessary to have mental tenacity at the plate, but to avoid physical tension. If I freed my mind of all distracting thoughts, I could tell what a pitch was going to be when it got about halfway to the plate."[3]

In a later interview, Musial told the *Sporting News* that he had the ability to tell when a pitcher intended to throw him a fastball—his favorite pitch to hit—stating, "I had a sixth sense. I don't know what else you call it, but it never deceived me."[4] Yet, Musial presented a far less scientific approach to hitting when he said, "You wait for a strike, then you knock the shit out of it."[5]

NL pitchers feared Musial more than any other hitter in the senior circuit. Hall of Fame hurler Warren Spahn suggested that, "Once Musial timed your fastball, your infielders were in jeopardy."[6] Dodger pitcher Preacher Roe discussed the technique he employed whenever he faced Musial, admitting, "I throw him four wide ones, then try to pick him off first base."[7]

In spite of the difficulties Musial presented to opposing pitchers whenever he stepped into the batter's box, they had a difficult time developing a personal dislike for him. Friendly, affable, good-natured, considerate, and modest, Musial was loved by everyone in the game, especially his teammates, whom he often entertained on road excursions by playing his harmonica. Musial had an endearing quality to his personality that few could resist, and he remained extremely humble throughout the years in spite of the excellence he displayed on the ball field.

Ty Cobb wrote an article for *Life* magazine that came out just before the start of the 1952 campaign in which he essentially stated that the modern ballplayer couldn't compare to the men who played the game during his time; however, he singled out Musial as an exception, proclaiming that he believed the St. Louis outfielder to be a "better player than Joe DiMaggio was in his prime."[8] Displaying the humility for which he became so well noted, Musial responded to the article by saying, "Cobb is baseball's greatest. I don't want to contradict him, but I can't say that I was ever as good as Joe DiMaggio."[9]

After winning the NL pennant in Musial's first four full seasons, the Cardinals never again finished atop the league standings while Stan the Man played for them. Nevertheless, Musial continued to excel for another decade as he went on to establish himself as one of the greatest hitters in baseball history. He had another fabulous season in 1949, placing among the league leaders with 36 home runs, 123 RBIs, 128 runs scored, and a .338 batting average, while topping the circuit in hits, triples, doubles, on-base percentage, and total bases. Musial subsequently captured the next three league batting titles, posting averages of .346, .355, and .336 in 1950, 1951, and 1952, respectively.

Although Musial compiled batting averages of .337 in 1953 and .330 in 1954, he failed to win the batting championship either year. Yet, he made baseball history on May 2, 1954, when he became the first major-league player to hit five home runs in a doubleheader. Musial concluded the campaign with 35 homers, 126 RBIs, and a league-leading 120 runs scored. In fact, even though Musial was not generally thought of as being a pure home run hitter, he averaged thirty-one long balls per season from 1948 to 1957.

After being named Sportsman of the Year by *Sports Illustrated* in 1957 for hitting 29 home runs, driving in 102 runs, and batting a league-leading .351 at the age of 36, Musial began to show a decline in offensive productivity the following year. Although he batted .337 in 1958, he hit only seventeen homers and knocked in just sixty-two runs. His batting average fell below .300 for the first time in his career the following year, and, when he failed to reach that mark in either of the next two seasons as well, speculation began that the Cardinal great's playing days were nearing an end. Musial, however, put an end to such talk when he rebounded in 1962 to finish third in the league with a .330 batting average, while also hitting nineteen home runs and driving in eighty-two runs. He played one more year before finally calling it quits at the conclusion of the 1963 campaign, at the age of forty-three.

Stan Musial ended his career with 475 home runs, 1,951 RBIs, 1,949 runs scored, a lifetime batting average of .331, a .417 on-base percentage, a .559 slugging percentage, 3,630 hits, 177 triples, and 725 doubles. He is the Cardinals' all-time leader in homers, RBIs, runs scored, hits, triples, doubles, total bases (6,134), bases on balls (1,599), games played (3,026), plate appearances (12,717), and official at bats (10,972). He also ranks among the team's all-time leaders in batting average, on-base percentage, and slugging percentage. An amazingly consistent performer, Musial compiled 1,815 hits at home during the course of his career, while also accumulating 1,815 hits on the road. He also struck out a total of only 696 times in his twenty-two big-league seasons. A solid outfielder as well, Musial compiled a total of thirty-one assists in 1943 and 1944, before splitting his time between left field and first base for much of the remainder of his career. In addition to being named NL MVP on three separate occasions, Musial finished second in the balloting four other times. Longtime Dodger announcer Vin Scully once said, "How good was Stan Musial? He was good enough to take your breath away."[10]

Immediately following Musial's retirement, President Lyndon Johnson named him director of the National Council on Physical Fitness. Musial later briefly served as Cardinals general manager, a position he held during the team's 1967 world championship season. The members of the Baseball Writers' Association of America (BBWAA) elected him to the National Baseball Hall of Fame in his first year of eligibility, in 1969.

Musial continued to grace us with his presence until January 19, 2013, when he passed away at the age of ninety-two, at his home in Ladue, a St. Louis suburb. Upon hearing of his passing, fellow Hall of

Famer Willie Mays said, "I never heard anybody say a bad word about him—ever."[11] Hall of Fame president Jeff Idelson stated, "Stan will be remembered in baseball annals as one of the pillars of our game. The mold broke with Stan. There will never be another like him."[12]

Meanwhile, Cardinals chairman William DeWitt Jr. expressed his sentiments by proclaiming, "We have lost the most beloved member of the Cardinals family."[13] In discussing Musial's legacy on ESPN's *Sports Century* several years earlier, Bob Costas noted, "He didn't hit a homer in his last at bat; he hit a single. He didn't hit in fifty-six straight games. He married his high school sweetheart and stayed married to her—never married a Marilyn Monroe. He didn't play with the sheer joy and style that goes alongside Willie Mays's name. None of those easy things are there to associate with Stan Musial. All Musial represents is more than two decades of sustained excellence and complete decency as a human being."[14]

CAREER HIGHLIGHTS

Best Season

Musial had a number of fabulous seasons, with his 1946, 1949, 1951, and 1954 campaigns ranking among his very best. In the first of those years, Stan the Man hit 16 homers; knocked in 103 runs; and led the league with a .365 batting average, 228 hits, 20 triples, 50 doubles, 124 runs scored, 366 total bases, and a .587 slugging percentage. Although Musial failed to win the batting title three years later, he finished second in the league with a mark of .338 and also placed near the top of the league rankings with 36 homers, 123 RBIs, 128 runs scored, and a .624 slugging percentage. Meanwhile, he topped the circuit with 207 hits, 13 triples, 41 doubles, 382 total bases, and a .438 on-base percentage. Musial posted comparable numbers in 1951 and 1954, leading the league with a .355 batting average, 124 runs scored, and 355 total bases in the first of those years, while batting .330, knocking in 126 runs, amassing 359 total bases, and topping the circuit with 120 runs scored and 41 doubles in the second of those campaigns.

Nevertheless, there can be no doubting that Musial had his best year in 1948, when he put together one of the greatest seasons in NL history. Musial led the league in nine different offensive categories and came within one home run of capturing the Triple Crown, en route to winning his third Most Valuable Player Award. Stan the Man established career highs with 39 home runs, 131 RBIs, 135 runs scored, 230 hits, 429 total bases, a .376 batting average, a .450 on-base percentage, and a .702 slugging percentage, while banging out 18 triples and 46 doubles. His mark of .376 left him forty-three points ahead of the runner-up in the league batting race, while his .702 slugging percentage gave him the largest margin of victory in that category since Rogers Hornsby's 1925 season.

Memorable Moments and Greatest Performances

Musial had several memorable hits and extraordinary days at the plate in his twenty-two seasons with the Cardinals. On September 22, 1948, he registered five hits in a game for the fourth time during the season, tying him with Ty Cobb (1922) for the most five-hit performances in a single year. He hit for the cycle at Brooklyn on July 24, 1949, and then put together the longest hitting streak of his career the following year, when he batted safely in thirty consecutive games before finally failing to get a hit on July 27.

An outstanding All-Star Game performer throughout his career, Musial won the 1955 Midsummer Classic for the NL when he led off the bottom of the twelfth inning with a home run that gave the senior circuit a 6–5 victory.

Among the many milestones Musial reached throughout the course of his career, he surpassed Mel Ott as the NL's all-time extra-base hits leader on August 12, 1956. Stan the Man subsequently collected the 3,000th hit of his career by doubling against the Cubs in a pinch-hitting role at Wrigley Field on May 13, 1958. The following season, Musial hit a game-winning home run on May 7 that made him the first major-league player ever to hit 400 homers and amass 3,000 hits. During the course of the 1962 campaign, he established himself as the NL's all-time leader in hits, RBIs, and runs scored. On July 8 of that same year, the forty-one-year-old Musial became the oldest player ever to hit three home runs in one game.

However, Musial saved arguably his greatest performance for the New York Giants, homering five times against the eventual world champions in the course of a May 2, 1954 doubleheader played at Busch Stadium in St. Louis. He hit two of the round-trippers against future Hall of Fame pitcher Hoyt Wilhelm. Musial's five homers on the day established a new major-league record that only Nate Colbert of the San Diego Padres has since been able to match.

Notable Achievements

Hit more than thirty home runs six times.

Knocked in more than 100 runs ten times, surpassing 120 RBIs on three occasions.

Scored more than 100 runs eleven times, topping 120 runs scored six times.

Batted over .340 on seven occasions, surpassing the .360 mark twice.

Collected more than 200 hits six times.

Topped twenty triples twice.

Surpassed fifty doubles three times, topping forty two-baggers on six other occasions.

Topped 400 total bases once (429 in 1948).

Compiled on-base percentage in excess of .440 four times.

Posted slugging percentage in excess of .600 on six occasions, topping the .700 mark once (.702 in 1948).

Led NL in batting average seven times, hits six times, doubles eight times, triples five times, total bases six times, runs scored five times, RBIs twice, on-base percentage six times, slugging percentage six times, and walks once.

Holds Cardinal career records for most home runs (475), RBIs (1,951), runs scored (1,949), hits (3,630), total bases (6,134), doubles (725), triples (177), extra-base hits (1,377), bases on balls (1,599), games played (3,026), plate appearances (12,717), and at bats (10,972).

One of only two players in major-league history to hit five home runs in one day.

Three-time NL MVP (1943, 1946, 1948).

Twelve-time *Sporting News* All-Star selection.

Two-time *Sporting News* Major League Player of the Year (1946, 1951).

Named *Sports Illustrated's* Sportsman of the Year in 1957.

Twenty-four-time NL All-Star (1943, 1944, 1946, 1947, 1948, 1949, 1950, 1951, 1952, 1953, 1954, 1955, 1956, 1957, 1958, 1959, 1960, 1961, 1962, 1963). Note: The All-Star Game was played twice a year from 1959 to 1962 to raise money for the players' pension funds, and Musial played in both games in those four years.

Four-time NL champion (1942, 1943, 1944, 1946).

Three-time world champion (1942, 1944, 1946).

Elected to Baseball Hall of Fame by members of BBWAA in 1969.

NOTES

1. "Stan Musial Quotes," *Baseball Almanac*, www.baseball-almanac.com/quotes/quomusl.shtml (accessed August 30, 2012).
2. "Stan Musial," *Answers*, www.answers.com/topic/stan-musial (accessed August 30, 2012).
3. "Stan Musial," www.answers.com/topic/stan-musial.
4. "Stan Musial," www.answers.com/topic/stan-musial.
5. "Stan Musial Quotes," www.baseball-almanac.com/quotes/quomusl.shtml.
6. Warren Spahn, quoted in "Stan Musial Quotes," www.baseball-almanac.com/quotes/quomusl.shtml.
7. Preacher Roe, quoted in "Stan Musial Quotes," www.baseball-almanac.com/quotes/quomusl.shtml.
8. Ty Cobb, "They Don't Play Baseball Any More," *Life*, XXXII (March 17, 1952).
9. "Stan Musial Quotes," www.baseball-almanac.com/quotes/quomusl.shtml.
10. Vin Scully, quoted in "Stan Musial Quotes," www.baseball-almanac.com/quotes/quomusl.shtml.
11. Willie Mays, quoted in Associated Press, "Hall of Famer Stan Musial Dies at 92," *Fox Sports*, January 19, 2013, http://msn.foxsports.com/mlb/story/stan-musial-the-man-dies-st-louis-cardinals-at-92-01913 (accessed January 20, 2013).
12. Jeff Idelson, quoted in Associated Press, "Hall of Famer Stan Musial Dies at 92," http://msn.foxsports.com/mlb/story/stan-musial-the-man-dies-st-louis-cardinals-at-92-01913.
13. William DeWitt Jr., quoted in Associated Press, "Hall of Famer Stan Musial Dies at 92," http://msn.foxsports.com/mlb/story/stan-musial-the-man-dies-st-louis-cardinals-at-92-01913.
14. Bob Costas, quoted in *Sports Century: Fifty Greatest Athletes—Stan Musial*, ESPN, 1999.

2

ROGERS HORNSBY

Albert Pujols provided Rogers Hornsby with stiff competition for the number two spot in these rankings, compiling numbers in his eleven years with the Cardinals that surpassed the figures Hornsby posted in most offensive categories in parts of thirteen seasons in St. Louis. In addition to hitting more than twice as many home runs as Hornsby as a member of the team (445 to 193), Pujols knocked in more runs, scored more times, collected more hits, amassed more doubles, and posted a higher slugging percentage. Hornsby holds his only statistical edges over Pujols in triples, batting average, and on-base percentage. Further strengthening the case for Pujols is the fact that he won three National League Most Valuable Player Awards while playing for the Cardinals, while Hornsby captured the trophy just once during his time in St. Louis; however, it must be considered that the senior circuit did not name a MVP from 1920 to 1923, which represented some of Hornsby's greatest years. The slugging second baseman likely would have laid claim to the honor at least another two or three times had the NL not placed a temporary moratorium on presenting the award. It ended up being an extremely close call, but Hornsby's two Triple Crowns and six straight seasons of leading the league in batting average, on-base percentage, and slugging percentage ultimately enabled him to edge out Pujols for the runner-up position.

The winner of seven batting championships and nine slugging titles in all, and the owner of the second highest career batting average in major-league history, Rogers Hornsby is considered by many baseball historians to be the greatest right-handed hitter ever to play the game. Easily the most prolific offensive second baseman of all time, Hornsby dominated the NL during the 1920s, much as Babe Ruth ruled the American League. Hornsby won two MVP Awards during the decade, captured seven batting titles, and led the league in on-base and slugging percentage eight times each. Perhaps his most remarkable achievement, however, is that he batted a combined .402 from 1921 to 1925.

Born in Winters, Texas, on April 27, 1896, Rogers Hornsby got his somewhat unusual first name from his mother Mary, whose maiden name was Rogers. Already competing against grown men by the time he reached fifteen years of age, Hornsby knew at a relatively early age that a career in the major leagues awaited him. He spent a few years playing semipro ball, before beginning his minor-league career in the Texas-Oakland League in 1914. A St. Louis Cardinals scout discovered Hornsby the following year, after which he purchased his contract for $500.

The slightly built Hornsby didn't prove to be much of a hitter in the minor leagues. Standing five feet, eleven inches tall and weighing only 155 pounds, he displayed little power at the plate, at the same time failing to hit for a particularly high batting average. Called up to St. Louis late in 1915, Hornsby batted only .246 in his fifty-seven official at bats; however, after observing Hornsby, Cardinals manager Miller Huggins suggested the young infielder put on some weight. Heeding his manager's advice, Hornsby spent the winter of 1915 working on his uncle's farm. After reporting to spring training in 1916 some 20 pounds heavier, Hornsby won a starting job in the St. Louis lineup. Splitting his time primarily between third base and shortstop, the twenty-year-old infielder batted .313 and finished among the league leaders in triples, on-base percentage, and slugging percentage.

Hornsby spent each of the next two seasons at shortstop for the Cardinals, performing somewhat erratically in the field but developing into one of the NL's better hitters. He finished second in the league in batting average and on-base percentage in 1917, while topping the circuit in triples, slugging percentage, and total bases. After his numbers fell off somewhat during the war-shortened 1918 campaign, Hornsby had another solid season in 1919. Splitting his time between all four infield positions, Hornsby placed among the league leaders in batting average, hits, total bases, on-base percentage, and slugging percentage.

Twenty-four years of age and an additional twenty pounds heavier by the start of the 1920 season, Hornsby had matured both physically and mentally. Ready for his breakout season, he moved to second base, a position he manned for the remainder of his career. Feeling more comfortable in the field, Hornsby began his onslaught on NL pitchers by hitting .370, en route to capturing the first of his six consecutive batting titles. He also placed among the league leaders with 20 triples and 96 runs scored, while topping the circuit with 94 RBIs, 218 hits, 44 doubles, 329 total bases, a .431 on-base percentage, and a .559 slugging percentage.

The NL began using a livelier ball in 1921, causing power numbers to increase dramatically throughout the senior circuit. Hornsby proved to be no exception, more than doubling his previous seasonal high in home runs by hitting twenty-one long balls. While Hornsby's 21 homers earned him a second-place finish in the league rankings, he topped the circuit with 126 RBIs, 131 runs scored, 18 triples, 44 doubles, 235 hits, a .397 batting average, 378 total bases, a .458 on-base percentage, and a .639 slugging percentage. He somehow managed to improve upon his performance the following year, leading the league in nine different offensive categories, en route to winning the Triple Crown for the first of two times. In addition to topping the circuit with 42 home runs, 152 RBIs, and a .401 batting average, the slugging second sacker finished first with 141 runs scored, 250 hits, 46 doubles, 450 total bases, a .459 on-base percentage, and a .722 slugging average.

Injuries limited Hornsby to 107 games in 1923, but he still managed to lead the league in batting for the fourth straight year with a mark of .384. Fully healthy again in 1924, Hornsby posted the highest single-season batting average of the modern era by hitting a remarkable .424. He also hit 25 home runs; drove in 94 runs; and led the league with 121 runs scored, 227 hits, 43 doubles, a .507 on-base percentage, and a .696 slugging percentage. All this came en route to finishing a close second to Dodger hurler Dazzy Vance in the MVP balloting. Hornsby claimed his first MVP trophy the following year, when he became the only player in NL history to win two Triple Crowns. In addition to topping the circuit with 39 home runs, 143

RBIs, and a .403 batting average, Hornsby led the league with a .489 on-base percentage, a .756 slugging percentage, and 381 total bases.

Hornsby's incredible success as a hitter could be attributed to a number of factors. In addition to possessing amazing natural ability, he employed a near-fanatical training regimen that included abstinence from smoking and drinking, as well as avoidance of reading and attending movies during the season for fear of ruining his batting eye. A perfectionist at the plate, Hornsby rarely swung at bad pitches, and he always stood in the far back corner of the batter's box and strode into the pitcher's delivery with a perfectly level swing. Opposing teams often tried to pitch him low and away, but his diagonal stride afforded him excellent plate coverage, enabling him to drive outside pitches to the opposite field with power. A remarkably consistent hitter, Hornsby posted lifetime batting averages of .359 at home and .358 on the road. He made such an impression on Ted Williams that "The Splendid Splinter" states in his autobiography, *My Turn at Bat*, that he considered Hornsby to be the greatest hitter for average and power in the history of baseball.[1] Williams adds in his book, *Ted Williams' Hit List*, "He (Hornsby) came very close to being the perfect hitter, if such a creature exists."[2]

Meanwhile, Frankie Frisch, for whom the Cardinals traded Hornsby at the conclusion of the 1926 campaign, commented, "He's (Hornsby's) the only guy I know who could hit .350 in the dark."[3] Hornsby's keen batting eye and overall greatness as a hitter earned him so much respect around baseball that legend has it umpire Bill Klem once told a rookie pitcher who complained to him he thought he had thrown Hornsby a strike, "Son, when you pitch a strike, Mr. Hornsby will let you know."[4]

An outstanding base runner as well, Hornsby possessed exceptional running speed, enabling him to frequently turn singles into doubles, and doubles into triples. In fact, Hornsby accumulated thirty inside-the-park home runs during the course of his career. Hall of Fame manager Al Lopez says of Hornsby in a January 8, 1963 article in the *Chicago American*, "he was one of the speediest men we ever had in baseball."[5] Long after Hornsby's playing career ended, he often found himself being compared to a young Mickey Mantle in terms of running speed. Hall of Fame third baseman Pie Traynor, who saw both men play, insisted that Hornsby would have beaten Mantle to first base from the right-hand batter's box.

While no one ever questioned Hornsby's greatness as a hitter, the second baseman has often been criticized throughout the years for his defense. Generally considered to be a mediocre fielder at best, Hornsby frequently struggled with pop-ups, committing as many as fifty-two errors while playing shortstop for the Cardinals in 1917. Still, in 1918, a reporter for the *Washington Post* described Hornsby as the "outstanding fielding shortstop in the western circuit of the National League and perhaps the finest fielding shortstop in the entire league."[6]

After moving to second base in 1920, Hornsby led the league in putouts, assists, and double plays. Meanwhile, Hall of Fame shortstop and manager Hughie Jennings describes him as one of the best-fielding second basemen in the game in an August 26, 1925 article in the *Los Angeles Times*.[7] Hornsby's average of 3.31 assists per game is the seventh highest of any second baseman in baseball history; therefore, the reviews on Hornsby's fielding prowess appear to be somewhat mixed.

Nevertheless, as much as Hornsby's fielding ability has come into question throughout the years, the quality of his character has perhaps been scrutinized even more closely. Most accounts of the time reveal Hornsby to be cold, contentious, heartless, and brutally frank. He only cared about winning, showing little or no compassion for anyone who happened to stand in his way. Hornsby once stated, "I've always played hard. If that's rough and tough, I can't help it. I don't believe there's any such thing as a good loser. I wouldn't sit down and play a game of cards with you right now without wanting to win. If I hadn't felt that way I wouldn't have got very far in baseball."[8] He added, "I've cheated, or someone on my team has cheated, in almost every single game I've been in."[9] Displaying the tremendous self-confidence and borderline arrogance that helped make him such a great hitter, Hornsby once proclaimed, "I don't like to sound egotistical, but every time I stepped up to the plate with a bat in my hands, I couldn't help but feel sorry for the pitcher."[10]

Meanwhile, sportswriter and baseball historian Lee Allen once discussed Hornsby's abrasive nature, saying, "He was frank to the point of being cruel and as subtle as a belch."[11] Another writer characterized

Hornsby as a "liturgy of hatred," while noted baseball writer Fred Lieb claimed that the Hall of Fame second baseman confessed to being a member of the Ku Klux Klan.

Hornsby's truculent manner helps to explain the nomadic existence he led during the second half of his career. After leading the Cardinals to the world championship in 1926 as the team's player-manager despite batting only .317, the star second baseman found himself traded to the Giants for Frankie Frisch by St. Louis owner Sam Breadon following a contract dispute between the two men that ended an increasingly contentious relationship. Hornsby had a big year for the Giants in 1927, hitting 26 home runs, driving in 125 runs, scoring 133 others, and batting .361. Nevertheless, New York dispatched him to Boston at season's end after he spent most of the year quarrelling with the Giants' equally belligerent manager, John McGraw. The second baseman had another outstanding season for the Braves in 1928, batting a league-leading .387, but he quickly wore out his welcome there as well. Hornsby joined the Chicago Cubs in 1929, leading his new team to the pennant and capturing league MVP honors for the second time in his career by hitting 39 homers, knocking in 149 runs, batting .380, collecting 229 hits, and topping the circuit with 156 runs scored, 409 total bases, and a .679 slugging percentage.

The 1929 campaign proved to be Hornsby's last as a full-time player. A broken leg kept him out of Chicago's lineup for all but forty-two games the following season, one in which he replaced Joe McCarthy as the team's manager. Serving as player-manager in 1931, the thirty-five-year-old Hornsby batted .331 and compiled a league-leading .421 on-base percentage in 100 games; however, after appearing in only nineteen games for the Cubs in 1932 as the result of a heel spur, Hornsby was fired as manager and subsequently traded back to his original team, the Cardinals. He split the 1933 season between the Cardinals and St. Louis Browns, ending his career with the Browns in 1937.

Rogers Hornsby retired from the game with 301 home runs, 1,584 RBIs, 1,579 runs scored, 2,930 hits, a .358 lifetime batting average, a magnificent .434 on-base percentage, and a .577 slugging percentage. Only Ty Cobb (.367) posted a higher lifetime batting average. In parts of 13 seasons with the Cardinals, Hornsby hit 193 home runs, knocked in 1,072 runs, scored 1,089 others, amassed 2,110 hits, collected 143 triples and 367 doubles, batted .359, compiled a .427 on-base percentage, and posted a .568 slugging percentage. He ranks among the Cardinals' all-time leaders in virtually every offensive category, holding franchise records for highest career batting average and on-base percentage among players with at least 2,000 plate appearances. He also ranks second to Stan Musial in triples. Meanwhile, Hornsby holds single-season team records for highest batting average (.424), on-base percentage (.507), and slugging percentage (.756), as well as most hits (250) and total bases (450). In fact, Hornsby posted the five highest single-season batting averages of any Cardinals player since 1900.

After his playing career ended, Hornsby had numerous stints as both a manager and scout; however, his autocratic style of managing and critical nature made it extremely difficult for him to relate to players. After serving briefly as a scout for the fledgling New York Mets in 1962, Hornsby died of a heart attack in 1963, shortly after undergoing cataract surgery.

In spite of Hornsby's contentious nature, his reputation as a truly great baseball player remains unsullied. While Stan Musial still reigned supreme in the city of St. Louis during the 1950s, a writer asked former Cardinals owner Sam Breadon if Stan the Man was his greatest player ever. The man who once feuded with Hornsby before finally trading him away to the Giants considered the question for a few moments before responding, "No, I couldn't say that. There was Hornsby."[12]

CARDINAL CAREER HIGHLIGHTS

Best Season

Hornsby performed magnificently for the Cardinals in 1921, 1922, 1924, and 1925, and any of those campaigns would have made a good choice for his best season. In the first of those years, Hornsby led the league in nine different offensive categories, including batting average (.397), RBIs (126), runs scored (131), and hits (235). He topped the senior circuit in eight categories in 1924, en route to posting a .424

batting average, which represents the highest mark compiled by any player in the "modern era." Hornsby had an absolutely fabulous year in 1925, earning NL MVP honors and winning the Triple Crown by leading the league with 39 home runs, 143 RBIs, and a .403 batting average. He also scored 133 runs, collected 203 hits, and topped the circuit with 381 total bases, a .489 on-base percentage, and a career-high .756 slugging percentage.

Nevertheless, most baseball historians consider Hornsby's 1922 campaign to be the finest of his career and, arguably, the greatest any NL player has ever turned in. "The Rajah" won the first of his two Triple Crowns by leading the league with a .401 batting average and a career-high forty-two homers and 152 RBIs. He also topped the circuit with 141 runs scored, 250 hits, 46 doubles, a .459 on-base percentage, a .722 slugging percentage, and a NL record 450 total bases. Hornsby finished nearly fifty points ahead of the league runner-up, Ray Grimes, in the batting race. Meanwhile, his forty-two homers doubled the amount posted by Philadelphia's Cy Williams, who finished second to him in that category. No other NL player has ever had a more dominant season.

Memorable Moments and Greatest Performances

Although Hornsby built his reputation primarily on his hitting, he tied a major-league record in 1917 by recording fourteen assists in a game at shortstop; however, as one might expect, Hornsby registered most of his greatest feats as a Cardinal at the plate. On July 20, 1922, he gave the Cardinals a 7–6 win over the Boston Braves by hitting a two-out, ninth-inning homer with two men on base. The blast was Hornsby's twenty-fifth round-tripper of the year, breaking Gavvy Cravath's previous twentieth-century single-season NL mark. Two weeks later, on August 5, Hornsby established a new all-time NL record by hitting his twenty-eighth homer of the campaign, surpassing in the process Ned Williamson, who homered twenty-seven times for Chicago in 1884.

On September 23, 1922, Hornsby became the first NL player to reach the forty-homer plateau when he hit a solo blast against the Giants during a 7–5 loss at New York's Polo Grounds. Just one week later, on October 1, Hornsby concluded his record-setting campaign by collecting three hits in five times at bat during a 7–1 victory over the Cubs. Hornsby's three safeties on the season's final day put him at .401 for the year, making him the first NL player since Ed Delahanty in 1899 to surpass the .400 mark, and the only player in major-league history to hit at least forty home runs and bat over .400 in the same season. Hornsby's magical 1922 campaign included a career-best thirty-three-game hitting streak, which lasted from August 13 through September 19.

Notable Achievements

- Hit more than thirty home runs twice.
- Knocked in more than 125 runs three times.
- Scored more than 120 runs four times.
- Batted over .400 three times, topping the .370 mark on three other occasions.
- Collected more than 200 hits five times.
- Surpassed twenty triples once.
- Topped forty doubles five times.
- Surpassed 400 total bases once.
- Compiled on-base percentage in excess of .500 once, surpassing the .450 mark four other times.
- Posted slugging percentage in excess of .700 twice.
- Led NL in batting average six times, on-base percentage six times, slugging percentage seven times, total bases six times, RBIs four times, runs scored three times, hits four times, doubles four times, home runs twice, triples twice, and bases on balls once.
- Only player in major-league history to hit more than forty home runs and bat over .400 in the same season.
- Holds twentieth-century single-season NL records for most total bases (450), highest batting average (.424), and highest slugging percentage (.756).
- Holds Cardinal single-season records for highest batting average (.424), highest on-base percentage (.507), highest slugging percentage (.756), most hits (250), and most total bases (450).

Holds Cardinal career records for highest batting average (.359) and on-base percentage (.427) of any player with at least 2,000 plate appearances.

NL MVP in 1925.

Two-time NL Triple Crown winner (1922, 1925).

Two-time *Sporting News* All-Star selection. Note: *Sporting News* made its first picks in 1925.

1926 NL champion.

1926 world champion.

Elected to Baseball Hall of Fame by members of the Baseball Writers' Association of America in 1942.

NOTES

1. Ted Williams, with John Underwood, *My Turn at Bat: The Story of My Life* (New York: Simon and Schuster, 196).
2. Ted Williams, with Jim Prime, *Ted Williams' Hit List* (Indianapolis, IN: Masters Press, 1996), 71.
3. Frankie Frisch, quoted in "Hornsby, Rogers," *National Baseball Hall of Fame and Museum*, www.baseballhall.org/hof/hornsby-rogers (accessed September 1, 2012).
4. Bill Klem, quoted in "Rogers Hornsby Quotes," *Baseball Almanac*, www.baseball-almanac.com/quotes/quohorn.shtml (accessed September 1, 2012).
5. Al Lopez, quoted in "Rogers Hornsby Quotes," www.baseball-almanac.com/quotes/quohorn.shtml.
6. "Rogers Hornsby Quotes," www.baseball-almanac.com/quotes/quohorn.shtml.
7. Hughie Jennings, quoted in *Los Angeles Times*, Auguest 26, 1925.
8. "Rogers Hornsby Quotes," www.baseball-almanac.com/quotes/quohorn.shtml.
9. "Rogers Hornsby Quotes," www.baseball-almanac.com/quotes/quohorn.shtml.
10. "Rogers Hornsby Quotes," www.baseball-almanac.com/quotes/quohorn.shtml.
11. Lee Allen, quoted in "Rogers Hornsby Quotes," www.baseball-almanac.com/quotes/quohorn.shtml.
12. Sam Breadon, quoted in Williams, *Ted Williams' Hit List*, 74.

3

ALBERT PUJOLS

One of the most prolific right-handed batters in baseball history, Albert Pujols attained a level of excellence in the course of his eleven seasons in St. Louis that only a few other players could even approach. Averaging more than forty home runs and just fewer than 121 RBIs per season during his time with the Cardinals, Pujols also posted a batting average of .328, en route to establishing himself as the only player in major-league history to hit more than 30 home runs, drive in more than 100 runs, and bat at least .300 in each of his first 10 seasons. Along the way, the man known as "The Machine" for the routine manner with which he consistently produces extraordinary offensive numbers year after year earned ten top-five finishes in the National League Most Valuable Player voting, winning the award three times. He also helped the Cardinals capture three NL pennants and two world championships.

Born in the Dominican Republic on January 16, 1980, Jose Alberto Pujols moved to the United States at the age of sixteen, after which he attended Fort Sage High School in Independence, Missouri. Pujols played college baseball for just one year before the Cardinals selected him in the thirteenth round with the 402nd overall pick of the 1999 Major League Baseball Draft. Ordinarily, a player with Pujols's ability would not have lasted nearly as long as he did; however, few teams expressed interest in him due to uncertainty about his age, his build, and which position he would eventually play.

After joining the Cardinals prior to the start of the 2001 campaign, the six-foot, three-inch, 230-pound Pujols spent his rookie season moving around the diamond, seeing a significant amount of playing time at first base, third base, right field, and left field. Wherever the team put him in the field, however, he managed to produce at the plate, unanimously winning NL Rookie of the Year honors by finishing among the league leaders with 37 home runs, 130 RBIs, 112 runs scored, 47 doubles, and a .329 batting average. Pujols's fabulous rookie campaign included a forty-eight consecutive game on-base streak that lasted from July 28 to September 22.

Continuing to split his time between the infield and outfield his second year in the league, Pujols again posted exceptional offensive numbers, earning a second-place finish to Barry Bonds in the NL MVP balloting by hitting 34 homers, driving in 127 runs, scoring 118 others, and batting .314. Splitting the 2003 campaign between left field and first base, Pujols knocked in 124 runs and established new career highs by hitting 43 home runs and leading the league with 137 runs scored, 212 hits, 51 doubles, 394 total bases, and a .359 batting average. At one point during the season, he put together a thirty-game hitting streak, tying him with Stan Musial for the second longest such streak in franchise history, behind only Rogers Hornsby's club mark of thirty-three straight games. Pujols also joined Hornsby as the only players in Cardinals history to surpass forty homers and 200 hits in the same season. At the end of the campaign, the twenty-three-year-old slugger again finished second to Bonds in the MVP voting.

Pujols's prodigious slugging, particularly at such an early age, earned him the respect and admiration of everyone around the league. Tony La Russa, the Cardinals manager during most of Pujols's time with the team, noted, "He just hits line drives that go out of the park. That's why he's a .330 hitter. He's a great hitter. He catches it, and it goes. He's a high-average hitter with power."[1] La Russa added, "He is the whole package as far as a player. He commits to defense just like he does offense. He has natural talent."[2]

Former Cardinals teammate Scott Rolen suggested, "His approach is so mature at the plate. He doesn't get himself out."[3] Tino Martinez, another former teammate of Pujols, commented, "Left-hander, right-hander, soft thrower, power guy, fastballs away, fastballs in—he doesn't have any holes."[4] Former Pirates manager Lloyd McClendon marveled, "I've never seen anything like it. He's quick to the ball with his bat, he hits to all fields, he rarely goes out of the strike zone, and no situation seems to rattle him."[5] Meanwhile, former teammate

Adam Wainwright proclaimed, "I don't know how anybody could ever be better than he is. . . . Ever. . . . No offense to Henry Aaron and all those guys. I'm sorry, Hank. Albert Pujols is really, really good."[6]

Pujols finally settled in at first base full time in 2004, a year in which he helped lead the Cardinals to the NL pennant by hammering 46 homers, knocking in 123 runs, batting .331, collecting 51 doubles, and topping the circuit with 133 runs scored and 389 total bases, despite being plagued by plantar fasciitis during the season's second half.

After earning four consecutive top-five finishes in the league MVP balloting, Pujols claimed the honor for himself in 2005, placing among the league leaders with 41 home runs, 117 RBIs, 360 total bases, a .330 batting average, a .430 on-base percentage, and a .609 slugging percentage, while topping the circuit with 129 runs scored. "Prince Albert's" 117 RBIs enabled him to join Ted Williams, Joe DiMaggio, and Al Simmons as the only players ever to surpass the century mark in that category in each of their first five seasons. His forty-one home runs also made him the first Cardinals player to reach the forty-homer plateau three straight times.

Pujols continued his onslaught against NL pitching in 2006 and 2007, combining for a total of 81 home runs, 240 RBIs, and 218 runs scored, while posting batting averages of .331 and .327. He subsequently captured league MVP honors in both 2008 and 2009, extending to nine the number of consecutive seasons he hit more than 30 home runs, knocked in more than 100 runs, and batted over .300. After hitting .357 in 2008, Pujols posted a mark of .327 in 2009, drove in 135 runs, and topped the senior circuit with 47 homers, 124 runs scored, 374 total bases, a .443 on-base percentage, and a .658 slugging percentage. He hit five grand slams during the course of the campaign, tying Ernie Banks's single-season NL record.

Pujols followed up his back-to-back MVP seasons with another big year in 2010, batting .312 and leading the league with 42 home runs, 118 RBIs, and 115 runs scored, en route to earning his fourth runner-up finish in the MVP voting. He also won the second Gold Glove of his career. A small fracture in his left wrist sustained during a collision at first base forced Pujols to miss almost three weeks of the ensuing campaign, preventing him from extending to eleven his streak of consecutive seasons with at least thirty home runs and 100 RBIs, and a batting average in excess of .300. Nevertheless, The Machine again posted solid numbers, concluding the year with 37 homers, 99 RBIs, 105 runs scored, and a .299 batting average. And Pujols likely cared little about failing to extend his streak after he helped lead the Cardinals to their second world championship in four years with a memorable performance against the Texas Rangers in Game 3 of the World Series. The Cardinals slugger concluded the contest with five hits, three home runs, six RBIs, and four runs scored, enabling his team to come away with a 16–7 victory, en route to defeating the favored Rangers in seven games.

Unfortunately, Pujols and the Cardinals failed to reach an agreement on a new long-term contract when the first baseman became eligible to pursue free agency at season's end. Opting instead to sign with the Los Angeles Angels of Anaheim, who offered him a huge ten-year deal, Pujols left the city and fans he maintained he still loved to play on the West Coast. Although brokenhearted upon learning of his departure, Cardinals fans took solace in the knowledge that Pujols helped lead their team to three pennants and two world championships during his time in St. Louis. They also drew consolation from the realization that they had witnessed arguably the finest player of his generation perform for them for eleven seasons.

In his 11 years with the Cardinals, Albert Pujols hit 445 home runs, drove in 1,329 runs, scored 1,291 others, collected 2,073 hits, batted .328, compiled a .420 on-base percentage, and posted a .617 slugging percentage. He ranks among the Cardinals' all-time leaders in most statistical categories, with only Stan Musial hitting more home runs, knocking in more runs, collecting more doubles, amassing more total bases, and drawing more bases on balls as a member of the team. Meanwhile, only Mark McGwire posted a higher slugging percentage. Pujols's extraordinary performance throughout the course of his eleven seasons in St. Louis prompted Matt Holliday to say of his former teammate, "The guy's a once-in-a-generation player."[7]

Pujols hasn't been nearly as prolific since leaving St. Louis, hitting as many as 30 home runs just once, and failing to bat higher than .285 in any of his three seasons with the Angels. Nevertheless, he has remained a productive hitter, driving in 105 runs in both 2012 and 2014. Pujols enters the 2015 campaign with career totals of 520 home runs, 1,603 RBIs, 1,514 runs scored, 2,519 hits, and 561 doubles, a lifetime batting average of .317, and a career OPS of .991.

CARDINAL CAREER HIGHLIGHTS

Best Season

There are so many great seasons from which to choose, with Pujols performing particularly well from 2003 to 2006, and in 2008 and 2009. The slugging first baseman smashed 46 homers, knocked in 123 runs, batted .331, and led the NL with 133 runs scored and 389 total bases in 2004. He followed that up with 41 homers, 117 RBIs, a .330 batting average, and a league-leading 129 runs scored in 2005. Pujols subsequently established career highs with 49 home runs, 137 RBIs, and a league-leading .671 slugging percentage in 2006. After a slightly less spectacular 2007 campaign, Pujols posted fabulous numbers, en route to earning league MVP honors in each of the next two seasons. In addition to hitting 37 home runs, driving in 116 runs, and batting .357 in 2008, he topped the circuit with a .653 slugging percentage that helped him compile a career-best 1.114 on-base plus slugging percentage (OPS). The following year, Pujols posted numbers nearly identical to the figures he compiled in 2006, concluding the campaign with 135 RBIs, a .327 batting average, and a league-leading 47 homers, 124 runs scored, 374 total bases, a .443 on-base percentage, and a .658 slugging percentage.

Nevertheless, I ultimately decided to go with Pujols's 2003 campaign. Although he finished second to Barry Bonds in the MVP balloting, he established career highs with 137 runs scored, 212 hits, 51 doubles, 394 total bases, and a .359 batting average, en route to leading the league in each category. Pujols also hit 43 home runs, knocked in 124 runs, compiled a .439 on-base percentage, and posted a .667 slugging percentage, finishing the year with a 1.106 OPS that fell just .008 points short of matching the career-high mark of 1.114 he compiled in 2008.

Memorable Moments and Greatest Performances

Pujols produced a number of memorable hits and had several huge games as a member of the Cardinals from 2001 to 2011. On July 20, 2004, he went 5-for-5, with 4 runs scored, 5 RBIs, and 3 home runs, including a game-winning, two-run blast against LaTroy Hawkins, as the Cardinals defeated the Chicago Cubs, 11–8. Pujols subsequently had a fabulous 2004 postseason, leading his team to a three-games-to-one victory over the Dodgers in the National League Division Series (NLDS) by hitting a game-winning, three-run homer against Wilson Alvarez that gave the Cardinals a 3–2 win in the series finale. The slugging first baseman continued his hot-hitting against Houston in the National League Championship Series (NLCS), collecting three hits, including a game-winning home run, during a 6–4 St. Louis victory in Game 2. Pujols eventually won NLCS MVP honors by batting .500, hitting 4 home runs, and driving in 9 runs, as the Cardinals defeated the Astros in seven games.

Pujols excelled for the Cardinals again in the 2005 playoffs, collecting five hits in nine official at bats during the Cardinals' three-game sweep of the Padres in the NLDS. He then came up with the team's biggest hit of the year in Game 5 of the NLCS. With the Astros leading the series, three games to one, and the Cardinals facing elimination in the top of the ninth inning, Pujols turned a 4–2 Cardinal deficit into a 5–4 victory with a two-out, three-run home run against Brad Lidge that landed on the train tracks in the back of Houston's Minute Maid Park. Although Houston ended up eliminating the Cardinals in Game 6, Pujols finished the NLCS with 2 home runs, 6 RBIs, and a .304 batting average.

On April 10, 2006, Pujols hit the first Cardinals' home run at the new Busch Stadium during a 6–4 St. Louis win over Milwaukee. Less than one week later, on April 16, he hit three consecutive home runs and drove in five runs against the Cincinnati Reds. Pujols hit the last of his three homers in the bottom of the ninth inning against David Weathers, turning an apparent 7–6 loss into an 8–7 Cardinal victory. The next day, Pujols hit a homer in his first at bat, giving him homers in four consecutive trips to the plate. The blast made him the thirty-fifth player in baseball history to accomplish the feat. Later in the year, on September 3, Pujols turned in another memorable performance, knocking in five runs and homering three times against Ian Snell in a 6–3 victory over the Pittsburgh Pirates.

Still, Pujols turned in the most memorable performance of his career against the Texas Rangers in Game 3 of the 2011 World Series. After hitting 2 home runs, driving in 9 runs, and batting .478 during the Cardinals' six-game victory over Milwaukee in the NLCS, Pujols found himself struggling against Texas pitching in the first two games of the Fall Classic; however, he broke out of his slump in Game 3, leading the Cardinals to a 16–7 win by becoming just the third player in baseball history to hit three home runs in one World Series game.

Pujols began his evening by grounding out to third base. He followed that up with a pair of singles, before beginning his virtuoso performance by hitting a three-run home run in the top of the sixth inning that put the Cardinals in front by a score of 11–6. Pujols subsequently homered again in the seventh and ninth innings, ending the game with five hits, three home runs, four runs scored, and six RBIs. In the process, he tied World Series single-game records for hits and RBIs, and he established a new single-game mark for total bases. He also became the first player in the history of the Fall Classic to collect hits in four consecutive innings. Noted baseball writer and analyst Tom Verducci later described the events of the evening, saying, "Lincoln at Gettysburg. Hendrix at Woodstock. Pujols at Arlington. It was, quite simply, the greatest night by one player in the history of the 620 World Series games ever played."[8]

Notable Achievements

Hit more than forty home runs six times.

Hit three home runs in one game during the regular season three times.

Knocked in more than 120 runs six times.

Scored more than 120 runs four times.

Batted over .330 five times, surpassing the .350 mark on two occasions.

Collected more than 200 hits once.

Topped fifty doubles twice, surpassing the forty mark on four other occasions.

Drew more than 100 bases on balls three times.

Compiled on-base percentage in excess of .450 once (.462 in 2008).

Posted slugging percentage in excess of .600 seven times.

Led NL in runs scored five times, total bases four times, slugging percentage three times, home runs twice, RBIs once, batting average once, on-base percentage once, hits once, and doubles once.

Second all-time on Cardinals in home runs, RBIs, doubles, total bases, walks, and slugging percentage.

Only player in major-league history to hit more than 30 home runs, drive in more than 100 runs, and bat at least .300 in each of his first 10 seasons.

One of only three players in baseball history to hit three home runs in one World Series game (October 22, 2011, Game 3).

Holds World Series record for most total bases in one game (sixteen).

Three-time NL MVP (2005, 2008, 2009).

2004 NLCS MVP.

2001 NL Rookie of Year.

Six-time Silver Slugger winner (2001, 2003, 2004, 2008, 2009, 2010).

Two-time Gold Glove winner (2006, 2010).

Seven-time *Sporting News* All-Star selection.

Three-time *Sporting News* Major League Player of Year (2003, 2008, 2009).

Sporting News Player of the Decade for 2000–2009.

Nine-time NL All-Star (2001, 2003, 2004, 2005, 2006, 2007, 2008, 2009, 2010).

Three-time NL champion (2004, 2006, 2011).

Two-time world champion (2006, 2011).

NOTES

1. Tony La Russa, quoted in "Albert Pujols: What They Say," *JockBio.com*, www.jockbio.com/Bios/Pujols/Pujols_they-say.html (accessed September 4, 2012).
2. La Russa, quoted in "Albert Pujols: What They Say," www.jockbio.com/Bios/Pujols/Pujols_they-say.html.
3. Scott Rolen, quoted in "Albert Pujols: What They Say," www.jockbio.com/Bios/Pujols/Pujols_they-say.html.
4. Tino Martinez, quoted in "Albert Pujols: What They Say," www.jockbio.com/Bios/Pujols/Pujols_they-say.html.
5. Lloyd McClendon, quoted in "Albert Pujols: What They Say," www.jockbio.com/Bios/Pujols/Pujols_they-say.html.
6. Adam Wainwright, quoted in "Albert Pujols: What They Say," www.jockbio.com/Bios/Pujols/Pujols_they-say.html.
7. Matt Holliday, quoted in "Albert Pujols: What They Say," www.jockbio.com/Bios/Pujols/Pujols_they-say.html.
8. Tom Verducci, quoted in "Albert Pujols: What They Say," www.jockbio.com/Bios/Pujols/Pujols_they-say.html.

4

BOB GIBSON

Longtime teammates and fellow Hall of Famers Bob Gibson and Lou Brock proved to be the leading contenders for the number four spot in these rankings. Brock was an outstanding hitter and a terrific base stealer who helped change the way the game was played with his thievery on the base paths. But Gibson was a more dominant player, establishing himself in the course of his career as one of the greatest big-game pitchers in baseball history. In addition to winning two Cy Young Awards and one National League Most Valuable Player trophy, Gibson earned World Series MVP honors twice, leading the Cardinals to victory in the 1964 and 1967 Fall Classics. The integral role Gibson played in winning each of those championships pushed him well ahead of Brock, who had to settle for a number five ranking here.

The greatest pitcher in St. Louis Cardinals history, Bob Gibson won more games (251), threw more innings (3,884), struck out more batters (3,117), started more games (482), threw more complete games (255), and tossed more shutouts (56) than any other Cardinals hurler. Spending his entire seventeen-year career in St. Louis, Gibson led the Cardinals to three NL pennants and two world championships, compiling an overall record of 7–2 in World Series play, along with a brilliant 1.89 ERA. A tremendous competitor, Gibson also proved to be one of the most intimidating pitchers of his time, causing many of his opponents' knees to weaken when they stepped into the batter's box to face him. The hard-throwing right-hander approached each start with a warlike attitude prompted by his poor upbringing and the difficulties he encountered during the early stages of his professional baseball career.

Born in Omaha, Nebraska, on November 9, 1935, Bob Gibson never knew his father, losing him to tuberculosis three months prior to his birth. Nevertheless, the younger Gibson persevered through a difficult childhood that included various problems, such as rickets and a serious case of asthma. Growing up in the ghetto without a father caused young Bob to lean heavily on his older brother, Josh, for guidance. Since Josh was fifteen years his senior, Bob learned most of life's lessons from his elder sibling, who instilled in him at an early age a sense of pride, dignity, self-respect, and determination.

Overcoming his earlier illnesses, Gibson starred in baseball, basketball, and track and field while attending Omaha Technical High School. After earning a full athletic scholarship to play basketball at Creighton University, Gibson continued to further his education and athletic career, excelling in both baseball and basketball in college.

Offered contracts by the Harlem Globetrotters basketball team and the St. Louis Cardinals upon his graduation, Gibson delayed the start of his baseball career for one year, choosing to join the Globetrotters for a brief period of time. However, he eventually decided to devote all of his attention to baseball, spending the entire 1958 season playing in the Cardinals' minor-league system.

Called up to the Cardinals for parts of both the 1959 and 1960 campaigns, Gibson saw limited action at the major-league level in each of those years, spending most of his time shuttling back and forth between St. Louis and the club's minor-league affiliates in Omaha and Rochester. Gibson finally joined the Cardinals for good in 1961, gradually earning a spot in the St. Louis starting rotation throughout the course of the season despite the somewhat backward thinking of Cardinals manager Solly Hemus. Filled with several preconceived notions about black players that unfortunately remained far too prevalent in the game at that time, Hemus found himself questioning Gibson's intellect and heart, making it quite clear to the young right-hander that he didn't think him capable of succeeding at the major-league level. The racial prejudice that Gibson experienced during his early days as a Cardinal helped fuel the tremendous drive and resolve he took with him to the mound the remainder of his career.

After concluding the 1961 campaign with a record of 13–12 and a respectable 3.24 ERA, Gibson began to thrive in his second full season, after Johnny Keane assumed the managerial reins of the Cardinals. Keane, who had managed Gibson in the minor leagues, treated the young hurler with much more respect than did Hemus, inserting him into the starting rotation full time and leaning on him heavily to help alter the losing mindset previously instilled in many of the team's players. Gibson ended up compiling a record of 15–13, leading the league with 5 shutouts, and placing among the leaders with a 2.85 ERA, 208 strikeouts, and 15 complete games, en route to earning his first All-Star selection.

Gibson developed into one of the NL's elite pitchers in 1963, posting a record of 18–9, compiling a 3.39 ERA, throwing 255 innings and 14 complete games, and again ranking among the league leaders with 204 strikeouts. As the twenty-seven-year-old right-hander grew increasingly secure in his role on the club, he also began to assume a position of leadership among his teammates, working with close friend and roommate Bill White to eliminate the use of racial slurs among the players. The Cardinals ended up developing a strong sense of camaraderie and team unity that was free of much of the racial tension that existed throughout the country at that time.

After finishing second in the senior circuit the previous year, six games behind the first-place Dodgers, the Cardinals captured their first NL pennant in 18 years in 1964, with Gibson serving as the ace of their pitching staff by finishing 19–12, with a 3.01 ERA, 17 complete games, 287 innings pitched, and 245 strikeouts. Gibson did yeoman's work down the stretch, tossing four innings of two-hit relief on the final day of the regular season to clinch the pennant for St. Louis, after throwing nine full innings just two days earlier. He then won two of his three starts against New York in the World Series, enabling the Cardinals to upset the favored Yankees in seven games. A weary Gibson earned Series MVP honors by throwing twenty-seven innings, tossing two complete games, and establishing a new Series record by striking out thirty-one batters.

Gibson followed up his outstanding performance in the Fall Classic by surpassing twenty wins in each of the next two seasons. He reached that plateau for the first time in 1965, finishing the campaign with a record of 20–12, a 3.07 ERA, and 6 shutouts, and placing third in the league with 20 complete games, 299 innings pitched, and 270 strikeouts. The hard-throwing right-hander subsequently finished 21–12 in 1966, with a 2.44 ERA, 20 complete games, 280 innings pitched, 225 strikeouts, and a league-leading 5 shutouts.

Gibson had his quest for a third consecutive twenty-win season short-circuited by a line drive off the bat of Roberto Clemente that broke his leg in July 1967, forcing him to miss almost two full months; however, he returned to the Cardinals in time to lead them to victory over the Boston Red Sox in the World Series. Starting Game 1, Game 4, and Game 7 for St. Louis, Gibson won all three contests, throwing 3 complete games, collecting 26 strikeouts, and allowing Boston a total of only 3 earned runs on just 14 hits. His extraordinary performance earned him World Series MVP honors for the second time in his career.

Gibson put on display for all to see in that year's Fall Classic the fierce competitiveness that characterized his persona. While many baseball fans around the nation had an opportunity to see that side of Gibson for the first time, those more familiar with him were already keenly aware of the qualities that made him one of the most intimidating pitchers ever to take the mound. Longtime Cardinals announcer Jack Buck states, "Bob Gibson was the toughest athlete I have ever seen. The night before he pitched, you'd call his hotel room and he was there, in the room. The next day at the ballpark, don't talk to him—even if you're a member of his team."[1]

Author David Halberstam, whose book *October 1964* discusses the events surrounding the 1964 World Series between the Cardinals and Yankees, says, "When Bob Gibson pitched, it transcended baseball. It was an act of war."[2] Halberstam goes on to explain that it wasn't so much that Gibson loved to win, but, rather, that he hated to lose, since doing so brought back memories of his poor ghetto upbringing.

Rusty Staub, who faced Gibson many times throughout the years as a member of the Astros, Expos, and Mets, suggests, "If you wanted to put the term 'true warrior' to a baseball player, he (Gibson) was it."[3] Dusty Baker spent his early years in the NL facing Gibson as a member of the Atlanta Braves. Reflecting on the impression Gibson made on him, Baker notes, "He was the only guy that ever intimidated me when I was at the plate."[4] Pete Rose says, "He'd knock you on your ass if you hugged the plate like you're not supposed to."[5]

Discussing Gibson's confrontational nature and mean streak he took with him to the mound, Maury Wills proclaims, "Some pitchers were kinda' chicken. . . . They'd think twice before throwing at you. But Gibson didn't mind that. He'd meet you halfway."[6] Frank Hyland, a writer for the *Atlanta Journal-Constitution*, states flatly, "Bob Gibson was the most intimidating pitcher that ever played the game."[7]

While Gibson acknowledges that he viewed opposing batters as his mortal enemies, he didn't see anything terribly unusual about the attitude with which he pitched, suggesting, "I might have had a little chip on my shoulder. . . . That's the way I pitched. That's the way Drysdale pitched. That's the way Koufax pitched. That's the way you played the game in those days."[8] Gibson adds, "When I went to an All-Star Game, I tried my best not to associate a lot with the other guys on the team because two days later, three days later, they would be trying to beat my brains out."[9]

In 1968, Gibson picked up right where he left off the previous year, earning NL Cy Young and MVP honors with one of the most amazing performances ever turned in by a pitcher. In a season that came to be known as "The Year of the Pitcher" for the dominance hurlers in both leagues displayed over hitters, Gibson proved to be the most dominant pitcher of all. Complementing his blazing fastball with a practically unhittable slider, Gibson concluded the campaign with a record of 22–9, 28 complete games, 305 innings pitched, and a league-leading 1.12 ERA, 268 strikeouts, and 13 shutouts. Although he subsequently failed to lead the pennant-winning Cardinals to victory over the Tigers in the World Series, Gibson again pitched remarkably well against the American League's (AL) representative in the Fall Classic. After setting a new World Series record by striking out seventeen Detroit batters in Game 1, Gibson fanned eighteen more hitters in his next two starts, breaking his own Series record by compiling a total of thirty-five strikeouts during the course of the Fall Classic. He concluded the Series with a record of 2–1, a 1.67 ERA, 3 complete games, 1 shutout, and a total of only 18 hits allowed in 27 innings of work.

Although Gibson understandably never again reached quite the same level of dominance, he remained an exceptional pitcher for four more years before Father Time finally began to catch up with him. After posting 20 wins, a 2.18 ERA, 269 strikeouts, 314 innings pitched, and a league-leading 28 complete games in 1969, Gibson won his second Cy Young Award the following year. He concluded the 1970 campaign with a record of 23–7, a 3.12 ERA, 274 strikeouts, 23 complete games, and 294 innings pitched. Gibson subsequently won a total of 35 games in the course of the next two seasons, pitching particularly well in 1972, when he finished 19–11, with a 2.46 ERA, 208 strikeouts, 23 complete games, and 278 innings pitched. However, that proved to be his last great year. Swelling in Gibson's knee limited the thirty-seven-year-old right-hander to only twenty-five starts in 1973, and he pitched just one more full season after that, calling it quits after making only fourteen starts in 1975.

Gibson retired at the end of the year with a lifetime record of 251–174, with an outstanding 2.91 ERA, and as the Cardinals all-time leader in most statistical categories for pitchers. An exceptional all-around athlete, he also won nine Gold Gloves, hit 24 home runs, and batted .206 in the course of his career. Following his retirement, Gibson spent several seasons serving as Joe Torre's pitching coach in Atlanta, before returning to St. Louis, where he spent five years hosting a pregame and postgame show for the Cardinals on radio station KMOX.

CAREER HIGHLIGHTS

Best Season

Was there ever any doubt? Gibson's performance during the course of the 1968 campaign ranks among the greatest ever turned in by any hurler. Although 1968 came to be known as "The Year of the Pitcher," no other pitcher in either league reached the same level of dominance. In addition to winning 22 games, throwing 305 innings, and tossing 28 complete games, Gibson struck out a league-leading 268 batters and led the majors with a 1.12 ERA and 13 shutouts. His microscopic ERA remains the lowest produced by any starting pitcher since the "dead-ball era," and the lowest single-season mark ever compiled by any hurler who worked more than 300 innings. Meanwhile, Gibson's thirteen shutouts left him just three short of Grover Cleveland Alexander's major-league record sixteen whitewashes, which the latter tossed in 1916.

Dominating opposing batters in overwhelming fashion throughout the campaign, Gibson allowed only two earned runs in ninety-two innings of work from June 2 to July 30, tossing forty-seven consecutive scoreless innings at one point, en route to compiling a 0.20 ERA in that stretch of time. He held opposing hitters to a batting average of just .184 during the course of the season, while also limiting them to a .233 on-base percentage and a .236 slugging percentage. Gibson lost five games by a score of 1–0, meaning that he surrendered more than one run in only four of his nine losses.

Looking back at his amazing performance, Gibson says, "The thing I remember most about the '68 season is that I didn't do anything wrong too often, and that's unusual. When you go out there with the confidence that you can do anything you want to do—and I did."[10] He adds, "When I look back on '68, it seems as though I'm looking back at somebody else's career—not my own—because it was something that only happens once in a lifetime."[11]

Memorable Moments and Greatest Performances

Gibson threw a no-hitter against the hard-hitting Pittsburgh Pirates on August 14, 1971, baffling the members of a lineup that included the likes of Al Oliver, Richie Hebner, and Manny Sanguillen, as well as Hall of Famers Willie Stargell and Roberto Clemente. Nevertheless, Gibson is most remembered for his extraordinary postseason pitching. After earning World Series MVP honors by defeating the Yankees twice in the 1964 Fall Classic, Gibson improved upon his performance in the 1967 Series, defeating the Boston Red Sox three times, en route to earning Series MVP honors for the second time. He began the 1967 Fall Classic by allowing Boston just two runs on six hits, while striking out ten, during a 2–1 St. Louis victory in Game 1. He followed that up with a five-hit shutout in Game 4, giving the Cardinals a 3–1 lead in the Series. After the Red Sox came back to even the Series at three games apiece, Gibson outdueled Boston ace Jim Lonborg in the decisive seventh contest. Gibson threw his third complete game of the Series, striking out ten batters, while allowing only three hits and two runs, in leading the Cardinals to a 7–2 victory that clinched their second world championship in four years. Gibson punctuated his performance with a fifth-inning solo home run against the AL Cy Young Award winner.

However, Gibson pitched probably the most memorable game of his career in the following year's Fall Classic. Facing the Detroit Tigers in the opening contest, Gibson tossed a five-hit shutout and established a World Series record that still stands by striking out seventeen batters. After allowing a leadoff single to Mickey Stanley in the ninth inning, Gibson finished the game by striking out Tiger sluggers Al Kaline, Norm Cash, and Willie Horton, fanning Kaline and Cash for the third time each. Recalling the events of the day, Detroit outfielder Jim Northrup remarked, "We were fastball hitters, but he blew the ball right by us. And he had a nasty slider that was jumping all over the place."[12] Gibson's effort in Game 1 remains one of the most dominant pitching performances in World Series history.

Notable Achievements

Five-time 20-game winner.

Won at least eighteen games three other times.

Compiled an ERA below 3.00 on seven separate occasions, with a mark of 1.12 in 1968, representing the lowest by any starting pitcher since the "dead-ball era."

Struck out more than 200 batters nine times, surpassing 250 strikeouts on four occasions.

Threw at least twenty complete games seven times.

Threw more than 300 innings twice.

Led NL pitchers in wins once, ERA once, complete games once, strikeouts once, and shutouts four times.

First NL pitcher to strike out more than 200 batters nine times.

Holds records for most strikeouts in a World Series (thirty-five) and most strikeouts in a World Series game (seventeen in Game 1 in 1968).

Holds Cardinal career records for most wins (251), strikeouts (3,117), shutouts (56), innings pitched (3,884), complete games (255), and games started (482).

Holds Cardinal single-season records for lowest ERA (1.12 in 1968), most shutouts (13 in 1968), and most strikeouts (274 in 1970).

Two-time NL Cy Young Award winner (1968, 1970).
1968 NL MVP.
Two-time World Series MVP (1964, 1967).
Two-time *Sporting News* All-Star selection (1968, 1970).
Two-time *Sporting News* Pitcher of the Year (1968, 1970).
Nine-time NL All-Star (1962, 1965, 1966, 1967, 1968, 1969, 1970, 1972). Note: The All-Star Game was played twice a year from 1959 to 1962 to raise money for the players' pension funds, and Gibson played in both games in 1962.
Nine-time Gold Glove winner (1965, 1966, 1967, 1968, 1969, 1970, 1971, 1972, 1973).
Three-time NL champion (1964, 1967, 1968).
Two-time world champion (1964, 1967).
Elected to Baseball Hall of Fame by members of the Baseball Writers' Association of America in 1981.

NOTES

1. Jack Buck, quoted in *A Century of Success: 100 Years of Cardinals Glory*, Major League Baseball Productions, 1992.
2. David Halberstam, quoted in *Sports Century: Bob Gibson*, ESPN, 2003.
3. Rusty Staub, quoted in *Sports Century: Bob Gibson*.
4. Dusty Baker, quoted in *Sports Century: Bob Gibson*.
5. Pete Rose, quoted in *Sports Century: Bob Gibson*.
6. Maury Wills, quoted in *Sports Century: Bob Gibson*.
7. Frank Hyland, quoted in *Sports Century: Bob Gibson*.
8. Bob Gibson, quoted in *Sports Century: Bob Gibson*.
9. Bob Gibson, quoted in *Sports Century: Bob Gibson*.
10. Bob Gibson, quoted in *A Century of Success: 100 Years of Cardinals Glory*.
11. Bob Gibson, quoted in *A Century of Success: 100 Years of Cardinals Glory*.
12. Jim Northrup, quoted in "Bob Gibson Quotes," *Baseball Almanac*, www.baseball-almanac.com/quotes/bob_gibson_quotes.shtml (accessed September 8, 2012).

5

LOU BROCK

Even though Lou Brock compiled a lifetime batting average of .293, amassed more than 3,000 hits, and established himself throughout the course of his career as one of the greatest base stealers of all time, baseball experts often dispute the lofty status he reached during his nineteen big-league seasons. They tend to point to the nine years in which he struck out more than 100 times—a rather large number for a leadoff hitter, particularly during the 1960s and 1970s. They also argue that he struck out more times than he scored in eleven different campaigns; that he fanned more than twice as many times as he walked during his career (1,730 to 761); and that he led all National League outfielders in errors seven times, committing no fewer than ten miscues each year from 1964 to 1973.

Taking all those factors into consideration, a strong case could certainly be made for slotting fellow Hall of Fame left fielder Joe Medwick just ahead of Brock in these rankings. Medwick hit more home runs than Brock in far fewer at bats as a member of the Cardinals. He also knocked in more runs, hit for a higher batting average, and posted better on-base and slugging percentages. But Brock scored more than 600 more runs than Medwick tallied as a Cardinal, collected almost twice as many hits, and stole 860 more bases. Medwick may have been a better hitter than Brock, but the latter accomplished more during his time in St. Louis. Furthermore, Brock's extraordinary baserunning ability made him a tremendous offensive force, enabling him to overcome any advantages Medwick may have had as a pure hitter. Brock wreaked havoc on the base paths, upsetting the defenses of opposing teams and allowing the men who followed him in the Cardinals batting order to get better pitches to hit. Brock did more than Medwick to make the other players around him better, which ultimately earned him a higher place in these rankings.

Former Phillies and Cubs shortstop Larry Bowa once said of Lou Brock, "Everybody in the park knows he's going to run and he makes it anyway."[1] Meanwhile, Brock suggested, "Baserunning arrogance is just like pitching arrogance or hitting arrogance. You are a force, and you have to instill that you are a force to the opposition. You have to have utter confidence."[2]

Brock's confidence, intelligence, and speed made him the premier base stealer of his time. Identified, along with Maury Wills, by Hall of Fame pitcher Tom Seaver as one of two players that helped change the manner in which the game was played during the 1960s, Brock helped revolutionize the art and science of base-stealing. An extremely cerebral player who was among the first to study game films, Brock used an 8 mm movie camera from the dugout to film opposing pitchers and study their windups and pickoff moves to detect weaknesses he could exploit. The outfielder's great speed and intellectual approach to his craft eventually enabled him to set numerous stolen base records during his time with the Cardinals. In addition to establishing a new single-season mark by stealing 118 bases in 1974, the speedy outfielder broke Major League Baseball's long-standing career mark by swiping 938 bags in the course of nineteen big-league seasons, spent mostly with the Cardinals. Although Rickey Henderson eventually surpassed both figures, Brock remains one of the greatest base stealers in the history of the sport, and one of the most exciting players ever to grace the diamond. More than just a superb base runner, Brock also established himself during his years in St. Louis as an outstanding hitter and an exceptional clutch performer, compiling a lifetime batting average of .391 in World Series play.

Born in El Dorado, Arkansas, on June 18, 1939, Louis Clark Brock got a relatively late start in baseball, failing to play the game at an organized level until he reached the eleventh grade. Nevertheless, he learned a great deal about the sport by listening to Cardinals radio broadcaster Harry Caray describe the way major-league hitters stood at the plate. After graduating from Southern University and A&M College in Baton Rouge, Louisiana, Brock signed with the Chicago

Cubs as an amateur free agent in 1960. He subsequently spent most of the next two seasons playing in the minor leagues, before earning a spot on the club's major-league roster in spring training of 1962. Although the young outfielder showed occasional glimpses of the greatness that awaited him, stealing a total of forty bases and becoming just the second player to hit a home run into the center-field bleachers at New York's Polo Grounds, Brock disappointed Cubs management during his two full seasons in Chicago, posting batting averages of just .263 and .258, striking out a total of 218 times, and playing erratically in the outfield. Finally losing patience with Brock, the Cubs made him the centerpiece of a six-player trade they completed with the Cardinals on June 15, 1964, which netted them former twenty-game winner Ernie Broglio.

The deal, which has since gone down as one of the most lopsided trades in baseball history, ended up giving the Cardinals exactly what they needed. Lacking team speed and a dynamic presence at the top of their batting order, the Cardinals finished six games behind the pennant-winning Dodgers the previous year. With their offense struggling again the first few months of the 1964 campaign, the Redbirds stood in eighth place at the time of the trade, with a record of only 28–31; however, with Brock batting .348, stealing 33 bases, collecting 146 hits, and scoring 81 runs in the final 103 games, the Cards surged to first place, capturing the pennant on the season's final day.

Right fielder Mike Shannon discusses the impact Brock made in St. Louis during the final few months of the season, saying, "What happened with Brock is he gave us something we didn't have. We didn't have a leadoff hitter, and we didn't have speed. He gave us all that, and, consequently, when that happens, it lifts everyone up. It gives everyone a little enthusiasm."[3] Tim McCarver, the team's young catcher at the time, adds, "The dominant thing about Lou Brock, to me, was that he was a low-ball hitter with power. I can remember several shots back in '63 where he hammered that ball down and in. So, I thought of him, ironically, more as a power hitter."[4]

Brock did indeed have excellent power, but he sacrificed hitting home runs for getting on base and upsetting the opposing team's defense for the betterment of the team at the request of Cardinals manager Johnny Keane. The young outfielder concluded the 1964 campaign with a combined batting average of .315, 43 stolen bases, 111 runs scored, and 200 hits, en route to earning a tenth-place finish in the league Most Valuable Player voting. He subsequently helped the Cardinals defeat the Yankees in the World Series by batting .300, hitting 1 homer, driving in 5 runs, and scoring twice in the course of the 7 games.

Brock continued to evolve into one of the NL's top outfielders in 1965, batting .288, scoring 107 runs, establishing new career highs with 16 home runs and 69 RBIs, and finishing second to Maury Wills in the senior circuit with 63 steals. Brock ended Wills's six-year reign as stolen base champ the following year, when he led the league in thefts for the first of four consecutive times by swiping seventy-four bags. He also batted .285 and scored 94 runs.

Brock had one of his finest all-around seasons in 1967, helping the Cardinals capture the first of two straight pennants by becoming the first player to surpass twenty home runs and fifty steals in the same season. In addition to swiping a league-leading 52 bases, he topped the circuit with 113 runs scored, batted .299, collected 206 hits, and established career highs by hitting 21 homers and driving in 76 runs. His outstanding performance earned him his first All-Star nomination and a seventh-place finish in the NL MVP voting. Brock subsequently performed magnificently against Boston in the World Series, teaming up with Bob Gibson to lead the Cardinals to a seven-game victory over their American League counterparts. Brock collected twelve hits in twenty-nine times at bat against Red Sox pitching, for a .414 batting average. He also homered once, scored eight times, and established a new World Series record by stealing seven bases.

Brock had a somewhat less productive 1968 campaign, batting .279, hitting only 6 home runs, knocking in just 51 runs, and scoring only 92 times. Nevertheless, he earned an eighth-place finish in the NL MVP balloting by becoming the first player since Honus Wagner in 1908 to top the senior circuit in triples (14), doubles (46), and stolen bases (62) in the same season. He followed that up with another sensational World Series performance, this time in a losing effort against the Detroit Tigers. Brock batted .464 against the Tigers, collecting thirteen hits in twenty-eight official trips to the plate. He also homered twice, drove in five runs, scored six others, and tied his own

World Series record that he had established just one year earlier by swiping seven bases.

After two more solid seasons in which he posted batting averages of .298 and .304, combined to score 211 runs, and stole a total of 104 bases, Brock had another exceptional year in 1971, batting .313, collecting 200 hits, compiling a career-high .385 on-base percentage, and leading the league with 126 runs scored and 64 stolen bases. He followed that up with two more outstanding seasons, batting .311 and topping the circuit with 63 steals in 1972, before batting .297, scoring 110 runs, and swiping a league-leading 70 bases in 1973, en route to earning a sixth-place finish in the MVP voting.

Considered by most people to be approaching the latter stages of his career heading into the 1974 campaign, Brock remarkably shattered Maury Wills's single-season stolen base record (104 in 1962) by swiping 118 bags at the age of thirty-five. His amazing performance earned him a second-place finish in the league MVP balloting and recognition by the *Sporting News* as Major League Baseball's Player of the Year.

Brock continued to perform extremely well in each of the next two seasons, posting batting averages of .309 and .301, while stealing a total of 112 bases; however, he experienced a precipitous drop-off in offensive production in 1977, batting just .272 and proving successful in only 35 of his 59 stolen base attempts. After batting just .221 and stealing only seventeen bases in a part-time role the following year, Brock rebounded in 1979 to bat .304 and steal twenty-one bases at the age of forty. He announced his retirement at season's end, concluding his Hall of Fame career with a .293 batting average, 3,023 hits, 1,610 runs scored, 149 home runs, 900 RBIs, and a then-record 938 stolen bases. Brock's numbers in his 16 years with the Cardinals include a batting average of .297, 2,713 hits, 1,427 runs scored, 129 home runs, 814 RBIs, and 888 steals. In addition to stealing more bases than any other Cardinals player, he ranks second to Stan Musial in hits, runs scored, games played (2,289), plate appearances (9,932), and official at bats (9,125). He also is among the team's all-time leaders in doubles (434), triples (121), and total bases (3,776). Following his playing career, Brock became a special instructor coach for the Cardinals, mentoring young players on the art of baserunning.

CARDINAL CAREER HIGHLIGHTS

Best Season

Although Brock's record-setting 118 steals earned him *Sporting News* Player of the Year honors in 1974, he actually performed better in both 1967 and 1971, collecting more hits, scoring more runs, amassing more total bases, and compiling a significantly higher slugging percentage in each of those campaigns. My first instinct was to go with 1967 since, in addition to batting .299 and leading the league with 113 runs scored and 52 stolen bases, Brock established career highs in home runs (21), RBIs (76), hits (206), total bases (325), and slugging percentage (.472); however, he walked only 24 times the entire year, enabling him to compile an on-base percentage of just .327—not a very good figure for a leadoff hitter. Brock hit fewer home runs (7), knocked in fewer runs (61), collected 6 fewer hits (200), amassed fewer total bases (272), and posted a lower slugging percentage (.425) in 1971, but he also hit for a higher batting average (.313), stole more bases (64), and led the league with a career-high 126 runs scored. Perhaps most significant is the fact that he drew more bases on balls (76) than he did in any other season, enabling him to compile an on-base percentage of .385, representing the highest mark of his career. He also finished the season with an on-base plus slugging percentage of .810, which surpassed the mark he posted in 1967 by eleven percentage points. It's an extremely close call, but the feeling here is that Brock had his best all-around season in 1971, since he reached base and scored more runs that year than in any other.

Memorable Moments and Greatest Performances

Brock turned in a number of memorable performances for the Cardinals, with his exceptional World Series play heading the list. He collected four hits, stole two bases, and scored two runs in Game 1 of the 1967 Fall Classic, in leading St. Louis to a 2–1 win over Boston. Brock subsequently led his team to victory in Game 7 by collecting another 2 hits and stealing 3 more bases, en route to finishing the Series with 12 hits, 7 stolen bases, a .414 batting average, and 8 runs scored.

Brock amazingly topped that performance in the following year's World Series, hitting 2 home runs, knocking in 5 runs, scoring 6 others, collecting 13 hits, batting .464, and stealing another 7 bases in a losing effort to the Detroit Tigers. Particularly effective in a 10–1 Cardinals victory in Game 4, Brock homered, tripled, doubled, stole a base, and drove in four runs.

Yet, ironically, Brock is perhaps remembered best for his baserunning mistake in Game 5 of the Series. With the Cardinals up three games to one and leading the Tigers by a score of 3–2 in the fifth inning, Brock attempted to score from second base on a single to left field by Julian Javier; however, Detroit left fielder Willie Horton threw him out at the plate when Brock inexplicably tried to score standing up. The play helped shift the momentum of the Series, with the Tigers coming back to win the contest by a score of 5–3, and eventually going on to defeat the Cardinals in seven games.

Brock's baserunning blunder notwithstanding, he accomplished some truly extraordinary things throughout the years with both his bat and his thievery on the base paths. The left fielder experienced a power surge at the beginning of the 1967 campaign, becoming the first player to hit five home runs in the season's first four games. Four years later, he put together a twenty-six-game hitting streak that remains one of the longest in Cardinals history. On May 26, 1975, Brock hit for the cycle during a 7–1 win over the San Diego Padres. He accomplished his greatest feat as a hitter, however, on August 13, 1979, when he joined the select 3,000-hit club by singling off Chicago's Dennis Lamp during a 3–2 Cardinals victory over the Cubs.

But Brock experienced the vast majority of his most memorable moments on the base paths. On September 10, 1974, he stole his 104th and 105th bases of the season during an 8–2 loss to the Phillies, breaking in the process Maury Wills's single-season record. The two thefts gave him a total of 740 for his career, also enabling him to break Max Carey's long-standing NL mark of 738 steals. A little less than three years later, on August 29, 1977, Brock stole two bases against the San Diego Padres, giving him 893 for his career, and moving him past Ty Cobb, into first place all-time among "modern-day" players.

Brock became the all-time stolen base champ on September 23, 1979, when he stole the 938th and final base of his career against the Mets, surpassing in the process nineteenth-century speedster Billy Hamilton, who compiled 937 steals during the course of his career.

Notable Achievements

Hit more than twenty home runs once (twenty-one in 1967).

Scored more than 100 runs seven times.

Batted over .300 on eight occasions.

Stole more than fifty bases twelve straight times.

Collected at least 200 hits four times.

Finished in double digits in triples five times.

Topped forty doubles once (forty-six in 1968).

Led NL in stolen bases eight times, runs scored twice, doubles once, and triples once.

Second all-time in career stolen bases.

Holds records for most hits (thirteen) and stolen bases (seven) in a World Series in 1968.

Holds records for most stolen bases (fourteen) in World Series play and highest batting average (.391) of anyone who played in at least twenty Series games.

Holds Cardinal single-season stolen base record (118 in 1974).

Holds Cardinal career record for most stolen bases (888).

Second all-time on Cardinals in hits (2,713), runs scored (1,427), games played (2,289), plate appearances (9,932), and official at bats (9,125).

Second in NL MVP voting in 1974.

1974 *Sporting News* All-Star selection.

1974 *Sporting News* Major League Player of the Year.

Six-time NL All-Star (1967, 1971, 1972, 1974, 1975, 1979).

Three-time NL champion (1964, 1967, 1968).

Two-time world champion (1964, 1967).

Elected to Baseball Hall of Fame by members of the Baseball Writers' Association of American in 1985.

NOTES

1. Larry Bowa, quoted in "Lou Brock Quotes," *Lou Brock.com*, www.cmgww.com/baseball/brock/quotes.htm (accessed September 10, 2012).
2. Lou Brock, "Lou Brock Quotes," www.cmgww.com/baseball/brock/quotes.htm.
3. Mike Shannon, quoted in *A Century of Success: 100 Years of Cardinals Glory*, Major League Baseball Productions, 1992.
4. Tim McCarver, quoted in *A Century of Success: 100 Years of Cardinals Glory*.

6

JOE MEDWICK

Known as much for his terrible temper and surly disposition as he was for his exceptional hitting ability, Joe Medwick established himself as the National League's finest all-around batsman during the latter half of the 1930s. The last NL player to win the Triple Crown, Medwick topped the senior circuit in both RBIs and doubles three straight years, from 1936 to 1938, averaging 138 RBIs and fifty-six doubles in that span of time. One of the leaders of the famed "Gas House Gang" in St. Louis, the Cardinals left fielder brawled with opposing players and teammates alike as he continued to terrorize NL pitchers throughout the decade. Medwick reached a level of unpopularity so great among players in the senior circuit that he prompted one former teammate, who preferred to remain anonymous, to state when the outfielder announced his retirement, "When he dies, half the National League will go to his wake just to make sure that son-of-a-bitch is dead."[1]

Born to Hungarian immigrants in Carteret, New Jersey, on November 24, 1911, Joseph Michael Medwick was one of the greatest all-around athletes in the Garden State's history. After excelling in track, football, basketball, and baseball in high school, Medwick turned down a football scholarship to Notre Dame to sign with the Cardinals organization.

Medwick experienced a great deal of success while advancing through the St. Louis farm system the next two years, posting lofty batting averages and solid power numbers in the Middle Atlantic League in 1930, and the Texas League the following year. While playing in the minors, Medwick acquired the nickname "Ducky Wucky" for the unusual manner in which he waddled when he walked. The moniker was eventually shortened to "Ducky," one that Medwick found somewhat more tolerable, although he preferred to be called by his other nickname of "Muscles."

Medwick made his major-league debut with the Cardinals in September 1932, batting .349 in the twenty-six games in which he appeared. He replaced former NL batting champion Chick Hafey as the team's regular left fielder the following year, batting .306, hitting 18 home runs, driving in 98 runs, and scoring 92 others in his first full season. Medwick also surpassed forty doubles for the first of seven consecutive times.

Medwick had another solid year in 1934, helping St. Louis capture the NL pennant by hitting 18 homers, knocking in 106 runs, scoring 110 others, batting .319, and topping the senior circuit with 18 triples, en route to earning All-Star honors for the first of seven straight times. It was during the World Series, however, that he truly made a name for himself. In addition to homering once, knocking in 5 runs, and batting .379 during the Cardinals' seven-game victory over the Detroit Tigers, Medwick initiated a brawl in the sixth inning of the final contest by knocking down Tiger third baseman Marv Owen with an overly aggressive slide, even though the Cardinals already held an insurmountable 9–0 lead. Medwick's act eventually prompted baseball commissioner Kenesaw Mountain Landis to remove him from the contest "for his own good" when irate Tiger fans began throwing fruits and bottles at him when he returned to his position in the outfield in the bottom of the inning.

Medwick's antagonistic gesture toward Owen really should not have come as much of a surprise to anyone. A combative and hard-nosed player who epitomized the Gas House Gang's aggressive style of play, Medwick typically slid hard into every base and rarely backed down from an altercation. He even fought with members of his own team from time to time, decking teammate Ed Heusser on one particular occasion when the St. Louis pitcher censured him for failing to hustle on a fly ball. Other incidents included run-ins with fellow Cardinals slugger Ripper Collins and pitcher Tex Carlton, who angered Medwick when he walked in front of the outfielder one too many times during a photograph session. Medwick once even threatened to take out both Dean brothers (Dizzy and Daffy) with a bat. Medwick's contentious nature provided a considerable amount of fodder for his critics, who often found fault with his actions.

However, even Medwick's harshest critics found it difficult to disparage his performance on the field the next few seasons. A bad-ball hitter who drove opposing pitchers' offerings to all fields with power, the muscular outfielder began an extraordinarily productive five-year run in 1935. Medwick surpassed 100 RBIs in each of those seasons, scored more than 100 runs and collected more than 200 hits four times each, and topped 20 homers and the .350 mark in batting three times each. After placing among the league leaders with 23 home runs, 126 RBIs, 132 runs scored, 224 hits, and a .353 batting average in 1935, Medwick batted .351 and topped the circuit with 138 RBIs, 223 hits, and a NL record 64 doubles the following year. He had his greatest season in 1937, when he captured the NL Triple Crown and league Most Valuable Player honors by topping the circuit with 31 home runs, 154 RBIs, and a .374 batting average. He also led all NL players with 111 runs scored, 237 hits, 56 doubles, 406 total bases, and a .641 slugging percentage. Medwick led the league in both RBIs and doubles for the third straight time the following year.

Although Medwick posted outstanding numbers again in 1939, finishing near the top of the league rankings with 117 RBIs, 98 runs scored, 201 hits, 48 doubles, and a .332 batting average, the Cardinals traded him to the Dodgers at the end of the year in a move that likely reflected the frustration team management felt toward its confrontational star. Medwick's violent behavior eventually caught up with him, prompting former St. Louis teammate Bob Bowman to hit him in the head with a fastball just six days after the star outfielder switched teams. Knocked out by the pitch, a concussed Medwick had to be carried off the field. Although he remained a solid hitter the next several years, Medwick never again posted huge offensive numbers. After hitting 18 home runs, knocking in 88 runs, scoring 100 others, and batting .318 for the pennant-winning Dodgers in 1941, he failed to hit more than 7 home runs, drive in 100 runs, or score more than 69 runs in any single season the remainder of his career. The Dodgers dealt Medwick to the Giants midway through the 1943 campaign, after which he remained in New York the next two years before joining the

Boston Braves for one season. From Boston, it was back to Brooklyn for one more year, before Medwick returned to the Cardinals, ending his career in 1948 in the same city it began sixteen years earlier.

Joe Medwick announced his retirement at the conclusion of the 1948 campaign with career totals of 205 home runs, 1,383 RBIs, 1,198 runs scored, 2,471 hits, 113 triples, 540 doubles, and a .324 batting average. His numbers as a member of the Cardinals include 152 home runs, 923 RBIs, 811 runs scored, 1,590 hits, 81 triples, 377 doubles, and a .335 batting average. Despite spending only seven full seasons in St. Louis, Medwick ranks among the team's all-time leaders in RBIs (eighth), triples (eighth), doubles (fourth), and batting average (fifth).

Medwick mellowed somewhat after his playing career ended. A mainstay at many baseball events, he became a minor-league batting instructor in the Cardinals organization in 1966. Elected to the National Baseball Hall of Fame by the members of the Baseball Writers' Association of America (BBWAA) in 1968, Medwick died of a heart attack in St. Petersburg, Florida, two years later, at the age of sixty-three.

CARDINAL CAREER HIGHLIGHTS

Best Season

Medwick performed brilliantly for the Cardinals from 1935 to 1939, playing particularly well the first three years. He finished second in the NL in six different offensive categories in 1935, including batting average (.353), slugging percentage (.576), RBIs (126), runs scored (132), hits (224), and doubles (46), en route to earning a fifth-place finish in the MVP voting. He followed that up by batting .351; scoring 115 runs; and topping the circuit with 138 RBIs, 223 hits, 64 doubles, and 367 total bases in 1936. His efforts earned him a fourth-place finish in the MVP balloting.

Nevertheless, Medwick's 1937 campaign would have to be considered the finest of his career. The slugging outfielder earned NL MVP honors by leading the league in eight different offensive categories. In addition to winning the Triple Crown by topping the circuit with a career-best 31 home runs, 154 RBIs, and .374 batting average, he finished first with 111 runs scored, 56 doubles, 237 hits, 406 total bases, and a .641 slugging percentage, establishing career highs in the last three categories as well. Medwick's 154 RBIs represent an all-time Cardinals single-season record. Meanwhile, his 56 doubles, 237 hits, and 406 total bases also give him one of the top three single-season marks in each of those categories.

Memorable Moments and Greatest Performances

Medwick accomplished a number of outstanding batting feats for the Cardinals, including hitting .379 for them in the 1934 World Series, with a homer and five RBIs. His exceptional effort included a dominant Game 1 performance in which he went 4-for-5, with a homer, 2 RBIs, and 2 runs scored during an 8–3 St. Louis victory.

Among Medwick's more memorable regular-season performances, he became just the third player in NL history to collect six extra-base hits in one day when he banged out five doubles and a triple during a Cardinals doubleheader sweep of the Reds on May 30, 1935. He again torched the Reds' pitching staff one month later when he hit for the cycle at Cincinnati on June 29.

Medwick equaled a NL record when he hit safely in ten consecutive trips to the plate in July 1936. After collecting seven straight hits during a July 19 doubleheader, he continued his streak by hitting safely in each of his first three plate appearances on July 21. New York's Carl Hubbell finally ended Medwick's streak by retiring him in his fourth trip to the plate.

Medwick peppered Philadelphia pitching for four extra-base hits, including two homers and two doubles, during a 15–3 Cardinals win over the Phillies on May 12, 1937. He subsequently hit safely four times for the NL during an 8–3 loss to the junior circuit in that year's annual All-Star Game on July 7. Less than one month later, Medwick set a Cardinals franchise record by collecting four doubles against Milwaukee during a 7–6 Cardinals win on August 4.

Still, Medwick is probably remembered best for the fireworks he set off in the final game of the 1934 World Series. Expanding somewhat on the events surrounding the incident I touched upon earlier in this chapter, the Cardinals held a 9–0 lead when Medwick drove a ball off the center-field wall in the top of the sixth inning. Sliding into third base with his spikes high, even though the ball had yet to be returned to the infield, Medwick knocked Tiger third baseman Marv Owen to the ground. After Owen said something to Medwick, the St. Louis left fielder began kicking him, causing blows to be exchanged between the two men. With the umpires choosing not to eject either player following their scuffle, Tiger fans began pelting Medwick with fruits and bottles when he returned to his position in the outfield in the bottom of the frame. Commissioner Kenesaw Mountain Landis, who witnessed the entire episode from the stands, subsequently summoned Medwick, Cardinals manager Frankie Frisch, and the umpiring crew to his box, where he decided to remove the St. Louis left fielder from the contest "for his own good." The incident remains one of the most famous in the annals of the Fall Classic.

Notable Achievements

Hit more than twenty home runs three times, topping thirty homers once.

Knocked in more than 100 runs six times, topping 120 RBIs on four occasions.

Scored more than 100 runs five times.

Batted over .300 on nine occasions, surpassing the .350 mark three times.

Collected more than 200 hits four times.

Finished in double digits in triples five times.

Amassed more than forty doubles seven times, topping fifty twice and sixty once.

Collected more than 400 total bases once (406 in 1937).

Amassed more than 350 total bases two other times.

Compiled on-base percentage in excess of .400 once (.414 in 1937).

Posted slugging percentage in excess of .600 once (.641 in 1937).

Led NL in RBIs three times, doubles three times, total bases three times, hits twice, home runs once, batting average once, runs scored once, triples once, and slugging percentage once.

Holds major-league record for most consecutive seasons (seven) with forty or more doubles.

Holds NL single-season record for most doubles (sixty-four in 1936).

Holds Cardinals single-season records for RBIs (154 in 1937) and doubles (sixty-four in 1936).

1937 NL MVP.

1937 NL Triple Crown winner.

Five-time *Sporting News* All-Star selection (1935, 1936, 1937, 1938, 1939).

Six-time NL All-Star (1935, 1936, 1937, 1938, 1939, 1940).

1934 NL champion.

1934 world champion.

Elected to Baseball Hall of Fame by members of BBWAA in 1968.

NOTE

1. "Bad to the Bone: Joe Medwick," *Dead Ball Era.com*, www.thedeadballera.com/BadboneMedwick.html (accessed September 11, 2012).

7

DIZZY DEAN

One of the most colorful and charismatic pitchers ever to play the game, Dizzy Dean rivaled Carl Hubbell as the National League's finest hurler during the mid-1930s. Although an injury prevented Dean from continuing his period of excellence for more than a few short seasons, the legendary Cardinals right-hander experienced a level of success from 1932 to 1937 that gained him admittance to Cooperstown following his playing career. The last NL pitcher to win thirty games in a season, Dean proved to be particularly dominant from 1934 to 1936, compiling an overall record of 82–32 during that three-year period, winning one Most Valuable Player Award, finishing second in the balloting two other times, and leading the Cardinals to victory in the 1934 World Series. Had a sore arm not limited his effectiveness in subsequent seasons, eventually bringing his career to a premature end, the small-town country boy with the bold and brazen, yet endlessly engaging personality may well have gone on to establish himself as one of the greatest pitchers in baseball history.

Born in Lucas, Arkansas, on January 16, 1910, Jay Hanna Dean had no formal training in baseball, learning to pitch primarily by spending much of his youth playing ball with his younger brother Paul on his family's farm. As sportswriter Red Smith once wrote, "As a ballplayer, (Dizzy) Dean was a natural phenomenon, like the Grand Canyon or the Great Barrier Reef. Nobody ever taught him baseball, and he never had to learn. He was just doing what came naturally when a scout named Don Curtis discovered him on a Texas sandlot and gave him his first contract."[1]

Curtis, a manager in the St. Louis Cardinals' farm system, first spotted Dean pitching for a semipro team at a tryout camp in San Antonio. After being signed to a contract by the Cardinals, Dean split the 1930 season between St. Joseph, Missouri, and Houston, posting a combined minor-league record of 25–10. The twenty-year-old right-hander with the blazing fastball made his major-league debut with the Cardinals on the season's final day, winning a complete-game three-hitter and allowing only one earned run. Dean subsequently spent the entire 1931 campaign back in Houston, compiling twenty-six victories and 303 strikeouts, before rejoining the Cardinals prior to the start of the 1932 season.

Pitching for the defending world champions, Dean posted a record of 18–15 as a rookie, along with a 3.30 ERA, 16 complete games, and a league-leading 191 strikeouts, 286 innings pitched, and 4 shutouts. He followed that up by finishing 20–18 for the fifth-place Cardinals in 1933, compiling an ERA of 3.04 in 293 innings of work, and topping all NL hurlers with 199 strikeouts and twenty-six complete games.

Despite posting a somewhat mediocre record of 38–33 in the course of his first two full seasons, Dean remained supremely confident heading into the 1934 campaign. Joined in the St. Louis starting rotation by his younger brother Paul (also known as "Daffy"), Dean boldly predicted, "Me and Paul will probably win forty games."[2] The Dean brothers actually ended up surpassing Dizzy's expectations, combining for a total of forty-nine victories, thereby supporting the elder Dean's contention that, "It ain't braggin' if you can back it up."[3]

Paul had a fine first year, winning nineteen games and placing among the league leaders with 150 strikeouts. But Dizzy served as the driving force behind the Cardinals' pennant-winning performance. The older of the Dean brothers compiled a record of 30–7; topped the circuit with 195 strikeouts and seven shutouts; and also finished among the leaders with a 2.66 ERA, 24 complete games, 312 innings pitched, and 7 saves. All this was en route to earning league MVP honors. He subsequently capped off his magnificent season by posting two victories for the Cardinals in the World Series, including a complete-game shutout over the Detroit Tigers in the decisive seventh contest.

Dean's great year made him one of the most popular men in the United States. As the southernmost and westernmost team in the major leagues at the time, the Cardinals were the favorite team of virtually everyone who lived south of the Mason-Dixon Line and west of the Mississippi River. Southerners, in particular, found themselves drawn to such players as the Dean brothers and Pepper Martin, all of whom emanated from that part of the country. Furthermore, the determination and grittiness of the Gas House Gang very much epitomized the attitude of most Americans, who drew inspiration from the Cardinals as they continued to struggle through the Great Depression.

As a result, Dizzy Dean became a folk hero of sorts, inspiring confidence in his fans with his assertive statements, while simultaneously entertaining them with his down-home, country-boy charm. Among his bolder remarks, Dean once proclaimed, "Anybody who's ever had the privilege of seeing me play knows that I am the greatest pitcher in the world."[4]

Ordinarily, such comments would have rubbed many people the wrong way, but Dean's sense of humor, ability to laugh at himself, and fun-loving manner enabled him to endear himself to virtually everyone who followed the sport. Teammate Pepper Martin once noted, "When old Diz was out there pitching it was more than just another ball game. It was a regular three-ring circus, and everybody was wide awake and enjoying being alive."[5]

Even the newspapers had fun with Dean. After being knocked unconscious with the return throw to first base while trying to break up a potential double play in Game 4 of the 1934 World Series, Dean was taken to the hospital for x-rays. The next morning's newspaper headline read, "X-RAY OF DEAN'S HEAD REVEALS NOTHING."[6]

Dean followed up his extraordinary 1934 season with another two sensational years in 1935 and 1936. He compiled an outstanding 3.04 ERA and a record of 28–12 in the first of those years, leading the league in wins for the second straight time. He also finished first among all NL hurlers with 325 innings pitched, 29 complete games, and 190 strikeouts, topping the circuit in the last category for the fourth consecutive time. Dean's outstanding performance earned him a second-place finish to Chicago's Gabby Hartnett in the NL MVP voting. He placed second in the balloting again the following year, trailing only Giants left-hander Carl Hubbell in the final tally. In addition to finishing second in the league to Hubbell with twenty-four victories, Dean placed second in the league rankings with 195 strikeouts. He also topped the circuit with 315 innings pitched, 28 complete games, and 11 saves.

Commenting years later on Dean's pitching brilliance, one-time Cardinals infielder Burgess Whitehead suggested, "Dizzy Dean went to the third grade in school, but he was absolutely the greatest right-handed pitcher I ever saw. He could stand 60'6"—the distance from home plate to the mound—and throw the ball in a knothole 99 times out of a hundred."[7]

Well on his way to another twenty-win campaign in 1937, Dean saw his days as a dominant pitcher come to an abrupt end midway through the season when a line drive off the bat of American League outfielder Earl Averill at the annual All-Star Game struck him in the foot, breaking his toe. Attempting to return to the mound too soon following the injury, Dean subsequently changed his pitching motion in an effort to put less pressure on his toe when he landed after completing his delivery to home plate. The change in his pitching mechanics caused Dean to injure his arm, resulting in the loss of his once overpowering fastball. He spent the remainder of his career primarily as a junk-ball pitcher, depending mostly on guile and off-speed pitches to maneuver his way past opposing lineups.

After finishing the 1937 season with a record of 13–10, Dean found himself traded to the Chicago Cubs, with whom he spent the next four years. Although he never again posted big numbers, the sore-armed hurler pitched effectively for the pennant-winning Cubs in 1938, compiling a record of 7–1 and an exceptional ERA of 1.81 in his ten starts. Dean appeared in a total of only thirty games for Chicago during the course of the next three seasons, finally announcing his retirement in 1941. He ended his playing career with a won-lost record of 150–83 and an ERA of 3.02. Dean compiled an overall record of 134–75, a 2.99 ERA, 141 complete games, and 23 shutouts in his years with the Cardinals.

After retiring from the game, Dean became a broadcaster for several teams, including the Cardinals and St. Louis Browns. Always extremely candid, and never at a loss for words, Dean stated on the air in 1947 that he believed he could do a better job than nine out of the ten hurlers on the staff of the pitching-poor Browns. Taken up on his offer by team management, Dean made a brief comeback at the age of thirty-seven, pitching four scoreless innings on the season's final day, before permanently returning to the broadcast booth.

Dean announced games nationally from 1952 to 1965, entertaining baseball fans across the country with his wit, colorful personality, and frequent malapropisms. He gained admittance to Cooperstown during that time, being elected to the Hall of Fame by the members of the Baseball Writers' Association of America (BBWAA) in 1953. Dean remained in sportscasting for more than a quarter of a century, finally settling down with his wife Patricia in her hometown of Bond, Mississippi. He died of a heart attack at the age of sixty-four in Reno, Nevada, on July 17, 1974.

Expressing the sentiments of most baseball fans from an earlier generation, Jim Murray wrote the following in the *Los Angeles Times* two days later:

> Well, we're all ten years older today. Dizzy Dean is dead, and 1934 is gone forever. Another part of our youth fled. You look in the mirror and the small boy no longer smiles back at you . . . just that sad old man. The Gas House Gang is now a duet. Dizzy died the other day at the age of eleven or twelve. The little boy in all of us died with him. But, for one brief shining afternoon in 1934, he brought joy to that dreary time when most needed it. Dizzy Dean. It's impossible to say without a smile, but then who wants to try? If I know Diz, he'll be calling God 'podner' someplace today. I hope there's golf courses or a card game or a slugger who's a sucker for a low outside fastball for Diz. He might have been what baseball's all about.[8]

CARDINAL CAREER HIGHLIGHTS

Best Season

Although Dean is perhaps remembered most for winning thirty games in 1934, he actually pitched almost as well the following year, posting only two fewer victories, throwing five more complete games and fourteen more innings, and striking out only five fewer batters. But 1934 has always been recognized as Dean's signature season, and with good reason. In addition to winning 30 games, compiling a 2.66 ERA that represented his best mark as a full-time starter, tossing 24 complete games and 312 innings, and leading all NL hurlers with 195 strikeouts, a career-high 7 shutouts, and a winning percentage of .811, Dean allowed fewer base runners per 9 innings pitched than he did in 1935, posting a WHIP (walks plus hits allowed per innings pitched) of 1.165, as opposed to the mark of 1.233 he compiled the ensuing campaign.

Memorable Moments and Greatest Performances

Dean pitched a number of memorable games during his years with the Cardinals. On July 30, 1933, he established a new twentieth-century major-league record (since broken) by striking out seventeen Chicago Cubs during an 8–2 Cardinals win. The following year, he clinched the pennant for St. Louis and posted his thirtieth win of the campaign by shutting out the Reds, 9–0, on September 30. Earlier in the year, Dean put together a ten-game winning streak, en route to finishing the season with a record of 30–7.

Perhaps Dean's most satisfying victory, however, came against Detroit in that year's World Series. Dean shut out the Tigers on only six hits in Game 7 of the Fall Classic, enabling the Cardinals to capture their third world championship with an 11–0 win in Detroit. Dean concluded the Series with 2 wins in his 3 starts, a 1.73 ERA, 2 complete games, and 17 strikeouts in 26 innings of work.

Notable Achievements

Four-time 20-game winner, posting thirty victories once (1934).
Compiled an ERA below 3.00 twice.
Threw more than twenty complete games four times.
Threw more than 300 innings three times.
Led NL pitchers in: wins twice, winning percentage once, strikeouts four times, complete games three times, innings pitched three times, shutouts twice, and saves once.

Last NL pitcher to win thirty games in a season.
Third all-time among Cardinals pitchers in strikeouts (1,095).
1934 NL MVP.
Finished second in NL MVP voting twice (1935, 1936).
Three-time *Sporting News* All-Star selection (1934, 1935, 1936).
Four-time NL All-Star (1934, 1935, 1936, 1937).
1934 NL champion.
1934 world champion.
Elected to Baseball Hall of Fame by members of BBWAA in 1953.

NOTES

1. Red Smith, quoted in "Quotes by Dizzy Dean," *Dizzy Dean.com*, www.dizzydean.com/quotes.htm (accessed September 12, 2012).
2. Dizzy Dean, "Quotes by Dizzy Dean," www.dizzydean.com/quotes.htm.
3. Dean, "Quotes by Dizzy Dean," www.dizzydean.com/quotes.htm.
4. Dean, "Quotes by Dizzy Dean," www.dizzydean.com/quotes.htm.
5. Pepper Martin, quoted in "Quotes by Dizzy Dean," www.dizzydean.com/quotes.htm.
6. Quoted in "Quotes by Dizzy Dean," www.dizzydean.com/quotes.html.
7. Burgess Whitehead, quoted in *A Century of Success: 100 Years of Cardinals Glory*, Major League Baseball Productions, 1992.
8. Jim Murray, quoted in "Quotes by Dizzy Dean," www.dizzydean.com/quotes.htm.

8

FRANKIE FRISCH

Although Frankie Frisch eventually established himself as the unquestioned leader of the Cardinals' famed "Gas House Gang," he hardly found himself being welcomed with open arms when he first arrived in St. Louis prior to the start of the 1927 campaign. Even though Frisch played exceptionally well for the New York Giants the previous few years, Cardinals fans openly voiced their disapproval when their team acquired him for fellow future Hall of Fame second baseman Rogers Hornsby during the off-season. St. Louis fans acknowledged the excellence of Frisch, who batted well over .300 in each of the previous six seasons, while leading the National League in runs scored, hits, stolen bases, and total bases at different times. But they bristled at the idea of parting with Hornsby, who had been the senior circuit's dominant player since the beginning of the decade.

In spite of the cool reception he initially received, Frisch quickly won over St. Louis fans with his outstanding hitting and defense, superb baserunning, and aggressive style of play, which became a trademark of the Cardinals in subsequent seasons. The second baseman had one of his finest all-around years in 1927, leading the league with 48 stolen bases and placing among the leaders with a .337 batting average, 112 runs scored, and 208 hits, en route to earning a second-place finish in the league Most Valuable Player voting at season's end. Frisch continued to ingratiate himself to Cardinals fans in the years that followed, leading St. Louis to four pennants and two world championships between 1928 and 1934.

Born to German immigrants in the Bronx, New York, on September 9, 1898, Frank Francis Frisch ended up attending Fordham

University, where he starred in baseball, football, basketball, and track. Shortly after graduating from college in June 1919, Frisch joined the New York Giants without playing as much as a single game of minor-league ball. The switch-hitting infielder spent the final three months of the campaign filling in at both second and third base, failing to distinguish himself as a hitter by batting only .226, but leaving a lasting impression on Giants manager John McGraw by stealing fifteen bases in only fifty-four games.

In spite of his early struggles at the plate, "The Fordham Flash," as Frisch came to be known, quickly became a favorite of his new manager, who admired the young infielder's speed, athleticism, versatility, and aggressiveness. McGraw installed Frisch as the team's starting third baseman early the following year, before naming him team captain shortly thereafter. Frisch responded by batting .280, driving in 77 runs, and finishing third in the league with 34 stolen bases.

McGraw used Frisch extensively at both second and third base in each of the next two seasons, during which time the young infielder established himself as one of the senior circuit's most dynamic players. After batting .341, driving in 100 runs, scoring 121 others, collecting 211 hits and 17 triples, and leading the NL with 49 stolen bases in 1921, Frisch batted .327, scored 101 runs, and stole 31 bases the following year. The Giants defeated the Yankees in the World Series both years, with Frisch compiling batting averages of .300 and .471 in the two Fall Classics.

Led by Frisch, who became the team's full-time second baseman in 1923, the Giants captured the NL pennant in each of the next two seasons as well. Frisch topped the circuit with 223 hits in 1923, while also placing among the leaders with a .348 batting average, 111 RBIs, 116 runs scored, and 29 stolen bases. He followed that up in 1924 by batting .328, compiling 15 triples, and leading the league with 121 runs scored, en route to earning a third-place finish in the league MVP voting. Although the Giants lost the World Series both years, Frisch posted batting averages of .400 and .333 in the losing efforts.

Frisch played well in both 1925 and 1926, but McGraw took out much of his frustration on his team's captain when the Giants failed to win the pennant either year. After being berated by McGraw in front of the entire team for missing a sign during an August 1926 loss, Frisch left the team, bringing an end to his previously close relationship with his manager. The Giants traded Frisch and pitcher Jimmy Ring to the St. Louis Cardinals at the end of the season for the equally unhappy Rogers Hornsby, whose relationship with St. Louis management had deteriorated as well.

Faced with the unenviable task of trying to replace the NL's greatest player in St. Louis, Frisch exhibited the same fire and competitiveness with which he played the game his entire career. In addition to posting outstanding offensive numbers, he led all league second basemen in fielding average, while also compiling an all-time single-season record 641 assists and 1,059 chances at second base. Sportswriter Damon Runyon praised Frisch for his fielding ability, saying, "His range was such that he played second base, some of center field, and a slice of right field, too."[1]

Frisch's exceptional all-around performance in 1927 earned him a second-place finish in the league MVP voting, prompting longtime *St. Louis Post-Dispatch* sportswriter Bob Broeg to later say, "Frisch didn't make them forget The Rajah (Hornsby), but he made them remember The Flash."[2]

Frisch continued to excel at second base for the Cardinals in each of the next four seasons, leading them to the NL pennant in 1928, 1930, and 1931, and to the world championship in the last of those years. In addition to batting over .300 and scoring more than ninety runs each season, he annually finished among the league leaders in stolen bases. Frisch had one of his finest offensive seasons in 1930, batting .346, scoring 121 runs, and driving in a career-high 114 runs. He followed that up by hitting .311 and topping the senior circuit with twenty-eight stolen bases in 1931, en route to leading the Cardinals to the world championship and capturing league MVP honors.

Although Frisch's offensive numbers fell off somewhat in subsequent seasons, he remained the leader and driving force behind the St. Louis "Gas House Gang" squad that won the World Series in 1934. Named player-manager of the Cardinals in 1933, Frisch led a rowdy and raucous collection of hardnosed players that included the Dean brothers, Joe Medwick, Leo Durocher, Pepper Martin, and Ripper Collins to victory over the Detroit Tigers in the 1934 Fall Classic. The fiery and combative Cardinals took on the personality of their skipper, whose hitting style reflected his overall attitude, according to Hall of Fame pitcher Burleigh Grimes, who said, "That Frisch was a sassy kid . . . but he had a lot of guts. I'd try to drive him back but he'd still lean in there and hit me to left field."[3]

Frisch adopted the same aggressive approach to managing, taking every possible opportunity to confront, embarrass, and intimidate umpires. He furiously disputed any call made against St. Louis, hurling his glove around the field and stomping his cap into shreds.

Frisch continued to manage the Cardinals until 1938, one year after he retired as an active player. The second baseman ended his career with a .316 batting average, 2,880 hits, 1,244 RBIs, 1,532 runs scored, and 419 stolen bases. One of the most difficult men in baseball to strike out, he fanned more than twenty times in a season just twice in his career, whiffing a total of only 272 times in more than 10,000 total plate appearances. Frisch never struck out more than seventeen times in any of his eleven seasons with the Cardinals, compiling a .312 batting average during his time in St. Louis. He also knocked in 720 runs, scored 831 others, collected 1,577 hits, and stole 195 bases as a member of the team.

After leaving the Cardinals organization, Frisch did radio play-by-play for the Boston Braves in 1939, before managing the Pittsburgh Pirates from 1940 to 1946. He rejoined the Giants in 1947, the same year that the members of the Baseball Writers' Association of America (BBWAA) elected him to the Hall of Fame. Frisch served one year as a radio announcer for the Giants, and another as a coach, before taking over the managerial reins of the Chicago Cubs for three seasons in 1949. Frisch resumed his announcing career with the Giants in 1952, although a heart attack he suffered in September 1956 forced him to subsequently curtail his activities. Frisch later served as a member of the Hall of Fame's Veterans Committee, eventually becoming chairman of the group. During his time on the committee, Frisch used his strong and persuasive personality to get many of his former Giants and Cardinals teammates who had previously been passed on by the members of the BBWAA elected to Cooperstown. Among those players who Frisch argued for extensively were George Kelly, Fred Lindstrom, Jesse Haines, Dave Bancroft, Chick Hafey, Ross Youngs, and Rube Marquard—whose selections have since been questioned by many.

Frisch died in Wilmington, Delaware, on March 12, 1973, from injuries suffered during a car accident he was involved in near Elkton, Maryland, one month earlier. The seventy-four-year-old Frisch had been returning to his home in Rhode Island from a Veterans Committee meeting in Florida when he lost control of his car.

CARDINAL CAREER HIGHLIGHTS

Best Season

Frisch won NL MVP honors in 1931, when he helped lead the Cardinals to the pennant by batting .311, scoring 96 runs, driving in 82 others, and topping the circuit with 28 steals; however, he posted much better overall numbers in both 1927 and 1930. Frisch batted .337 in the first of those years, knocked in 78 runs, scored 112 others, collected 208 hits, and led the league with 48 stolen bases. He compiled even better numbers in 1930, when he batted .346, scored 121 runs, and established career highs by driving in 114 runs, collecting 46 doubles, and posting on-base and slugging percentages of .407 and .520, respectively. It must be considered, however, that the NL experimented with using a livelier ball in both 1929 and 1930, causing offensive numbers to increase dramatically throughout the senior circuit. As a result, Frisch placed in the league's top 10 in only three offensive categories in 1930, in spite of the lofty numbers he produced. On the other hand, the second baseman ranked among the league leaders in six different offensive categories in 1927, en route to earning a second-place finish to Pittsburgh's Paul Waner in the MVP voting. Furthermore, Frisch accumulated almost 200 more assists in the field in 1927 than he did in 1930 (641 to 473), establishing in the process a major-league record for second basemen that still stands. All things considered, Frisch had his best all-around year for the Cardinals in 1927.

Memorable Moments and Greatest Performances

Although Frisch hit only 105 home runs during the course of his career, never hitting more than twelve round-trippers in any single season, he experienced a brief power surge early in 1928, homering in three of the Cardinals' first four games. Later that same year, on September 28, Frisch sparked St. Louis to a seven-run rally in the top of the fifteenth inning against Boston by stealing home. The Cardinals ended up winning the contest, 10–3, with Frisch's theft making him the only NL player ever to steal home on two separate occasions in extra innings. On July 5, 1930, Frisch tied Miller Huggins's NL record by accepting sixteen chances during a 6–4 St. Louis victory over Cincinnati.

Although Frisch hit only four home runs in the course of the entire 1931 campaign, he delivered one of the Cardinals' biggest long balls of the season on June 16. With St. Louis trailing Philadelphia, 1–0, in the bottom of the ninth inning, George Watkins tied the game with a one-out homer. Frisch followed Watkins's blast with one of his own, giving the Cardinals a 2–1 victory.

Nevertheless, Frisch hit arguably the most memorable home run of his career against the American League in the 1933 All-Star Game. Although the Nationals ended up losing the inaugural All-Star tilt by a score of 4–2, Frisch hit the first home run for the senior circuit in the history of the Midsummer Classic in the sixth inning, accounting for his team's only two runs.

Notable Achievements

- Knocked in more than 100 runs once (114 in 1930).
- Scored more than 100 runs three times.
- Batted over .300 seven times, surpassing the .330 mark on three occasions.
- Collected more than 200 hits once (208 in 1927).
- Finished in double digits in triples twice.
- Amassed more than forty doubles twice.
- Compiled on-base percentage in excess of .400 once (.407 in 1930).
- Posted slugging percentage in excess of .500 once (.520 in 1930).
- Stole more than forty bases once (forty-eight in 1927).
- Led NL in stolen bases twice (1927, 1931).
- Led NL second basemen in fielding percentage three times and assists once.
- Holds single-season major-league record for most assists by a second baseman (641 in 1927).

1931 NL MVP.

Two-time *Sporting News* All-Star selection (1930, 1931).

Three-time NL All-Star (1933, 1934, 1935).

Four-time NL champion (1928, 1930, 1931, 1934).

Two-time world champion (1931, 1934).

Elected to Baseball Hall of Fame by members of BBWAA in 1947.

NOTES

1. Damon Runyon, quoted in "Frisch, Frankie," *National Baseball Hall of Fame and Museum*, www.baseballhall.org/hof/frisch-frankie (accessed September 14, 2012).

2. Bob Broeg, quoted in "Frisch, Frankie," www.baseballhall.org/hof/frisch-frankie.

3. Burleigh Grimes, quoted in "Frankie Frisch," *Baseball-Reference*, www.baseball-reference.com/bullpen/Frankie_Frisch (accessed September 14, 2012).

9

OZZIE SMITH

Generally considered to be the greatest defensive shortstop in baseball history, Ozzie Smith earned the nickname "The Wizard" throughout the course of his career for his brilliance in the field. The winner of a National League record thirteen consecutive Gold Gloves, Smith gained widespread acclaim during his playing days for his ability to perform the seemingly impossible with his glove. More than just a defender, Smith was an artist in the field, incorporating into his game a combination of baseball, ballet, and gymnastics. Whether diving for a hard-hit ball up the middle, ranging far into the hole to rob a batter of an apparent base hit, or gathering in a short pop fly hit to the outfield, Smith displayed an incredible amount of quickness and dexterity in the field that separated him from virtually every other player who has ever manned his position. Meanwhile, although Smith represented a liability at the plate early in his career, he eventually turned himself into a solid offensive performer as well, excelling on the base paths and even winning the NL Silver Slugger Award in 1987, as the senior circuit's best-hitting shortstop. Smith's outstanding all-around play helped the Cardinals capture four division titles, three NL pennants, and one world championship in his fifteen years with the team.

Born in Mobile, Alabama, on December 26, 1954, Osborne Earl Smith developed his baseball skills playing in California after moving with his family to Watts, Los Angeles, at the age of six. After Smith graduated from California Polytechnic State University, San Luis Obispo, the San Diego Padres selected him in the fourth round of the 1977 amateur draft.

Smith made his major-league debut with the Padres the following year, earning their starting shortstop job in spring training after appearing in only sixty-eight games in the minor leagues. Although the twenty-three-year-old shortstop failed to distinguish himself at the plate in his first big-league season, hitting only 1 home run, driving in just 46 runs, batting only .258, and compiling on-base and slugging percentages of just .311 and .312, respectively, he displayed enough on the bases (40 steals) and in the field to earn a second-place finish in the NL Rookie of the Year balloting. Early in the year, on April 28, 1978, Smith made what he later stated he considered to be the finest defensive play of his career when he dove to his left to snare a grounder hit by Atlanta's Jeff Burroughs. The ball took a bad hop and skipped behind Smith's head, prompting the shortstop to thrust out his bare right hand. Snagging the ball as he fell to the ground, he rose quickly to his feet and threw out Burroughs at first base.

Smith continued to excel in the field for the Padres in each of the next three seasons, earning Gold Glove honors in both 1980 and 1981, and establishing a major-league record that still stands by amassing 621 assists in the first of those years. However, his struggles at the plate continued, with Smith failing to bat any higher than .230 in any of those campaigns, even though he stole a career-high fifty-seven bases in 1980. After Smith batted just .222 in 1981 and demanded a pay raise from the Padres, San Diego elected to trade him to the Cardinals for Garry Templeton, who had worn out his welcome in St. Louis.

Whitey Herzog's Cardinals, who emphasized speed and defense in spacious Busch Stadium, proved to be a perfect match for Smith. Since the Cardinals usually found themselves involved in low-scoring contests, they relied heavily on the brilliant young shortstop's ability to thwart late-inning rallies with his fielding excellence. Herzog later argued that Smith typically saved seventy-five runs per year with his glove.

With Smith manning shortstop for them, the Cardinals won their first world championship in fifteen years in 1982. They also enjoyed pennant-winning seasons in 1985 and 1987. Smith continued to earn Gold Glove honors year after year, leading NL shortstops in assists and fielding percentage virtually every season. He also gradually evolved into an effective offensive player. Learning how to use his home ballpark's artificial surface to his advantage, Smith shortened his swing and eventually became quite adept at chopping down on the ball to make better use of his outstanding running speed. After seeing his offensive numbers rise steadily his first three years in St. Louis, Smith established new career highs with 6 home runs, 54 RBIs, a .276 batting average, a .355 on-base percentage, and a .361 slugging percentage in 1985. Although the Cardinals eventually lost that year's World Series to the Kansas City Royals in seven games, Smith gave St. Louis fans one of the greatest thrills they ever experienced when he homered against Dodger closer Tom Niedenfuer in the bottom of the ninth inning of Game 5 of the National League Championship Series (NLCS), to give the Cardinals a 3–2 victory and a 3–2 lead in the series.

After performing well again in 1986, Smith had arguably his finest all-around season the following year, stealing 43 bases and posting career highs in RBIs (75), runs scored (104), hits (182), doubles (40), batting average (.303), on-base percentage (.392), and slugging percentage (.383). He also committed only ten errors in the field. Smith's outstanding all-around performance helped the Cardinals capture their second NL pennant in three years, earning him a second-place finish in the league Most Valuable Player voting.

Smith continued to play exceptional defense in subsequent seasons, even though he gradually lost some of his mobility and arm strength. Compensating as he grew older for his somewhat diminished natural gifts, he became an expert at positioning himself in the field and improving his throwing mechanics to get rid of the ball more quickly. Despite displaying less range in the field than he had earlier in his career, Smith established a new NL record for fewest errors in a season by a shortstop when he committed only eight miscues the entire 1991 campaign. He also batted .285 and scored ninety-six runs that year. Smith collected his 2,000th hit and stole his 500th base the following season, while also notching his thirteenth consecutive Gold Glove, breaking in the process a NL record previously held by Willie Mays and Roberto Clemente.

Smith remained the Cardinals' full-time starting shortstop for three more years, before a serious shoulder injury cut into his playing time significantly in 1995. He played one more year, announcing his retirement at the conclusion of the 1996 campaign to assume a position in the broadcast booth. He ended his career having compiled more assists (8,375) and participated in more double plays (1,590) than any other shortstop in major-league history (Omar Vizquel has since surpassed the latter figure). Smith also collected 2,460 hits during the course of his 19-year career, scored 1,257 runs, stole 580 bases, batted .262, and posted a .337 on-base percentage. His numbers as a member of the Cardinals include 1,944 hits, 991 runs scored, 433 stolen bases, a .272 batting average, and a .350 on-base percentage. He ranks among the team's all-time leaders in games played (third), plate appearances (third), at bats (third), bases on balls (third), stolen bases (third), hits (seventh), runs scored (seventh), and doubles (tenth).

Following his playing career, Smith served as host of the television show *This Week in Baseball* for three years beginning in 1997, before pursuing numerous business ventures. The members of the Baseball Writers' Association of American (BBWAA) elected him to the Hall of Fame the first time his name appeared on the ballot in 2002. Speaking of the man who became known as The Wizard, longtime Cardinals announcer Jack Buck once stated, "He is the greatest defensive shortstop to ever play the game."[1]

CARDINAL CAREER HIGHLIGHTS

Best Season

Although Smith stole a career-high 57 bases, scored 80 runs, and batted .270 in 1988, the 1987 and 1991 campaigns would have to be considered his two finest. In addition to batting .285, compiling a .380 on-base percentage, stealing 35 bases, and scoring 96 runs in 1991, Smith established a new NL record for shortstops by committing only eight errors in the field, en route to earning Gold Glove honors for the twelfth straight time. The Wizard made two more miscues in the field four years earlier, when he committed a total of ten errors, but he also accepted 132 more chances, enabling him to compile the exact same fielding percentage (.987). Furthermore, Smith had easily his most productive offensive season in 1987, establishing career highs with 75 RBIs, 104 runs scored, 182 hits, 40 doubles, a .303 batting average, a .392 on-base percentage, and a .383 slugging percentage. His outstanding all-around performance enabled him to earn his only top-10 finish in the NL MVP voting, with the shortstop placing second to Andre Dawson in the balloting.

Memorable Moments and Greatest Performances

As one might expect, Smith provided Cardinals fans with their most indelible images of him with his extraordinary glove work. The Wizard made several remarkable plays in the field during his time in St. Louis, turning in perhaps his most memorable effort when he hauled in a short fly ball to left field with a headlong, diving, over-the-shoulder catch that seemed to defy the laws of gravity.

Smith also reached a number of milestones while wearing a St. Louis uniform. With the Cardinals celebrating their 100th anniversary in 1992, Smith stole the 500th base of his career on April 26, and then followed that up exactly one month later by collecting his 2,000th hit on May 26. On July 14, 1994, he recorded four assists during an 8–1 Cardinals' loss to Colorado, moving him past Luis Aparicio into first place all-time among shortstops. Smith added to his collection of fielding records on September 15, 1995, when he established himself as the all-time leader among players at his position by turning in his 1,554th double play.

Nevertheless, Smith ironically created his greatest memory for Cardinals fans with his bat, doing so by hitting a game-winning home run against Los Angeles right-hander Tom Niedenfuer in the bottom of the ninth inning of Game 5 of the 1985 NLCS. After dropping the first two contests to the Dodgers, St. Louis rallied to even the series at two games apiece. Facing the Dodgers' ace reliever with one man out, no one on base, and the score tied at 2–2 in the bottom of the ninth inning of Game 5, Smith hit a low inside fastball over the right-field wall, reaching the seats from the left-hand side of the plate for the first time in 3,010 career at bats. Smith's unexpected blast elicited cries of "Go crazy folks. . . . Go crazy" from legendary Cardinals broadcaster Jack Buck. Cardinals fans later voted it the greatest moment in Busch Stadium history.

Notable Achievements

Scored more than 100 runs once (104 in 1987).
Batted over .300 once (.303 in 1987).

Surpassed forty doubles once (forty in 1987).

Stole more than thirty bases nine times, topping forty steals on three occasions.

Led NL shortstops in assists three times, putouts once, and fielding percentage seven times.

Holds major-league record for most assists by a shortstop (8,375).

Holds NL records for most double plays (1,590) and career games (2,511) at shortstop.

Third all-time on Cardinals in games played (1,990), plate appearances (8,242), at bats (7,160), bases on balls (876), and stolen bases (433).

Finished second in 1987 NL MVP voting.

1985 NLCS MVP.

1987 NL Silver Slugger winner at shortstop.

Won eleven consecutive Gold Gloves (1982, 1983, 1984, 1985, 1986, 1987, 1988, 1989, 1990, 1991, 1992).

Five-time *Sporting News* All-Star selection.

Fourteen-time NL All-Star (1982, 1983, 1984, 1985, 1986, 1987, 1988, 1989, 1990, 1991, 1992, 1994, 1995, 1996).

Three-time NL champion (1982, 1985, 1987).

1982 world champion.

Elected to Baseball Hall of Fame by members of BBWAA in 2002.

NOTE

1. Jack Buck, quoted in *A Century of Success: 100 Years of Cardinals Glory*, Major League Baseball Productions, 1992.

10

JIM BOTTOMLEY

Johnny Mize proved to be a tremendous offensive force during his time in St. Louis, winning a batting title and leading the National League in home runs twice, RBIs once, and slugging percentage and total bases three times each. He finished second in the league Most Valuable Player voting in back-to-back years and earned All-Star honors in four out of five seasons at one point. Even though Mize didn't have the advantage accorded Jim Bottomley of playing in the hitting-dominated 1920s, he typically hit more home runs than his predecessor at first base for the Cardinals, drove in nearly as many runs, scored just as many times, hit for just as high a batting average, and compiled higher on-base and slugging percentages. Overall, Mize would have to be considered superior to Bottomley as a hitter; however, Mize spent only six seasons in St. Louis, while Bottomley played for the Cardinals nearly twice as long. As a result, the latter posted better numbers than Mize in virtually every offensive statistical category during his time with the team. In addition to compiling more home runs than Mize, Bottomley collected many more RBIs, runs scored, hits, doubles, and triples. Doing so enabled Bottomley to claim the number ten spot in these rankings, just ahead of Mize, who had to settle for an eleventh-place finish.

Although most Cardinals fans are not nearly as familiar with Jim Bottomley as they are with several of the other forthcoming players included here, the slugging first baseman earned this lofty spot in these rankings by establishing himself as one of the NL's top run producers during the 1920s. Despite spending several of his peak seasons in St. Louis playing in the shadow of the great Rogers Hornsby, the man who came to be known as "Sunny Jim" for his smiling face and pleasant demeanor eventually gained induction into the Baseball Hall of Fame largely on the strength of his propensity for driving in huge numbers of runs. Bottomley averaged 126 RBIs per year for the Cardinals from 1924 to 1929, topping the senior circuit in that category on two separate occasions. He also batted over .360 twice and accomplished the rare feat of compiling more than 20 home runs, 20 triples, and 20 doubles in the same season in 1928, when he captured NL MVP honors.

Born in Oglesby, Illinois, on April 23, 1900, James Leroy Bottomley grew up in nearby Nokomis, Illinois, where he attended high school. After signing with the Cardinals in 1920, Bottomley spent the next two years advancing through Branch Rickey's farm system. The left-handed-hitting first baseman arrived in St. Louis for the first time in August 1922, after which he established himself as the team's first baseman of the future by batting .325 and driving in thirty-five runs, in only 151 official at bats in the season's final six weeks. Convinced that the twenty-two-year-old first sacker had all the tools necessary to excel at the major-league level, Rickey traded veteran first baseman Jack Fournier to Brooklyn during the off-season to make room for Bottomley in the Cardinals' starting lineup. Rewarding Rickey for the faith he showed in him, Bottomley had an exceptional rookie season. He knocked in 94 runs; amassed 14 triples, 34 doubles, and 194 hits; and finished second in the league to teammate Hornsby with a .371 batting average and a .425 on-base percentage.

Although Bottomley's batting average slipped to .316 in 1924, he had a solid second season, hitting 14 home runs, driving in 111 runs, and scoring 87 others. He had the greatest day of his career on September 16 of that year, when he drove in a record twelve runs against the Dodgers, with two homers, a double, and three singles. Bottomley's 6-for-6 afternoon ended up being one of two such performances he turned in during the course of his career.

Bottomley developed into one of the NL's top players in 1925, finishing among the league leaders with 21 home runs, 128 RBIs, a .367 batting average, a .578 slugging percentage, and 358 total bases, while topping the circuit with 44 doubles and 227 hits. He followed that up with another big year in 1926, when he led the league with 120 RBIs, 40 doubles, and 305 total bases. Bottomley also batted .299, scored 98 runs, and placed among the league leaders with 19 home runs and 14 triples. He subsequently performed exceptionally well against New York in the World Series, batting .345 and knocking in five runs, in helping the Cardinals upset the heavily favored Yankees in seven games.

Batting fourth in the St. Louis lineup, immediately behind Rogers Hornsby, certainly provided Bottomley with numerous opportunities to drive in runs, but the first baseman maintained his outstanding run production after Hornsby left the Cardinals at the conclusion of the 1926 campaign. Bottomley drove in 124 runs for St. Louis in 1927, while also hitting 19 home runs and batting .303. He then had arguably his finest all-around season in 1928, becoming just the second player in major-league history to surpass 20 homers, 20 triples, and 20 doubles in the same year (Chicago's Frank Schulte was the first). In addition to leading the NL with 31 home runs and 20 triples, Bottomley accumulated 42 doubles, scored a career-high 123 runs, batted .325, and topped the circuit with 136 RBIs and 362 total bases, en route to leading the Cardinals to their second pennant in three years. Although St. Louis ended up being swept by the Yankees in the World Series, Bottomley found some consolation in being named the NL's MVP at season's end.

Bottomley had one more big year left in him before his skills gradually began to diminish. He finished among the NL leaders with twenty-nine home runs and 137 RBIs in 1929, while also batting .314 and scoring 108 runs. Although he failed to produce similar numbers for the pennant-winning Cardinals in either of the next two seasons, he still managed to bat .304 and knock in ninety-seven runs in 1930, despite missing almost three weeks of the season with an injury. Injuries subsequently limited Bottomley to only 108 games in 1931. Nevertheless, he performed well for the eventual world champions, driving in seventy-five runs and finishing a close third in the NL batting race with a mark of .3482 (teammate Chick Hafey batted .3489, while Giants first baseman Bill Terry hit .3486).

After Bottomley appeared in only ninety-one games for the Cardinals in 1932, the team traded him to Cincinnati during the off-season to make room at first base for another choice member of Branch Rickey's farm system, Ripper Collins. Bottomley spent 3 years in Cincinnati, never hitting more than 13 home runs, driving in more than 83 runs, or batting higher than .284. He returned to St. Louis in 1936 as a member of the Browns. Reunited with former Cardinals teammate Roger Hornsby, who managed the American League's St. Louis entry for parts of five seasons, Bottomley had a solid season, batting .298 and knocking in ninety-five runs.

After serving the Browns primarily as a pinch hitter during the first half of the 1937 campaign, the thirty-seven-year-old Bottomley was named to succeed Hornsby as manager of the team. He served the Browns in that capacity until the season ended, being replaced by another former Cardinals player, Gabby Street. Bottomley subsequently announced his retirement, leaving the game with a lifetime batting average of .310, 219 home runs, 1,422 RBIs, 1,177 runs scored, 2,313 hits, 151 triples, and 465 doubles. Bottomley's 219 homers, 151 triples, and 465 doubles made him the first of two players (Lou Gehrig being the other) to reach the 150 mark in all three categories. In parts of 11 seasons with the Cardinals, Bottomley hit 181 home runs, knocked in 1,105 runs, scored 921 others, collected 1,727 hits, amassed 344 doubles and 119 triples, batted .325, and posted on-base and slugging percentages of .387 and .537, respectively. He ranks among the franchise's all-time leaders in home runs (eighth), RBIs (fourth), runs scored (tenth), hits (tenth), doubles (eighth), triples (fifth), and total bases (seventh).

Following his retirement as an active player, Bottomley managed briefly in the minor leagues, before moving to Bourbon, Missouri, where he raised Hereford cattle. He later returned to baseball as a scout for the Cubs and a minor-league manager in the Appalachian League. Plagued by heart problems later in life, Bottomley suffered a heart attack while serving in the latter capacity. He spent the last years of his life in nearby Sullivan, Missouri, where he was eventually laid to rest after dying of another heart attack at the age of fifty-nine. The Veterans Committee elected Bottomley to the Hall of Fame posthumously fifteen years later, in 1974.

CARDINAL CAREER HIGHLIGHTS

Best Season

Although Bottomley had several outstanding seasons for the Cardinals, he performed particularly well for them in 1925 and 1928.

Despite being overshadowed by teammate Rogers Hornsby (who won the Triple Crown) in the first of those years, Bottomley earned a seventh-place finish in the NL MVP voting by finishing among the league leaders with 21 home runs, 128 RBIs, 12 triples, 358 total bases, a .367 batting average, a .413 on-base percentage, and a .578 slugging percentage, while also topping the circuit with 227 hits and 44 doubles. Bottomley captured NL MVP honors three years later, when he batted .325, collected 187 hits and 42 doubles, compiled a .402 on-base percentage and a .628 slugging percentage, scored 123 runs, and led the league with 31 homers, 136 RBIs, 20 triples, and 362 total bases. It's a close call, but I ultimately elected to go with his 1928 campaign. In addition to winning the MVP Award by establishing career highs in home runs, triples, runs scored, total bases, and slugging percentage, he accomplished the rare feat of amassing at least 20 homers, 20 triples, and 20 doubles in the same season. Furthermore, he compiled a career-best on-base plus slugging percentage of 1.030, surpassing in the process the figure he posted in 1925 (.992) by thirty-eight percentage points.

Memorable Moments and Greatest Performances

Bottomley had several memorable games while playing for the Cardinals. He tied a major-league record by collecting three triples in one game, doing so on two separate occasions. Bottomley accomplished the feat for the first time during a 10–5 St. Louis victory over Boston on May 15, 1923. He duplicated his earlier effort against the Cubs in the second game of a doubleheader sweep of Chicago by St. Louis on June 21, 1927. Less than one month later, on July 15, 1927, Bottomley hit for the cycle, collecting five hits in five trips to the plate during a 9–7 Cardinals win over the Phillies.

Bottomley had one of his finest days at the plate on July 6, 1929, when, after hitting two home runs in a loss to the Phillies in the first game of a doubleheader, he led the Cardinals to a 28–6 victory in the nightcap by hitting a grand slam and driving in seven runs. He also collected six hits in six trips to the plate on two separate occasions, doing so for the second time during a 16–2 St. Louis victory over Pittsburgh in the second game of an August 5, 1931 doubleheader.

Bottomley's effort in the nightcap followed a first-game performance in which he hit safely another four times.

However, Bottomley had the greatest game of his career against Brooklyn at Ebbets Field on September 16, 1924, when he went 6-for-6 for the first time, amassing in the process a major-league record twelve RBIs during a 17–3 Cardinals win. The slugging first baseman collected two home runs, a double, and three singles during the contest, driving home four runs with a fourth-inning grand slam.

Notable Achievements

Hit more than twenty home runs three times, topping thirty homers once.

Knocked in more than 100 runs six times, surpassing 120 RBIs on five occasions.

Scored more than 100 runs twice.

Batted over .300 nine times, topping the .360 mark twice.

Collected more than 200 hits once (227 in 1925).

Finished in double digits in triples seven times, amassing twenty three-baggers once (1928).

Topped forty doubles three times.

Surpassed 350 total bases twice.

Compiled on-base percentage in excess of .400 four times.

Posted slugging percentage in excess of .600 once (.628 in 1928).

Surpassed 20 homers, 20 triples, and 20 doubles in same season once (1928).

Led NL in RBIs twice, doubles twice, total bases twice, home runs once, triples once, and hits once.

Led NL first basemen in putouts twice.

Holds major-league record for most RBIs in one game (twelve on September 16, 1924).

1928 NL MVP.

1925 *Sporting News* All-Star selection.

Four-time NL champion (1926, 1928, 1930, 1931).

Two-time world champion (1926, 1931).

Elected to Baseball Hall of Fame by members of Veterans Committee in 1974.

11

JOHNNY MIZE

The National League's premier slugger and top first baseman for nearly a decade, Johnny Mize hit 359 career home runs despite spending three peak seasons serving in the military during World War II. A home run hitter who rarely struck out, Mize led the NL in homers and slugging percentage four times each, while also topping the senior circuit in RBIs and total bases three times each and leading the league in runs scored, batting average, triples, and doubles once each. Blessed with a keen batting eye, Mize compiled a lifetime on-base percentage of .397, while striking out only 524 times in almost 7,400 total plate appearances. The big first baseman's proficiency as a hitter eventually earned him a spot in Cooperstown in spite of the fact that he played regularly in the major leagues for only eleven full seasons.

Born in Demorest, Georgia, on January 7, 1913, John Robert Mize originally signed with the Cardinals as an amateur free agent as a seventeen-year-old in 1930; however, he didn't make his major-league debut with the team until six years later. Mize elected to attend Piedmont College before beginning his professional playing career. He then needed to have corrective surgery to repair an upper-leg bone spur that threatened to end his career before it began. After Mize spent a brief amount of time in the St. Louis farm system, the Cardinals sold him to Cincinnati for $55,000 on December 13, 1934. The Reds later returned the twenty-one-year-old first sacker to the Cardinals, however, due to concerns about the health of his leg.

Finally arriving in St. Louis in 1936, Mize won the starting first base job in spring training and subsequently went on to hit 19 home runs, knock in 93 runs, and bat .329 in his first big-league season. The poise Mize exhibited at the plate prompted Cincinnati Reds manager Charlie Dressen to refer to him as the "greatest rookie I've ever seen."[1]

Standing six feet, two inches and weighing close to 220 pounds, Mize possessed little foot speed and only marginal range in the field, but he had sure hands and an extremely quick bat that soon earned him the nickname "The Big Cat." And, despite his burly appearance, Mize displayed a great deal of finesse at the plate, rarely swinging at bad pitches and hitting for a high batting average, especially in his early years in the league.

Mize followed up his outstanding rookie campaign with an exceptional sophomore season, finishing second to teammate Joe Medwick in the NL batting race with a mark of .364. The big first baseman also placed among the league leaders with 25 home runs, 113 RBIs, 103 runs scored, 204 hits, 40 doubles, 333 total bases, a .427 on-base percentage, and a .595 slugging percentage, en route to earning a top-10 finish in the NL Most Valuable Player voting and the first All-Star selection of his young career.

Mize had another productive year in 1938, hitting 27 homers, knocking in 102 runs, batting .337, and leading the league with 16 triples, 326 total bases, and a .614 slugging percentage. Continuing to perform at an extremely high level in 1939, Mize led the league in four different offensive categories, topping the circuit with 28 homers, a .349 batting average, a .626 slugging percentage, and 353 total bases. He also finished among the leaders with 108 RBIs, 104 runs scored, 197 hits, 14 triples, 44 doubles, 92 walks, and a .444 on-base percentage. Mize's outstanding all-around performance earned him a second-place finish in the league MVP balloting.

Swinging more for the fences in 1940 caused Mize's batting average to drop somewhat to .314. Nevertheless, the slugger ended up leading the NL with 43 home runs, 137 RBIs, 368 total bases, and a .636 slugging percentage. He also placed near the top of the league rankings with 111 runs scored, 13 triples, and a .404 on-base percentage, en route to earning his second straight runner-up finish in the MVP voting.

Although Mize put up solid numbers again in 1941, concluding the campaign with 100 RBIs and a league-leading thirty-nine doubles, he showed decreased offensive production in virtually every statistical category. Following his pattern of trading away players before their skills began to decline, Cardinals general manager Branch Rickey dealt the twenty-nine-year-old first baseman to the New York Giants for three prospects at the end of the year.

Mize went on to perform extremely well for the Giants in parts of five seasons, even though he ended up missing three full years after he enlisted in the U.S. Navy in March 1943. Mize surpassed forty homers and 100 runs scored twice each as a member of the Giants. He also knocked in more than 100 runs three times and batted over .300 on three separate occasions. He had his best year for them in 1947, when he batted .302 and established career highs by leading the league with 51 home runs, 138 RBIs, and 137 runs scored. Mize's forty-two strikeouts that season made him the only player ever to strike out fewer than fifty times while also hitting fifty homers.

Mize's proficiency as a hitter could be largely attributed to his keen batting eye and great patience at the plate. Sportswriter Tom Meany once wrote, "Taking a pitch, Mize actually followed the ball with his eyes right into the catcher's mitt, and he maintains that he actually could see the ball hit the bat."[2]

Meanwhile, Stan Musial, who played briefly with Mize in St. Louis, discussed the poise and grace his former teammate exhibited in the batter's box, saying, "Did you ever see a pitcher knock him down at the plate? Remember how he reacted when brushed back? He'd just lean back on his left foot, bend his body back, and let the pitch go by. Then he'd lean back into the batter's box and resume his stance, as graceful as a big cat."[3]

The Giants ended up selling Mize to the Yankees for $40,000 in August 1949, and the veteran first baseman went on to become a key contributor to five consecutive world championship clubs on the other side of town. Although he remained a part-time player during his time with the Yankees, Mize produced whenever the team called upon him, providing a powerful left-handed bat against opposing right-handers and serving as a pinch hitter deluxe.

While with the Yankees, Mize continued to impress all those who observed his hitting style. Manager Casey Stengel noted, "His bat doesn't travel as far as anybody else's. He just cocks it and slaps, and when you're as big as he is, you can slap a ball into the seats. That short swing is wonderful."[4]

Mize announced his retirement from the game at the conclusion of the 1953 season. He ended his career with 359 home runs, 1,337 RBIs, 1,118 runs scored, 2,011 hits, and a .312 batting average. His numbers in six full seasons in St. Louis include 158 home runs, 653 RBIs, 546 runs scored, 1,048 hits, 66 triples, 218 doubles, a .336 batting average, a .419 on-base percentage, and a .600 slugging percentage. Mize ranks in the Cardinals' all-time top 10 in batting average (fourth), on-base percentage (fifth), slugging percentage (third), and home runs (tenth).

Although Mize's relatively modest career numbers prevented him from gaining admittance to Cooperstown during his initial period of eligibility, the members of the Veterans Committee eventually elected him to the Hall of Fame knowing that he lost three peak seasons due to time spent serving in the military during World War II. They also voted for him on the strength of his impressive .397 career on-base percentage, .562 slugging percentage, 10 All-Star selections, and six top-10 finishes in the league MVP voting. Likely resonating with the voters as well were Mize's all-time record six 3-homer games, his outstanding walk-to-strikeout ratio of better than 1.5 to 1, and the fact that he homered in all of the 15 major-league parks in use during his career.

Following his playing career, Mize served briefly as a coach with the Kansas City Athletics, before working for a housing development in St. Augustine, Florida, during the 1970s. He eventually returned to Demorest, Georgia, where he spent the last few years of his life before passing away at the age of eighty in June 1993.

Discussing Mize in his book, *Ted Williams' Hit List*, "The Splendid Splinter" said the following of his contemporary:

> Mize was one of the really outstanding hitters in baseball history. . . . Every place he played, from the time he started to play baseball till the time he quit, he was a premier hitter. . . . When he ambled up to the plate, people expected big things because he made things happen. I always thought he was one of the very best.[5]

Johnny Mize likely never received a greater compliment from anyone.

CARDINAL CAREER HIGHLIGHTS

Best Season

It really was a toss-up between Mize's 1939 and 1940 campaigns, and either one of those years would have made a good choice. Mize proved to be somewhat more productive in 1940, hitting more home runs (43 to 28), driving in more runs (137 to 108), scoring more times (111 to 104), amassing more total bases (368 to 353), and posting a slightly higher slugging percentage (.636 to .626), en route to leading the NL in four different offensive categories; however, Mize also topped the senior circuit in four departments in 1939, when he established career highs in batting average (.349), on-base percentage (.444), and doubles (44). His 197 hits and ninety-two bases on balls earned him top-five finishes in each of those categories as well, enabling him to compile an on-base percentage that exceeded the mark he posted the following year by forty points. Mize also compiled a career-best on-base plus slugging percentage of 1.070, which surpassed the figure he posted in 1940 by thirty-one percentage points. It's awfully close, but we'll go with Mize's 1939 performance.

Memorable Moments and Greatest Performances

Although Mize had a number of exceptional days at the plate for the Cardinals, he gained much of his notoriety during his time in St. Louis by demonstrating a propensity for accumulating home runs in huge bunches. Mize homered three times in one game four times as a member of the Cardinals, en route to establishing an all-time major-league record by accomplishing the feat a total of six times throughout the course of his career.

Mize homered three times in one contest for the first time on July 13, 1935, doing so during a 10–5 St. Louis loss to Boston. He duplicated his earlier effort almost exactly three years later, blasting three homers against the Giants in leading the Cardinals to a 7–1 victory in the second game of a doubleheader. Mize established a new NL record on May 13, 1940, when he hit three home runs in one game for the third time in his career, doing so during a fourteen-inning, 8–8 tie with the Cincinnati Reds. The slugging first baseman established a new major-league mark later in the year when he went deep three times in the first game of a September 8 doubleheader.

Notable Achievements

Hit more than forty home runs once.
Hit three home runs in one game four times.
Knocked in more than 100 runs five times.
Scored more than 100 runs three times.
Batted over .300 six times, surpassing the .330 mark on three occasions.
Collected more than 200 hits once.
Finished in double digits in triples three times.
Amassed more than forty doubles twice.
Amassed more than 350 total bases twice.
Compiled on-base percentage in excess of .400 six times.
Posted slugging percentage in excess of .600 three times.
Led NL in home runs twice, RBIs once, batting average once, triples once, doubles once, total bases three times, and slugging percentage three times.
Led NL first basemen in fielding percentage with a mark of .994 in 1936.
Finished second in NL MVP voting twice (1939, 1940).
Four-time NL All-Star (1937, 1939, 1940, 1941).
Elected to Baseball Hall of Fame by members of Veterans Committee in 1981.

NOTES

1. Charlie Dressen, quoted in "Quotes about Johnny Mize," *Johnny Mize.com*, www.johnnymize.com/quotes.htm (accessed September 13, 2012).
2. Tom Meany, quoted in "Quotes about Johnny Mize," www.johnnymize.com/quotes.html.
3. Stan Musial, quoted in "Quotes about Johnny Mize," www.johnnymize.com/quotes.html.
4. Casey Stengel, quoted in "Quotes about Johnny Mize," www.johnnymize.com/quotes.html.
5. Ted Williams, with Jim Prime, *Ted Williams' Hit List* (Indianapolis, IN: Masters Press, 1996), 123.

12

ENOS SLAUGHTER

An aggressive, hardnosed player with a win-at-all-costs mentality, Enos "Country" Slaughter spent thirteen years in a St. Louis Cardinals uniform, establishing himself during that time as one of the National League's top outfielders. Featuring a smooth swing that made him a reliable "contact" hitter, Slaughter compiled a batting average in excess of .300 in eight of his thirteen seasons in St. Louis, never batting any lower than .276 or striking out more than fifty-three times during that time. Also a solid outfielder with a strong and accurate throwing arm, Slaughter led all NL right fielders in putouts three times and assists twice. The hustling outfielder's outstanding all-around play helped lead the Cardinals to the world championship in both 1942 and 1946. Slaughter continued his winnings ways after he left St. Louis at the conclusion of the 1953 campaign, helping the Yankees capture three American League pennants and two world championships from 1956 to 1958. Slaughter's legacy of winning would have been even greater had he not spent three of his peak seasons serving in the military during World War II.

Born in Roxboro, North Carolina, on April 27, 1916, Enos Bradsher Slaughter acquired the nickname "Country" early in his professional career due to his rural farm upbringing. Signed by the Cardinals as an amateur free agent in 1935, Slaughter rose rather quickly through Branch Rickey's vast farm system, arriving in St. Louis in 1938. Discovering almost immediately that the Cubs had offered $100,000 for him, the twenty-two-year-old outfielder persuaded Rickey to increase his salary from $400 to $600 a month.

Although the era of the "Gas House Gang" had begun to wind down by the time Slaughter joined the Cardinals in 1938, their aggressive, rough-and-tumble style of play suited him perfectly. Rebuked once for not hustling by manager Eddie Dyer while playing in the minor leagues, Slaughter vowed never again to give less than 100 percent on the ball field. He subsequently became the quintessential hustler, even running hard to first base following walks. Meanwhile, Slaughter continued to take with him to the field every day the same fire and passion with which he played the game while growing up in Roxboro.

Stan Musial, who spent ten seasons playing alongside Slaughter in the Cardinals outfield, proclaimed, "Enos Slaughter was a tough competitor. He came to play. When he put his uniform on, you knew he was out to beat you."[1] Musial added, "He was one of the great hustlers of baseball. He loved baseball. He always ran hard and played hard."[2]

After posting decent numbers in 112 games as a rookie, Slaughter developed into one of the Cardinals' best players in 1939, driving in 86 runs, scoring 95 others, placing among the league leaders with 193 hits and a .320 batting average, and topping the circuit with 52 doubles. He also led all NL outfielders with 348 putouts and eighteen assists. Slaughter followed that up with another .300 season in 1940, before having his 1941 campaign ended prematurely on August 11, when he broke his collarbone trying to avoid a collision with Cardinals centerfielder Terry Moore. Chasing down a line drive hit to deep right-center, Slaughter averted running into Moore; however, in doing so, he slammed into the right-field wall at Sportsman's Park, putting him out for the rest of the season.

Returning to the Cardinals fully healthy in 1942, Slaughter had one of his finest all-around years. In addition to finishing among the NL leaders with 98 RBIs, 100 runs scored, 88 walks, a .318 batting average, a .412 on-base percentage, and a .494 slugging percentage, he topped the senior circuit with 188 hits, 17 triples, and 292 total bases, en route to earning All-Star honors for the second straight time and a second-place finish in the league Most Valuable Player voting. Slaughter subsequently helped lead the Cardinals to a five-game victory over the Yankees in the World Series by homering once, driving in two runs, and making several outstanding plays in the outfield.

Only twenty-six years old at the conclusion of the 1942 campaign, and apparently just reaching his peak, Slaughter ended up missing the next three years after he enlisted in the U.S. Air Force following the World Series. He spent his first two years in the military serving as a physical education instructor, in charge of 200 troops. In the last year of his enlistment, Slaughter toured the South Pacific with several other major-league stars, playing exhibition games at Tinian, Saipan, Guam, and Iwo Jima. He received his discharge from the service on March 1, 1946, enabling him to return to the Cardinals for the beginning of the 1946 campaign.

Showing no ill-effects from his three-year layoff, Slaughter batted .300 in his first year back, scored 100 runs, collected 183 hits, and established career highs with 18 home runs and a league-leading 130 RBIs. His exceptional performance enabled him to finish third in the NL MVP voting, behind teammate Stan Musial and Brooklyn outfielder Dixie Walker. Slaughter experienced his greatest moment of glory, however, in that year's World Series, earning a permanent place in baseball lore with his "Mad Dash" around the bases in the decisive seventh contest. Slaughter's effort, in which he scored the game-winning run all the way from first base on a double to short left-center by teammate Harry Walker, remains one of the most memorable moments in World Series history.

Slaughter continued to post solid numbers for the Cardinals in his seven remaining years in St. Louis, driving in better than 90 runs four more times, scoring more than 90 runs and batting over .300 three more times each, and compiling an on-base percentage in excess of .400 another two times. He had one of his finest seasons in 1949, when he earned another third-place finish in the NL MVP balloting. This came after knocking in 96 runs; scoring 92 others; collecting 191 hits; amassing a league-leading 13 triples; and establishing career highs with a .336 batting average, a .418 on-base percentage, and a .511 slugging percentage.

However, with the St. Louis front office deciding to adopt a youth movement by the mid-1950s, Slaughter suddenly became expendable to them. On April 11, 1954, just two days before the start of the regular season, the Cardinals traded the thirty-seven-year-old outfielder to the Yankees for outfielder Bill Virdon, pitcher Mel Wright, and minor-league outfielder Emil Tellinger. Taking the news hard, Slaughter cried openly at the thought of leaving the only family with which he had been associated in professional baseball. Meanwhile, Cardinals manager Eddie Stanky summed up the move by saying, "A player like Slaughter just can't stand sitting on the bench, and, while I am not trying to put myself on a pedestal by comparing myself with him, I couldn't stand it, either."[3]

Slaughter spent the next six years as a part-time player, shuttling back and forth between New York and Kansas City. He helped the Yankees win three pennants and two world championships during his time with them, before ending his career as a backup outfielder/ pinch hitter with the Milwaukee Braves in 1959. Slaughter concluded his 19-year big-league career with 169 home runs, 1,304 RBIs, 1,247 runs scored, 2,383 hits, 413 doubles, 148 triples, a .300 lifetime batting average, a .382 on-base percentage, and a .453 slugging percentage. In Slaughter's 13 years in St. Louis, he hit 146 home runs, knocked in 1,148 runs, scored 1,071 others, collected 2,064 hits, accumulated 366 doubles and 135 triples, batted .305, and compiled on-base and slugging percentages of .384 and .463, respectively. He ranks among the Cardinals' all-time leaders in games played (1,820), plate appearances (7,713), at bats (6,775), RBIs, runs scored, hits, triples, doubles, total bases (3,138), and walks (838).

Following his playing days, Slaughter retired to his 240-acre farm near Roxboro, where he harvested tobacco, watermelon, and assorted vegetables. Not yet ready to say good-bye to the game he loved so dearly, he ended up coaching baseball at Duke University for seven years before retiring from the sport for good. The members of the Veterans Committee elected Slaughter to the Hall of Fame in 1985. The Cardinals retired his number 9 in 1996, making him one of just nine St. Louis players to be so honored. Three years later, the team dedicated a statue to him, depicting his famous "Mad Dash" around the bases in the 1946 World Series.

Enos Slaughter passed away three years later, on August 12, 2002, at the age of eighty-six, after fighting a lengthy battle with non-Hodgkin's lymphoma. Many friends and former teammates paid their final respects to the man known as "Country" at his funeral in Allensville Methodist Church. Among those in attendance was Lou

Brock, who developed a relationship with his Cardinal predecessor after he joined the team in 1964. Speaking of his longtime friend, Brock stated, "Enos and I are in the Hall of Fame together. History finds us together. That is one thing that binds me to him. And, I'll tell you this, the name of Enos Slaughter will be spoken for generations to come. Players like Enos and Stan (Musial) really helped me to see what being a Cardinal meant. He's been my friend for a long time."[4]

CARDINAL CAREER HIGHLIGHTS

Best Season

Although Slaughter never had what could be referred to as a "career year," he had a number of outstanding seasons, any one of which would have made a good choice. He batted .320 in 1939, knocked in 86 runs, scored 95 others, and established career highs with 193 hits and a league-leading 52 doubles. Slaughter had his most productive season in 1946, when he established career highs with eighteen home runs and a league-leading 130 RBIs. He also scored 100 runs, batted .300, compiled a .374 on-base percentage and a .465 slugging percentage, and amassed 283 total bases, en route to earning a third-place finish in the NL MVP voting. Slaughter again placed third in the MVP balloting three years later, when he drove in 96 runs, scored 92 others, collected 191 hits, accumulated 290 total bases, and established career highs by batting .336 and posting on-base and slugging percentages of .418 and .511, respectively.

In the end, however, I elected to go with Slaughter's 1942 campaign. In addition to knocking in 98 runs and scoring 100 others, he batted .318, compiled a .412 on-base percentage, posted a .494 slugging percentage, and topped the senior circuit with 188 hits, 17 triples, and 292 total bases, en route to earning a second-place finish to teammate Mort Cooper in the NL MVP voting. Slaughter may have posted slightly better offensive numbers in one or two other seasons, but he placed in the league's top five in nine different offensive categories in 1942—more than he did in any other season. He also finished fourth in the senior circuit with fifteen outfield assists.

Memorable Moments and Greatest Performances

Slaughter had his greatest day at the plate for the Cardinals on June 29, 1947, when he knocked in ten runs during a doubleheader split with the Cincinnati Reds. After the Cardinals lost the opener by a score of 9–7, Slaughter led them to a 17–2 win in the nightcap by driving in seven runs with a single and a pair of doubles; however, Slaughter will always be remembered most for the tremendous hustle he displayed during his "Mad Dash" in Game 7 of the 1946 World Series. With the Fall Classic deadlocked at three games apiece and the Cardinals and Red Sox tied at 3–3, with two men out in the bottom of the eighth inning of the decisive seventh contest, Slaughter took off from first base on a hit-and-run with Harry Walker batting for St. Louis. Walker stroked a line drive to left-center field, where Boston's centerfielder fielded the ball with Slaughter heading toward third. Red Sox shortstop Johnny Pesky received the cutoff throw with Slaughter barely having reached third base, but Slaughter ignored the third base coach's stop sign and continued to barrel on toward home plate. Pesky, likely caught off guard by Slaughter's decision, hesitated for one brief moment, allowing the hustling base runner to slide across home plate with the run that ended up giving the Cardinals a 4–3 win and a World Series victory. Subsequently referred to as Slaughter's "Mad Dash," the play was ranked number 10 on the *Sporting News'* 2001 list of Baseball's 25 Greatest Moments.

Notable Achievements

Knocked in more than 100 runs three times.

Scored 100 runs three times.

Batted over .300 eight times, surpassing the .320 mark on three occasions.

Finished in double digits in triples seven times.

Surpassed fifty doubles once (fifty-two in 1939).

Compiled on-base percentage in excess of .400 three times.

Posted slugging percentage in excess of .500 twice.

Led NL in RBIs once, hits once, doubles once, triples twice, and total bases once.

Led NL outfielders in assists twice, putouts once, and fielding percentage once.

Ranks among Cardinals all-time leaders in RBIs (third), runs scored (fifth), hits (fifth), total bases (fifth), doubles (sixth), triples (third), bases on balls (fourth), games played (fourth), plate appearances (fourth), and official at bats (fifth).

Finished second in NL MVP voting in 1942.

Two-time *Sporting News* All-Star selection (1942, 1946).

Ten-time NL All-Star (1941, 1942, 1946, 1947, 1948, 1949, 1950, 1951, 1952, 1953).

Two-time NL champion (1942, 1946).

Two-time world champion (1942, 1946).

Elected to Baseball Hall of Fame by members of Veterans Committee in 1985.

NOTES

1. Stan Musial, quoted in *A Century of Success: 100 Years of Cardinals Glory*, Major League Baseball Productions, 1992.

2. Stan Musial, "Enos Slaughter Stats," *Baseball Almanac*, www.baseball-almanac.com/players/player.php?p=slaugen01 (accessed September 18, 2012).

3. Eddie Stanky, quoted in Joseph Wancho, "Enos Slaughter," *Society for American Baseball Research*, http://sabr.org/bioproj/person/fd6550d9 (accessed September 18, 2012).

4. Lou Brock, quoted in Wancho, "Enos Slaughter," http://sabr.org/bioproj/person/fd6550d9.

13

KEN BOYER

Ken Boyer and Ted Simmons ended up vying for the number thirteen spot, with the two men posting comparable numbers in most offensive categories during their time in St. Louis. Boyer compiled better overall numbers than Simmons in most departments, hitting more home runs, driving in more runs, scoring more times, and collecting more hits, but he also appeared in 100 more games with the Cardinals, enabling him to accumulate 600 more total plate appearances than Simmons, whose offensive production rivaled that of Boyer. To get an idea of how evenly matched Boyer and Simmons were as offensive players, one needs only look at the batting averages, on-base percentages, and slugging percentages they compiled while wearing a Redbird uniform. Boyer batted .293 and posted on-base and slugging percentages of .356 and .475, respectively. Meanwhile, Simmons batted .298, compiled an on-base percentage of .366, and posted a slugging percentage of .459 in his 13 years with the Cardinals.

Two factors ultimately pushed Boyer ahead of Simmons in these rankings, the first of which ended up being the former's superior leadership skills. Although the Cardinals clubs of the early 1960s featured such outstanding leaders as Bob Gibson, Bill White, and Dick Groat, Boyer served as team captain, providing veteran leadership to a still developing squad that had not yet learned how to win. Furthermore, Boyer handled himself better defensively at the hot corner than Simmons did behind home plate. While Simmons developed a reputation for being just a marginal defensive receiver throughout the course of his career, Boyer was considered to be one of the finest defensive third basemen of his time, winning a total of five Gold Gloves in his eleven years in St. Louis. More than anything, that last fact moved Boyer comfortably ahead of Simmons, into the number thirteen position in these rankings.

One of the most overlooked and underrated players in the rich history of the Cardinals, Ken Boyer rarely receives the credit he deserves for being one of the finest all-around third basemen in National League history. Overshadowed by Eddie Mathews for much of his career, Boyer also had to contend with Ron Santo for preeminence among players who manned the hot corner in the senior circuit his final few seasons. As a result, Boyer gained widespread recognition as the NL's top player at his position in only two or three of his fifteen major-league seasons. Nevertheless, the Cardinals captain earned All-Star honors seven times, won five Gold Gloves, and finished in the top ten in the league Most Valuable Player voting four times, winning the award in 1964, when he led his team to the world championship.

Born in Liberty, Missouri, on May 20, 1931, Kenton Lloyd Boyer grew up the fifth of fourteen children in Alba, Missouri. The third eldest of seven brothers, Boyer had little difficulty fielding a team to compete in pick-up baseball games as a youngster. In fact, two of his siblings—Cloyd and Clete—went on to play in the major leagues as well.

After graduating from Alba High School in 1949, Boyer received an invitation to attend a special tryout camp at Sportsman's Park in St. Louis. Although he usually played either the infield or outfield, Cardinals scout Runt Marr believed that Boyer's strong arm made him a potential candidate to join the St. Louis starting rotation. Signed by the Cardinals to a $6,000 bonus, Boyer spent most of his first two minor-league seasons working as a pitcher; however, as he later recalled, "I had no control. No curve, and not much of a fastball."[1]

While Boyer struggled as a pitcher, he performed so well at the plate that the Cardinals eventually decided to shift him to third base. Playing every day for the first time as a professional, Boyer finished the 1951 campaign with 90 RBIs and a .306 batting average, while also doing a solid job at third base. Apparently ready to advance to the next level of the St. Louis farm system, Boyer temporarily put his baseball career on hold when he was drafted by the U.S. Army. He spent the next two years serving overseas, although he continued to play ball for the army, performing in exhibition games in Germany and Africa.

Boyer resumed his professional playing career after being discharged from the army in October 1953. He spent the 1954 season with the Cardinals' Double-A affiliate, making such a strong impression on the members of the St. Louis front office that they traded away starting third baseman Ray Jablonski at the end of the year to create a spot for him in the starting lineup.

The 24-year-old Boyer had a solid rookie season for the Cardinals, hitting 18 home runs, driving in 62 runs, and batting .264, while also fielding his position well. He developed into a star the following year, when he hit 26 homers, knocked in 98 runs, scored 91 others, and batted .306, en route to earning his first selection to the NL All-Star team. Boyer displayed his versatility in 1957, when the Cardinals moved him to center field to allow rookie Eddie Kasko to break in at third base. Even though he did a creditable job in the outfield, Boyer allowed the defensive switch to affect his hitting, concluding the campaign with just 19 home runs, 62 RBIs, and a .265 batting average.

Back at his more familiar position of third base in 1958, Boyer excelled both at the bat and in the field for the Cardinals. In addition to hitting 23 home runs, driving in 90 runs, scoring 101 others, and batting .307, he won the first of four straight Gold Gloves for his outstanding defensive work at the hot corner. His forty-one double plays that year equaled the second-highest total in league history to that point. Named captain of the Cardinals prior to the start of the 1959 campaign, Boyer drew praise from manager Solly Hemus, who said, "Boyer is the guy everybody walks up to in the clubhouse and talks to."[2]

Although quiet and reserved, Boyer wielded a considerable amount of influence in the Cardinals clubhouse. Rather than yelling and screaming, he preferred to lead by example, and he usually managed to get his point across through subtle prodding. Boyer also later received a great deal of credit from several of his black teammates for helping to create the racial harmony on the Cardinals that, in many ways, made them the first truly integrated team in the major leagues.

Fred Hutchinson, who preceded Hemus as St. Louis manager, once said of his third baseman, "Ken is the kind of player you wish you had twelve of, so you could play nine and have three on the bench just to stir things up. He's the kind of guy you dream about: terrific speed, great arm, and brute strength. There's nothing he can't do."[3]

Hutchinson's assessment was quite accurate. In addition to possessing outstanding power, the six-foot, two-inch, 200-pound Boyer had good speed. After stealing a career-high twenty-two bases as a rookie, he finished in double digits in stolen bases another four times. Furthermore, even though he never hit more than thirty-two home runs in a season, Boyer surpassed the twenty-homer mark a total of eight times with the Cardinals, despite playing his home games in Sportsman's Park—an extremely difficult park for right-handed power hitters like him.

Boyer put together two straight excellent years after being named team captain, hitting a total of sixty home runs in 1959 and 1960, while also driving in a total of 191 runs and batting over .300 both years. He went on a twenty-nine-game hitting streak in 1959 that represented the longest such string in the major leagues since Stan Musial hit in thirty consecutive games for the Cardinals nine years earlier. Boyer finished tenth in the league MVP voting in 1959, before placing sixth in the balloting the following year.

Boyer had his finest season to date in 1961, when he hit 24 homers, knocked in 95 runs, and placed among the league leaders with 109 runs scored, 194 hits, and a .329 batting average, en route to earning his third straight top-ten finish in the league MVP voting. After another solid campaign in 1962, in which he hit 24 homers, knocked in 98 runs, scored 92 others, and batted .291, Boyer reached the 100-RBI mark for the first time in his career the following season. In addition to finishing second in the senior circuit with 111 RBIs, Boyer hit 24 home runs, batted .285, and won the last of his 5 Gold Gloves.

Boyer had arguably his finest season in 1964, leading the Cardinals to the NL pennant by hitting 24 homers for the fourth consecutive time, scoring 100 runs, batting .295, and topping the circuit with 119 RBIs. Boyer's outstanding campaign, coupled with the Cardinals' first-place finish, enabled him to edge out several other leading candidates for NL MVP honors.

Shortly after the Cardinals clinched the pennant on the season's final day, veteran St. Louis shortstop Dick Groat proclaimed, "Ken

Boyer is the best third baseman in the major leagues. He's carried our club all year. Without him, we would be a second-division team. You can't be chosen the number one third baseman by your fellow players unless you're great like Ken. He's a ballplayer's ballplayer."[4]

Boyer capped off his brilliant year with a clutch performance against the New York Yankees in the World Series. After winning Game 4 with a grand slam home run, Boyer homered, collected 3 hits, and scored 3 runs in the decisive Game 7, leading his team to its first world championship since 1946. His younger brother Clete hit a home run for New York in the final contest as well, making the Boyer brothers the only pair of siblings to ever homer in the same World Series game.

After appearing in virtually every game for the Cardinals in each of the three previous seasons, Boyer began to experience back problems in 1965 that limited both his playing time and offensive production. Missing more than 10 of his team's games for just the second time in his career, Boyer concluded the campaign with uncharacteristically low numbers that included only 13 home runs, 75 RBIs, 71 runs scored, and a .260 batting average. The Cardinals elected to trade their thirty-four-year-old captain to the New York Mets for journeyman third baseman Charlie Smith at the end of the year, bringing Boyer's time in St. Louis to an end. He spent parts of two seasons in New York, before splitting his final two and a half years between the Chicago White Sox and Los Angeles Dodgers. Failing to regain his earlier form, Boyer finished out his career as a part-time player with the Dodgers in 1969, retiring at season's end with 282 home runs, 1,141 RBIs, 1,104 runs scored, 2,143 hits, and a .287 batting average. His numbers with the Cardinals include 255 home runs, 1,001 RBIs, 988 runs scored, 1,855 hits, a .293 batting average, a .356 on-base percentage, and a .475 slugging percentage. Boyer ranks among the team's all-time leaders in home runs (third), RBIs (sixth), runs scored (eighth), total bases (sixth), hits (eighth), bases on balls (ninth), games played (eighth), plate appearances (seventh), and at bats (sixth).

Following his playing career, Boyer became a Cardinals coach in 1971, serving the team in that capacity for two seasons. After managing in the minor leagues for several years, he took over the managerial reigns of the Cardinals in 1978, leading the team to a third-place finish the following year. Replaced at the helm by Whitey Herzog early in 1980, Boyer anticipated managing the St. Louis Triple-A affiliate; however, lung cancer forced him to give up the job. Boyer lost his battle with cancer some two years later, passing away in St. Louis, Missouri, on September 7, 1982, at the age of 51. The Cardinals retired his number 14 in 1984, making him the only player not in the Hall of Fame to be so honored.

Stan Musial, whose kindness and encouragement made a strong impression on Boyer early in his career, said of his former teammate, "Kenny Boyer was a pillar of strength in the Cardinal organization. It was kind of an understood thing that Kenny took care of the players coming into the organization. He took people under his wing—it was kind of like a father image."[5]

CARDINAL CAREER HIGHLIGHTS

Best Season

A remarkably consistent performer, Boyer posted outstanding numbers year after year, making this an extremely difficult decision. No fewer than eight different seasons could easily be classified as the best of his career. I finally narrowed it down to 1960, 1961, 1963, and 1964—any of which would have made a good choice. Boyer hit a career-high 32 homers in the first of those campaigns, while also knocking in 97 runs, scoring 95 others, batting .304, and compiling a career-best on-base plus slugging percentage (OPS) of .932. The following year, he posted a .329 batting average that represented the highest mark of his career. Boyer also hit 24 homers, drove in 95 runs, compiled a .930 OPS, and established career highs with 109 runs scored and 194 hits in 1961. Two years later, he hit 24 home runs, knocked in 111 runs, and batted .285.

Nevertheless, I ultimately decided to go with Boyer's 1964 campaign. In addition to leading the NL with a career-high 119 RBIs, he hit 24 homers, scored 100 runs, batted .295, collected 185 hits, and amassed 307 total bases, nearly equaling the career-best total of 314 he accumulated in 1961. More importantly, Boyer led the Cardinals to the NL pennant, en route to earning league MVP honors. He punctuated his exceptional year by hitting 2 homers, driving in 6 runs, and scoring 5 others during the Cardinals' seven-game World Series victory over the Yankees.

Memorable Moments and Greatest Performances

Boyer put together a twenty-nine-game hitting streak in 1959 that represented the longest in the major leagues since Stan Musial hit safely in thirty consecutive games for the Cardinals in 1950. Boyer's streak began against the Giants on August 10, and ended against the Cubs on September 13. He went 41-for-117 during that stretch of time, compiling in the process a batting average of .350.

Boyer also hit for the cycle twice in his career, doing so for the first time in the second game of a doubleheader sweep of the Cubs on September 14, 1961. Boyer's performance climaxed a 7-for-11 day that he ended in style with a game-winning homer in the bottom of the eleventh inning. Boyer hit for the cycle again on June 16, 1964, leading the Cardinals to a 7–1 win over Houston.

Still, Boyer unquestionably delivered his most memorable blow against the Yankees in Game 4 of the 1964 World Series. With New York holding a two-games-to-one advantage in the Fall Classic and leading Game 4 by a score of 3–0, Boyer stepped up to the plate to face Al Downing with the bases loaded in the top of the sixth inning. The Cardinals captain cleared the bases with a grand slam home run that gave his team a 4–3 lead it never relinquished. The blast completely shifted the momentum of the Series, providing much of the impetus for the Cardinals to eventually defeat the Yankees in seven games. Boyer also homered in the decisive seventh contest, concluding the Series with two homers and six RBIs.

Notable Achievements

Hit more than thirty home runs once (thirty-two in 1960).
Third all-time on Cardinals with 255 home runs.
Knocked in more than 100 runs twice.
Scored more than 100 runs three times.
Batted over .300 five times.

Finished in double digits in triples three times.

Compiled slugging percentage in excess of .500 three times.

Led NL with 119 RBIs in 1964.

Led NL third basemen in double plays five times, assists twice, and putouts once.

1964 NL MVP.

Five-time Gold Glove winner (1958, 1959, 1960, 1961, 1963).

Five-time *Sporting News* All-Star selection.

1964 *Sporting News* Major League Player of the Year.

Seven-time NL All-Star (1956, 1959, 1960, 1961, 1962, 1963, 1964).

1964 NL champion.

1964 world champion.

NOTES

1. Ken Boyer, quoted in www.kenboyer.com/quotes.html (accessed September 18, 2012).
2. Solly Hemus, quoted in www.kenboyer.com/quotes.html (accessed September 18, 2012).
3. Fred Hutchinson, quoted in Mike Shalin and Neil Shalin, *Out by a Step: The 100 Best Players Not in the Baseball Hall of Fame* (Lanham, MD.: Diamond Communications, 2002), 40.
4. Dick Groat, quoted in Shalin and Shalin, *Out by a Step*, 42.
5. Stan Musial, quoted in "Ken Boyer Stats," *Baseball Almanac*, www.baseball-almanac.com/players/player.php?p=boyerke01 (accessed September 18, 2012).

14

TED SIMMONS

One of the best hitting catchers in National League history, Ted Simmons spent most of his career being overshadowed by Johnny Bench, who established himself as the era's greatest receiver. Yet, even though Bench typically compiled better power numbers than Simmons, the latter hit for a higher batting average and posted a superior on-base percentage. Sparky Anderson, Bench's longtime manager in Cincinnati, once claimed, "I don't think there were ever very many catchers who could hit like Ted Simmons. He wasn't like Bench. John was death and destruction. For pure hitting, though, Simmons was the best catcher I ever saw."[1]

Although Ivan Rodriguez eventually surpassed both marks, Simmons retired from the game with more hits (2,472) and doubles (483) than any other catcher in major-league history. A switch-hitter with good power from both sides of the plate, Simmons also established the NL career record (since broken) for most home runs by a switch-hitter (182). In all likelihood, Simmons's reputation as a somewhat below-average receiver is the only thing keeping him out of the Hall of Fame.

Born in Highland Park, Michigan, on August 9, 1949, Ted Lyle Simmons began his professional career almost immediately after he graduated from Michigan's Southfield High School. Selected by the Cardinals in the first round of the 1967 amateur draft with the tenth overall pick, Simmons spent the next three years advancing through the St. Louis farm system, excelling as a hitter wherever he went. After earning brief call-ups at the end of the 1968 and 1969 campaigns, the twenty-year-old Simmons joined the Cardinals for good in 1970.

Assuming a part-time role in his first full year in the league, Simmons posted modest numbers, batting just .243 and driving in only 24 runs in 82 games and 284 official at bats.

Simmons took over as the team's starting catcher in 1971, concluding the campaign with 7 homers, 77 RBIs, and a .304 batting average. He earned the first of three straight All-Star selections the following season by batting .303, hitting 16 home runs, driving in 96 runs, and finishing third in the league with 36 doubles. Simmons's 96 RBIs and 16 homers established new Cardinals records by a receiver. He compiled solid numbers in each of the next two seasons as well, concluding the 1973 campaign with 91 RBIs, 192 hits, and a .310 batting average, before batting .272 and establishing new career highs with 20 homers and 103 RBIs in 1974.

Even though Simmons failed to make the NL All-Star Team for the fourth consecutive time in 1975, he had arguably his finest season for the Cardinals. Appearing in 157 of the team's 162 games (all but three behind home plate), the switch-hitting receiver hit 18 home runs, knocked in 100 runs, scored 80 others, finished second in the league with a career-best .332 batting average, and placed fourth in the circuit with 193 hits. His outstanding all-around performance earned him a sixth-place finish in the league Most Valuable Player voting.

As Simmons continued to establish himself as one of the NL's top hitters, the man nicknamed "Simba" by his teammates for his long locks also developed a reputation for being a hardnosed player with an intense desire to win. A volatile competitor who spoke his mind openly to opponents and teammates alike, Simmons once fought with Cardinals pitcher John Denny in the runway between the clubhouse and the dugout during a game at Busch Memorial Stadium.

Yet, Simmons also had a more cerebral side, prompting pitcher Dan Quisenberry to comment on one occasion, "He (Simmons) didn't sound like a baseball player. He said things like 'nevertheless' and 'if, in fact.'"[2] Simmons once revealed the intellectual side to his persona when he noted, "The ball jumps off the bat and you're running to first, drifting outside the line to start you on your way to second. The ultimate pleasure in baseball is that abstract moment when everything comes together and flows naturally."[3]

Still, Simmons built his reputation primarily on his hitting, gaining widespread recognition throughout the course of his career as one of the finest line-drive hitters in the game. After a slightly subpar 1976 campaign, Simmons returned to top form in 1977, batting .318, hitting 21 homers, driving in 95 runs, and scoring 82 others. The following year, he finally broke Johnny Bench's nine-year stranglehold as the starting catcher for the NL in the All-Star Game, earning the assignment by hitting 22 home runs, knocking in 80 runs, and batting .287. Simmons had another solid year in 1979, before winning the only Silver Slugger Award of his career the following year by hitting 21 homers, driving in 98 runs, scoring 84 others, and batting .303.

Unfortunately, the 1980 campaign ended up being Simmons's last in St. Louis. After feuding with Cardinals manager Whitey Herzog, Simmons found himself included in a seven-player trade the team completed with the Milwaukee Brewers at the end of the year. Simmons subsequently spent five years in Milwaukee, having his best season for the Brewers in 1983, when he batted .308 and knocked in a career-high 108 runs. As a member of the 1982 American League champion Brewers, Simmons competed against the Cardinals in that year's World Series, hitting two home runs against his former team in a losing effort. From Milwaukee, Simmons moved on to Atlanta, where he spent his final three seasons serving primarily as a utility player and pinch hitter. He retired at the end of 1988, with 248 career home runs, 1,389 RBIs, 1,074 runs scored, 2,472 hits, 483 doubles, a .285 batting average, a .348 on-base percentage, and a .437 slugging percentage. In parts of 13 seasons in St. Louis, Simmons hit 172 home runs, knocked in 929 runs, scored 736 others, collected 1,704 hits, amassed 332 doubles, compiled a .298 batting average, and posted on-base and slugging percentages of .366 and .459, respectively. He ranks among the team's all-time leaders in RBIs (seventh), home runs (ninth), total bases (ninth), bases on balls (tenth), intentional bases on balls (second), and plate appearances (tenth).

Following his playing career, Simmons became a major-league executive. He started out on that path in October 1988, when Cardinals general manager Dal Maxvill named him director of player development for St. Louis.

Although the stigma of being a below-average defensive receiver during his career continues to surround Simmons, there are those who consider that to be something of an injustice. Former fellow catcher Randy Hundley once suggested, "People knock his (Simmons's) defense, but he was a lot better defensive player than he got credit for."[4] Rusty Staub once stated, "People have a tendency to label players. He (Simmons) wasn't a bad defensive catcher. I've seen some bad defensive catchers, and Simmons wasn't one of them. And he could hit with anybody. He was a grinder."[5] Meanwhile, Hall of Famer Rod Carew proclaimed, "Simmons could do everything. I think he was very underrated. Everyone talked about Johnny Bench, but they should talk about this guy."[6]

CARDINAL CAREER HIGHLIGHTS

Best Season

Simmons had several outstanding years for the Cardinals, with 1973, 1975, 1977, and 1980 heading the list. Although Simmons hit only 13 home runs in the first of those years, he knocked in 91 runs, collected 192 hits, and batted .310. He hit 21 homers, drove in 95 runs, batted .318, compiled a .408 on-base percentage, and posted a .500 slugging percentage in 1977, en route to compiling a career-high .908 on-base plus slugging percentage (OPS). Simmons also had another good year in 1980, when he hit 21 homers, knocked in 98 runs, and batted .303. However, I ultimately decided to go with Simmons's 1975 campaign. In addition to hitting 18 home runs and driving in 100 runs, he established career highs with 193 hits, 285 total bases, and a .332 batting average, finishing second in the league to Bill Madlock in the last category. Simmons also concluded the campaign with a .396 on-base percentage and a .491 slugging percentage, giving him an OPS of .887, which fell only twenty-one points short of the career-high mark he established two years later.

Memorable Moments and Greatest Performances

Despite being labeled by many people as a below-average defensive receiver, Simmons caught two no-hitters during his time in St.

Louis. After calling the signals for Bob Gibson's 1971 no-no, he served as backstop when Bob Forsch threw the first of his two no-hitters in 1978. Still, there is little doubt that Cardinals fans remember Simmons mostly for the outstanding hitting he exhibited in his eleven years as a full-time player in St. Louis. He homered from both sides of the plate in the same game three different times for the Cardinals. Simmons had arguably his best game for the team on August 18, 1980, leading St. Louis to a 10–1 victory over Cincinnati by going 4-for-4, with 2 home runs, 3 RBIs, and 4 runs scored.

Notable Achievements

Hit more than twenty home runs five times.
Hit home runs from both sides of plate in same game three times.
Knocked in more than 100 runs twice.
Batted over .300 six times.
Collected forty doubles once (1978).
Compiled on-base percentage in excess of .400 once (.408 in 1977).
Posted slugging percentage in excess of .500 four times.
Finished second in NL with .332 batting average in 1975.
Led NL in intentional bases on balls twice.
Led NL catchers in putouts and assists two times each.
1980 Silver Slugger winner.
Three-time *Sporting News* All-Star selection (1977, 1978, 1979).
Six-time NL All-Star (1972, 1973, 1974, 1977, 1978, 1979).

NOTES

1. Sparky Anderson, quoted in Mike Shalin and Neil Shalin, *Out by a Step: The 100 Best Players Not in the Baseball Hall of Fame* (Lanham, MD: Diamond Communications, 2002), 121.

2. Dan Quisenberry, quoted in "The Greats," *Pete's Baseball Quotes*, www.peterga.com/baseball/quotes/greats.htm (accessed September 25, 2012).

3. Ted Simmons, quoted in "Ted Simmons Stats," *Baseball Almanac*, www.baseball-almanac.com/players/player.php?p=simmote01 (accessed September 25, 2012).

4. Randy Hundley, quoted in Shalin and Shalin, *Out by a Step*, 122.

5. Rusty Staub, quoted in Shalin and Shalin, *Out by a Step*, 122.

6. Rod Carew, quoted in Shalin and Shalin, *Out by a Step*, 123.

15

JIM EDMONDS

Known affectionately to Cardinals fans as "Jimmy Baseball," Jim Edmonds reached a level of popularity during his time in St. Louis shared by a scant few during the course of the past two decades. A classic five-tool player, Edmonds thrilled Cardinals fans with his soaring home runs and breathtaking outfield catches, en route to gaining general recognition as one of the finest all-around players in the game. After being acquired from the Anaheim Angels for two players prior to the start of the 2000 campaign, Edmonds spent eight years in St. Louis, earning six Gold Gloves, one Silver Slugger, and two top-five finishes in the National League Most Valuable Player voting during that time. Along the way, he helped the Cardinals advance to the playoffs six times, capture two pennants, and win one world championship.

Born in Fullerton, California, on June 27, 1970, James Patrick Edmonds signed with the California Angels just six days before celebrating his eighteenth birthday after the team selected him in the seventh round of the 1988 amateur draft. He spent most of the next five years working his way up the Angels' farm system, finally making his major-league debut with them in September 1993. Edmonds appeared in eighteen games during the final three weeks of the season, batting just .246 and driving in only four runs. After assuming a part-time role the following year, Edmonds became a regular member of California's starting outfield in 1995, earning his first All-Star selection by hitting 33 home runs, knocking in 107 runs, batting .290, and finishing third in the league with 120 runs scored.

Edmonds posted solid numbers in each of the next two seasons before having another big year in 1998. In addition to hitting 25 homers and driving in 91 runs, Edmonds scored 115 times, batted .307, collected a career-high 184 hits, and won his second consecutive Gold Glove for his brilliant play in center field.

Blessed with a world of natural ability, Edmonds tended to make the game of baseball look too easy at times. The Southern California native often drew criticism from teammates, some of whom objected to his laid-back attitude. Edmonds irritated some players with the somewhat casual demeanor he brought with him to the field much of the time, while he angered others who felt he never made the effort to fulfill his enormous potential.

Angels starter Chuck Finley once commented, "He (Edmonds) can definitely play the game when he wants to. Jimmy's biggest problem is Jimmy."[1] Meanwhile, Mo Vaughn, who became the Angels' team leader and spokesman after he signed with them as a free agent prior to the start of the 1999 campaign, proclaimed, "Jim Edmonds is one of the most talented guys I've ever played with. The responsibility is what's in question."[2]

Edmonds' somewhat tenuous relationship with several of his teammates grew increasingly precarious when a shoulder injury he sustained in the spring of 1999 ended up limiting him to only fifty-five games that season. With Edmonds due to become a free agent at the end of the ensuing campaign and his commitment to the team being questioned by some, the Angels elected to trade him to the Cardinals for pitcher Kent Bottenfield and second baseman Adam Kennedy just two weeks before the start of the 2000 regular season.

Taking his Gold Glove and smooth left-handed swing with him to St. Louis, Edmonds proved to be a huge success in his first year with his new team. Appearing in 154 games for the Cardinals, Edmonds hit 42 home runs, knocked in 108 runs, batted .295, walked a career-high 103 times, and finished third in the league with 129 runs scored. The center fielder earned the third Gold Glove of his career, All-Star honors for the second time, and a fourth-place finish in the NL MVP voting.

Edmonds followed that up with four more outstanding seasons for the Cardinals, averaging 35 home runs, 98 RBIs, and 95 runs scored for them from 2001 to 2004. He also batted over .300 in three of those years. After hitting 30 homers, driving in 110 runs, scoring 95 others, and batting .304 in 2001, Edmonds homered 28 times and established career highs with a .311 batting average and a .420 on-base percentage in 2002. He totaled 81 home runs and 200 RBIs the next two seasons, performing particularly well in 2004, when he hit 42 homers, knocked in 111 runs, scored 102 others, and batted .301, en route to earning a fifth-place finish in the league MVP balloting. Edmonds continued to excel during the 2004 postseason, helping the Cardinals advance to the World Series by winning Game 6 of the National League Championship Series (NLCS) with a two-run homer in the bottom of the twelfth inning, before making a spectacular defensive play in center during the team's Game 7 victory.

Such efforts prompted Cardinals teammate Scott Rolen to say, "Offensively and defensively, he's (Edmonds) a great, great player. He amazes me every day. You talk about players, he's a player. It's not just the numbers that you put up. It's on both sides of the ball. It's understanding the game. He's as good as it gets."[3]

Providing Cardinals fans with thrills both in the field and at the bat during his time in St. Louis, Edmonds made several spectacular catches that helped him further his reputation as one of the game's premier defensive outfielders. He made arguably his most memorable play as a member of the Cardinals on July 16, 2004, when he robbed Cincinnati's Jason LaRue of a certain home run. LaRue drove a ball to deep center field that Edmonds pursued at full speed onto the warning track. Scaling the wall upon reaching it, Edmonds extended his entire right arm over the fence and snared the ball, ending the game in the process.

Unfortunately, Edmonds's reckless style of play resulted in the center fielder incurring numerous injuries that limited his effectiveness his last two years in St. Louis. After posting solid numbers again in 2005, Edmonds missed huge portions of both 2006 and 2007, spending much of that time struggling with postconcussion syndrome, which caused dizziness and blurred vision. Unable to perform as he once did, Edmonds found himself traded to San Diego at the conclusion of the 2007 campaign. With Edmonds struggling mightily throughout the course of the season's first month, the Padres released him on May 9, 2008. The center fielder subsequently signed with the Chicago Cubs, with whom he spent the remainder of the year.

After failing to receive an acceptable offer from any major-league team at the end of the year, Edmonds elected to sit out all of 2009; however, he returned to the big leagues in 2010, splitting the campaign between Milwaukee and Cincinnati before officially announcing his retirement on February 18, 2011. Edmonds ended his 17-year playing career with 393 home runs, 1,199 RBIs, 1,251 runs scored, 1,949 hits, a .284 batting average, a .376 on-base percentage, and a .527 slugging percentage. His numbers as a member of the Cardinals include 241 home runs, 713 RBIs, 690 runs scored, 1,033 hits, a .285 batting average, a .393 on-base percentage, and a .555 slugging percentage. Edmonds ranks among the team's all-time leaders in home runs (fourth), slugging percentage (seventh), and bases on balls (eighth).

CARDINAL CAREER HIGHLIGHTS

Best Season

Edmonds had his two best seasons for the Cardinals in 2000 and 2004. In the first of those years, he hit 42 homers, drove in 108 runs, scored a career-high 129 runs, collected 306 total bases, batted .295, and compiled on-base and slugging percentages of .411 and .583, respectively. Edmonds hit another 42 homers four years later, drove in a career-high 111 runs, scored 102 others, amassed 320 total bases, batted .301, posted an on-base percentages of .418, and compiled a career-best .643 slugging percentage. It was an extremely close call, but I decided to go with 2004, since the 1.061 on-base plus slugging percentage Edmonds posted that year exceeded his 2004 mark by sixty-seven percentage points.

Memorable Moments and Greatest Performances

Although Edmonds provided Cardinals fans with several memorable moments with his spectacular defense in center field, he also performed a number of outstanding batting feats during his years in St. Louis. On April 12, 2000, Edmonds tied Chick Hafey's seventy-one-year-old team record by reaching base safely for the twelfth consecutive time. Nearly one year later, on April 4, 2001, Edmonds became the first player to hit two fair balls into the upper deck at Coors Stadium when he homered twice during a 13–9 loss to Colorado.

On April 8, 2003, Edmonds collected four hits and five RBIs during a 15–12 victory over Colorado, becoming in the process just the sixth major-league player to notch seven extra base hits in the course of two consecutive games. Just four days earlier, he hit two homers and doubled twice against Houston. Almost three months later, on June 28, Edmonds tied a major-league record by collecting four extra-base hits for the second time in the year. He homered twice during the contest, leading the Cardinals to a 13–9 win over the Royals.

Edmonds absolutely terrorized Atlanta's vaunted pitching staff in the 2000 National League Division Series, leading the Cardinals to a three-game sweep of the defending NL champions by hitting 2 home runs, smashing 4 doubles, driving in 7 runs, and batting .571. He subsequently homered once and knocked in five runs during the Cardinals' five-game loss to the Mets in the NLCS.

Nevertheless, Edmonds experienced the most surreal moment of his career on October 20, 2004, when he delivered a two-run, game-winning homer in the bottom of the twelfth inning of Game 6 of the NLCS that evened the series at three games apiece. Edmonds's one-out blast against Astros reliever Dan Miceli gave the Cardinals a 6–4 victory, propelling them into Game 7, which they won to claim their first World Series berth in seventeen years.

Notable Achievements

Hit more than thirty home runs four times, surpassing forty homers twice.
Knocked in more than 100 runs three times.
Scored more than 100 runs twice.
Batted over .300 three times.
Surpassed thirty doubles five times.
Walked more than 100 times twice.
Compiled on-base percentage in excess of .400 four times.
Posted slugging percentage in excess of .600 twice.
Led NL center fielders in assists three times.
Fourth all-time on Cardinals with 241 home runs.

2004 Silver Slugger winner.

Six-time Gold Glove winner (2000, 2001, 2002, 2003, 2004, 2005).

2004 *Sporting News* All-Star selection.

Three-time NL All-Star (2000, 2003, 2005).

Two-time NL champion (2004, 2006).

2006 world champion.

NOTES

1. Chuck Finley, quoted in "Jim Edmonds," *Baseball Library.com*, www.baseballlibrary.com/ballplayers/player.php?name=Jim_Edmonds_1970&page=summary (accessed September 27, 2012).

2. Mo Vaughn, quoted in "Jim Edmonds," www.baseballlibrary.com/ballplayers/player.php?name=Jim_Edmonds_1970&page=summary.

3. Scott Rolen, quoted in "Jim Edmonds Stats," *Baseball Almanac*, www.baseball-almanac.com/players/player.php?p=edmonji01 (accessed September 27, 2012).

16

RED SCHOENDIENST

An outstanding leader both on and off the field, Red Schoendienst gained universal respect throughout his professional career for his talent, heart, sound judgment, and calm demeanor. One of the finest fielding second basemen of his day, Schoendienst accumulated 4,616 putouts and 5,243 assists during the course of his career, while also participating in 1,368 double plays and committing only 170 errors in 10,029 total chances, en route to compiling an exceptional .987 fielding percentage. A solid switch-hitter as well, Schoendienst posted a .289 lifetime batting average and collected 2,449 hits in nineteen big-league seasons, fifteen of which he spent with the Cardinals. After his playing career ended, Schoendienst remained an important member of the Cardinals organization, serving the team at different times as a coach and field manager. Assuming the club's managerial reins from Johnny Keane in 1965, Schoendienst subsequently spent the next twelve years calling the signals from the Cardinals' dugout, piloting his team to back-to-back pennants in 1967 and 1968, and to the world championship in the first of those years. In all, Schoendienst contributed to four pennant winners and three world championship teams as a player, coach, and manager during his time in St. Louis.

Born in Germantown, Illinois, on February 2, 1923, Albert Fred Schoendienst first displayed his tremendous will and determination when he signed a minor-league contract with the Cardinals in 1942, after earlier suffering a severe eye injury while serving in the Civilian Conservation Corps. Excelling in his first full season of minor-league ball, Schoendienst earned International League Most Valuable Player honors in 1943, before enlisting in the U.S. Army later that year. He spent most of 1944 serving his country, before receiving a discharge early in 1945 because of an injured shoulder and vision problems resulting from his earlier eye injury. Compensating for the difficulties he subsequently experienced seeing the ball batting right-handed against right-handed pitching, Schoendienst taught himself how to switch-hit, eventually developing into one of the best switch-hitters in the game.

Joining the Cardinals a few months after his discharge, Schoendienst earned the team's starting left-field job in spring training. He did well as a rookie, batting .278, scoring 89 runs, and leading the National League with twenty-six stolen bases. Schoendienst moved to second base the following year, after which he manned the position for the Cardinals for the next decade. Batting .281, scoring 94 runs, and leading all NL second sackers with a .984 fielding percentage, Schoendienst earned All-Star honors for the first of ten times in his career, helping St. Louis capture the league championship in the process.

Schoendienst performed well for the Cardinals in each of the next two seasons, before earning the first of his four top-ten finishes in the NL MVP voting in 1949 by batting .297, scoring 102 runs, and collecting 190 hits. He followed that up by amassing a league-leading forty-three doubles in 1950, while putting together a streak at one point during the season in which he handled 320 consecutive chances in the field without making an error.

Blessed with sure hands and quick reflexes, Schoendienst quickly developed into the senior circuit's premier defensive second baseman. He led all NL players at his position in fielding percentage a total of seven times, compiling in 1956 a mark of .9934, which remained a league record until Ryne Sandberg surpassed it thirty years later. In discussing Schoendienst, Stan Musial once said of his longtime teammate, "The greatest pair of hands I've ever seen."[1]

Schoendienst made his fifth and sixth appearances on the NL All-Star Team in 1951 and 1952, placing tenth in the league MVP balloting in the second of those years after batting .303, scoring 91 runs, amassing 188 hits, and collecting 40 doubles during the regular season. He then had the greatest season of his career in 1953. That year, he earned a fourth-place finish in the MVP voting by hitting 15 homers; driving in 79 runs; finishing second in the batting race with a mark of

.342; and placing among the league leaders with 107 runs scored, 193 hits, and 35 doubles. Schoendienst spent two more full seasons in St. Louis, batting .315, knocking in 79 runs, and scoring 98 others in 1954, before seeing his average slip to .268 the following year, with only 51 RBIs and 68 runs scored.

Believing that the thirty-three-year-old Schoendienst had already seen his best days, the Cardinals elected to include him in a nine-player trade they completed with the Giants on June 14, 1956, which netted them shortstop Alvin Dark, among others. Schoendienst remained in New York almost exactly one year, being dealt to the Milwaukee Braves for three players on June 15, 1957. The veteran second baseman proved to be a huge pickup for the Braves, as he helped the team win the next two NL pennants. Performing particularly well for his new team in the first of those years, Schoendienst concluded the 1957 campaign with 15 homers, 65 RBIs, 91 runs scored, a .309 batting average, and a league-leading 200 hits. In addition to posting excellent offensive numbers, Schoendienst provided outstanding leadership to a developing Braves team that included young veterans Hank Aaron and Eddie Mathews. Aaron later recalled, "He (Schoendienst) was just a tremendous ballplayer. He and I dressed side by side, and I'll never forget how much he taught me about the game. He was a terrific leader."[2] Schoendienst's all-around contributions to the team earned him a third-place finish in the NL MVP voting.

Bruised ribs, a broken finger, and pleurisy limited Schoendienst to only 106 games in 1958, although he started all seven games in Milwaukee's World Series loss to the Yankees. Diagnosed with tuberculosis during the subsequent off-season, Schoendienst sat out all but five games in 1959, after having part of a lung removed. Yet, he once again showed his fighting spirit, returning to the Braves the following year to assume a part-time role with the team. Released by Milwaukee at the conclusion of the 1960 campaign, Schoendienst returned to St. Louis, where he spent the final three years of his career serving the Cardinals as a utility infielder and pinch-hitter. Excelling in his new role, Schoendienst posted batted averages of .300 and .301 in 1961 and 1962, leading the league with twenty-two pinch-hits in seventy-two attempts in the second of those two seasons.

Schoendienst made only six pinch-hitting appearances for the Cardinals in 1963, before officially announcing his retirement as an active player midway through the season. He ended his playing career with 84 home runs, 773 RBIs, 1,223 runs scored, 2,449 hits, a .289 batting average, a .337 on-base percentage, and a .387 slugging percentage. In parts of 15 seasons in St. Louis, he hit 65 homers, knocked in 651 runs, scored 1,025 others, collected 1,980 hits, batted .289, compiled a .338 on-base percentage, and posted a .388 slugging percentage. He ranks sixth all-time on the Cardinals in runs scored and base hits.

Although Schoendienst appeared in his last game with the Cardinals on July 7, 1963, he remained with them long thereafter, continuing to serve the team as a coach under manager Johnny Keane until the latter handed in his resignation following the conclusion of the 1964 World Series. Named by the St. Louis front office as Keane's replacement, Schoendienst piloted the Cardinals for the next twelve years, leading them to two pennants and one world championship, as well as earning NL Manager of the Year honors in both 1967 and 1968. Fired at the end of the 1976 season, Schoendienst spent two years coaching for the A's before accepting a similar position back in St. Louis in 1979. He again served as Cardinals manager for six weeks in 1980, when Whitey Herzog temporarily left the dugout to become general manager. Schoendienst remains a valued member of the Cardinals organization, currently holding the title of "special assistant coach." The members of the Veterans Committee elected Schoendienst to the Baseball Hall of Fame in 1989, seven years before the Cardinals retired his number 2.

CARDINAL CAREER HIGHLIGHTS

Best Season

Although Schoendienst also put up good numbers in 1949, 1952, and 1954, there can be no doubting that he had his best season for the Cardinals in 1953. In addition to collecting 193 hits and recording 35 doubles, Schoendienst established career highs in several offensive categories, including home runs (15), RBIs (79), runs scored (107), batting average (.342), on-base percentage (.405), and slugging percentage (.502). His on-base plus slugging percentage of .907 exceeded the next-highest mark he compiled in that category by more than 100 points. Schoendienst also had an exceptional year in the field, leading all NL second basemen in putouts (365), assists (430), and fielding percentage (.983).

Memorable Moments and Greatest Performances

Schoendienst had one of his greatest days at the plate for the Cardinals on June 6, 1948, leading his team to a doubleheader sweep of the Phillies by banging out five doubles and a homer. Coupled with Schoendienst's three doubles from one day earlier, his homer and three doubles in the opener gave him a total of seven extra-base hits in the course two games, tying a major-league record.

Schoendienst proved to be a huge thorn in the side of the Pirates throughout the years, saving some of his best games for them. On July 8, 1951, exactly one year after going 5-for-5 against them in Pittsburgh, the Cardinals second baseman led his team to a victory over the Pirates in the second game of a doubleheader by homering from both sides of the plate. Schoendienst had another big day against Pittsburgh on May 20, 1953, driving in six runs, with a home run, two doubles, and a single during an 11–6 Cardinals win over the Pirates.

Schoendienst also authored the longest batting streak of the entire 1954 campaign, hitting safely in twenty-eight consecutive games, before having his successful run ended by Chicago's Bob Rush on July 10.

However, Schoendienst delivered arguably his most memorable blow in a game that didn't even count in the standings. After Ralph Kiner tied the 1950 All-Star Game at 3–3 with a ninth-inning home run, Schoendienst won the annual Midsummer Classic for the senior circuit with a blast in the top of the fourteenth.

Notable Achievements

Scored more than 100 runs twice.
Batted over .300 four times.
Surpassed forty doubles twice.
Compiled on-base percentage in excess of .400 once (.405 in 1953).

Posted slugging percentage in excess of .500 once (.502 in 1953).

Topped twenty stolen bases once (twenty-six in 1945).

Led NL in doubles once and stolen bases once.

Finished second in NL in batting once and hits once.

Led NL second basemen in assists three times, putouts three times, and fielding percentage six times.

Ranks among Cardinals all-time leaders in runs scored (sixth), hits (sixth), doubles (seventh), total bases (eighth), games played (fifth), plate appearances (fifth), and at bats (fourth).

1953 *Sporting News* All-Star selection.

Nine-time NL All-Star (1946, 1948, 1949, 1950, 1951, 1952, 1953, 1954, 1955).

1946 NL champion.

1946 world champion.

Elected to Baseball Hall of Fame by members of Veterans Committee in 1989.

NOTES

1. Stan Musial, quoted in www.schoendienst.com/quotes.html (accessed September 28, 2012).

2. Hank Aaron, quoted in www.schoendienst.com/quotes.html (accessed September 28, 2012).

17

CHICK HAFEY

Chick Hafey served as a full-time starting outfielder in only four of his eight seasons in St. Louis, appearing in as many as 130 games just twice. Health and vision problems likely prevented him from ever maximizing his full potential. Meanwhile, many baseball historians tend to view his numbers with a considerable amount of cynicism since he compiled them during an excellent era for hitters. Nevertheless, Hafey's reputation as one of the most complete players of his time prompted me to assign him this rather lofty spot in my rankings.

Considered to be one of the finest right-handed hitters of the 1920s and 1930s, Chick Hafey drew praise from various quarters, including none other than the great Rogers Hornsby, who called his onetime teammate the greatest right-handed batter he ever saw. A line-drive hitter with home run power as well, Hafey was said to hit the ball harder than any other right-handed batter of his generation, with the exception of Jimmie Foxx. One of the first position players in the major leagues to wear eyeglasses, Hafey excelled at the plate even though he experienced difficulties with his eyesight throughout his playing career. The owner of the fourth-highest slugging percentage in Cardinals history, Hafey hit more than 25 home runs, knocked in more than 100 runs, and scored more than 100 runs three times each during his time in St. Louis, while also posting a batting average in excess of .330 on four separate occasions. Also an outstanding outfielder, Hafey possessed outstanding speed and one of the most powerful throwing arms in all of baseball.

Born in Berkeley, California, on February 12, 1903, Charles James Hafey originally signed with the Cardinals as a pitcher in 1923, after attending Berkeley High School; however, after witnessing Hafey repeatedly drive balls over the outfield wall during batting practice one day, Branch Rickey decided to have the youngster converted into an outfielder. Advancing rapidly through Rickey's expansive farm system, Hafey joined the Cardinals for the first time late in 1924, compiling a .253 batting average and driving in twenty-two runs in only ninety-one official at bats in the season's final month.

After beginning the 1925 campaign back in the minor leagues, Hafey returned to the Cardinals early in the season to post a .302 batting average and knock in fifty-seven runs in ninety-three games the remainder of the year. Apparently ready to assume a starting job in the St. Louis outfield, Hafey ended up missing half of 1926 while recovering from multiple beanings that further affected his already somewhat blurred vision. Plagued throughout his career by a chronic sinus condition that required several operations, Hafey eventually took to wearing eyeglasses, finding it necessary to rotate among three different pairs due to the variable nature of his vision. Yet, despite his poor eyesight, he managed to begin an extremely productive stretch in 1927 that gained him general recognition as one of the finest hitters in the game.

Although Hafey appeared in only 103 games in 1927, he knocked in sixty-three runs and finished sixth in the National League with eighteen home runs. He also topped the senior circuit with a .590 slugging percentage, while also placing among the leaders with a .329 batting average and a .401 on-base percentage. Hafey followed that up with three straight seasons in which he surpassed 25 homers, 100 RBIs, and 100 runs scored. He also batted over .330 and compiled a slugging percentage in excess of .600 in each of those campaigns. After batting .337, hitting 27 homers, driving in 111 runs, and collecting 46 doubles in 1928, Hafey batted .338 and established career highs with 29 home runs, 125 RBIs, and 47 doubles in 1929. He had another big year in 1930, when he batted .336, hit 26 homers, knocked in 107 runs, and reached career highs with 108 runs scored, a .407 on-base percentage, and a .652 slugging percentage.

During the most productive stretch of his career, Hafey gained general recognition as one of the premier hitters of his day. Predominantly a pull hitter, Hafey became known for hitting vicious line drives over third base and down the left-field line. New York Giants third baseman Fred Lindstrom once noted the following:

> When Hafey hits that jackrabbit at you, you don't have time to think. Only your instinct of self-preservation functions. You put up your hands to protect yourself. Sometimes the ball sticks; other times it whistles by you like a shot. I am afraid to think of what may happen someday if the third baseman doesn't get his hands up fast enough.[1]

Although Hafey built his reputation primarily on his hitting, he also excelled in the field, gaining widespread acclaim for the outstanding range and powerful throwing arm he exhibited in the outfield. After spending his first four seasons splitting his time between all three outfield positions, he eventually settled in as the Cardinals' everyday left fielder, manning that spot his final four years with the team. Displaying the strong throwing arm that prompted the Cardinals to originally sign him as a pitcher, Hafey led all NL left fielders in assists in both 1928 and 1930.

Hafey began the 1931 campaign late after holding out during spring training for $15,000. He eventually signed for $12,500, but Branch Rickey fined him $2,100 for not being in playing shape. Hafey responded by knocking in 95 runs, scoring 94 others, and winning the batting title with a mark of .349. The slugging outfielder waited until the season's final day to lay claim to the batting crown, getting a hit in his last at bat to edge out New York's Bill Terry and teammate Jim Bottomley in the closest batting race ever. Hafey concluded the campaign with a mark of .3489, while Terry and Bottomley finished with averages of .3486 and .3482, respectively.

Hafey again held out at the start of the ensuing campaign, demanding that the previous year's fine be added to his 1932 salary; however, when Rickey offered to increase his salary only $500, to $13,000, an insulted Hafey left the Cardinals' spring training facility and drove home to California, where he waited until April 11 to find out that he had been traded to the last-place Cincinnati Reds for two players and $50,000. Rickey subsequently replaced him in left field with Joe Medwick.

The Reds agreed to pay Hafey the $15,000 he sought, after which the outfielder posted a batting average of .344 in his first year with his new club. Sinus problems limited him to just eighty-three games and 253 official at bats, enabling him to hit only two home runs and drive in just thirty-six. Although Hafey appeared in more than 140 games for Cincinnati in each of the next two seasons, he failed to compile the type of offensive numbers he typically posted in St. Louis, combining for a total of only twenty-five home runs and 129 RBIs, while batting right around .300 each year. Continuing to struggle with sinus and vision problems, Hafey announced his retirement early in 1935, after playing in only fifteen games. He attempted a comeback with the Reds in 1937, serving the team as a backup outfielder, before retiring for good at the end of the year.

Hafey ended his career with 164 home runs, 833 RBIs, 777 runs scored, 1,466 hits, a .317 batting average, a .372 on-base percentage, and a .526 slugging percentage. In parts of eight seasons in St. Louis, he hit 127 home runs, knocked in 618 runs, scored 542 others, collected 963 hits, compiled a .326 batting average, and posted on-base and slugging percentages of .379 and .568, respectively. In addition to tying Rogers Hornsby for the fourth-highest slugging percentage in team history, Hafey ranks eighth in batting average and sixth in on-base plus slugging percentage (OPS) (.948).

Following his retirement, Hafey purchased farmland near Calistoga, California, where he eventually raised cattle and sheep. He lived a quiet life, staying away from the baseball scene for the most part; however, he returned briefly in 1971, when the Veterans Committee elected him to the Hall of Fame. Suffering from ill health that included attacks of asthma and stomach problems, Hafey passed away less than two years later, at the age of seventy, on July 2, 1973.

Hafey's selection to the Hall of Fame is one of many made by the members of the Veterans Committee that has drawn a considerable amount of criticism throughout the years. The relative brevity of Hafey's career left him with rather modest career totals, prompting many to suggest that the outfielder's induction into Cooperstown can be mostly attributed to the presence of Frankie Frisch on the committee, Frisch being his longtime teammate in St. Louis. Nevertheless, those who saw Hafey at the height of his career would not likely find fault with his admission to the Hall.

Years after engaging in numerous salary disputes with Hafey, Branch Rickey often mentioned how great a player he considered the outfielder to be. The man noted for his ability to judge talent stated, "I always thought that if Hafey had been blessed with normal eyesight and good health, he might have been the best right-handed hitter baseball had ever known."[2]

CARDINAL CAREER HIGHLIGHTS

Best Season

Hafey is perhaps remembered most for winning the closest batting race in NL history with a mark of .349 in 1931. He also hit 16 homers, knocked in 95 runs, scored 94 others, compiled a .404 on-base percentage, and posted a .569 slugging percentage that year, en route to earning his only top-ten finish in the NL Most Valuable Player voting. But Hafey actually compiled slightly better overall numbers in each of the three previous seasons, posting similar batting averages and on-base percentages, while hitting more home runs, driving in more runs, scoring more times, and compiling higher slugging percentages.

Hafey compiled almost identical batting averages of .337, .338, and .336 from 1928 to 1930, surpassing 25 home runs, 100 RBIs, and 100 runs scored each year, while also compiling a slugging percentage in excess of .600 in each of those campaigns. After hitting twenty-seven homers and driving in 111 runs in 1928, he established career highs with twenty-nine home runs and 125 RBIs in 1929. Hafey followed that up by hitting 26 homers; knocking in 107 runs; and establishing career bests with 108 runs scored, a .407 on-base percentage, and a .652 slugging percentage in 1930. However, the NL experimented with a livelier ball in both 1929 and 1930, causing offensive numbers to increase dramatically throughout the senior circuit. As a result, Hafey placed in the league's top five in only two offensive categories in the first of those years, and just one in the second campaign. On the other hand, he finished among the league leaders in five different categories in 1928, placing third in home runs (27), fourth in RBIs

(111), second in doubles (46), third in slugging percentage (.604), and fifth in total bases (314). Hafey also finished eighth in batting average (.337), seventh in runs scored (101), and fifth in OPS (.990). All things considered, his 1928 performance would have to be considered the finest of his career.

Memorable Moments and Greatest Performances

Hafey had one of his best days at the plate for the Cardinals on July 28, 1928, when he led his team to a doubleheader sweep of the Phillies by banging out two home runs and four doubles. Hafey's performance made him the first major leaguer to collect six extra-base hits in a doubleheader.

A little less than a year later, on July 9, 1929, Hafey set a Cardinals record (later tied by Jim Edmonds) by reaching base safely in his eleventh and twelfth straight plate appearances. By collecting two hits before Philadelphia's Phil Collins finally retired him, Hafey also extended to ten his consecutive hits streak, tying the NL record in the process.

On May 7, 1930, Hafey accomplished the rare feat of knocking in five runs in one inning. He did so in the fifth frame of a 16–11 Cardinals victory over the Phillies. Hafey had another big day at the plate later in the year, going 4-for-4, with two homers, during a 5–4 St. Louis loss to Boston on July 24. Almost one month later, on August 21, Hafey hit for the cycle during a 16–6 Cardinals victory over the Phillies in St. Louis.

Hafey, however, had the biggest day of his career on August 23, 1931, when he went 5-for-5, hit 2 home runs, and drove in 8 runs during a 16–1 Cardinals win over Boston in the first game of a doubleheader. Hafey collected four RBIs on one swing of the bat, hitting one of his homers with the bases full.

Notable Achievements

Hit more than twenty-five home runs three times.

Knocked in more than 100 runs three times.

Scored more than 100 runs three times.

Batted over .300 six times, topping the .330 mark on four occasions.

Surpassed forty doubles twice.
Compiled on-base percentage in excess of .400 three times.
Posted slugging percentage in excess of .600 three times.
Led NL in batting average once and slugging percentage once.
Led NL left fielders in assists twice.
Ranks among Cardinals all-time leaders in batting average (eighth), slugging percentage (tied for fourth), and OPS (sixth).
Four-time NL champion (1926, 1928, 1930, 1931).
Two-time world champion (1926, 1931).
Elected to Baseball Hall of Fame by members of Veterans Committee in 1971.

NOTES

1. Fred Lindstrom, quoted in "Chick Hafey Stats," *Baseball Almanac*, www.baseball-almanac.com/players/player.php?p=hafeych01 (accessed September 29, 2012).
2. Branch Rickey, quoted by Greg Erion, "Chick Hafey," *Society for American Baseball Research*, www.sabr.org/bioproj/person/96ae4951 (accessed September 29, 2012).

18

KEITH HERNANDEZ

Keith Hernandez and Joe Torre compiled extremely comparable numbers during their time in St. Louis. Hernandez appeared in almost 250 more games and accumulated almost 600 more official at bats than Torre as a Cardinal, enabling him to score some 200 more runs, amass 155 more hits, collect 100 more doubles, and accumulate almost 20 more triples. But Torre hit seventeen more home runs than Hernandez in a Redbirds uniform, and he also drove in runs at a faster pace, compiling only thirty-seven fewer RBIs. Hernandez batted .299 as a Cardinal and posted on-base and slugging percentages of .385 and .448, respectively. Torre compiled a batting average of .308, posted an on-base percentage of .382, and compiled a slugging percentage of .458. Therefore, the statistical matchup between the two men is quite close.

Both Hernandez and Torre won a batting title and captured National League Most Valuable Player honors while playing for the Cardinals. Hernandez helped lead St. Louis to the world championship in 1982, while the Cardinals never finished any higher than second in any of Torre's six seasons with them, doing so three times. Hernandez held his biggest edge over Torre, however, on the defensive end, earning Gold Glove honors in each of his final five seasons in St. Louis. That is the thing that ultimately pushed him ahead of Torre in these rankings.

Considered by many baseball experts to be the greatest fielding first baseman in the history of the game, Keith Hernandez won more Gold Gloves (eleven) than any other player at his position. Possessing outstanding range, superb instincts, and tremendous self-confidence,

Hernandez revolutionized play at first base in much the same manner that Brooks Robinson changed the way the position of third base was defended. Hernandez's quickness, strong and accurate throwing arm, and total lack of fear enabled him to charge attempted sacrifice bunts with abandon, taking away from the batter the entire right side of the infield in such situations. While managing the Cincinnati Reds, Pete Rose once compared bunting against Hernandez to "driving the lane against Bill Russell."[1]

During the course of his career, Hernandez established major-league records for first basemen by leading his league in double plays six times. He also topped all NL first sackers in assists five times, putouts four times, and fielding average once, while compiling the third most assists (1,682) of any first baseman in history. Also an outstanding hitter, Hernandez posted a lifetime batting average of .296 and a career on-base percentage of .384, leading the NL in both offensive categories once. He also topped the senior circuit in runs scored twice and doubles once.

Born in San Francisco, California, on October 20, 1953, Keith Hernandez grew up in Pacifica and Millbrae, California. The son of a Mexican father and a Scots-Irish mother, Hernandez starred in baseball at Capuchino High School, in San Bruno, from which he graduated in 1971. Despite excelling on the diamond his first two years at Capuchino, Hernandez received few college scholarship offers since he developed a reputation for having a poor attitude after sitting out his entire senior year due to a dispute with a coach. He played briefly at the College of San Mateo, a local community college, before being selected by the St. Louis Cardinals in the forty-second round of the 1971 Major League Baseball Draft.

Although the six-foot, 195-pound Hernandez displayed a strong affinity for playing first base early in his minor-league career, he failed to impress at the plate, compiling a batting average that hovered around the .250 mark in each of his first two seasons. However, the lefty-swinging Hernandez began to show improvement as a hitter in 1973, after being promoted to the Cardinals' Triple-A affiliate in Tulsa. The first baseman batted .333, with five home runs and a .525 slugging percentage during the season's second half, before hitting .351 for the Oilers in the first five months of the 1974 campaign. Hernandez's increased offensive production earned him a promotion to St. Louis in late August. He appeared in fourteen games for the Cardinals during the season's final month, batting .294 and driving in the first two runs of his major-league career.

Hernandez split the 1975 season between Tulsa and St. Louis, batting just .250 for the Cardinals in just fewer than 200 official at bats, while also hitting three home runs and knocking in twenty runs. Nevertheless, he made a strong impression on St. Louis management with his exceptional fielding ability, committing only two errors in 507 chances, for an outstanding .996 fielding percentage.

Hernandez's excellent glove work convinced the Cardinals to give him an opportunity to break into the team's starting lineup the following year. Gradually establishing himself as the club's regular first baseman throughout the course of the season, Hernandez batted .289, hit 7 homers, and drove in 46 runs.

Hernandez developed into one of the NL's top first basemen the ensuing campaign, batting .291, hitting 15 home runs, knocking in 91 runs, scoring 90 others, and finishing third in the senior circuit with 41 doubles. Although Hernandez posted less-impressive offensive numbers in 1978, he ended up winning the first of his major-league record eleven consecutive Gold Gloves at first base.

Hernandez took his game to the next level in 1979, batting a league-leading .344, driving in a career-high 105 runs, placing second in the senior circuit with 210 hits and a .417 on-base percentage, and leading the league with 116 runs scored and 48 doubles. The twenty-five-year-old first baseman's brilliant year earned him his first All-Star nomination and a first-place tie with Pittsburgh's Willie Stargell in the league MVP voting.

Hernandez also put up outstanding numbers for the Cardinals in each of the next three seasons, performing particularly well in 1980, when he batted .321, hit 16 home runs, knocked in 99 runs, and led the NL with 111 runs scored and a .408 on-base percentage. Two years later, he helped lead St. Louis to the world championship by driving in 8 runs against Milwaukee in the World Series, after batting .299, knocking in 94 runs, and stealing a career-high 19 bases during the regular season.

However, Hernandez's relationship with Cardinals manager Whitey Herzog grew increasingly hostile during the early 1980s, a period during which the first baseman developed an addiction to cocaine. Herzog, who eventually came to view the free-spirited Hernandez as a cancer to his team, finally decided to part ways with arguably the Cardinals' best player on June 15, 1983, trading him to the last-place New York Mets for pitchers Neil Allen and Rick Ownbey. After being criticized for accepting less than equal value from the Mets for the All-Star first baseman, Herzog attempted to defend the deal by hinting at Hernandez's use of drugs. Hernandez threatened a libel suit, but the Pittsburgh drug trials held two years later substantiated Herzog's remarks.

At the aforementioned trials, a number of major-league players, including Hernandez, Dale Berra, Lee Lacy, Lee Mazzilli, John Milner, Dave Parker, Willie Aikens, Vida Blue, Tim Raines, and Lonnie Smith, testified against a pair of small-time cocaine dealers, who were tried and convicted in federal prosecutions. Parker's testimony revealed some of the earliest cocaine use among those called in for questioning. Meanwhile, Hernandez claimed during his testimony that about 40 percent of all major-league players used cocaine in 1980, describing it as the "love affair year between baseball and the drug."[2]

Although the players that appeared in court were known to have used the drug, none of them went to jail since they were granted full immunity. Hernandez's testimony helped to vindicate Herzog, who never regretted making the trade. The St. Louis manager replaced Hernandez at first base shortly thereafter with fellow All-Star Jack Clark, who helped the Cardinals win two more pennants in the next four years.

Meanwhile, Hernandez initially balked at the idea of coming to New York to play for a Mets team that typically finished at or near the bottom of the NL East rankings; however, he eventually changed his mind after the Mets' front office assured him that such talented youngsters as Dwight Gooden and Darryl Strawberry would soon be joining him in New York.

Hernandez's decision proved to be a wise one, since the Mets became a contending team shortly thereafter, winning the world championship in 1986 and advancing to the National League Championship Series (NLCS) in 1988. Displaying a level of intensity he failed to exhibit in St. Louis, Hernandez evolved into the Mets' team leader, even being named the first captain in franchise history prior to the start of the 1987 campaign. At the same time, he excelled on the field, batting over .300 three times and driving in more than ninety runs twice from 1984 to 1987, en route to earning All-Star honors three times and two top-five finishes in the NL MVP balloting. Hernandez also won six more Gold Gloves while playing for the Mets.

Hernandez found playing in the city of New York much to his liking. Reenergized by the change in scenery, and quite comfortable with the celebrity status he quickly attained in the Big Apple, he became a New York icon. He enjoyed the city's nightlife, became a fixture at Manhattan's most popular clubs, and dated celebrities, all while providing outstanding leadership on the field to his younger teammates.

Larry Bowa, who spent most of his career competing against Hernandez as a member of the Phillies and Cubs, joined the Mets for the final month of the 1985 campaign, after which he announced his retirement. Hernandez made a lasting impression on Bowa during their brief time together, with the longtime shortstop later saying the following:

> You watch the things that this guy did in the field, it was amazing. This guy could go to the mound . . . he was like a pitching coach out there. Talk about leadership qualities—he was probably as good a leader as anybody I've ever seen. He would settle a pitcher down, tell him the situation, what to do.[3]

Bowa added, "He's as good a first baseman as I've ever seen for doing everything. Bunt plays . . . his bunt plays were unbelievable! First and second, he'd charge and throw to third. Man on first, he'd charge and throw to second—he could do it with anybody."[4]

In spite of the tremendous impact Hernandez made in New York, his days in a Mets uniform became numbered when injuries forced him to miss huge portions of the 1988 and 1989 campaigns. With the ability of the veteran first baseman to properly lead his younger Mets teammates already being called into question by some when New York failed to return to the World Series in either 1987 or 1988,

Hernandez lost even more credibility when he found himself unable to take the field for much of his last two years with the team.

A well-publicized confrontation with Darryl Strawberry, who perhaps admired Hernandez more than anyone else on the team at one point, essentially marked the beginning of the end for the first baseman in New York. After Hernandez batted just .233 and drove in only nineteen runs in seventy-five games in 1989, the Mets chose not to resign their thirty-six-year-old captain when his contract expired at the end of the year. Hernandez subsequently signed as a free agent with the Cleveland Indians, with whom he spent the 1990 campaign before announcing his retirement at season's end. Hernandez left the game with 162 home runs, 1,071 RBIs, 1,124 runs scored, 2,182 hits, a lifetime batting average of .296, a career on-base percentage of .384, and a lifetime slugging percentage of .436. His numbers as a member of the Cardinals include 81 home runs, 595 RBIs, 662 runs scored, 1,217 hits, a .299 batting average, a .385 on-base percentage, and a .448 slugging percentage.

After retiring from the game as an active player, Hernandez turned to broadcasting, eventually earning a spot as a color commentator on New York Mets' television broadcasts. He continues to serve in that capacity.

CARDINAL CAREER HIGHLIGHTS

Best Season

Hernandez had an outstanding year for the Cardinals in 1980, when he hit 16 home runs, knocked in 99 runs, batted .321, collected 191 hits, amassed 39 doubles, posted a .494 slugging percentage, and led the NL with 111 runs scored and a .408 on-base percentage. Nevertheless, Hernandez's 1979 campaign would have to be considered the finest of his career. In addition to topping the senior circuit with 116 runs scored, 48 doubles, and a .344 batting average, he established career highs with 105 RBIs, 210 hits, 11 triples, a .417 on-base percentage, and a .513 slugging percentage, en route to earning a share of the league MVP trophy.

Memorable Moments and Greatest Performances

Hernandez helped lead the Cardinals to their first world championship in fifteen years in 1982 by performing exceptionally well during the postseason. After batting .333 during the Cardinals' three-game sweep of Atlanta in the NLCS, he homered once and knocked in eight runs against Milwaukee in the World Series. Hernandez helped St. Louis overcome a three-games-to-two deficit in the Fall Classic by hitting a home run during a 13–1 Cardinals victory in Game 6; however, he delivered his biggest hit of the World Series in the decisive seventh contest, when his bases-loaded single in the sixth inning turned a 3–1 Cardinals deficit into a 3–3 tie. George Hendrick then knocked in what proved to be the game-winning run with a RBI single.

Notable Achievements

Knocked in more than 100 runs once (105 in 1979).
Scored more than 100 runs twice.
Batted over .300 three times, surpassing the .320 mark twice.
Surpassed 200 hits once (210 in 1979).
Finished in double digits in triples once (eleven in 1979).
Topped forty doubles twice.
Surpassed 100 walks once (100 in 1982).
Compiled on-base percentage in excess of .400 four times.
Posted slugging percentage in excess of .500 once (.513 in 1979).
Led NL in runs scored twice, batting average once, on-base percentage once, doubles once, and intentional bases on balls once.
Led NL first basemen in putouts three times and assists twice.
1979 NL Co-MVP.
1980 Silver Slugger winner.
Five-time Gold Glove winner (1978, 1979, 1980, 1981, 1982).
Two-time *Sporting News* All-Star selection (1979, 1980).
Two-time NL All-Star (1979, 1980).
1982 NL champion.
1982 world champion.

NOTES

1. Pete Rose, quoted in www.keithhernandez.com/quotes.html (accessed September 30, 2012).

2. Keith Hernandez, quoted in Craig Calcaterra, "A Few Words on Cocaine in Baseball," *NBC Sports Hardball Talk*, March 17, 2010, www.hardballtalk.nbcsports.com/2010/03/17/a-few-words-on-cocaine-in-baseball (accessed September 30, 2012).

3. Larry Bowa, quoted in Mike Shalin and Neil Shalin, *Out by a Step: The 100 Best Players Not in the Baseball Hall of Fame* (Lanham, MD: Diamond Communications, 2002), 79.

4. Bowa, quoted in Shalin and Shalin, *Out by a Step*, 80.

19

JOE TORRE

Joe Torre recently entered the Baseball Hall of Fame for having managed the New York Yankees to ten American League East titles, six AL pennants, and four world championships from 1996 to 2007; however, most people tend to forget the degree to which Torre excelled on the field during his eighteen-year playing career. The former catcher-first baseman-third baseman batted over .300 in five of his fifteen full big-league seasons, surpassing the .320 mark on three separate occasions. He also hit more than 20 home runs six times, knocked in more than 100 runs five times, and accumulated more than 200 hits twice, en route to earning nine All-Star nominations and two top-five finishes in the National League Most Valuable Player voting. Torre made the All-Star team in four out of his six seasons in St. Louis, winning NL MVP honors in 1971, when he put together the greatest season ever turned in by a Cardinals third baseman.

Born in Brooklyn, New York, on July 18, 1940, Joseph Paul Torre followed in his brother Frank's footsteps when he signed with the Milwaukee Braves as an amateur free agent in 1960 after graduating from Brooklyn's James Madison High School. The younger Torre made his major-league debut with the Braves later that year, joining them in the season's final week after displaying his outstanding hitting ability by winning the Northern League batting championship with a .344 batting average while playing for the Class A Eau Claire Braves. Returned to the minor leagues for more seasoning at the end of the year, Torre arrived in Milwaukee to stay early in 1961, earning a second-place finish in the NL Rookie of the Year balloting by batting .278 and driving in forty-two runs in 113 games.

After spending most of 1962 platooning with veteran receiver Del Crandall, Torre became a full-time starter the following year, spending most of his time behind home plate, while also seeing a significant amount of playing time at first base. He continued to serve the Braves in that capacity the next few seasons, establishing himself during that time as the NL's premier catcher, as well as one of the senior circuit's better hitters. Torre had his two best years for the team in 1964 and 1966, earning a fifth-place finish in the NL MVP voting in the first of those years by hitting twenty home runs and placing among the league leaders with 109 RBIs and a .321 batting average. After the Braves left Milwaukee at the conclusion of the 1965 campaign, Torre found Atlanta's tiny Fulton County Stadium very much to his liking, hitting a career-high thirty-six homers in 1966, while also driving in 101 runs and batting .315. However, when injuries contributed greatly to a decrease in Torre's offensive production in each of the next two seasons, the Braves elected to trade the right-handed-hitting slugger to the Cardinals for former NL MVP Orlando Cepeda prior to the start of the 1969 campaign.

With Tim McCarver holding down the starting catching job in St. Louis, Torre moved to first base in his first year with his new team, seeing only occasional action behind home plate. Although playing in spacious Busch Stadium caused Torre's home run total to drop to eighteen, the Cards' new first baseman managed to drive in 101 runs and bat .289. Torre split his time between catcher and third base the following year, after the Cardinals traded McCarver to Philadelphia and regular third sacker Mike Shannon found himself sidelined by a career-ending illness. Despite manning a more demanding defensive position much of the time, Torre ended up improving upon his numbers, hitting 21 homers, knocking in 100 runs, scoring 89 others, collecting 203 hits, finishing second in the NL batting race with a mark of .325, and establishing new career highs with 311 total bases and a .398 on-base percentage.

Torre moved to third base full-time in 1971, enabling him to thrive at the plate as never before. Having shed more than thirty pounds during the previous off-season, and no longer affected by the rigors of catching every day, Torre had the greatest season of his career. In addition to hitting 24 home runs, scoring 97 runs, compiling a .421 on-base percentage, and posting a .555 slugging percentage, he topped the senior circuit with 137 RBIs, a .363 batting average, 230 hits, and 352 total bases. Torre's fabulous performance helped lead the Cardinals to a respectable second-place finish in the NL East, earning him league MVP honors in the process.

Sparky Anderson, who managed the Cincinnati Reds that year, later commented, "Joe Torre showed me a lot by winning a batting title there. It's hard to hit home runs there (Busch Stadium), so he became a line-drive hitter. He learned to use the middle and not try to do what can't be done."[1] Outfielder Tom Grieve, who later played under Torre when the latter managed the Mets, once noted, "That great year he had when he hit .363 was amazing. And you think about the way Joe ran, he sure didn't get any bunt hits or infield hits—he earned every bit of that."[2]

The 1971 campaign ended up being Torre's last big year. Although he put up solid numbers for the Cardinals in each of the next three seasons, he never came close to reaching the same level of offensive production. After Torre totaled just thirty-five home runs and 220 RBIs from 1972 to 1974, the Cardinals traded him to the New York Mets for veteran pitcher Ray Sadecki and minor leaguer Tommy Moore. Torre subsequently spent parts of three years in New York, seeing his numbers continue to drop before announcing his retirement as an active player on June 18, 1977, just eighteen days after being named New York's player-manager. Torre ended his playing career with 252 home runs, 1,185 RBIs, 996 runs scored, 2,342 hits, a .297 batting average, a .365 on-base percentage, and a .452 slugging percentage. In his six years in St. Louis, he hit 98 homers, drove in 558 runs, scored 455 others, accumulated 1,062 hits, batted .308, and compiled on-base and slugging percentages of .382 and .458, respectively.

Although Torre retired as an active player midway through the 1977 campaign, he continued to manage the Mets until the end of 1981. Relieved of his managerial duties in New York after experiencing little in the way of success his five years there, Torre subsequently piloted the Atlanta Braves for three years, leading them to a division title in 1982; however, after Atlanta finished second in each of the next two seasons, Torre again found himself without a job. Always one to land on his feet, however, he became a popular broadcaster for the

Angels, before returning to the dugout to manage the Cardinals from the tail end of 1990 to the early portion of 1995.

After being relieved of his duties by the Cardinals forty-seven games into the 1995 campaign, Torre resurfaced once more, returning to New York to manage the Yankees. Overcoming numerous obstacles that included a 1999 bout with prostate cancer, Torre led the Yankees on an extraordinarily successful run, during which they captured six AL pennants and four world championships.

Torre left New York after he failed to reach agreement with team management on a new long-term contract at the conclusion of the 2007 campaign. He subsequently managed the Los Angeles Dodgers for three years, before being appointed by baseball commissioner Bud Selig as the new executive vice president for baseball operations for Major League Baseball. He continues to serve in that capacity.

CARDINAL CAREER HIGHLIGHTS

Best Season

Although Torre had an exceptional year for the Cardinals in 1970, hitting 21 homers, driving in 100 runs, collecting 203 hits, batting .325, and compiling on-base and slugging percentages of .398 and .498, respectively, his performance that season paled in comparison to the effort he put forth the following campaign, when he had easily the greatest season of his career. Torre hit 24 home runs in 1971; placed among the league leaders with 97 runs scored, 34 doubles, a .421 on-base percentage, and a .555 slugging percentage; and topped the senior circuit with a .363 batting average, 137 RBIs, 230 hits, and 352 total bases. Torre's 230 hits tie him with Stan Musial (1948) for the fourth-highest single-season total in Cardinals history. Meanwhile, his 137 RBIs place him in a four-way tie for the seventh-highest total in club history.

Memorable Moments and Greatest Performances

Torre provided Cardinals fans with a memorable moment on August 28, 1970, when he hit a ninth-inning home run against Don Sutton to give St. Louis a 1–0 victory over Los Angeles. Torre's blast made a winner out of Jerry Reuss, who pitched a two-hitter for the Cardinals. Sutton surrendered only five hits to the Cardinals.

Torre had his biggest day at the plate for the Cardinals on June 27, 1973, when he led his team to a 15–4 win over the Pirates by hitting for the cycle. He began his day by doubling in the first inning. He followed that up with a homer in the third and a triple in the fourth, before hitting into a double play and drawing a base on balls in his next two trips to the plate. Although Torre asked Red Schoendienst to pinch-run for him after walking in the eighth inning, the Cardinals manager left him in the contest, allowing him to complete his cycle by singling in the ninth inning.

Notable Achievements

Hit more than twenty home runs twice.
Knocked in more than 100 runs three times.
Batted over .300 twice, surpassing .325 mark on both occasions.
Topped 200 hits twice.
Compiled on-base percentage in excess of .400 once (.421 in 1971).
Posted slugging percentage in excess of .500 once (.555 in 1971).
Led NL in RBIs once, batting average once, hits once, and total bases once.
Led NL third basemen in putouts once.
Led NL first basemen in assists once.
1971 NL MVP.
1971 *Sporting News* All-Star selection.
1971 *Sporting News* Major League Player of the Year.
Four-time NL All-Star (1970, 1971, 1972, 1973).

NOTES

1. Sparky Anderson, quoted in Mike Shalin and Neil Shalin, *Out by a Step: The 100 Best Players Not in the Baseball Hall of Fame* (Lanham, MD.: Diamond Communications, 2002), 129.

2. Tom Grieve, quoted in Shalin and Shalin, *Out by a Step*, 128.

20

JESSE HAINES

Although he isn't nearly as well known to Cardinals fans as either Bob Gibson or Dizzy Dean, who clearly rank as the two greatest pitchers in team history, Jesse Haines established himself during the course of his eighteen years in St. Louis as one of the finest hurlers ever to take the mound for the Redbirds. Spending virtually his entire career with the Cardinals, the right-handed knuckleball artist won more games, tossed more complete games, and threw more innings than any other pitcher in franchise history, with the exception of Gibson. Along the way, Haines surpassed twenty victories on three separate occasions, helping the Cardinals capture five National League pennants and three world championships.

Born in Clayton, Ohio, on July 22, 1893, Jesse Joseph Haines spent several seasons toiling in the minor leagues before finally making his major-league debut with the Cincinnati Reds in 1918, just two days before celebrating his twenty-fifth birthday. Haines appeared in just one game for the Reds, before they returned him to Kansas City of the American Association. Hardly considered to be a top prospect due to his advanced age and merely average fastball, Haines nonetheless managed to post an exceptional 21–5 record for Kansas City in 1919. With the Cardinals desperately in need of pitching in 1920, field manager and team president Branch Rickey convinced the club's directors to purchase the twenty-six-year-old right-hander for $10,000.

Pitching for a St. Louis team that finished fifth in the NL in 1920 with a record of 75–79, Haines won only thirteen of his thirty-three decisions. Nevertheless, he pitched well for the Cardinals, compiling a 2.98 ERA, tossing 19 complete games, and placing among the league leaders with 301.7 innings pitched and 120 strikeouts. The Cardinals posted a winning record in each of the next three campaigns, enabling Haines to compile an overall mark of 49–34 during that time. Particularly effective in 1923, Haines finished 20–13, threw 266 innings, and placed among the league leaders with a 3.11 ERA and 23 complete games.

Mediocre finishes by the Cardinals in 1924 and 1925 caused Haines to post a losing record both years; however, the thirty-three-year-old veteran proved to be a huge contributor to a St. Louis team that captured the NL pennant in 1926. Serving the Cardinals as both a starter and reliever, Haines concluded the campaign with a record of 13–4, a 3.25 ERA, and 14 complete games in 20 starts. He subsequently helped lead his team to an upset win over the heavily favored Yankees in the World Series, posting two victories, including a 4–0 shutout in Game 3.

Having incorporated into his pitching repertoire a knuckleball that complemented his rather mediocre fastball, Haines developed into the ace of the Cardinals' pitching staff in 1927. In easily his finest season, Haines finished 24–10, with a 2.72 ERA and a league-leading twenty-five complete games and six shutouts. He followed that up with a mark of 20–8 for the 1928 NL champion Cardinals, while also compiling a 3.18 ERA and tossing twenty complete games.

Although most knuckleballers tend to grip the ball with their fingertips, Haines instead grasped it with his knuckles, allowing him to throw it with more velocity than most others. Discussing his specialty pitch in an article that appeared in the May 1928 edition of *Baseball Magazine*, Haines notes the following:

> My favorite ball is the knuckler. I hold the ball tight against the knuckles of my pitching hand and throw it with every ounce of speed I can put behind it. When it's breaking right, it swoops down a good deal like a curve, only faster and with a sharper break than a curve. I don't believe any batter in uniform likes to face a good knuckleball when it's sweeping in with a lot of zip and breaking right.[1]

After pitching extremely well for the Cardinals during the 1928 regular season, Haines faltered somewhat in the World Series, allowing the Yankees six runs (three earned) in six innings of work in his lone start, as New York swept St. Louis in four straight games. Haines's poor performance likely caused him a considerable amount of consternation, since he tended to take each loss very badly. Known as a pleasant and kind fellow off the field, Haines couldn't stand defeat, also developing a reputation throughout the years for losing his temper when defensive lapses made by teammates cost him games. Center fielder Terry Moore, who joined the Cardinals during the latter stages of Haines's career, once commented, "When I saw how hard a nice old man like Pop could take it after losing a game, I realized why he'd been a consistent winner . . . and the Cardinals, too. I never forgot how much Haines expected of himself, and of others."[2]

Gradually acquiring the nickname "Pop" as his hair grew thinner, Haines became a father figure to the Cardinals' younger players, whom he treated with patience and kindness. Meanwhile, his knuckler helped keep him in the big leagues after he lost the ability to get out opposing batters with any of his other pitches. After helping the Cardinals win the NL pennant in 1930 and 1931 by posting an overall record of 25–11, primarily as a starter, Haines spent his final six years in St. Louis working mostly out of the bullpen, although he occasionally took on a spot-starting assignment as well. Pitching past his forty-fourth birthday, he finally retired after the Cardinals released him at the conclusion of the 1937 campaign.

Haines ended his career with a record of 210–158, a 3.64 ERA, 208 complete games, 23 shutouts, and 3,209 innings pitched. In addition to ranking second all-time among Cardinals pitchers in wins, complete games, and innings pitched, Haines appeared in more games than any other hurler in team history (554). He also ranks among the club's all-time leaders in games started (third), strikeouts (seventh), and shutouts (fifth).

After retiring from the game as an active player, Haines served the Dodgers as pitching coach in 1938. In one of the many controversial selections they made under the leadership of longtime Cardinals second baseman Frankie Frisch, the members of the Veterans Committee elected Haines to the Baseball Hall of Fame in 1970. He passed away eight years later, two weeks after celebrating his eighty-fifth birthday.

CAREER HIGHLIGHTS

Best Season

Although Haines pitched extremely well for the Cardinals in 1923 and 1928, posting 20 victories in each of those years, he unquestionably had his finest season in 1927. In addition to finishing fourth in the N.L. with a 2.72 ERA and placing second in the circuit with 24 wins, a .706 winning percentage, and 301 innings pitched, Haines led all league hurlers with 25 complete games and 6 shutouts. He also allowed fewer hits than innings pitched for the first time in his career, surrendering 273 hits to opposing batters, en route to earning an eighth-place finish in the NL Most Valuable Player voting.

Memorable Moments and Greatest Performances

Haines pitched arguably the greatest game of his career on July 17, 1924, hurling a no-hitter against Boston at Sportsman's Park in St. Louis. The no-no was the first thrown by a St. Louis pitcher since 1876. Haines pitched another memorable game four years earlier, when he worked seventeen innings before finally losing a 3–2 decision to Chicago's brilliant right-hander, Grover Cleveland Alexander.

Yet, Haines pitched the two most important games of his career against the Yankees in the 1926 World Series. He gave the Cardinals a 2–1 lead in the Series by hurling a five-hit shutout in Game 3, punctuating his outstanding performance by hitting a two-run homer in the fourth inning of his team's 4–0 triumph. Haines took the mound again for Game 7, holding the Yankees to just two runs through the first six innings before a blister he developed on his throwing hand contributed to him loading the bases with two men out in the bottom of the seventh. Grover Cleveland Alexander, who evened the Fall Classic at three games apiece one day earlier with a complete-game 10–2 victory, subsequently added to his legacy of greatness by squelching New York's rally, coming out of the St. Louis bull pen to strike out Tony Lazzeri with the bags full, before retiring the Yankees in each of the next two frames. Haines received credit for the win, concluding the Series with a record of 2–0 and a 1.08 ERA.

Although the Cardinals ended up losing the 1930 World Series to Philadelphia in six games, Haines again pitched brilliantly for his team in Game 4, evening the Series at two games apiece by outdueling A's staff ace Lefty Grove. Haines went the distance, allowing the A's just one run on four hits, in pitching the Cardinals to a 3–1 victory.

Notable Achievements

Won at least twenty games three times.
Compiled ERA below 3.00 three times.
Threw more than 300 innings twice.
Led NL pitchers in complete games once and shutouts once.
Threw more than twenty complete games three times.
Cardinals all-time leader in games pitched (554).
Second all-time among Cardinals pitchers in wins (210), complete games (208), and innings pitched (3,204).
Five-time NL champion (1926, 1928, 1930, 1931, 1934).
Three-time world champion (1926, 1931, 1934).
Elected to Baseball Hall of Fame by members of Veterans Committee in 1970.

NOTES

1. Jesse Haines, quoted in "Jesse Haines Stats," *Baseball Almanac*, www.baseball-almanac.com/players/player.php?p=haineje01 (accessed October 2, 2012).

2. Terry Moore, quoted in "Haines, Jesse," *National Baseball Hall of Fame and Museum*, www.baseballhall.org/hof/haines-jesse (accessed October 2, 2012).

21

MARK MCGWIRE

There likely will be some people who consider Mark McGwire's twenty-first-place finish in these rankings to be something of a slight to the man who holds the top two single-season home run marks in franchise history. McGwire also posted the highest career slugging percentage of anyone who ever played for the Cardinals. "Big Mac" reached iconic-like status during his relatively short stay in St. Louis, leading the nation on a memorable journey throughout the summer of 1998 as he doggedly pursued, and eventually broke, Roger Maris's long-standing single-season home run record. McGwire followed that up with a phenomenal 1999 campaign in which he established himself as one of only two players in baseball history to surpass fifty homers in four straight seasons. Nevertheless, the fact remains that McGwire spent parts of only five seasons in St. Louis, and that he appeared in more than 100 games for the Redbirds in just two of those. Even more significant is the fact that even though McGwire and the Cardinals have since done everything possible to sway public opinion to their side, the slugger has, in many ways, come to symbolize that period in baseball history often referred to as the "Steroid Era." In the process, at least in this writer's opinion, he has embarrassed himself and sullied the reputation of one of the most storied franchises in the history of the sport. That being the case, I found it impossible to place McGwire any higher than twenty-first on this list.

Born in Pomona, California, on October 1, 1963, Mark David McGwire played college baseball at the University of Southern California, before being selected by the Oakland Athletics in the first round of the 1984 amateur draft with the tenth overall pick. Spending barely two full seasons in the minor leagues, McGwire arrived in Oakland in late August 1986, after which he batted .189 and hit his first three major-league homers during the course of the final few weeks of the regular season.

McGwire earned a spot in the national limelight the following year, when he won American League Rookie of the Year honors by batting .289, knocking in 118 runs, and topping the junior circuit with 49 home runs and a .618 slugging percentage. An immediate fan favorite, the slugging first baseman was named to the AL All-Star team in each of his first six seasons, even though he posted batting averages of only .231, .235, and .201 in three of those campaigns. After hitting 42 homers, driving in 104 runs, batting .268, and leading the league with a .585 slugging percentage in 1992, McGwire found himself struggling to stay on the field in each of the next two seasons due to an assortment of injuries. Appearing in a total of only seventy-four games in the course of the 1993 and 1994 campaigns, McGwire hit just eighteen home runs and knocked in only forty-nine runs those two years.

Despondent over his inability to remain healthy, McGwire later admitted that he seriously considered retiring at one point. Recalling a conversation he had with his father, McGwire told the *New York Times*, "I remember telling him, 'I want to retire. I want to get away.' At the time, I knew my swing was developing, but I couldn't get away from the injuries. I seriously thought about retiring, but my dad talked me out of it."[1]

Instead of retiring, McGwire turned to steroids, admitting to Bob Costas during a January 2010 television interview that he tried them briefly after the 1989 season, but that he did not begin using them regularly until the winter following his injury-riddled 1993 campaign. Telling Costas that he took steroids solely to stay on the field, McGwire claimed, "I used very, very low dosages. There's no way I wanted to look like Lou Ferrigno or Arnold Schwarzenegger."[2] He added, "I don't want to use it as a crutch, but there was no drug testing. I didn't use it for strength. I used it to help me recover from injuries."[3]

Despite his statements to the contrary, McGwire gradually grew into a man of gargantuan-like proportions. Returning to the A's in 1995 having added nearly forty pounds of muscle onto his frame, the six-foot, five-inch slugger hit thirty-nine home runs and drove in ninety runs, in only 104 games and 317 official at bats, before a heel injury sidelined him for the remainder of the year. Fully healthy in 1996 for the first time in four years, McGwire drove in 113 runs and established new career highs with 104 runs scored, 116 walks, a .312 batting average, as well as a league-leading 52 homers, .467 on-base percentage, and .730 slugging percentage.

However, it wasn't until 1997 that McGwire began developing into a truly legendary figure. Traded to the Cardinals from the A's for three players at the end of July, McGwire hit twenty-four homers and knocked in forty-two runs in fifty-one games with his new team, concluding the campaign with 123 RBIs and a league-leading fifty-eight home runs. He subsequently joined Sammy Sosa in a memorable home run race the following season, establishing a new single-season mark (since broken) by hitting seventy round-trippers. McGwire also knocked in 147 runs; scored 130 others; batted .299; and led the National League with 162 walks, a .470 on-base percentage, and a .752 slugging percentage. Big Mac followed that up with a similarly productive 1999 campaign in which he scored 118 runs, walked 133 times, and topped the senior circuit with 65 home runs and 147 RBIs.

The 1999 season turned out to be McGwire's last great year, since injuries relegated him to part-time status in each of the next two seasons. After hitting thirty-two homers and driving in seventy-three runs in only eighty-nine games in 2000, McGwire announced his retirement at the conclusion of the ensuing campaign after posting a batting average of just .187, despite hitting twenty-nine homers in only ninety-seven games. He ended his career with 583 home runs, 1,414 RBIs, 1,167 runs scored, 1,626 hits, a .263 batting average, a .394 on-base percentage, and a .588 slugging percentage. His numbers as a member of the Cardinals include 220 home runs, 473 RBIs, 394 runs scored, 469 hits, a .270 batting average, a .427 on-base percentage, and a .683 slugging percentage. McGwire ranks among the club's all-time leaders in slugging percentage (first), on-base percentage (tied for second), on-base plus slugging percentage (first), and home runs (sixth).

Yet, in spite of his tremendous slugging feats, McGwire's career remains shrouded in controversy, with his accomplishments being tainted in the eyes of many by his involvement with performance-enhancing drugs. After stating repeatedly, "I'm not here to talk about the past . . . I only want to look ahead to the future,"[4] when asked about steroids during the Congressional hearings held on March 17, 2005, McGwire finally elected to "come clean" nearly five years later, admitting that he used steroids when he broke baseball's single-season home run record in 1998.

McGwire did his best to present himself in a sympathetic light while making his admission, stating the following during a 2010 interview with the *New York Times*:

> It's something I'm certainly not proud of. I'm certainly sorry for having done it. Someday, somehow, somewhere I knew I'd probably have to talk about this. I guess the steppingstone was being offered the hitting-coach job with the Cardinals. At that time, I said, 'I need to come clean about this.'[5]

McGwire later told Bob Costas during a one-on-one television interview that he actually wanted to open up to the members of Congress, but that his lawyers warned him that doing so could subject him to prosecution or a grand jury hearing. McGwire told Costas, "My lawyers were downstairs trying to get immunity for me. I wanted to talk. I kept telling myself, 'I want to get this off my chest.' Well, we didn't get immunity. So, here I am in a situation where I have two scenarios: a possible prosecution or possible grand-jury testimony."[6]

McGwire continued, saying the following:

> Well, you know what happens when there's a prosecution? They bring in your whole family, they bring in your whole friends, they bring in ex-teammates, coaches, anybody that's surrounding you. How the heck am I going to bring those people in for some stupid act that I did? So you know what I did? We agreed to not talk about the past. And it was not enjoyable to do that.[7]

He added, "I was not going to lie. I wanted to tell the truth."[8] McGwire also said, "I wish I had never touched steroids. It was foolish, and it was a mistake. I truly apologize. Looking back, I wish I had never played during the Steroid Era."[9]

Still, one has to wonder just how sincere McGwire's apology truly was, especially when it is considered that his admission of guilt happened to coincide with his resurfacing as hitting coach for the Cardinals. McGwire certainly did not seem to be experiencing any sort of remorse as he moved inexorably toward establishing a new home run record in 1998, reveling in the adulation heaped upon him by fans and the media. Shortly after breaking Roger Maris's thirty-seven-year-old mark, McGwire expressed his feelings to a national audience by stating, "Absolutely incredible. What can I say? I'm almost speechless. It's been awesome. The last week and a half, my stomach has been turning and my heart beating a million miles a minute. What a feat!"[10] Do those sound like the words of someone with a guilty conscience? Furthermore, McGwire displayed his arrogance and lack of compunction when he told Costas that he believed he "absolutely"[11] could have broken the record without using steroids, pointing to his home run-hitting prowess going back to Little League.

McGwire's involvement with steroids, and the belief held by many writers that he wouldn't even have approached the figures he compiled throughout the course of his career had he not artificially enhanced his performance, have prevented the former slugger from gaining much support in the Hall of Fame balloting since he first became eligible for induction in 2007. Only time will tell if the writers eventually soften their stance on him. In the meantime, after spending three years in St. Louis as hitting coach, McGwire accepted a similar position in Los Angeles, where he has spent the past two seasons coaching Dodger batsmen.

CARDINAL CAREER HIGHLIGHTS

Best Season

Although McGwire also had a monstrous 1999 campaign, scoring 118 runs, walking 133 times, and leading the NL with 65 homers and 147 RBIs, he clearly had his best season one year earlier. In addition to eclipsing the existing single-season home run mark by hitting 70 round-trippers, Big Mac knocked in 147 runs, scored 130 others, batted .299, accumulated a career-best 383 total bases, and topped the senior circuit with 162 bases on balls, a .470 on-base percentage, and a .752 slugging percentage. McGwire's 162 walks established a new NL record (since broken), as did his thirty-eight home runs hit at home. McGwire also set a new major-league mark by averaging one homer every 7.27 at bats. His dominant performance earned him a second-place finish to Sammy Sosa in the league Most Valuable Player voting.

Memorable Moments and Greatest Performances

McGwire hit a number of memorable home runs for the Cardinals during his relatively brief stay in St. Louis. On September 16, 1997, he launched a 517-foot blast that cleared the left-field scoreboard at Busch Stadium. McGwire topped his earlier feat on May 16, 1998, when he hit the longest home run in Busch Stadium history, driving the opposing pitcher's offering an estimated 545 feet. However, McGwire experienced his greatest moment later that year, when he homered off Chicago Cubs' right-hander Steve Trachsel on September 8, breaking in the process Roger Maris's thirty-seven-year-old single-season record.

Engaged in a memorable home run race with Chicago slugger Sammy Sosa, McGwire and his Cardinals began an early September home stand against the Cubs, with McGwire holding a slight fifty-nine to fifty-six lead over Sosa in their personal battle. After tying Maris's previous major-league record by hitting his sixty-first homer one day earlier, McGwire established a new mark on September 8, when he pulled one barely over the left-field wall against Trachsel with two men out in the fourth inning, for his sixty-second of the campaign. McGwire subsequently received congratulations from each of Chicago's infielders as he circled the bases, after which his teammates mobbed him when he crossed home plate. Sosa ran in from right field to congratulate McGwire, with the two sluggers embracing one another as the Maris family cheered from the stands. A celebration ensued, with baseball commissioner Bud Selig presiding over the festivities. Although much of the luster has since been removed from McGwire's accomplishment by his admitted use of steroids, the events of the evening remain vivid in the memory of anyone who witnessed them.

Notable Achievements

Hit more than sixty home runs twice, reaching the seventy-homer plateau once (1998).

Set new major-league single-season home run record in 1998, with seventy (since broken).

Knocked in 147 runs twice.

Scored more than 100 runs twice.

Batted over .300 once (.305 in 2000).

Walked more than 130 times twice.

Compiled on-base percentage in excess of .400 four times.

Posted slugging percentage in excess of .600 four times, surpassing the .700 mark twice.

Led NL in home runs twice, RBIs once, walks once, on-base percentage once, and slugging percentage once.

Holds Cardinals single-season records for most home runs (seventy) and walks (162).

Holds Cardinals career record for highest slugging percentage (.683).

Second in 1998 NL MVP voting.

1998 Silver Slugger winner.

1998 *Sporting News* All-Star selection.

Three-time NL All-Star (1998, 1999, 2000).

NOTES

1. Mark McGwire, quoted in Tyler Kepner, "McGwire Admits That He Used Steroids," *New York Times*, January 11, 2010, www.nytimes.com/2010/01/12/sports/baseball/12mcgwire.html?pagewanted=all (accessed November 28, 2012).

2. McGwire, quoted in Kepner, "McGwire Admits That He Used Steroids," www.nytimes.com/2010/01/12/sports/baseball/12mcgwire.html?pagewanted=all.

3. McGwire, quoted in Kepner, "McGwire Admits That He Used Steroids," www.nytimes.com/2010/01/12/sports/baseball/12mcgwire.html?pagewanted=all.

4. Mark McGwire, quoted in Associated Press, "Statements Made by Mark McGwire to Congress in 2005," January 12, 2010, http://sports.espn.go.com/mlb/news/story?id=4816607 (accessed November 28, 2012).

5. McGwire, quoted in Kepner, "McGwire Admits That He Used Steroids," www.nytimes.com/2010/01/12/sports/baseball/12mcgwire.html?pagewanted=all.

6. McGwire, quoted in Kepner, "McGwire Admits That He Used Steroids," www.nytimes.com/2010/01/12/sports/baseball/12mcgwire.html?pagewanted=all.

7. McGwire, quoted in Kepner, "McGwire Admits That He Used Steroids," www.nytimes.com/2010/01/12/sports/baseball/12mcgwire.html?pagewanted=all.

8. McGwire, quoted in Kepner, "McGwire Admits That He Used Steroids," www.nytimes.com/2010/01/12/sports/baseball/12mcgwire.html?pagewanted=all.

9. Mark McGwire, quoted in "McGwire Apologizes to La Russa, Selig," *ESPN.com*, January 12, 2010, http://sports.espn.go.com/mlb/news/story?id=4816607 (accessed November 28, 2012).

10. Mark McGwire, quoted in "Mark McGwire Admits to Using Steroids Says 'Roids Didn't Help Him," *Crooks and Liars.com*, January 11, 2010, http://crooksandliars.com/john-amato/mark-mcgwire-admits-using-steroids (accessed November 28, 2012).

11. McGwire, quoted in Kepner, "McGwire Admits That He Used Steroids," www.nytimes.com/2010/01/12/sports/baseball/12mcgwire.html?pagewanted=all.

22

CURT FLOOD

Choosing between Curt Flood and Willie McGee for the number twenty-two spot in these rankings proved to be a difficult task, since the two center fielders posted extremely similar numbers while playing for the Cardinals. Flood appeared in seventy-seven more games and accumulated almost 600 more official at bats than McGee did as a member of the team, enabling him to compile slightly better overall numbers. But, while Flood hit more home runs, collected more hits, scored more times, and amassed more doubles than McGee, the latter knocked in more runs, accumulated more triples, and stole many more bases (301 to 88). Furthermore, little separated the two men in terms of their batting averages, on-base percentages, and slugging percentages. Flood batted .293, compiled a .343 on-base percentage, and posted a .390 slugging percentage during the course of his 12 years in St. Louis. McGee finished with marks of .294, .329, and .400, respectively, in his 13 years with the Cardinals, giving him an on-base plus slugging percentage (OPS) of .729, which nearly matched Flood's mark of .733.

Looking beyond the numbers, neither man possessed much power at the plate, and they both tended to be free swingers who failed to draw many bases on balls. McGee's superiority as a base stealer proved to be easily the biggest advantage he held over Flood, who, in spite of his outstanding speed, did not steal a lot of bases. It could also be argued that McGee made more of an impact during his time with the team, earning National League Most Valuable Player honors in 1985; Flood never finished any higher than fourth in the balloting. But, while McGee failed to earn a single point in any other MVP election,

Flood placed in the top twenty in the voting a total of five times. Flood also reached a greater level of consistency during his years with the Cardinals. After struggling at the plate his first three seasons, Flood batted over .300 in six of his final nine years with the club, posting a mark below .285 just once during that time. Although McGee led the NL in hitting twice, compiling averages of .353 in 1985 and .335 in 1990, he tended to perform a bit more erratically at the plate, also posting marks of .256, .236, .253, and .251 in other seasons. Perhaps the biggest edge Flood held over McGee, however, ended up being his superiority as an outfielder. That is not to in any way suggest that McGee did not play outstanding defense. His exceptional running speed allowed him to cover a considerable amount of territory in center field, enabling him to earn Gold Glove honors on three separate occasions. But throughout the course of his career Flood established himself as one of the finest defenders in the game, rivaling Willie Mays as the NL's best ball hawk in center field. In addition to leading all senior circuit outfielders in fielding percentage twice, Flood finished first in putouts four times, en route to winning seven consecutive Gold Gloves. That is the thing that ultimately prompted me to place him just ahead of McGee in these rankings.

Curt Flood will always be mostly remembered for the courage and self-sacrifice he displayed when he elected to challenge baseball's reserve clause after being traded by the Cardinals to Philadelphia at the conclusion of the 1969 campaign. He will also be unfairly remembered for misplaying a ball in the seventh game of the 1968 World Series that led to a Detroit victory over St. Louis. However, in truth, thoughts of Flood should also evoke memories of someone who typically batted .300, ran the bases well, and patrolled center field as well as anyone in the game. In addition to topping the .300 mark in batting on six occasions, Flood surpassed 200 hits twice and scored more than ninety runs four times. Meanwhile, he displayed grace, elegance, outstanding speed, and marvelous instincts while tracking down fly balls in the outfield.

Hall of Fame shortstop Lou Boudreau once commented, "I haven't seen a thing that Flood can't do. He gets as good a jump on the ball as Mays does. He has absolutely no fear of the walls."[1] Roger Maris, who played alongside Flood in the St. Louis outfield for two seasons, at one time marveled, "His swiftness is something amazing. When I first played beside him in the spring he really surprised me. I'd think to myself 'that one's in there.' But Curt would catch it. He has to be the best."[2] Meanwhile, Bill Virdon, who once played a pretty fair center field himself for the Pirates, once suggested, "When you have a man who can play center field the way Flood does and can get 200 hits a season, you've really got something."[3]

Born in Houston, Texas, on January 18, 1938, Curtis Charles Flood grew up in Oakland, California, graduating from McClymonds High School, where he played in the same outfield as future Cincinnati Reds stars Frank Robinson and Vada Pinson. After Robinson signed with the Reds as an amateur free agent in 1953, Flood and Pinson followed suit, inking contracts with the club three years later. Robinson, Pinson, and Flood all experienced a great deal of racial prejudice while coming up through Cincinnati's farm system, particularly when performing for the team's minor-league clubs based in the south. Those experiences left a lasting impression on all three men, causing the sensitive Flood to closely examine in future years the somewhat oppressive nature of the relationship that existed between owners and players at the time.

Flood appeared in a total of only eight games with the Reds in 1956 and 1957, before the team elected to trade him to the Cardinals prior to the start of the 1958 campaign. He subsequently earned the starting center-field job in St. Louis as a rookie, batting .261 in his first full major-league season. He struggled at the plate in each of the next two seasons, posting batting averages of .255 and .237, while driving in a total of only sixty-four runs and scoring just sixty-one others. Flood also walked a total of only fifty-one times during the course of those two campaigns, compiling in the process on-base percentages that barely exceeded .300.

Although Flood remained an extremely aggressive hitter throughout the remainder of his career, he began to show a bit more selectivity at the plate in 1961, enabling him to raise his batting average and on-base percentage to .322 and .391, respectively. Despite seeing both marks fall off somewhat the following year, Flood really came into his own in 1962, beginning an extremely successful seven-year run during which he established himself as one of the NL's top outfielders. In addition to batting .296, he compiled easily his best numbers in most offensive categories, including home runs (12), RBIs (70), runs scored (99), hits (188), doubles (30), and total bases (264). He also finished second among all NL outfielders with 387 putouts.

Flood continued his ascension into stardom the following year, batting .302, driving in 63 runs, scoring 112 others, collecting 200 hits, stealing a career-high 17 bases, and winning the first of his seven consecutive Gold Gloves by leading all NL outfielders in putouts for the first of four times, with a total of 403. He subsequently earned the first of his three All-Star nominations in 1964, helping the Cardinals capture their first pennant in 18 years by batting .311, scoring 97 runs, and topping the senior circuit with 211 hits.

Flood posted solid numbers for the Cardinals in each of the next four campaigns as well, performing particularly well in 1965, when he batted .310, scored 90 runs, accumulated 191 hits, hit 11 homers, and knocked in a career-high 83 runs. He compiled the highest batting average of his career in 1967, posting a mark of .335, before earning a fourth-place finish in the NL MVP voting the following year by batting .301, leading all league outfielders in putouts for the third time, and topping all circuit center fielders in assists for the second of three times. The Cardinals won the pennant in both 1967 and 1968, defeating the Red Sox in seven games in the World Series in the first of those years, before losing to the Tigers in the ensuing Fall Classic.

With St. Louis seeking to acquire troubled superstar Dick Allen from Philadelphia, and with Flood rapidly approaching his thirty-second birthday, the Cardinals included their longtime center fielder in a seven-player deal with the Phillies on October 7, 1969; however, upon learning of the trade, Flood balked at the idea of going to Philadelphia, which fielded a poor team and played its games in an old stadium before fans known for their racial intolerance. Stating that he considered his inclusion in the deal consummated between the two clubs to be an "impersonal" act, Flood refused to report to the Phillies, choosing instead to fight the reserve clause, which essentially bound a player to a team for perpetuity, unless the team decided otherwise.

Flood first expressed his chagrin by sending a letter to baseball commissioner Bowie Kuhn, in which he demanded that he be declared a free agent. The following is the contents of Flood's letter to Kuhn:

December 24, 1969

> After twelve years in the major leagues, I do not feel I am a piece of property to be bought and sold irrespective of my wishes. I believe that any system [that] produces that result violates my basic rights as a citizen and is inconsistent with the laws of the United States and of the several States.
>
> It is my desire to play baseball in 1970, and I am capable of playing. I have received a contract offer from the Philadelphia club, but I believe I have the right to consider offers from other clubs before making any decision. I, therefore, request that you make known to all major league clubs my feelings in this matter, and advise them of my availability for the 1970 season.[4]

Since Flood received a then-generous salary of $90,000 from the Cardinals in his last year with the club, the public and the media initially reacted to his proclamation with great surprise, branding the outfielder an ingrate, a destroyer of tradition, and even a blasphemer. After having his appeal denied by Commissioner Kuhn, Flood expressed to Marvin Miller, founder and executive director of the Players Association, his desire to sue Major League Baseball. Miller later recalled, "I told him that, given the courts' history of bias toward the owners and their monopoly, he didn't have a chance in hell of winning. More important than that, I told him, even if he won, he'd never get anything out of it—he'd never get a job in baseball again."[5]

Miller revealed that Flood subsequently asked him if his action would benefit other players. Miller said, "I told him 'Yes, and those to come.'"[6] Miller added that Flood responded by saying, "That's good enough for me."[7] When Miller realized that Flood understood the odds against him and remained determined to go ahead with the case, he told him, "You're a union-leader's dream."[8]

Flood's case eventually reached the U.S. Supreme Court, with the court ruling against the contention made by Flood's attorney that baseball's reserve clause violated the nation's antitrust laws by depressing wages and limiting a player to one team; however, even though Flood lost his case by a count of five to three, federal judge

Irving Ben Cooper recommended that changes be made to the reserve system through negotiation between players and owners. Less than six years later, his recommendation became a reality, with free agency being instituted as part of the game, changing the face of baseball forever.

As Miller had predicted, Flood never benefited from the revolution he helped begin. After sitting out the entire 1970 season, he signed with the Washington Senators for $110,000 prior to the start of the 1971 campaign, after the team acquired him from Philadelphia for three nondescript players; however, after appearing in only thirteen games with the Senators, Flood left the team on April 27, announcing his retirement in a letter to Senators' owner Bob Short before departing for Denmark. Flood ended his playing career with 85 home runs, 636 RBIs, 851 runs scored, 1,861 hits, and a .293 batting average. He ranks among the Cardinals' all-time leaders in hits (ninth), games played (sixth), plate appearances (eighth), and at bats (seventh).

A heavy drinker throughout most of his playing career, Flood drifted into alcoholism after he left the game. Plagued by increasing debt and bombarded with hate mail from fans who accused him of trying to destroy baseball, he grew increasingly despondent as the years passed, at one point being admitted to a psychiatric hospital in Barcelona, Spain.

Yet, Flood eventually managed to pull his life back together, returning to the United States and being presented in 1992 with the National Association for the Advancement of Colored People's Jackie Robinson Award for his contributions to black athletes. He experienced perhaps the most gratifying moment of his life in 1994, when he gave a speech on solidarity to the players as they prepared to go on strike, after which he received a standing ovation.

Decades of smoking and drinking finally caught up to Flood, leading to a diagnosis of throat cancer early in 1995. He died two years later, on January 20, 1997, just two days after his fifty-ninth birthday. Delivering the eulogy at Flood's funeral, Jesse Jackson stated, "Baseball didn't change Curt Flood. Curt Flood changed baseball. He fought the good fight."[9]

CARDINAL CAREER HIGHLIGHTS

Best Season

Although Flood also performed well in 1961, 1967, and 1968, he played his best ball from 1962 to 1965, batting at least .296, scoring at least 90 runs, and collecting at least 188 hits in each of those years. In addition to batting .296 and scoring ninety-nine runs in the first of those seasons, Flood hit a career-high twelve home runs and knocked in seventy runs. He followed that up by batting .302, amassing 200 hits, driving in 63 runs, and establishing career highs with 112 runs scored, 34 doubles, 9 triples, 267 total bases, and 17 steals in 1963. Although Flood knocked in only 46 runs for the pennant-winning Cardinals in 1964, he batted .311, scored 97 runs, and led the NL with 211 hits.

Nevertheless, I ultimately decided to go with Flood's 1965 campaign. In addition to hitting 11 homers and driving in a career-high 83 runs, he batted .310, scored 90 runs, collected 191 hits, and accumulated 30 doubles. Furthermore, he compiled a career-high .421 slugging percentage and walked a career-high fifty-one times, enabling him to post a .366 on-base percentage that ranked among the best of his career. His .788 OPS also surpassed the figure he compiled in any of the other three campaigns.

Memorable Moments and Greatest Performances

Leading off for the Cardinals against Sandy Koufax on August 17, 1958, Flood put his name in the record books when he hit a home run that second-place hitter Gene Freese followed with a blast of his own. The back-to-back round-trippers marked the fifth time in NL history that the first two batters in a game homered.

Flood had arguably his greatest day at the plate on August 16, 1964, collecting eight straight hits during a doubleheader split with the Dodgers. After going 4-for-4, with two doubles, against Sandy Koufax in the opener, Flood went 4-for-5, with a triple, in the nightcap.

Flood performed extremely well once again during a doubleheader split with the Phillies on September 6, 1965. After singling home a run, stealing a base, and hitting a three-run homer in the first contest, he delivered a two-run blast in the nightcap.

Flood had another big day at the plate when the Cardinals clinched the NL pennant on September 15, 1968. In this game, he led his team to a 7–4 win over the Astros by going 5-for-5.

An extraordinary fielder, Flood went through the entire 1966 campaign without committing an error, handling 396 consecutive chances flawlessly. His errorless streak, which began on September 3, 1965, continued well into 1967, finally ending on June 4, at a NL record 226 games and 568 total chances. On June 19, 1967, just two weeks after seeing his errorless streak come to an end, Flood pulled off the first unassisted double play made by a NL center fielder in thirty-four years during a 5–4 win over Houston.

Yet, ironically, the brilliant-fielding Flood is perhaps remembered most for a defensive miscue he committed in Game 7 of the 1968 World Series against the Detroit Tigers. With Bob Gibson and Mickey Lolich engaged in a 0–0 pitcher's duel heading into the seventh inning, the Tigers put runners on first and second with two men out. Detroit outfielder Jim Northrup then drove a line drive to deep left-center field that Flood momentarily misjudged. Taking one step in, Flood slipped as he attempted to regain his bearings, allowing the ball to sail well over his head for a triple that gave Detroit the first two runs of the game. Northrup later scored, and the Tigers added another run in the ninth inning to clinch their first world championship in twenty-three years, with a 4–1 victory. Although Flood received a considerable amount of criticism for his misplay after the contest, it should be noted that he likely would have had a difficult time catching Northrup's well-hit drive even if he had gotten a good jump on the ball.

Notable Achievements

Scored more than 100 runs once (112 in 1963).
Batted over .300 six times, surpassing the .320 mark twice.
Topped 200 hits twice.
Compiled perfect 1.000 fielding percentage in 1966.
Led NL in hits once (211 in 1964).

Led NL outfielders in putouts four times and fielding percentage twice.

Led NL center fielders in assists three times.

Holds NL record with 226 consecutive errorless games in center field.

Holds major-league record with 568 consecutive errorless chances in center field.

Ranks among Cardinals all-time leaders in hits (ninth), games played (sixth), plate appearances (eighth), and at bats (seventh).

Won seven consecutive Gold Gloves (1963, 1964, 1965, 1966, 1967, 1968, 1969).

1968 *Sporting News* All-Star selection.

Three-time NL All-Star (1964, 1966, 1968).

Three-time NL champion (1964, 1967, 1968).

Two-time world champion (1964, 1967).

NOTES

1. Lou Boudreau, quoted in Mike Shalin and Neil Shalin, *Out by a Step: The 100 Best Players Not in the Baseball Hall of Fame* (Lanham, MD.: Diamond Communications, 2002), 137.

2. Roger Maris, quoted in Shalin and Shalin, *Out by a Step*, 137.

3. Bill Virdon, quoted in Shalin and Shalin, *Out by a Step*, 137.

4. http://mlb.mlb.com/news/article.jsp?ymd=20070315&content_id=1844945&vkey=news_mlb&c_id=mlb&fext=.jsp.

5. Marvin Miller, quoted in Allen Barra, "How Curt Flood Changed Baseball and Killed His Career in the Process," *Atlantic*, July 12, 2011, www.theatlantic.com/entertainment/archive/2011/07/how-curt-flood-changed-baseball-and-killed-his-career-in-the-process/241783/ (accessed October 7, 2012).

6. Miller, quoted in Barra, "How Curt Flood Changed Baseball and Killed His Career in the Process," www.theatlantic.com/entertainment/archive/2011/07/how-curt-flood-changed-baseball-and-killed-his-career-in-the-process/241783/.

7. Miller, quoted in Barra, "How Curt Flood Changed Baseball and Killed His Career in the Process," www.theatlantic.com/entertainment/archive/2011/07/how-curt-flood-changed-baseball-and-killed-his-career-in-the-process/241783/.

8. Miller, quoted in Barra, "How Curt Flood Changed Baseball and Killed His Career in the Process," www.theatlantic.com/entertainment/archive/2011/07/how-curt-flood-changed-baseball-and-killed-his-career-in-the-process/241783/.

9. Jesse Jackson, quoted in Barra, "How Curt Flood Changed Baseball and Killed His Career in the Process," www.theatlantic.com/entertainment/archive/2011/07/how-curt-flood-changed-baseball-and-killed-his-career-in-the-process/241783/.

With a mark of .378, Jesse Burkett holds the Cardinals career record for highest batting average.
Photo courtesy of T. Scott Brandon

With the exception of Bob Gibson, Jesse Haines won more games than any other Cardinals pitcher.
Photo courtesy of RMYauctions.com

The National League's dominant player for much of the 1920s, Rogers Hornsby won 6 straight batting titles and 2 Triple Crowns for the Cardinals between 1920 and 1925.
Photo Courtesy of T. Scott Brandon.

Jim Bottomley proved to be one of the National League's top run-producers during the 1920s.
Photo courtesy of LegendaryAuctions.com

Chick Hafey ranks among the Cardinals all-time leaders in batting average, slugging percentage and OPS.

Photo courtesy of T. Scott Brandon

Dizzy Dean (right) pictured here with Cardinals player/ manager Frankie Frisch.

Copyright Leslie Jones Collection, Courtesy of the Trustees of the Boston Public Library, Print Dept.

Pepper Martin (right), seen here with his brother Stu, was one of the leaders of the Cardinals "Gas House Gang."

Copyright Leslie Jones Collection, Courtesy of the Trustees of the Boston Public Library, Print Dept.

Joe Medwick (left) and Dizzy Dean led the Cardinals to victory over the Detroit Tigers in the 1934 World Series.

Copyright Leslie Jones Collection, Courtesy of the Trustees of the Boston Public Library, Print Dept.

James "Ripper" Collins provided much of the power in the middle of the Cardinals' batting order during the early 1930s.
Photo courtesy of T. Scott Brandon.

The "Big Cat" Johnny Mize, pictured here with Boston first baseman Elbie Fletcher.
Copyright Leslie Jones Collection, Courtesy of the Trustees of the Boston Public Library, Print Dept.

Enos Slaughter (left) and Terry Moore comprised two-thirds of the outfield that helped lead the Cardinals to a five-game victory over the Yankees in the 1942 World Series.

Copyright Leslie Jones Collection, Courtesy of the Trustees of the Boston Public Library, Print Dept.

Marty Marion proved to be the finest defensive shortstop of his time.

Photo courtesy of T. Scott Brandon.

Mort (left) and Walker Cooper gave the Cardinals the National League's foremost battery during the early 1940s.

Pictured here with teammate Johnny Hopp, Stan Musial (right) holds virtually every Cardinals career batting record.

Stan "The Man" Musial—the greatest Cardinal of them all.
Photo courtesy of RMYauctions.com.

Whitey Kurowski made key contributions to four pennant-winning teams and three world championship ball clubs during his time in St. Louis.
Copyright Leslie Jones Collection, Courtesy of the Trustees of the Boston Public Library, Print Dept.

Harry "The Cat" Brecheen posted three victories over the Boston Red Sox in the 1946 World Series.
Photo courtesy of Mainlineautographs.com.

Red Schoendienst (center) chatting with two Cardinals teammates by the batting cage during pre-game warmups.
Photo Courtesy of Missouri State Archives.

Ken Boyer gave the Cardinals outstanding run production, a solid glove at third, and exceptional leadership in the clubhouse for more than a decade.

Photo Courtesy of Kevin Noland.

Curt Flood (foreground), seen here with Julian Javier, won seven consecutive Gold Gloves for the Cardinals during the 1960s.

Photo courtesy of City of Montreal Archives.

The 1969 Cardinals starting lineup featured (left to right): Lou Brock, Curt Flood, Vada Pinson, Joe Torre, Mike Shannon, Tim McCarver, Julian Javier, and Dal Maxvill.

Photo Courtesy of City of Montreal Archives.

Joe Torre (far right) and Bill White seen here talking with Montreal Expos manager Gene Mauch.

Photo courtesy of City of Montreal Archives.

Tim McCarver helped the Cardinals win three pennants and two world championships during the 1960s.
Photo courtesy of LegendaryAuctions.com.

Bob Gibson perhaps intimidated opposing batters more than any other pitcher of his time.
Photo courtesy of StlSportsHistory.com.

Lou Brock helped change the way the game was played with his thievery on the basepaths.

Photo Courtesy of Richard Albersheim of www.albersheims.com.

Steve Carlton won 77 games for the Cardinals, before posting another 241 victories for the Philadelphia Phillies.

Photo courtesy of Dexter Press.

Orlando Cepeda captured NL MVP honors for the Cardinals in 1967.
Photo courtesy of RMYauctions.com.

The greatest hitting catcher in Cardinals history, Ted Simmons batted over .300 six times as a member of the team.
Photo courtesy of MearsOnlineAuctions.com.

Bob Forsch (right), seen here with brother Ken, ranks third in Cardinals history with 163 wins.
Photo courtesy of Jeff Scott.

Keith Hernandez captured N.L. MVP honors in 1979 when he topped the Senior Circuit with a .344 batting average.
Photo Courtesy of Jeff Scott.

Garry Templeton (right), pictured here with Tony Scott, created a considerable amount of controversy during his time in St. Louis.

Photo courtesy of Cliff via Flickr.

Nicknamed "Silent George" by the media, George Hendrick batted over .300 three times and knocked in more than 100 runs twice for the Cardinals.

Photo courtesy of Mainlineautographs.com.

Bruce Sutter was the National League's top closer during his time in St. Louis.
Photo courtesy of Jeff Scott.

Willie McGee earned NL MVP honors in 1985 by scoring 114 runs, stealing 56 bases, and leading the league with a .353 batting average.
Photo courtesy of Phillip Hendon.

Joaquin Andujar surpassed 20 victories twice for the Cardinals during the 1980s.
Photo courtesy of Mainlineautographs.com.

John Tudor (left) seen here celebrating the clinching of the 1985 NL pennant with his teammates.
Photo courtesy of Mainlineautographs.com.

Ozzie Smith won 11 consecutive Gold Gloves at shortstop as a member of the Cardinals.
Photo Courtesy of Mark Harp.

Jack Clark provided most of the power in the Cardinals' lineup during the mid-1980s.
Photo courtesy of Mainlineautographs.com.

Ray Lankford excelled in all phases of the game for 13 seasons in St. Louis.
Photo by Jerry Reuss, reprinted courtesy of Jerry Reuss.

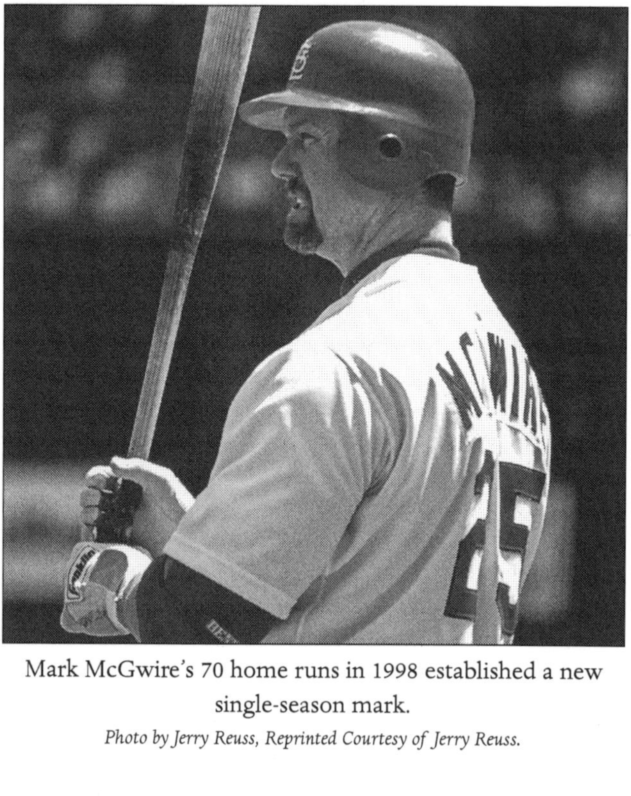

Mark McGwire's 70 home runs in 1998 established a new single-season mark.
Photo by Jerry Reuss, Reprinted Courtesy of Jerry Reuss.

Jim Edmonds provided the Cardinals with a powerful bat and exceptional defense in center field during his time in St. Louis.
Photo Courtesy of Jim French.

Albert Pujols established himself as arguably baseball's most dominant hitter during his time in St. Louis.
Photo Courtesy of David Herholz.

Scott Rolen helped lead the Cardinals to two pennants and one world championship in his six years with the team.
Photo Courtesy of Mike Martinez.

Edgar Renteria, seen here as a member of the Cincinnati Reds, starred at shortstop for the Cardinals for six seasons.
Photo courtesy of Keith Allison.

Chris Carpenter helped lead the Cardinals to three pennants and two world championships.

Photo Courtesy of Keith Allison.

Prior to earning a spot in the starting rotation, Adam Wainwright pitched exceptionally well out of the bullpen, starring in relief en route to helping the Cardinals capture the 2006 world championship.

Photo Courtesy of Michael Smith.

Yadier Molina's solid hitting and outstanding glove work behind home plate have made him invaluable to the Cardinals the past several seasons.
Photo Courtesy of Keith Allison.

23

WILLIE MCGEE

The Cardinals made one of their best trades ever on October 21, 1981, when they acquired minor-league outfielder Willie McGee from the New York Yankees for journeyman pitcher Bob Sykes. While Sykes never appeared in a single game for the Yankees, McGee spent parts of thirteen seasons in St. Louis. While there he won two batting titles, three Gold Gloves, and one National League Most Valuable Player trophy, earned All-Star honors four times, and helped the Cardinals capture three NL pennants and one world championship. Establishing himself with his outstanding play as one of the most popular Cardinals players of his time, McGee further ingratiated himself to St. Louis fans with his humble demeanor and strong personal character.

Born in San Francisco, California, on November 2, 1958, Willie Dean McGee entered the New York Yankees' farm system in 1977, after being selected by the team in the first round of that year's amateur draft with the fifteenth overall pick. Even though the Yankees found themselves desperately in need of someone with McGee's exceptional running speed by the early 1980s, their philosophy of pursuing veteran talent rather than promoting from within prevented them from advancing the young outfielder beyond the AA level of their minor-league system. Finally, after five long years in the minors, the twenty-three-year-old McGee received his long-awaited opportunity when New York dealt him to St. Louis.

After being assigned briefly to the Cardinals' Triple-A affiliate in Louisville, McGee arrived in St. Louis to stay in May 1982. Finding himself starting in center field for the Cardinals shortly thereafter, the switch-hitting McGee batted .296 and stole twenty-four bases in the season's final five months, earning in the process a third-place finish in the NL Rookie of the Year voting. McGee subsequently helped the Cardinals win their first world championship in fifteen years by excelling in the postseason. After batting .308, homering once, and driving in 5 runs during the Cardinals' three-game sweep of Atlanta in the National League Championship Series (NLCS), he hit 2 home runs and knocked in another 5 runs against Milwaukee in the World Series, putting on a memorable performance in Game 3 that saw him homer twice and make a spectacular catch in center field.

McGee continued to blossom in each of the next two seasons, posting batting averages of .286 and .291, scoring a total of 157 runs, and amassing a total of 82 stolen bases. He also earned All-Star honors and the first of his three Gold Gloves in 1983. McGee developed into a full-fledged star in 1985, leading the Cardinals to the NL East title and the league championship by driving in 82 runs, scoring 114 others, stealing a career-high 56 bases, and topping the senior circuit with a .353 batting average, 216 hits, and 18 triples, en route to earning NL MVP honors.

Along with fellow speedsters Vince Coleman and Ozzie Smith, McGee came to exemplify the style of play manager Whitey Herzog stressed in St. Louis during the 1980s. Playing in spacious Busch Stadium, with its artificial surface, the Cardinals typically found themselves engaged in low-scoring contests that necessitated the employment of solid fundamentals, exceptional team speed, sound baserunning, outstanding defense, and strong pitching. Although the knock-kneed McGee proved to be very much a free swinger who rarely walked and failed to hit many home runs, he adopted an approach at the plate that made him a successful major-league hitter. Predominantly a slap hitter with little power, McGee rarely attempted to drive the ball out of the ball park. Instead, he used his blinding speed to often turn singles into doubles, and doubles into triples. His extraordinary quickness also enabled him to excel on the base paths and in the outfield, even though he lacked outstanding instincts. McGee ended up stealing more than twenty bases six times during his time in St. Louis, surpassing forty thefts on three separate occasions. Although criticized at times for a lack of concentration in the field, he also led all NL center fielders in putouts and fielding percentage once each.

After a subpar, injury-plagued 1986 campaign, McGee rebounded in 1987 to bat .285 and establish career highs with 11 homers, 37 doubles, and 105 RBIs. Although the Cardinals subsequently ended up losing the World Series to Minnesota in seven games, McGee had an outstanding postseason, batting .308 against the Giants in the NLCS, before posting a mark of .370 against the Twins in the Fall Classic.

McGee compiled solid numbers again in 1988, but injuries forced him to suffer through a horrendous 1989 campaign in which he batted only .236 in fifty-eight games; however, he rebounded again the following year, compiling a league-leading .335 batting average in the season's first five months, before being dealt to the eventual American League champion Oakland Athletics for three prospects on August 29. After becoming a free agent at season's end, McGee signed on with the San Francisco Giants, spending the next four years on the West Coast, and batting over .300 another two times. McGee subsequently assumed a part-time role in Boston in 1995, before he followed his heart back to St. Louis, where he rejoined the Cardinals the following year after he became a free agent once again. McGee spent the remainder of his career in the city where it first began almost two decades earlier, serving the Cardinals primarily as a fourth outfielder and occasional pinch hitter his final four years, before announcing his retirement at the conclusion of the 1999 campaign. He ended his career with 79 home runs, 856 RBIs, 1,010 runs scored, 2,254 hits, 350 doubles, 94 triples, 352 stolen bases, a .295 batting average, a .333 on-base percentage, and a .396 slugging percentage. Throughout the course of his 13 years in St. Louis, McGee hit 63 homers, knocked in 678 runs, scored 760 others, collected 1,683 hits, accumulated 255 doubles and 83 triples, stole 301 bases, batted .294, compiled a .329 on-base percentage, and posted a .400 slugging percentage. He is sixth all-time among Cardinals players in stolen bases, and he also ranks seventh in triples.

After retiring as an active player, McGee worked with the Cardinals as a part-time instructor at training camp the following spring. He expressed no regret over leaving the game that he loved, stating, "I've had my shot. I don't have any desire to pick up a bat. . . . It's really strange, but I don't want to do it."[1]

CARDINAL CAREER HIGHLIGHTS

Best Season

Although McGee knocked in a career-high 105 runs for the Cardinals in 1987, he had easily his best season two years earlier, en route to capturing NL MVP honors. He hit ten homers and drove in eighty-two runs in 1985. McGee also established career bests that year with 114 runs scored; 56 stolen bases; 308 total bases; a .384 on-base percentage; a .503 slugging percentage; and a league-leading .353 batting average, 216 hits, and 18 triples. He also earned the second of his three Gold Gloves for his outstanding defensive work in center field.

Memorable Moments and Greatest Performances

McGee ironically had one of his greatest days at the plate for the Cardinals in a losing effort. He hit for the cycle and drove in six runs during a 12–11 loss to the Cubs at Wrigley Field on June 23, 1984.

McGee had another big offensive day on August 10, 1985, when he led the Cardinals to a doubleheader sweep of the Phillies by collecting seven hits in ten at bats. After collecting 3 hits in 5 trips to the plate in the opener, McGee went 4-for-5, with a home run, 4 RBIs, and 2 runs scored in the nightcap.

McGee got one of his most memorable hits as a member of the Cardinals in his second tour of duty with the club, stroking a two-out, pinch-hit home run in the bottom of the ninth inning of the St. Louis 1997 home opener to give the Cards a 2–1 victory.

However, there is little doubt that McGee will be remembered most fondly by Cardinals fans for his tremendous performance in Game 3 of the 1982 World Series. Although not known for his power, the fleet-footed center fielder led his team to a 6–2 win over Milwaukee by hitting two home runs, driving in four runs, and making an extraordinary leaping catch against the left-center field wall. Cardinals manager Whitey Herzog said after the contest, "I don't know if anyone has ever played a better World Series game than Willie. If he doesn't make that catch in the ninth, Mr. (Bruce) Sutter's in trouble."[2]

Notable Achievements

Knocked in more than 100 runs once (105 in 1987).
Scored more than 100 runs once (114 in 1985).
Batted over .300 four times, surpassing the .330 mark twice.
Topped 200 hits once (216 in 1985).
Finished in double digits in triples three times.
Compiled slugging percentage in excess of .500 once (.503 in 1985).
Stole more than forty bases three times, surpassing fifty steals once (fifty-six in 1985).
Led NL in batting average twice, hits once, and triples once.
Led NL outfielders in fielding percentage once (1986).
Led NL center fielders in putouts once (1986).
Ranks among Cardinals all-time leaders in stolen bases (sixth), triples (seventh), games played (ninth), and at bats (tenth).
1985 NL MVP.
1985 Silver Slugger winner.
Won three Gold Gloves (1983, 1985, 1986).
1985 *Sporting News* All-Star selection.
Four-time NL All-Star (1983, 1985, 1987, 1988).
Three-time NL champion (1982, 1985, 1987).
1982 world champion.

NOTES

1. Willie McGee, quoted in "Willie McGee Stats," *Baseball Almanac*, www.baseball-almanac.com/players/player.php?p=mcgeewi01 (accessed October 10, 2012).

2. Whitey Herzog, quoted in "Willie McGee Stats, www.baseball-almanac.com/players/player.php?p=mcgeewi01.

24

JESSE BURKETT

Jesse Burkett spent only three seasons playing for the National League entry situated in the city of St. Louis, joining the Perfectos in 1899, and remaining with the franchise another two years after it changed its name to the Cardinals. Nevertheless, the left-handed line-drive hitter earned a prominent place in these rankings by batting over .360 in each of those three seasons, compiling in the process two of the ten highest single-season batting averages in franchise history. An exceptional bunter who excelled at fouling off pitches, Burkett won three NL batting titles during the course of his career, posting an average in excess of .400 on two separate occasions, while also collecting more than 200 hits six times. An outstanding base runner as well, the five-foot, eight-inch, 155-pound Burkett stole more than thirty bases five times and scored more than 100 runs nine times, surpassing 140 runs scored on four occasions. Burkett also holds the major-league record for most inside-the-park home runs, being credited with fifty-five during his sixteen-year career.

Born in Wheeling, West Virginia, on December 4, 1868, Jesse Cail Burkett began his career in professional baseball as a pitcher, winning thirty-nine games for Worcester of the Atlantic Association in 1889; however, after experiencing little success on the mound as a rookie with the Giants in 1890, Burkett moved to the outfield, where he remained the next sixteen seasons. Concluding the 1890 campaign with a .309 batting average in more than 400 official at bats, Burkett spent most of 1891 in the minor leagues after being purchased by the Cleveland Spiders. Burkett earned a starting job in Cleveland's outfield the following year, however, finishing the season with a .275 batting average and 119 runs scored.

After the powers that be moved the pitcher's mound back from only fifty feet to sixty feet, six inches from home plate in 1893, NL players saw their batting averages rise dramatically. Burkett's mark proved to be no exception, with the speedy outfielder beginning an exceptional run during which he batted at least .341 for the Spiders in each of the next six seasons. He had his two best years for the club in 1895 and 1896, topping the circuit in batting average and base hits both seasons. After batting .405 and collecting 225 hits in 1895, Burkett compiled a batting average of .410 and amassed 240 hits the ensuing campaign. He also led the league with 160 runs scored and 317 total bases.

During his time in Cleveland, Burkett gradually shifted from right field to left field, which remained his primary position the rest of his career. Initially considered to be a below-average defensive player due to the somewhat erratic nature of his outfield play, Burkett eventually turned himself into a competent fielder. It was at the plate, however, that he truly excelled. Although Burkett had little power, he learned to take advantage of his outstanding running speed by slapping at the ball and developing a bunting technique that made him the finest bunter in the game. One reporter later remarked, "Burkett seldom failed to drop a bunt just where he wanted to. He could lay it down either side of the plate, stop it dead if need be, or drag it as the occasion required."[1]

Meanwhile, Burkett's ability to foul off difficult pitches proved to be one of the reasons for the introduction of the rule making foul balls strikes. One commentator later observed that the diminutive outfielder seemed to take special pleasure in fouling off tough pitches, noting, "He would do a snappy little jig after tipping off a good pitch, or snapping one on a low line into the left-field section of the grandstand or the left-field bleachers, very well pleased with himself."[2]

The pleasure Burkett derived from exasperating an opposing pitcher by spoiling one of his better offerings exhibited his truculent nature. Nicknamed "The Crab" by his Cleveland teammates, Burkett became noted for being cranky and unsociable. Known to challenge opponents with his fists and insult fans and umpires with strings of expletives, he had a bad temper, which made him an easy target for anyone who wished to get under his skin. Once benched for throwing a baseball at a crowd of hecklers in the stands, Burkett suffered the indignity of being ejected from both ends of a doubleheader on another occasion. One writer recalled, "Even when he was hitting .400, he played ball with a perennial scowl."[3]

In spite of his surly disposition, Burkett remained a key contributor to any success the Spiders experienced until the Robison brothers essentially disbanded the team at the conclusion of the 1898 campaign. After gaining control of the St. Louis franchise as well, the Spiders' owners transferred most of the club's best players to St. Louis in an effort to punish Cleveland fans for failing to support their team at the gate. Burkett joined legendary pitcher Cy Young in moving to St. Louis, helping the team improve its record from 39–111 to 84–67 by finishing second in the NL with a .396 batting average and 221 hits. Burkett also placed among the league leaders with 116 runs scored, a .463 on-base percentage, and a .500 slugging percentage.

Burkett followed up his exceptional 1899 campaign with two more outstanding years, posting a batting average of .363 in 1900, before topping the senior circuit with a mark of .376 in 1901. He also led the league with 142 runs scored, 226 hits, 306 total bases, and a .440 on-base percentage in the second of those years.

The 1901 season ended up being Burkett's last with the Cardinals. Persuaded to jump to the rival American League by St. Louis Browns manager Jimmy McAler, a former teammate of Burkett's in Cleveland, the outfielder spent the next three campaigns playing for the Browns, before spending the last of his sixteen major-league seasons with the Boston Pilgrims. After Burkett batted just .257 for Boston in 1905, the team released him at the end of the year. He ended his major-league playing career with 2,850 hits, 1,720 runs scored, 952 RBIs, 75 home runs, 182 triples, 320 doubles, a .338 batting average, a .415 on-base percentage, and a .446 slugging percentage. His Cardinal numbers include 650 hits, 346 runs scored, 214 RBIs, a .378 batting average, a .444 on-base percentage, and a .495 slugging percentage. Burkett's .378 batting average and .444 on-base percentage represent the highest marks ever posted by any Cardinals player.

After being released by Boston, Burkett purchased a franchise in the New England League (NEL) and moved it to Worcester, where he became the team's new manager and best player. He won the NEL batting crown in 1906, with a mark of .344, while also guiding Worcester to the first of four consecutive pennants.

After selling his ownership in the franchise, Burkett became the head coach at Holy Cross University in 1917, remaining in that position through 1920, when he accepted a coaching job with John McGraw's New York Giants. Disliked by most Giants players, he remained in New York just one year, returning to the minor leagues in 1923 to resume his managerial career. After piloting two different teams throughout the course of the next few seasons, Burkett worked occasionally as a scout and spring training instructor during the Depression, while also holding down a job with the Massachusetts State Highway Department. He died of heart disease at the age of eighty-four, on May 27, 1953, seven years after the members of the Old Timers Committee elected him to the Baseball Hall of Fame. Shortly after being inducted into Cooperstown, Burkett told a reporter, "It took them a long time, and I thought they weren't going to because everybody had forgotten me."[4]

CARDINAL CAREER HIGHLIGHTS

Best Season

Although Burkett posted his highest batting average (.396) and on-base percentage (.463) as a member of the Cardinals in 1899, he had his best all-around year for the club in 1901. In his last NL campaign, Burkett hit a career-high 10 home runs, drove in 75 runs, collected 15 triples, compiled a slugging percentage of .509, and topped the senior circuit with 142 runs scored, 226 hits, 306 total bases, a .376 batting average, and a .440 on-base percentage.

Memorable Moments and Greatest Performances

Despite being known mostly as a singles hitter, Burkett showed occasional glimpses of power during his time with the Cardinals. On September 8, 1899, he backed the solid pitching of Cy Young by singling once and hitting two home runs during a 12–3 St. Louis victory over Cincinnati. Ten months later, on July 8, 1900, Burkett hit two inside-the-park homers in the same game for the fourth time in his career. He also accomplished the feat twice for the Cardinals in 1899, doing so on July 29 and August 28. Burkett also tied a major-league record by leading off two straight games with a home run, getting the Cardinals off to a quick start on May 22 and May 23, 1901.

Notable Achievements

Scored more than 100 runs twice.
Batted over .360 three times, surpassing the .390 mark once.
Topped 200 hits three times.
Finished in double digits in triples twice.
Compiled on-base percentage in excess of .400 three times.
Posted slugging percentage in excess of .500 twice.
Stole more than thirty bases once (thirty-two in 1900).
Led NL in batting average once, runs scored once, hits once, on-base percentage once, and total bases once.
Holds Cardinals career records for highest batting average (.378) and highest on-base percentage (.444).
Elected to Baseball Hall of Fame by members of Old Timers Committee in 1946.

NOTES

1. Quoted in David Jones, "Jesse Burkett," *Society for American Baseball Research*, www.sabr.org/bioproj/person/53d6808e (accessed October 4, 2012).
2. Quoted in Jones, "Jesse Burkett," www.sabr.org/bioproj/person/53d6808e.
3. Quoted in Jones, "Jesse Burkett," www.sabr.org/bioproj/person/53d6808e.
4. Jesse Burkett, quoted in Jones, "Jesse Burkett," www.sabr.org/bioproj/person/53d6808e.

25

CHRIS CARPENTER

Despite missing a significant amount of playing time with shoulder and elbow problems in five of his eleven seasons with the Cardinals, Chris Carpenter proved to be one of the National League's premier pitchers during his time in St. Louis. The big right-hander posted at least fifteen victories in five of the six seasons he remained healthy, compiling an overall record of 95–44 for the Cardinals that gave him a winning percentage of .683 that ranks as one of the best in franchise history. Carpenter served as the ace of the Cardinals' pitching staff in most of those years, helping them capture three NL pennants and two world championships. Along the way, he developed a reputation as a tremendous big-game pitcher, compiling a postseason record of 10–4 and an impressive 3.00 ERA.

Born in Exeter, New Hampshire, on April 27, 1975, Christopher John Carpenter originally signed with the Toronto Blue Jays in August 1993, after the team selected him in the first round of that year's amateur draft with the fifteenth overall pick. He subsequently spent three full seasons working his way up through the Toronto farm system before finally earning a call-up to the major-league club in May 1997. Working primarily as a spot starter the remainder of the year, the twenty-two-year-old right-hander pitched mostly ineffectively, winning only three of his ten decisions, while posting an ERA of 5.09; however, Carpenter began to fulfill his potential after the team inserted him into the starting rotation early in the ensuing campaign, concluding 1998 with a record of 12–7 and an ERA of 4.37.

After suffering through an injury-plagued 1999 season, Carpenter battled periods of ineffectiveness in both 2000 and 2001. During that three-year stretch, he compiled an overall mark of just 30–31, along with ERAs of 4.38, 6.26, and 4.09.

Shoulder problems limited Carpenter to only thirteen starts in 2002, forcing him to undergo season-ending surgery in September. Growing increasingly impatient with the once-heralded right-hander, the Blue Jays removed Carpenter from their forty-man roster at season's end, after which they offered him a minor-league incentive deal. Refusing Toronto's offer, Carpenter became a free agent, allowing the Cardinals to sign him with the hope that he might be ready for the 2003 campaign; however, he sat out the entire season while recovering from a torn labrum.

His shoulder problems a thing of the past, Carpenter finally made his long-awaited debut with the Cardinals in 2004, helping them advance to the World Series by compiling a record of 15–5 and a 3.46 ERA. Nevertheless, he found himself unable to pitch in the Fall Classic, being shut down in September due to a nerve problem in his right biceps.

Fully healthy by the start of the 2005 campaign, Carpenter had his best season since first entering the big leagues eight years earlier, going 21–5, with a 2.83 ERA, 213 strikeouts, and a league-leading 7 complete games. His exceptional performance earned him NL Cy Young honors, his first All-Star selection, and an eighth-place finish in the league Most Valuable Player voting. Although the Cardinals subsequently failed to make it past the Houston Astros in the National League Championship Series (NLCS), Carpenter pitched extremely well for them during the postseason, posting a combined record of 2–0 against the Padres and Astros, along with a 2.14 ERA in twenty-one innings of work. He followed that up with another solid year in 2006, finishing the campaign with a record of 15–8, an ERA of 3.09, 184 strikeouts, 5 complete games, and a league-leading 3 shutouts. Carpenter then helped the Cardinals capture their first world championship in twenty-four years by throwing eight scoreless innings against Detroit in Game 3 of the World Series.

Unfortunately, Carpenter found himself unable to take the mound for virtually all of the next two seasons. After undergoing surgery early in 2007 to trim bone spurs in his pitching elbow, he experienced complications during the recovery process that forced him to have

Tommy John surgery, thereby putting him on the sidelines for practically all of 2008 as well.

Returning to the Cardinals early in 2009, Carpenter again established himself as the ace of the team's pitching staff, compiling a record of 17–4 and leading the league with a 2.24 ERA, en route to earning NL Comeback Player of the Year honors. Carpenter also finished second in the league Cy Young balloting.

After putting together another big year in 2010 in which he finished 16–9, with a 3.22 ERA, Carpenter helped the Cardinals win their second championship in five seasons in 2011. Although he finished the regular season with a record of only 11–9, he pitched exceptionally well during the postseason, posting huge victories over the Phillies in Game 5 of the National League Division Series (NLDS), as well as the Rangers in Game 7 of the World Series.

Carpenter's ability to excel under pressure came as no surprise to former Cardinals manager Tony LaRussa, who stated, "He's got great concentration. He's got a very strong mind."[1] Meanwhile, longtime Cardinals pitching coach Dave Duncan noted, "Chris is single-minded and has the ability to shut out things that would distract a lot of other pitchers."[2] LaRussa also raved about Carpenter's overall approach to pitching, commenting, "He gives us a chance to win, which is important. He competes like a maniac, which is important. How he handles a good game and a not-so-good game is important. If we get beat, it's all his fault. And if we win, he just did his job and he points out the other guys who made it happen."[3]

After pitching so spectacularly for the Cardinals throughout the 2011 postseason, Carpenter again had the injury bug bite him in 2012, missing all but three starts due to thoracic outlet syndrome, which caused him to experience nerve-related shoulder problems throughout the year. Undergoing surgery at midseason to resolve the issue, he returned to the team in September, after which he made three postseason starts for a Cardinals club that eventually lost to the San Francisco Giants in the NLCS. Although Carpenter initially expected to regain his spot in the St. Louis starting rotation in 2013, he suffered another setback during the offseason when he began experiencing the same symptoms that sidelined him for virtually all of 2012. Unable to make a full recovery, Carpenter announced his retirement on October

13, 2013, after which he accepted a front-office job with the Cardinals, serving their general manager as a special assistant. He left the game with a career record of 144–94 and an ERA of 3.76. During his time in St. Louis, Carpenter posted an overall mark of 95–44, along with an ERA of 3.07.

CARDINAL CAREER HIGHLIGHTS

Best Season

Carpenter pitched exceptionally well for the Cardinals in 2009, finishing the year with a record of 17–4, which gave him the NL's best winning percentage (.810). He also led all NL hurlers with a 2.24 ERA and posted a career-best 1.007 WHIP (walks plus hits allowed per innings pitched). Nevertheless, it would be difficult not to select the 2005 campaign as the finest of Carpenter's career. In addition to finishing second in the league with 213 strikeouts, 242 innings pitched, 4 shutouts, and a winning percentage of .808, Carpenter compiled a record of 21–5, which also placed him second in the senior circuit in wins. He also led all NL hurlers with seven complete games and finished among the league leaders with a 2.83 ERA. During the course of the campaign, Carpenter became the first Cardinals pitcher since Bob Gibson in 1970 to win ten consecutive road decisions, and the first since Gibson in 1968 to win eleven straight decisions overall. He also established himself as the first pitcher since the Deadball Era to make sixteen starts in succession in which he lasted at least seven innings and surrendered three runs or less to the opposition.

Memorable Moments and Greatest Performances

Although he is known much more for his outstanding work on the mound, Carpenter had an exceptional day at the plate on October 1, 2009, keying a 13–0 rout of the Cincinnati Reds with a grand slam home run, a double, and six RBIs. In driving in six runs during the contest, Carpenter became just the fourth pitcher since the advent of divisional play in 1969 to collect as many as six RBIs in one game, breaking in the process Bob Gibson's team record of five RBIs by a hurler, which the latter set on July 26, 1973.

Carpenter pitched arguably his best game for the Cardinals on June 14, 2005, when he surrendered just one hit to the Toronto Blue Jays during a 7–0 shutout. Almost exactly one year later, on June 13, 2006, he struck out a career-high thirteen batters during a 2–1 victory over the Pittsburgh Pirates. Carpenter worked the first seven innings, shutting out the Pirates on only three hits, before turning the game over to the bullpen.

Carpenter also pitched magnificently in a pair of 2009 starts. After being sidelined for virtually all of the two previous campaigns, he made his 2009 debut a memorable one, shutting out the Pirates on just one hit in seven innings. Later in the year, on September 7, Carpenter ran his record to 16–3 by shutting out the Brewers, 3–0, at Miller Park, on just one hit. He also struck out ten during the contest.

Carpenter turned in a memorable performance against Detroit in Game 3 of the 2006 World Series, giving the Cardinals a 2–1 lead in the Fall Classic by pitching his team to a 5–0 victory. Carpenter worked the first eight innings, surrendering only three hits to the hard-hitting Tigers.

Carpenter again demonstrated his ability to pitch well under pressure five years later, when he pitched the Cardinals into the postseason by tossing a complete-game shutout against Houston on the final day of the 2011 regular season. He followed that up by turning in an absolute gem against the Philadelphia Phillies in Game 5 of the NLDS. Facing his old friend Roy Halladay, Carpenter outdueled his former Toronto teammate, throwing a complete-game 1–0 shutout that put the Cardinals in the NLCS. He subsequently took the ball on short rest in Game 7 of the World Series, working six strong innings, in pitching his team to a 6–2 Series-clinching win over the favored Texas Rangers.

Notable Achievements

Surpassed twenty wins once (twenty-one in 2005).
Won at least fifteen games four other times.
Compiled ERA below 3.00 three times.
Struck out more than 200 batters once (213 in 2005).
Threw more than 220 innings four times.

Led NL pitchers in winning percentage once, ERA once, innings pitched once, complete games once, and shutouts once.

Owns best strikeouts-to-walks ratio of any Cardinals pitcher in history (3.666).

Ranks among Cardinals all-time leaders in strikeouts (second) and winning percentage (eighth).

2005 NL Cy Young Award winner.

2009 NL Comeback Player of the Year.

Two-time *Sporting News* Pitcher of the Year (2005, 2006).

Three-time NL All-Star (2005, 2006, 2010).

Three-time NL champion (2004, 2006, 2011).

Two-time world champion (2006, 2011).

NOTES

1. Tony LaRussa, quoted in "Chris Carpenter: What They Say," *JockBio.com*, www.jockbio.com/Bios/Carpenter/Carpenter_they-say.html (accessed October 11, 2012).

2. Dave Duncan, quoted in "Chris Carpenter: What They Say," www.jockbio.com/Bios/Carpenter/Carpenter_they-say.html.

3. LaRussa, quoted in "Chris Carpenter: What They Say," www.jockbio.com/Bios/Carpenter/Carpenter_they-say.html.

26

MORT COOPER

A couple of hurlers who pitched for the Cardinals' championship teams of the 1940s take up the next two spots in our rankings, with Mort Cooper and Harry Brecheen reaching similar levels of excellence during their years in St. Louis. Brecheen spent ten seasons in a Redbirds uniform, while Cooper remained with the team for only six full seasons, and parts of two others. As a result, Brecheen posted slightly better overall numbers than did Cooper with the Cardinals, winning more games, throwing more innings, tossing more complete games, and striking out more batters; however, it could be argued that Cooper pitched more effectively than Brecheen did during his time with the team. Brecheen compiled a record of 128–79 with the Cardinals, for a winning percentage of .618. He also posted an ERA of 2.91 and a WHIP (walks plus hits allowed per innings pitched) of 1.181. Cooper went 105–50, for a .677 winning percentage, while compiling an ERA of 2.77 and a WHIP of 1.206. Therefore, a valid argument could certainly be waged on either player's behalf. In the end, I elected to place Cooper one spot ahead of Brecheen due to the fact that he earned three top-ten finishes in the National League Most Valuable Player voting, winning the award in 1942; Brecheen placed in the top ten in the balloting just once, never finishing any higher than fifth.

Mort Cooper teamed up with younger brother Walker to form baseball's foremost battery during the first half of the 1940s. While the hard-hitting Walker started behind the plate for the Cardinals from 1942 to 1944, earning NL All-Star honors each season, Mort served as the ace of their pitching staff, posting more than twenty victories each year, and capturing league MVP honors in 1942, when he turned in one of the most dominant single-season pitching performances in franchise history. The hard-throwing right-hander compiled an overall record of 65–22 for the Cardinals those three seasons, leading them to three straight NL pennants and two world championships.

Born in Atherton, Missouri, on March 2, 1913, Morton Cecil Cooper had the good fortune to pitch for his home-state team when he joined the Cardinals at the tail end of 1938, after spending the previous few seasons pitching for Columbus in the American Association and Houston in the Texas League. Although no longer viewed as a top prospect due to his somewhat advanced age, the twenty-six-year-old right-hander established himself as an integral member of the St. Louis pitching staff the following year, compiling a record of 12–6 and an ERA of 3.25, while serving the team as both a starter and reliever. Cooper gradually worked his way into the Cardinals' starting rotation throughout the course of the next two seasons, posting an overall record of 24–23, despite being plagued by elbow problems that forced him to miss six weeks in 1941 after undergoing surgery.

Fully recovered from his surgery by 1942, Cooper emerged as the Cardinals' staff ace, leading them to the NL pennant by topping all hurlers in the senior circuit with a record of 22–7, a 1.78 ERA, and 10 shutouts. He also finished second in the league with 152 strikeouts and 279 innings pitched, while placing third with twenty-two complete games. Cooper's magnificent performance earned him NL MVP honors and the first of three consecutive *Sporting News* All-Star selections. He subsequently struggled against the Yankees in the World Series, losing Game 1 and posting an ERA of 5.54 in his two starts, but the Cardinals defeated New York in the final four contests, winning their first world championship since 1934.

Cooper pitched brilliantly again in 1943, concluding the campaign with a record of 21–8, a 2.30 ERA, 24 complete games, 274 innings pitched, and 6 shutouts, en route to earning All-Star honors for the second straight year and a fifth-place finish in the league MVP voting. He pitched much more effectively than he did in the previous year's World Series when the Cardinals once again faced the Yankees in the Fall Classic, winning the first of his two starts and limiting New York to just eleven hits in sixteen total innings of work. But New York turned the tables on St. Louis, taking the Series in five games, to deny the Cardinals their second consecutive world championship.

Cooper turned in his third straight exceptional campaign in 1944, placing among the NL leaders with a record of 22–7, an ERA of 2.46, 22 complete games, and 252 innings pitched, while topping the circuit with 7 shutouts. He then led the Cardinals to victory over the rival St. Louis Browns in the World Series by compiling a 1.13 ERA and surrendering only nine hits in sixteen innings of work in his two starts.

Cooper accomplished all he did those three years despite suffering from constant elbow pain he took with him to the mound before each start. Stan Musial states the following in his autobiography, *Stan Musial: The Man's Own Story*:

> This great pitcher (Cooper) used to chew aspirins on the mound to dull the pain caused by bone chips in his elbow. Mort had a very good fastball and a good fork ball. He didn't walk anybody. It was a pleasure to play behind him because he knew where he was going to pitch the hitters, and you could play them accordingly, confident of Cooper's control.[1]

Unfortunately, Cooper didn't remain in St. Louis much longer. He and brother Walker both staged contract holdouts in early 1945, prompting Cardinals management to dispose of both men shortly thereafter. While Walker was sold to the New York Giants at the end of the year, Cooper was dealt to the lowly Boston Braves after making only three starts for St. Louis in 1945. Although he pitched effectively for Boston in each of the next two campaigns, Cooper found it increasingly difficult to withstand the constant pain he experienced on the mound. After being traded to the Giants in early 1947, he appeared in only eight more games before the team eventually released him. Cooper ended his career with a record of 128–75, for a winning percentage of .631, and an ERA of 2.97. In parts of eight seasons in St. Louis, he went 105–50, with a 2.77 ERA, 105 complete games, and 28 shutouts. He ranks among the Cardinals' all-time leaders in shutouts (third) and winning percentage (ninth). Meanwhile, his ten shutouts in 1942 remain the second-highest single-season total ever compiled by a Cardinals pitcher (Bob Gibson threw thirteen in 1968).

Mort Cooper only lived another thirteen years after he threw his last pitch for the Cardinals. Complications from a lung condition ended his life on November 17, 1958. He was just forty-five years of age when he passed away.

CARDINAL CAREER HIGHLIGHTS

Best Season

Although Cooper also pitched exceptionally well for the Cardinals in both 1943 and 1944, the 1942 campaign would have to be considered his finest. In addition to posting a league-leading 22 victories, which tied his career high, he established career bests with a 1.78 ERA, 10 shutouts, 279 innings pitched, and 152 strikeouts, leading all NL hurlers in the first two categories. Cooper's 1.78 ERA ended up being the lowest mark compiled by any right-hander in the senior circuit from 1920 to 1967.

Memorable Moments and Greatest Performances

As one might expect, Cooper turned in a number of memorable pitching performances during the course of his MVP season of 1942. On May 20, he engaged in a classic pitching duel with Brooklyn staff ace Whit Wyatt, ending the Dodger right-hander's eight-game winning streak by shutting out Brooklyn, 1–0, on just two hits.

A little more than three months later, on August 25, Cooper and Wyatt again found themselves battling one another right down to the wire, this time in front of the largest night crowd in St. Louis history, to that point. After the two staff aces matched zeroes for the first twelve innings, both teams managed to push across a run in the thirteenth. Walker Cooper then made a winner out of his brother by delivering a RBI single in the bottom of the fourteenth, giving the elder Cooper a 2–1 victory.

Cooper again got the best of the Dodgers on September 11, allowing them just 3 hits during a 3–0 shutout at Ebbets Field. The right-hander's eighth shutout of the year moved St. Louis to within one game of first-place Brooklyn in the NL standings. Less than two weeks later, on September 24, Cooper assured the Cardinals of at least a tie for the pennant by tossing his tenth shutout of the year against Cincinnati. The 6–0 St. Louis victory, a two-hitter for Cooper, gave the right-hander the last of his twenty-two wins on the season.

Still, Cooper accomplished the greatest feat of his career in 1943, when he threw back-to-back one-hitters. After allowing the Dodgers just one hit during a 7–0 win on May 31, Cooper surrendered just one safety to Philadelphia during a 5–0 victory on June 4. Brooklyn's Billy Herman and Philadelphia's Jimmy Wasdell collected the only hits against Cooper in the two contests.

Although the Cardinals ended up losing the 1943 World Series to the Yankees in five games, Cooper redeemed himself somewhat for the rather mediocre performance he turned in against New York in the previous year's Fall Classic. After giving the Cardinals their only win of the Series in Game 2, he lost a heartbreaking 2–0 decision to American League MVP Spud Chandler in the Series finale.

Cooper pitched even better against the St. Louis Browns in the 1944 World Series, dominating the Browns' lineup in both his starts. After losing Game 1 by a score of 2–1 despite surrendering only two hits to the opposition, Cooper returned in Game 5 to give the Cardinals a 3–2 lead in the World Series by shutting out the Browns, 2–0. The Cardinals also took Game 6, clinching in the process their second world championship in three years. Cooper concluded the Series with a 1.13 ERA, allowing the Browns just nine hits in sixteen innings of work, while striking out sixteen.

Notable Achievements

Won more than twenty games three times.

Compiled ERA below 3.00 four times, posting a mark lower than 2.00 once (1.78 in 1942).

Completed more than twenty games three times.

Threw more than 250 innings three times.

Threw ten shutouts in 1942.

Led NL pitchers in wins twice, shutouts twice, and ERA once.

Third all-time among Cardinals pitchers in shutouts (twenty-eight).

1942 NL MVP.
Three-time *Sporting News* All-Star selection (1942, 1943, 1944).
Two-time NL All-Star (1942, 1943).
Three-time NL champion (1942, 1943, 1944).
Two-time world champion (1942, 1944).

NOTE

1. Stan Musial, quoted in "Mort Cooper Awards," *Baseball Almanac*, www.baseball-almanac.com/players/awards.php?p=coopermo01 (accessed October 12, 2012).

27

HARRY BRECHEEN

Nicknamed for the quickness and athleticism he displayed on the mound, Harry "The Cat" Brecheen spent ten full seasons with the Cardinals, serving as the ace of their pitching staff in several of those years. Working almost exclusively as a starter from 1944 to 1950, the left-handed screwball artist won at least fourteen games six straight times, compiling an overall record of 96–53 in that six-year stretch. In helping the Cardinals win three National League pennants and two world championships, Brecheen established himself as one of the finest big-game pitchers of his time, posting a record of 4–1 in World Series play, along with an extraordinary 0.83 ERA. One of only three left-handed pitchers in baseball history to win three games in a single World Series (Mickey Lolich and Randy Johnson are the others), Brecheen led the Cardinals to victory over the favored Boston Red Sox in the 1946 Fall Classic by tossing two complete games, en route to compiling a 0.45 ERA against a powerful lineup that included Ted Williams, Bobby Doerr, Dom DiMaggio, and Rudy York. Brecheen also fielded his position exceptionally well, retiring with the fourth-highest fielding percentage among pitchers (.983).

Born in Broken Bow, Oklahoma, on October 14, 1914, Harry David Brecheen didn't arrive in St. Louis to stay until after he had already turned twenty-eight years of age. After beginning his professional career in 1935, he spent the next two seasons in the minor leagues, posting a record of 21–6 for the Portsmouth Cubs of the Piedmont League in 1937, before the Cardinals purchased his contract. Assigned to the Houston Buffaloes of the Texas League, Brecheen subsequently spent another two years in the minors before making a brief appearance in

St. Louis in early 1940. He then spent virtually all of the next three campaigns at Columbus in the American Association.

Brecheen might have remained buried in the minor leagues even longer had a shortage of talent at the major-league level not developed in 1943, as a result of the U.S. involvement in World War II. Exempt from military service with a 4-F classification due to a spinal malformation and boyhood ankle injury, Brecheen finally received the opportunity he craved with the defending world-champion Cardinals in 1943. Working as a spot starter and reliever, the five-foot, ten-inch, 160-pound southpaw compiled a record of 9–6 and a 2.26 ERA in his first full season. He became a regular member of the team's starting rotation the following year, helping the Cardinals capture their third consecutive pennant by finishing 16–5, with a 2.85 ERA. Brecheen subsequently recorded a complete-game victory over the St. Louis Browns in Game 4 of the World Series, as the Cardinals defeated their rivals in six games.

With Mort Cooper traded away to Boston in early 1945, Brecheen emerged as the ace of the Cardinals' pitching staff, posting a record of 15–4, which gave him the league's best winning percentage (.789). He also placed among the leaders with a 2.52 ERA. Although Brecheen compiled a less impressive 15–15 record in 1946, he continued to pitch extremely well, finishing fifth among NL hurlers with an ERA of 2.49, while topping the circuit with five shutouts. It was during the World Series, however, that he created a permanent place for himself in Cardinals' lore, earning a victory in each of his three appearances, throwing two complete games, and allowing the Red Sox just one earned run and fourteen hits in twenty innings of work.

Brecheen followed up his exceptional World Series performance with a solid 1947 campaign, in which he finished 16–11, with a 3.30 ERA and eighteen complete games. He then had the finest season of his career in 1948, compiling a record of 20–7, and leading the league with a 2.24 ERA, 149 strikeouts, and 7 shutouts, en route to earning NL All-Star honors for the second straight year and a fifth-place finish in the league Most Valuable Player voting.

As Brecheen gradually established himself as one of the senior circuit's top starters, he also developed a reputation as the league's finest fielding pitcher. Blessed with exceptional quickness, agility, and cat-like reflexes that caused the nickname "The Cat" to become affixed to him, Brecheen became noted for his ability to field bunts and other slowly hit balls. He led all NL hurlers in fielding percentage on four separate occasions, compiling a perfect mark of 1.000 each time.

After his banner year of 1948, Brecheen finished in double digits in wins just once more before his skills began to diminish, posting a record of 14–11 in 1949. Failing to win more than eight games in any of the next three campaigns, the southpaw found himself released by the Cardinals at the end of the 1952 season. He subsequently signed with the St. Louis Browns, remaining with them one year, until they too released him at the conclusion of the 1953 campaign. Rapidly approaching his thirty-ninth birthday, Brecheen elected to announce his retirement, ending his career with a record of 133–92 and an ERA of 2.92. He compiled a mark of 128–79 as a member of the Cardinals, along with a 2.91 ERA, 122 complete games, and 25 shutouts. In addition to ranking among the team's all-time leaders in wins, shutouts, innings pitched, and games started, Brecheen held the franchise record for career strikeouts by a left-hander from 1951 to 1971, finally being surpassed by Steve Carlton in the last of those years. Brecheen's twenty-five career shutouts remain the Cardinal record for southpaws.

After being released by the Browns at the end of 1953, Brecheen remained with the team when they moved to Baltimore and changed their name to the Orioles the ensuing campaign, serving as Baltimore pitching coach from 1954 to 1967. He passed away in January 2004, at the age of eighty-nine, while staying at a nursing facility in Bethany, Oklahoma.

CARDINAL CAREER HIGHLIGHTS

Best Season

Even though he also performed extremely well in 1944 and 1945, Brecheen reached the apex of his career in 1948, posting his best numbers in virtually every statistical category. In addition to winning 20 games for the only time in his career, Brecheen threw 21 complete games, worked 233 innings, and led all NL hurlers with a 2.24 ERA, 149 strikeouts, and 7 shutouts. At one point during the season, the left-hander tossed thirty-two and two-thirds consecutive scoreless innings.

Memorable Moments and Greatest Performances

Brecheen pitched the best game of his career against Philadelphia on May 8, 1948, allowing just one man to reach base against him during a 5–0 Cardinals victory over the Phillies. Only an infield single by Johnny Blatnik in the seventh inning prevented Brecheen from throwing a perfect game.

Brecheen turned in another memorable pitching performance against Chicago on April 30, 1950, working thirteen scoreless innings, en route to winning a 1–0 decision. Del Rice's home run in the bottom of the thirteenth inning made a winner out of Brecheen, who surrendered just five hits to the Cubs, while striking out eight.

Nevertheless, Brecheen will always be remembered most for his magnificent performance in the 1946 World Series. After allowing the hard-hitting Red Sox just four singles during a 3–0 Cardinals' win in Game 2, Brecheen returned to the mound six days later to even the Fall Classic at three games apiece with a 4–1 complete-game victory. He subsequently entered Game 7 in the eighth inning on just one day's rest, throwing two scoreless innings and earning his third win of the Series when Enos Slaughter made his "Mad Dash" around the bases in the bottom of the frame.

Notable Achievements

Won twenty games once (1948).
Surpassed fifteen victories four other times.
Compiled ERA below 3.00 five times.
Threw more than twenty complete games once (twenty-one in 1948).
Led NL pitchers in winning percentage once, ERA once, strikeouts once, shutouts twice, and fielding percentage four times.
Ranks among Cardinals all-time leaders in wins (seventh), shutouts (fourth), innings pitched (eighth), and games started (sixth).
1948 *Sporting News* All-Star selection.
Two-time NL All-Star (1947, 1948).
Three-time NL champion (1943, 1944, 1946).
Two-time world champion (1944, 1946).

28

MARTY MARION

Unlike contemporaries Pee Wee Reese and Phil Rizzuto, Marty Marion has yet to be enshrined in Cooperstown. The latter also received less publicity than either of the other two men during his playing days. Yet, even though playing in the city of New York allowed Reese and Rizzuto to receive more in the way of accolades throughout the course of their careers, Marion gained general recognition as the finest fielding shortstop of his time. Known as "The Octopus" for the manner in which he gobbled up ground balls with his long arms, Marion led all National League shortstops in fielding percentage four times, while also topping all players at his position in putouts and assists twice each. Marion's exceptional fielding ability enabled him to earn three top-ten finishes in the league Most Valuable Player voting in spite of the fact that he typically posted rather modest offensive numbers. In fact, even though teammate Stan Musial compiled much better numbers in 1944, the baseball writers named Marion the NL's MVP for the overall contributions he made to a Cardinals team that captured its third straight pennant. In all, Marion played for four pennant winners and three world championship teams during his eleven years in a Cardinals uniform.

Born in Richburg, South Carolina, on December 1, 1917, Martin Whiteford Marion grew up in Atlanta, Georgia, where he played high school ball and briefly attended Georgia Tech University before signing with the Cardinals as an amateur free agent in 1936. After spending the next three years advancing through the Cardinals' farm system, where manager Burt Shotton nicknamed him "Slats" due to his slender frame, Marion arrived in St. Louis in 1940, earning the team's starting shortstop job in spring training. Although he committed a total of seventy-one errors in the field his first two seasons, Marion displayed exceptional range at shortstop, leading all NL players with 489 assists in 1941. He also handled himself well at the plate, posting a batting average of .278 as a rookie, before batting .252 the following season and leading all NL players with twenty-eight sacrifice hits.

Marion had one of his finest offensive seasons in 1942, batting .276, scoring 66 runs, and topping the senior circuit with 38 doubles, en route to earning a seventh-place finish in the league MVP voting. Deferred from military service because of a childhood leg injury, he subsequently had three of his best years while most of the game's top players served in the armed forces during World War II. After batting a career-high .280 in 1943, he helped lead the Cardinals to their third straight pennant the following year by batting .267, driving in 63 runs, and hitting a career-high 6 home runs, en route to earning NL MVP honors and the second of his seven All-Star selections. Marion followed that up with a .277 batting average in 1945, which helped him finish eighth in the MVP balloting.

It was during the war years that Marion also developed into the game's finest fielding shortstop, establishing himself as the glue of the Cardinals' infield. Disproving the previously held theory that players at that position had to be small men, the six-foot, two-inch, 170-pound Marion had long arms that reached for ground balls like tentacles, prompting writers to dub him "The Octopus." He took long, gliding strides and had tremendous reach, enabling him to cover more ground than any other shortstop of his time. Marion also possessed outstanding leaping ability, allowing him to snare many line drives that appeared headed for the outfield. Priding himself on his fielding ability, he often seemed to be obsessed with picking up pebbles that might cause a bad hop to come his way on the hard-baked Sportsman's Park infield.

Longtime teammate Stan Musial told the *St. Louis Post-Dispatch* in 1992, "He (Marion) could go in the hole better than anyone I ever saw. He had the most accurate arm you ever saw."[1] Cardinals manager Billy Southworth once said of his star shortstop, "He's the best ever. He anticipates plays perfectly, can go to his right or left equally as well, and has a truly great arm. Some of the things he does have to be seen to be believed."[2] Meanwhile, Negro Leagues legend Satchel Paige, who later played with Marion in St. Louis as a member of the Browns, stated, "Man, I've been in this game a lotta' years, but I ain't seen a better shortstop than Marty. . . . He's so good that all the other players stop what they are doing to watch him. I mean it. They just sit back and enjoy the show."[3]

A solid offensive player as well, Marion had two of his best years in 1947 and 1949, batting .272 each season, while knocking in seventy-four and seventy runs, respectively. After back and knee problems limited Marion to only 106 games in 1950, he took over as Cardinals manager in 1951, leading an aging team to a surprising third-place finish. Fired nonetheless at season's end, Marion moved crosstown to become player-manager of the Browns, serving in that capacity for the next two seasons before being dismissed after piloting the team to a last-place finish in 1953. He subsequently officially announced his retirement as an active player, ending his career with a .263 batting average and 1,448 hits. In his eleven seasons with the Cardinals, Marion batted .264 and collected 1,402 hits.

After retiring as an active player, Marion assumed the managerial reins of the Chicago White Sox, who he led to consecutive third-place finishes in 1955 and 1956, before stepping down at the conclusion of the 1956 campaign. Although Marion never again managed at the major-league level, he remained close to the game, later owning the Houston Buffs of the American Association and managing the stadium club at the Cardinals' first Busch Stadium. Marion lived until the ripe old age of ninety-three, eventually passing away in Ladue, Missouri, on March 15, 2011.

Although Marty Marion is generally ranked well behind Ozzie Smith on the list of outstanding Cardinals shortstops, not everyone agrees with that assessment. Terry Moore, the team's center fielder and captain when Marion first arrived in St. Louis in 1940, said the following years later:

> People always ask me what I think of Ozzie in comparison to Marty. I tell 'em I'd give Ozzie the nod as the best shortstop I've ever seen on Astroturf. But, if you put Ozzie on the

fields that Marion played on and put Marion on the fields that Ozzie played on, then I don't think you could compare them. I don't think Ozzie would have been the shortstop that Marion was in Marion's conditions.[4]

CARDINAL CAREER HIGHLIGHTS

Best Season

Although Marion captured NL MVP honors in 1944, when he batted .267, knocked in 63 runs, and hit a career-high 6 home runs, en route to helping the Cardinals win their third consecutive pennant, he actually posted better overall numbers in two or three other seasons. In addition to batting .276 and compiling a career-high .718 on-base plus slugging percentage (OPS) in 1942, he led the league with thirty-eight doubles, topping the senior circuit in a major offensive statistical category for the only time in his career. Marion also had one of his best offensive seasons in 1949, when he batted .272, drove in 70 runs, and scored 61 others.

Nevertheless, the feeling here is that Marion had his best all-around season in 1947. In addition to batting .272, compiling an OPS of .686, and knocking in a career-high 74 runs, he committed only 15 errors in the field, enabling him to compile a career-best .981 fielding percentage, which led all NL shortstops. He also finished second in the league with 452 assists and topped all players at his position with 329 putouts—the highest total of his career.

Memorable Moments and Greatest Performances

Hardly known for his power at the plate, Marion went on a brief power surge in 1950, when he homered in three straight games; however, he saved his finest offensive performance for the 1943 World Series, hitting a home run, driving in 2 runs, and collecting 5 hits in 14 official trips to the plate in a losing effort against the Yankees. Marion concluded the Fall Classic with a batting average of .357, an on-base percentage of .471, and a slugging percentage of .714, giving him an OPS of 1.185.

Notable Achievements

Led NL in doubles once (thirty-eight in 1942).

Led NL in sacrifice hits twice.

Led NL shortstops in assists twice, putouts twice, and fielding percentage four times.

1944 NL MVP.

1944 *Sporting News* Major League Player of the Year.

Two-time *Sporting News* All-Star selection (1944, 1945).

Eight-time NL All-Star (1943, 1944, 1945, 1946, 1947, 1948, 1949, 1950).

Four-time NL champion (1942, 1943, 1944, 1946).

Three-time world champion (1942, 1944, 1946).

NOTES

1. Stan Musial, quoted in Richard Goldstein, "Marty Marion, Cardinals' Slick-Fielding Shortstop, Dies at 93," *New York Times*, March 16, 2011, www.nytimes.com/2011/03/17/sports/baseball/17marion.html (accessed October 14, 2012).
2. Billy Southworth, quoted in Mike Shalin and Neil Shalin, *Out by a Step: The 100 Best Players Not in the Baseball Hall of Fame* (Lanham, MD: Diamond Communications, 2002), 112.
3. Satchel Paige, quoted in Shalin and Shalin, *Out by a Step*, 112.
4. Terry Moore, quoted in Shalin and Shalin, *Out by a Step*, 112.

29

BILL WHITE

The contributions Bill White made to the Cardinals during the course of his seven years in St. Louis cannot be measured by statistics alone. Although the powerfully built first baseman slugged more than 20 home runs, knocked in more than 100 runs, and batted over .300 three straight times from 1962 to 1964, he accomplished considerably more off the field, helping to raise the social consciousness of the entire organization by disproving several racial stereotypes that previously existed about black athletes. Intelligent, fair-minded, nonjudgmental, and judicious, White carried himself with class and dignity both on and off the field, holding himself and those around him to a higher standard than most. In so doing, he helped change the attitude formerly held by many in the game, paving the way for future generations of dark-skinned players to gain employment at the major-league level.

Born in Lakewood, Florida, on January 28, 1934, William DeKova White grew up in Warren, Ohio, after moving north with his family as an infant. With his father having left the family early in his childhood, young William was raised by his mother and grandmother, who passed on to him their wisdom, sense of purpose, self-discipline, and strong moral character. Although he eventually received a number of scholarship offers from larger schools after starring in baseball and football at Warren G. Harding High School, White elected to attend Ohio's Hiram College, since it had a reputation for preparing students well for medical school; however, he changed his plans after being offered a contract by New York Giants scout Tony Ravish following a tryout in 1953.

White made his pro debut in the Carolina League as a member of the Danville Leafs later that year, being the only player on the team of African American descent. Despite experiencing a considerable amount of racial prejudice during the campaign, the nineteen-year-old White ended up hitting twenty home runs and batting .298. He also performed well in each of the next two seasons, as he continued to work his way up the Giants' farm system, before finally being promoted to the majors in May 1956.

White had a solid rookie season for the Giants, apparently establishing himself as the team's first baseman of the future by hitting twenty-two home runs and driving in fifty-nine runs in 138 games. But, after spending all of 1957 and most of 1958 in the army, White returned to the Giants to find young sluggers Orlando Cepeda and Willie McCovey ahead of him on the club's depth chart at first base. Unhappy with his situation in San Francisco, White requested a trade, prompting the Giants to trade him to St. Louis prior to the start of the 1959 campaign.

With Stan Musial serving as the Cardinals' regular first baseman in 1959, White saw a limited amount of action at his natural position in his first year with his new team, spending most of his time in left field. Nevertheless, he didn't allow the defensive switch to adversely affect his hitting, finishing the year with a .302 batting average and seventy-two RBIs, en route to earning his first All-Star selection. After being shifted back to first base in 1960, White hit 16 homers, drove in 79 runs, scored 81 others, batted .283, and won the first of his seven consecutive Gold Gloves.

Even though White ended up posting solid numbers in each of his first two seasons with the Cardinals, he initially found it difficult to adapt to his new environment. Swinging mostly for the fences when he first arrived in St. Louis, the left-handed-hitting White compiled a batting average of only .091 after his first few weeks with his new team; however, after seeking out the advice of Cardinals' hitting coach Harry Walker, who taught him to use his hands, hit the ball back up the middle, and use the entire field, White straightened himself out, developing into one of the senior circuit's better hitters. More of a line-drive hitter than a pure slugger, White never posted huge home-run totals for the Cardinals. Nevertheless, he possessed enough natural physical strength to typically hit between twenty and twenty-five homers, establishing himself in the process as the team's other primary power threat, besides Ken Boyer.

White topped 20 homers for the first time as a member of the Cardinals in 1961, when he hit 20 round-trippers, knocked in 90 runs, scored 89 others, and batted .286. He followed that up with three straight seasons in which he hit at least 20 home runs, drove in more than 100 runs, and batted over .300. After hitting 20 homers, knocking in 102 runs, scoring 93 others, collecting 199 hits, and batting a career-high .324 in 1962, White batted .304 in 1963, while also establishing career highs with 27 home runs, 109 RBIs, 106 runs scored, 200 hits, and 323 total bases. The All-Star first baseman then helped lead the Cardinals to the National League pennant in 1964 by hitting 21 homers, driving in 102 runs, scoring 92 others, amassing 191 hits and 37 doubles, and batting .303, en route to earning a third-place finish in the league Most Valuable Player voting.

As he grew increasingly comfortable during his time in St. Louis, White established himself as one of the Cardinals' team leaders. Demonstrating patience, wisdom, and foresight in his dealings with others, he often found himself being approached by his teammates for advice. Particularly revered by the team's black players, the veteran first baseman gradually developed a reputation that prompted dark-skinned players on other teams to seek him out whenever they visited St. Louis. On one particular occasion, White took it upon himself to reprimand a young black player on an opposing team who failed to hustle during a game against the Cardinals. White approached the player after the contest, telling him, "Listen, you cut that crap out. We can't afford to do stuff like that. You're hurting *everybody* when you do that. A lot of people worked very hard for us to be here, and we're not going to blow this chance."[1] White's intelligence, strong will, and leadership qualities helped erase many of the myths that previously existed about black players, enabling racial harmony and a true sense of camaraderie that didn't exist in most places during the 1960s to develop on the Cardinals.

Although White posted solid numbers again in 1965, he experienced a decline in offensive production in virtually every offensive category, prompting the Cardinals to trade him to the Phillies at the end of the year. The veteran first baseman spent three years in

Philadelphia, having one more big season in 1966, when he hit twenty-two home runs and knocked in 103 runs. After experiencing less success the next two years, the thirty-five-year-old White found himself back in St. Louis, where he spent the last year of his career as a backup first baseman/pinch hitter. He announced his retirement at the end of 1969, with career totals of 202 home runs, 870 RBIs, 843 runs scored, and 1,706 hits. He also compiled a lifetime batting average of .286, a .351 on-base percentage, and a .455 slugging percentage. White hit 140 home runs, drove in 631 runs, scored 627 others, and collected 1,241 hits while playing for the Cardinals. He also batted .298 in his eight years in St. Louis, compiled a .357 on-base percentage, and posted a .472 slugging percentage.

Following his playing days, White began a successful career as an announcer, spending eighteen years in the New York Yankees broadcast booth working with Phil Rizzuto and Frank Messer. He gave up his announcing career after being named president of the NL in 1989, when Bart Giamatti vacated the position to assume the duties of baseball commissioner. The assignment made White the highest-ranking African American official in the history of American professional sports. He remained in that post for five years, presiding over the expansion of the major leagues in 1993, before announcing his resignation in March 1993.

CARDINAL CAREER HIGHLIGHTS

Best Season

White had three consecutive outstanding seasons for the Cardinals in which he batted over .300, hit at least 20 home runs, and knocked in more than 100 runs—any of which would have made a good choice. In addition to hitting 20 home runs, driving in 102 runs, scoring 93 others, and collecting 199 hits in 1962, he batted a career-high .324 and posted a career-best on-base plus slugging percentage (OPS) of .868. Two years later, White earned a third-place finish in the NL MVP voting, helping the Cardinals win their first pennant in 18 years by hitting 21 homers, knocking in 102 runs, scoring 92 others, amassing 191 hits, batting .303, and compiling an OPS of .829.

However, I ultimately decided to go with White's 1963 campaign, one in which he established career highs with 27 home runs, 109 RBIs, 106 runs scored, 200 hits, 323 total bases, and a .491 slugging percentage. White also batted .304, posted an OPS of .851 (the second-highest mark of his career), and appeared in all 162 games for the Cardinals, en route to earning a seventh-place finish in the league MVP balloting.

Memorable Moments and Greatest Performances

White became a part of history on April 12, 1960, when, batting third for the Cardinals in the top of the first inning, he recorded the first hit in the history of Candlestick Park—a single to right field off of Giants' starter Sam Jones. White had one of the finest offensive days of his career later in the year, hitting for the cycle in the first game of a doubleheader loss to Pittsburgh on August 14, 1960. He went 4-for-5, with two RBIs and one run scored during the contest.

White had another big day at the plate on July 13, 1964. He collected 6 hits, hit 2 home runs, and knocked in 5 runs during a doubleheader sweep of the Pittsburgh Pirates at Forbes Field.

White accomplished his greatest feat three years earlier, however, when he tied Ty Cobb's major-league record by collecting a total of fourteen hits in consecutive doubleheaders the Cardinals played on July 17 and July 18, 1961. After going 8-for-10 during a doubleheader sweep of the Cubs on July 17, White led St. Louis to another sweep of Chicago the very next day, collecting three hits in four trips to the plate in each contest. During the course of the two days, he went a combined 14-for-18, with a homer, a double, 2 triples, 6 RBIs, and 7 runs scored.

Notable Achievements

Hit more than twenty home runs five times.
Knocked in more than 100 runs three times.
Scored more than 100 runs once (106 in 1963).
Batted over .300 four times.
Surpassed 200 hits once (200 in 1963).
Finished in double digits in triples twice.

Led NL first basemen in fielding percentage once (.996 in 1964).
Finished third in 1964 NL MVP voting.
Six-time Gold Glove winner (1960, 1961, 1962, 1963, 1964, 1965).
Two-time *Sporting News* All-Star selection (1963, 1964).
Five-time NL All-Star (1959, 1960, 1961, 1963, 1964).
1964 NL champion.
1964 world champion.

NOTE

1. Bill White, quoted in David Halberstam, *October 1964* (New York: Villard Books, 1994), 199.

30

VINCE COLEMAN

Although he possessed somewhat questionable character off the field, Vince Coleman established himself as one of the greatest base stealers of all time during his time in St. Louis. In leading the National League in stolen bases in each of his six seasons with the Cardinals, "Vincent Van Go," as he came to be known, became the only player in major-league history to surpass 100 steals in three consecutive seasons. Coleman's thievery on the base paths made him a key contributor to two pennant-winning teams in St. Louis, even though he had only marginal hitting skills and virtually no power at the plate. A prototypical Cardinals player of the mid-1980s, Coleman used his speed to his advantage, pounding balls into Busch Stadium's artificial surface, stretching singles into doubles and doubles into triples, and putting constant pressure on his opponent with his exceptional running speed. Serving as leadoff man in St. Louis throughout his tenure there, Coleman finished among the league leaders in runs scored four times, crossing the plate more than 100 times on two separate occasions.

Born in Jacksonville, Florida, on September 22, 1961, Vincent Maurice Coleman starred in baseball and football at Raines High School in Jacksonville, before excelling at both sports at Florida A&M University. After setting a single-season A&M record by stealing sixty-five bases in sixty-nine attempts in 1981, Coleman decided to concentrate solely on baseball when the Cardinals selected him in the tenth round of the 1982 Major League Baseball Draft. He spent the next three seasons in the minor leagues, displaying his elite base-stealing ability by swiping 145 bags with Macon of the South Atlantic League in 1983, and pilfering another 101 bases for the Louisville Redbirds of the American Association the following year.

With the Cardinals trading away Lonnie Smith in early 1985 to make room in the outfield for Coleman, the young speedster nailed down the starting left-field job almost as soon as he arrived in St. Louis. He subsequently went on to shatter the rookie record for most thefts in a season by stealing 110 bases. He also scored 107 runs, collected 170 hits, batted .267, and finished second in the NL with 16 outfield assists, en route to earning NL Rookie of the Year honors and an eleventh-place finish in the league Most Valuable Player voting. However, Coleman ended up appearing in only three postseason games for the NL East champion Cardinals after he suffered a freak injury prior to the start of the fourth game of the National League Championship Series (NLCS). With the automatic tarpaulin at Busch Stadium being placed onto the field during pregame warm-ups to protect the playing surface from a light rain that began to fall, the tarpaulin rolled over Coleman's leg, chipping a bone in his knee, badly bruising his leg, and bringing his season to an abrupt end. The Cardinals went on to defeat the Dodgers in the NLCS, but they ended up losing the World Series to the Kansas City Royals in seven games.

Although Cardinals fans eventually forgave Coleman for his mishap that some felt cost their team the world championship, they had a far more difficult time overlooking the insensitivity and lack of awareness he displayed when he commented during the season, "I don't know nothin' about him. Why are you asking me about Jackie Robinson?"[1] Responding to Coleman's foolish remark, Robinson's widow, Rachel, stated, "I hope somehow he'll learn and be embarrassed by his own ignorance."[2]

Coleman followed up his rather eventful rookie campaign with a subpar second season in which he batted just .232; compiled an on-base percentage of just .301; and accumulated only 29 RBIs, 139 hits, and 168 total bases in 600 official at bats. Nevertheless, he still managed to score ninety-four runs and lead the league with 107 stolen bases. Coleman rebounded in 1987 to have arguably his finest all-around season. He struck out 126 times and posted relatively unimpressive totals in home runs (3), RBIs (43), doubles (14), and total bases (223). But he also raised his batting average to .289; finished among the league leaders with 121 runs scored, 180 hits, and 10 triples; and topped the circuit with 109 stolen bases.

Coleman failed to approach 100 steals in any of his three remaining years with the Cardinals. Yet, he still topped the senior circuit in stolen bases in each of those years, compiling totals of 81 in 1988, 65 in 1989, and 77 in 1990. After scoring ninety-four runs in the second of those campaigns, he batted a career-high .292 in 1990.

A free agent at the end of the 1990 season, Coleman signed a four-year, $11.95 million contract with the rival New York Mets, after which his career took a downward spiral. Plagued by injuries throughout the first three years of the deal, Coleman appeared in only 235 out of a possible 485 games from 1991 to 1993, stealing only ninety-nine bases and scoring just 146 runs during that period. Furthermore, he repeatedly angered Mets' management with his rebellious behavior and poor judgment off the field. In addition to frequently ignoring his coaches' signs on the base paths, Coleman quarreled with Coach Mike Cubbage at the tail end of the 1991 season, contributing to the eventual dismissal of Bud Harrelson as manager. Coleman subsequently engaged in a fight with Harrelson's successor, Jeff Torborg, in September 1992, resulting in the enigmatic outfielder being suspended without pay for the remainder of the year. Coleman finally reached a point of no return in New York during the second half of the 1993 campaign, when, just three months after injuring Dwight Gooden's arm by recklessly swinging a golf club in the clubhouse, he was charged with endangerment when he threw a lit firecracker into a crowd of fans waiting for autographs in the Dodger Stadium parking lot. The explosion injured three children, causing Coleman to be sentenced to 200 hours of community service. Coleman never played for the Mets again, with the team subsequently placing him on paid administrative leave for the rest of the season, before trading him to Kansas City at the end of the year.

Coleman spent a year and a half in Kansas City, stealing a total of seventy-six bases and scoring 100 runs, before splitting his final season and a half between Seattle, Cincinnati, and Detroit, serving primarily as a backup outfielder and pinch runner in all three places. Released by the Tigers in early 1997, Coleman announced his retirement, concluding his career with a .264 batting average, 1,425 hits, 849 runs scored, and 752 stolen bases. He hit only 28 home runs, knocked in just 346 runs, and compiled on-base and slugging percentages of only .324 and .345, respectively, in the course of 13 big-league seasons. Coleman batted .265 in his six years with the Cardinals, scored 566 runs, collected 937 hits, stole 549 bases, compiled an on-base percentage of .326, and posted a slugging percentage of .339. He stole more bases than anyone in team history, with the exception of Lou Brock.

CARDINAL CAREER HIGHLIGHTS

Best Season

Coleman had easily his finest all-around season in 1987, when, in addition to leading all NL left fielders with 15 assists, he batted .289, posted a career-best .363 on-base percentage, stole a league-leading 109 bases, and placed among the senior circuit leaders with a career-high 121 runs scored and 180 hits, en route to earning a twelfth-place finish in the NL MVP voting. Coleman stole second and third base in the same inning thirteen times that year, reaching the 500 stolen base plateau faster than any other player by recording his 500th steal in just his 804th game.

Memorable Moments and Greatest Performances

Coleman's thievery on the base paths enabled him to reach a number of milestones during his six years in St. Louis. He established a new rookie record on August 1, 1985, when he stole two bases in the first inning against the Chicago Cubs to run his season total to seventy-four, thereby eclipsing the mark of seventy-two that Philadelphia speedster Juan Samuel set just one year earlier. Later in the year, Coleman joined Rickey Henderson (three times), Lou Brock, and Maury Wills as the only twentieth-century players to steal as many as 100 bases in a season, when he swiped his 100th bag against the Phillies on September 19.

Coleman also ended up establishing a new major-league record by stealing fifty consecutive bases without being caught. He began his streak in September 1988, eventually breaking the previous mark of thirty-eight straight successful stolen base attempts (set by Davey

Lopes in 1975) by swiping two bags against the Pittsburgh Pirates on June 24, 1989. Coleman's streak finally ended a little more than a month later, on July 26, when Montreal receiver Nelson Santovenia gunned him down at second.

Notable Achievements

Scored more than 100 runs twice.

Finished in double digits in triples three times.

Stole more than 100 bases three times, surpassing sixty steals on three other occasions.

Ranks second to Lou Brock in Cardinals history with 549 career stolen bases.

Last man to steal 100 bases in a season (1987).

Led NL in stolen bases six straight times (1985, 1986, 1987, 1988, 1989, 1990).

Led NL left fielders with fifteen assists in 1987.

Holds major-league rookie record for most stolen bases in a season (110 in 1985).

Holds major-league record with fifty consecutive successful stolen base attempts (September 18, 1988–July 26, 1989).

Holds three of the top six single-season stolen base marks in major-league history (110 in 1985, number 3; 109 in 1987, number 4; 107 in 1986, number 6).

1985 NL Rookie of the Year.

Two-time NL All-Star (1988, 1989).

Two-time NL champion (1985, 1987).

NOTES

1. Vince Coleman, quoted in J. Kurp, "Most Hated Mets," *Surviving the Citi.com*, www.survivingtheciti.com/?p=1157 (accessed October 17, 2012).

2. Rachel Robinson, quoted in Kurp, "Most Hated Mets," www.survivingtheciti.com/?p=1157.

31

ADAM WAINWRIGHT

Although a strong case could also be made for John Tudor, the number thirty-one spot in these rankings ended up going to Adam Wainwright. It could certainly be argued that Tudor pitched more effectively than Wainwright during his time with the Cardinals. Tudor's .705 winning percentage far exceeds the mark of .643 that Wainwright has been able to compile thus far. The former also posted a better ERA, threw more complete games, tossed more shutouts, and allowed fewer base runners per inning pitched. But, while Tudor won only sixty-two games for the Cardinals, surpassing thirteen wins just once, Wainwright has already posted 119 victories, winning at least fourteen games on six separate occasions. Those are the figures that prompted me to give the nod to Wainwright.

An integral member of the St. Louis pitching staff for much of the past nine seasons, Adam Wainwright has excelled for the Cardinals as both a starter and reliever. After taking over for an injured Jason Isringhausen as the team's closer late in 2006, Wainwright has since evolved into a top-flight starter, posting 20 victories twice and 19 wins another two times, striking out more than 200 batters three times, and earning three top-three finishes in the National League Cy Young balloting. Along the way, the big right-hander has helped the Cardinals win four division titles, two pennants, and one world championship.

Born in Brunswick, Georgia, on August 30, 1981, Adam Parrish Wainwright originally intended to play baseball for Georgia Tech University when he graduated from Brunswick's Glynn Academy High School; however, he decided to forgo college when his favorite team, the Atlanta Braves, selected him in the first round of the 2000 amateur draft with the twenty-ninth overall pick.

As things turned out, Wainwright never got to play for the team he followed as a youngster, since the Braves included him in a five-player deal they completed with the Cardinals in December 2003 that netted them outfielder J. D. Drew. Wainwright spent the next two years in the minor leagues, before finally being called up to St. Louis in late 2005. Although he appeared in only two games for the Cardinals in the final three weeks of the campaign, he became a regular member of the team's bullpen the following year. Serving primarily as setup man for closer Jason Isringhausen, Wainwright pitched effectively, striking out seventy-two batters in seventy-five innings of work, while surrendering sixty-four hits to the opposition; however, when a severe injury forced Isringhausen to undergo season-ending hip surgery in September, Cardinals manager Tony La Russa inserted Wainwright into the role of closer.

The twenty-five-year-old rookie did an outstanding job as Isringhausen's replacement, helping the Cardinals hold off a late charge by Houston to win the NL Central Division title by posting two crucial saves in the season's final week. He then excelled during the postseason, closing out all three series for the Cardinals as they won their first world championship in twenty-four years.

With ace right-hander Chris Carpenter lost for virtually all of the 2007 campaign due to elbow surgery, and with Wainwright possessing a varied arsenal of pitches that includes a sinkerball, cut fastball, and excellent curveball, the latter moved into the starting rotation, where he gradually developed into the team's most reliable starter, compiling a record of 14–12 and an ERA of 3.70. Despite suffering a finger injury the following season that sidelined him for two and a half months, Wainwright pitched even more effectively in 2008, finishing the year with a record of 11–3 and an ERA of 3.20.

The return of Carpenter and the further maturation of Wainwright gave the Cardinals a pair of staff aces in 2009. While Carpenter posted seventeen victories and a league-leading 2.24 ERA, Wainwright finished 19–8, to lead all NL hurlers in wins. He also topped the senior circuit with 34 starts and 233 innings pitched, placed among the leaders with 212 strikeouts and a 2.63 ERA, and won the

Gold Glove Award by leading all NL pitchers with 27 putouts and a perfect 1.000 fielding percentage. Wainwright's outstanding performance earned him a third-place finish in the Cy Young voting. He also finished fifteenth in the Most Valuable Player balloting. Wainwright followed that up in 2010 by going 20–11, with a 2.42 ERA and 213 strikeouts, en route to earning All-Star honors for the first time and a second-place finish to Philadelphia's Roy Halladay in the Cy Young voting.

Wainwright's status as an elite pitcher became somewhat tenuous when the Cardinals announced during the subsequent off-season that the twenty-nine-year-old right-hander needed Tommy John surgery on his right elbow that would force him to miss the entire 2011 campaign. Yet, after the Cardinals somehow managed to win the World Series without him, Wainwright returned to their starting rotation at the beginning of 2012. Although he perhaps lacked some of the velocity he once had on his fastball, Wainwright finished the season with fourteen wins and a respectable 3.94 ERA.

Returning to top form in 2013, Wainwright earned All-Star honors for the second time and a runner-up finish in the Cy Young voting by placing among the league leaders with 219 strikeouts and a 2.94 ERA, compiling a record of 19–9 that tied him with Washington's Jordan Zimmerman for the most wins in the league, and topping the circuit with five complete games, two shutouts, and 241-2/3 innings pitched. Wainwright's exceptional fielding also enabled him to win his second Gold Glove. He had another outstanding season in 2014, ranking among the NL leaders with a record of 20–9, an ERA of 2.38, 5 complete games, and 227 innings pitched, while tossing a league-leading three shutouts.

Heading into 2015, Wainwright has posted a record of 119–66 and an ERA of 3.01 in parts of nine seasons with the Cardinals. With 1,306 career strikeouts to his credit, he has struck out more batters than any other Cardinals pitcher, with the exception of Bob Gibson. Wainwright's career strikeouts-to-walks ratio of 3.383 is the second-best in Cardinals history, while his average of 7.624 strikeouts per nine innings pitched places him third in team annals. Since Wainwright will not turn 34 until well after the 2015 season gets underway, there is still ample time for him to move up several places in these rankings.

CARDINAL CAREER HIGHLIGHTS

Best Season

Wainwright pitched brilliantly for the Cardinals in 2009, when he led all NL hurlers with 19 wins and 233 innings pitched. He also finished fourth in the league with 212 strikeouts, a .704 winning percentage, and a 2.63 ERA. However, he proved to be equally effective in 2013, when, in addition to ranking among the league leaders with 219 strikeouts and a 2.94 ERA, he topped all NL pitchers with 19 wins, 241-2/3 innings pitched, five complete games, and two shutouts. Yet, it could be argued that Wainwright had his finest all-around season in 2014, when he finished 20–9, with 179 strikeouts and five complete games, led the league with three shutouts, and posted the best marks of his career with a 2.38 ERA and a WHIP (walks plus hits allowed per innings pitched) of 1.031.

Nevertheless, I ultimately settled on Wainwright's exceptional 2010 campaign. En route to earning a second-place finish in the NL Cy Young balloting, Wainwright finished second in the league in wins (20), ERA (2.42), complete games (5), and shutouts (2), placed third in innings pitched (230-1/3), and finished fourth in strikeouts (213). Meanwhile, Wainwright's WHIP of 1.051, which nearly equaled the career-low mark he posted four years later, placed him third in the league rankings.

Memorable Moments and Greatest Performances

Wainwright's first at bat with the Cardinals proved to be a memorable one, as, on May 24, 2006, he became just the twenty-second player in baseball history to hit a home run on the first pitch thrown to him in the major leagues. The blast also made Wainwright one of only three players to homer in his first at bat and then win the game as a pitcher.

However, as one might expect, Wainwright has experienced most of his greatest moments on the mound, most notably during the 2006 postseason. Pitching extraordinarily well for the Cardinals throughout that year's playoffs and World Series, Wainwright threw nine and two-thirds innings of scoreless relief, allowing the opposition only seven hits and striking out fifteen, en route to earning four saves.

After Wainwright picked up a save and tossed three and two-thirds scoreless innings against San Diego in the National League Division Series, he saved another two games against the Mets in the National League Championship Series, enabling his team to advance to the World Series by closing out a tension-filled Game 7. Catcher Yadier Molina broke a 1–1 tie in the top of the ninth inning of the decisive seventh contest with a two-run homer. Wainwright then took the mound in the bottom half of the frame and proceeded to load the bases with two men out, before striking out Carlos Beltran on a practically unhittable 0–2 curveball that left the Mets' slugger standing frozen in the batter's box. The victory gave the Cardinals their second pennant in three seasons. Although the Cardinals' subsequent five-game World Series triumph over the Detroit Tigers proved to be somewhat less dramatic, Wainwright closed out that series as well, recording the final out with a strikeout of Tigers third baseman Brandon Inge.

Notable Achievements

Has won 20 games twice.
Has won 19 games two other times.
Has compiled ERA below 3.00 four times.
Has struck out more than 200 batters three times.
Has thrown more than 200 innings five times.
Has led NL pitchers in: wins twice; innings pitched twice; shutouts twice; and complete games once.
Has led NL pitchers in putouts once and fielding percentage twice.
Ranks among Cardinals all-time leaders in: strikeouts (2nd); wins (8th); WHIP (9th); strikeouts-to-walks ratio (2nd); strikeouts per nine innings pitched (3rd); and games started (8th)
Has finished in top five in NL Cy Young voting four times, placing second twice.
Two-time Gold Glove winner (2009, 2013).
Three-time NL All-Star (2010, 2013, 2014).
Two-time NL champion (2006, 2013).
2006 world champion.

32

JOHN TUDOR

Although John Tudor spent less than five full seasons with the Cardinals, he clearly earned a spot in these rankings with his exceptional performance during the course of his relatively brief stay in St. Louis. In two tours of duty with the club, the crafty left-hander compiled an outstanding overall record of 62–26, along with a sparkling 2.52 ERA. After being acquired from the Pittsburgh Pirates at the conclusion of the 1984 campaign, Tudor rewarded the Cardinals by putting together a magnificent 1985 season, in which he helped lead them to the National League East title by going 21–8, with a 1.93 ERA and a league-leading ten shutouts. While Tudor never again reached such heights during his time in St. Louis, he remained an extremely effective starter, posting an ERA below 3.00 in three of his four other years with the Cardinals, while winning forty-one of his fifty-nine decisions. Yet, Cardinals fans likely never fully appreciated Tudor due to the inaccurate picture of him the media painted to the general public.

Born in Schenectady, New York, on February 2, 1954, John Thomas Tudor grew up in Massachusetts, spending his earliest years living in Lynn, before moving with his family to Peabody at the age of nine. After attending Georgia Southern University in Statesboro, Georgia, Tudor was selected by the Boston Red Sox in the third round of the 1976 amateur draft. He subsequently spent more than three years in the minor leagues, finally earning a call-up to the majors in August 1979. Tudor made six starts in the final few weeks of the season, compiling a rather unimpressive ERA of 6.43. After starting out the ensuing campaign at Triple-A, the left-hander joined the Red Sox for good later in the year, establishing himself as a regular member of the team's starting rotation by season's end by compiling a record of 8–5 and an ERA of 3.02. Although Tudor made only eighteen appearances and eleven starts during the course of the strike-shortened 1981 campaign, he assumed a more prominent role on Boston's staff the following year, posting a record of 13–10 and an ERA of 3.63. After Tudor won thirteen games for the Red Sox again in 1983, they elected to trade the twenty-nine-year-old left-hander to Pittsburgh for outfielder/designated hitter Mike Easler. He spent just one season in Pittsburgh, going 12–11 with a 3.27 ERA for the Pirates in 1984, before being dealt to the Cardinals for veteran outfielder George Hendrick at the end of the year.

Pitching for a contending team for the first time in his career very much agreed with Tudor, who took his game up a notch after he joined the Cardinals in 1985. The southpaw started off the season slowly, winning just one of his first eight decisions; however, he ended up turning his season around, doing so with the help of his high-school catcher, who noticed a flaw in the hurler's delivery while watching a Cardinals game on television. Heeding the advice of his former teammate, Tudor adjusted his pitching motion, after which he became practically unbeatable the rest of the year. Tudor posted a record of 20–1 and an ERA of 1.37 in his final twenty-six starts, helping the Cardinals edge out the New York Mets for the NL East title in the process. In addition to finishing the campaign 21–8, with a 1.93 ERA, he tossed a league-leading ten shutouts, making him the last major-league pitcher to shut out the opposition that many times in one season.

Tudor's outstanding control (he walked only forty-nine batters in 275 innings of work), exceptional ball movement, ability to hit the corners of the plate and change speeds, and superb changeup all contributed greatly to the tremendous success he experienced in 1985. Yet, Cardinals manager Whitey Herzog suggested, "His (Tudor's) real key is when he throws inside with his fastball. That's his 'out' pitch."[1] Herzog also marveled years later,

> He didn't want any right-handed batters turning on his curveball, so he had a unique strategy. He never showed 'em one. That's right; in five years with the Cardinals, John Tudor never threw his curveball to a right-handed batter. That's

2,000-some hitters, at least. If you don't play ball for a living, you might not understand how crazy that is.[2]

Meanwhile, Phillies slugger Mike Schmidt stated the following:

> What makes Tudor so tough is that, first you see the ball in his hand, then you lose it in his uniform. And his delivery is exactly the same on every pitch. I don't know how he can have such a perfect fastball delivery and throw the ball twenty-five miles an hour slower. How many times a game do you see a batter swing at what he thinks is a fastball away, only to be halfway into the swing and realize that it's a changeup that's not due to arrive for a few more minutes?[3]

Chuck Tanner, who managed Tudor in Pittsburgh, believed that the hurler's intelligence enabled him to succeed even though he lacked an overpowering fastball. Discussing Tudor's pitching style, Tanner noted, "Puts a little on, takes a little off, throws the fastball when you're expecting something different and it looks like it's ninety-five miles per hour. He's a very smart pitcher."[4]

Although Tudor eventually won over Cardinals fans with his brilliant performance, they probably never really got to know him. Intelligent, introspective, and extremely forthright, he developed a reputation among members of the media for being uncooperative and aloof, even though his teammates described him differently. As Joe Henderson writes in an article called "The Man and the Image," which appears in the August 1986 issue of *Baseball Digest*,

> He (Tudor) was also combative, curt, and bluntly honest; when he considered a question stupid, he said so. It is the age of ten-second sound bites and TC mini-cams, and much of what the professional athlete must deal with really is trivial and repetitive. But the unwritten rule is that you play along, smile for the camera, babble banalities, and go on. Not this guy.[5]

Uncomfortable being in the spotlight, Tudor found it particularly difficult dealing with the members of the press corps as he continued to struggle early in 1985, often responding to their questions by rolling his eyes or answering in a few short words. Refreshingly devoid of ego, he did not particularly enjoy talking about himself, preferring instead to discuss the accomplishments of others. After getting the better of New York's Dwight Gooden in a memorable pitching duel in late 1985, writers asked Tudor if he felt he deserved to win the Cy Young Award. The left-hander responded by saying, "How could anyone even think that I deserve to win the award over Gooden? All his stats are better than mine. I don't want to get into that kind of thing."[6]

On another occasion, Tudor refused to accept praise for his brilliant 1985 performance, stating, "I have to give credit to the awesome defense I have behind me. . . . This defense has been a godsend to me. I can't say enough about it. It's phenomenal."[7]

Tudor ended up finishing runner-up to Gooden in the Cy Young voting, and placing second in the league to the New York right-hander in several statistical categories as well, including wins (21), ERA (1.93), complete games (14), and innings pitched (275). Tudor continued to perform well for the Cardinals in the 1985 postseason, winning one of two decisions against the Dodgers in the National League Championship Series, before dominating the Royals in his first two starts in the World Series. However, the season's workload finally caught up with him in Game 7 of the Fall Classic, one in which he lasted into only the third inning. Cardinals pitching coach Mike Roarke later recalled, "He'd try to throw pitches right down the middle, and they'd be a foot out of the strike zone. When that happens to a pitcher with perfect control, you know the arm just gave out."[8] Tudor subsequently displayed his anger over his poor performance by punching a rotating fan in the clubhouse, severely cutting his hand in the process.

Noted baseball columnist Peter Gammons later wrote, "The day before the game, Tudor had said, 'I know I'll pay the price forever. But I also may only be here once in my life. It's worth whatever price I have to pay.'"[9]

Tudor did indeed pay a steep price. Although he remained a good pitcher for the Cardinals in subsequent seasons, he managed to throw more than 200 innings just once more. After compiling a record of 13–7 and an ERA of 2.92 in 219 innings of work during the first five months of the 1986 campaign, Tudor sat out the final three weeks of the season with shoulder stiffness. He underwent surgery during the off-season to rectify the problem but ended up missing more than half of the ensuing campaign when New York Mets catcher Barry Lyons broke his leg when the receiver fell into the St. Louis dugout chasing a foul pop. Making only sixteen starts for the Cardinals throughout the course of the season, Tudor finished the year 10–2, with a 3.84 ERA.

After starting 1988 on the disabled list with an aching knee and a bothersome shoulder, Tudor compiled a record of 6–5 and an ERA of 2.29 in twenty-one starts with the Cardinals. In desperate need of a power hitter, St. Louis traded him to Los Angeles in mid-August for slugger Pedro Guerrero. An ailing elbow prevented Tudor from making more than twelve starts for the Dodgers through the end of 1989, after which he returned to the Cardinals as a free agent. The left-hander spent one more year in St. Louis, posting a record of 12–4 and an ERA of 2.40, before announcing his retirement at season's end. Tudor ended his career with a record of 117–72 and an ERA of 3.12. In addition to going 62–26 and compiling a 2.52 ERA with the Cardinals, he threw twenty-two complete games and tossed twelve shutouts. His 2.52 ERA represents the lowest mark posted by any Cardinals pitcher since the Deadball Era. Meanwhile, his .705 winning percentage is the third best in franchise history.

After retiring, Tudor returned to Massachusetts, where he continued living in the same simple and unpretentious manner he did throughout his playing career. He returned to baseball briefly, serving as a minor-league pitching instructor, first for the Cardinals, then for the Phillies, and finally for the Rangers, before leaving the game for good at the end of 1996.

Years later, Whitey Herzog noted the following:

> Nobody ever did more with less than my favorite cranky Yankee, John Tudor. John won me sixty-four ballgames and only lost twenty-seven (actually, 62–26) between 1985 and 1990, a record that still leaves me shaking my head, considering the stuff he had. Well, when you can't crack eighty-five on the radar gun, maybe a foul mood and a chip on your shoulder are just the right ticket. They sure didn't hurt John.[10]

CARDINAL CAREER HIGHLIGHTS

Best Season

Was there ever really any question? Tudor's 1985 campaign not only ranks as easily the finest of his career, but also one of the best ever turned in by a Cardinals pitcher. After starting off the season with a record of 1–7 and an ERA of 3.74 through May, Tudor won twenty of his final twenty-one decisions, compiling an ERA of 1.37 during that stretch. The left-hander concluded the campaign with a record of 21–8, 14 complete games, 275 innings pitched, 169 strikeouts, a spectacular 1.93 ERA, and a league-leading 10 shutouts and 0.938 WHIP (walks plus hits allowed per innings pitched). Tudor's ten shutouts tie him with Mort Cooper for the second-highest single-season total in Cardinals history (Bob Gibson registered thirteen shutouts in 1968). Tudor finished second in the league in wins, ERA, complete games, and innings pitched, with only Dwight Gooden's magnificent performance for New York preventing him from earning NL Cy Young honors.

Memorable Moments and Greatest Performances

Tudor threw a number of brilliant games during the course of the 1985 season, with his August 8 effort against Chicago ranking among his very best. The left-hander shut out the Cubs, 8–0, on just one hit, allowing only a fifth-inning single to Leon Durham.

A little more than a month later, on September 11, Tudor engaged in a memorable pitcher's duel with New York's Dwight Gooden, outdueling the eventual Cy Young Award winner by surrendering just three hits in ten innings, in recording a 1–0 victory that moved the Cardinals back into a first-place tie with New York in the NL East. Cesar Cedeno delivered the game's only run with a tenth-inning homer off reliever Jesse Orosco. The shutout was Tudor's third in succession.

Just a little more than two weeks later, on September 26, Tudor threw a four-hit shutout against Philadelphia, defeating the Phillies by a score of 5–0. The victory was Tudor's twentieth of the year, with his tenth shutout representing the most by a left-hander in the major leagues since Sandy Koufax tossed ten for the Dodgers in 1963.

Tudor again found himself involved in a pitcher's duel with a member of New York's pitching staff on October 1, battling Ron Darling in the opener of a three-game showdown between the two clubs for first place. Each hurler threw ten scoreless innings, before Darryl Strawberry hit a game-winning homer off St. Louis reliever Ken Dayley in the eleventh. New York's 1–0 win moved the Mets to within two games of the Cardinals in the NL East. St. Louis ended up winning the division, however, edging out New York by three games in the final standings. The Cardinals clinched first place four days later, when Tudor surrendered just four hits to Chicago in defeating the Cubs by a score of 7–1.

Although the Cardinals subsequently lost the World Series to Kansas City in seven games, Tudor pitched exceptionally well in his first two starts. After defeating the Royals by a score of 3–1 in the opening contest, he gave the Cardinals a commanding three-games-to-one lead in the Fall Classic by tossing a 3–0, five-hit shutout in Game 4. Unfortunately, Tudor didn't fare nearly as well in his final start, allowing the Royals five runs in just a little more than two innings of work in Game 7, after a blown call by the first-base umpire in the ninth inning of Game 6 led to a come-from-behind 2–1 win by Kansas City.

Notable Achievements

- Surpassed twenty victories once (twenty-one in 1985).
- Compiled ERA below 3.00 four times, finishing with a mark below 2.00 once (1.93 in 1985).
- Threw more than 250 innings once (275 in 1985).
- Threw ten shutouts once (1985).
- Led NL pitchers with ten shutouts in 1985.
- Ranks among Cardinals all-time leaders in ERA (second) and winning percentage (third).
- Finished second in 1985 NL Cy Young voting.
- 1990 NL Comeback Player of the Year.
- 1985 *Sporting News* All-Star selection.
- Two-time NL champion (1985, 1987).

NOTES

1. Whitey Herzog, quoted in Rory Costello, "John Tudor," *Society for American Baseball Research*, www.sabr.org/bioproj/person/b7e0addd (accessed October 19, 2012).

2. Herzog, quoted in Costello, "John Tudor," www.sabr.org/bioproj/person/b7e0addd.

3. Mike Schmidt, quoted in Costello, "John Tudor," www.sabr.org/bioproj/person/b7e0addd.

4. Chuck Tanner, quoted in Costello, "John Tudor," www.sabr.org/bioproj/person/b7e0addd.

5. Joe Henderson, quoted in "John Tudor Stats," *Baseball Almanac*, www.baseball-almanac.com/players/player.php?p=tudorjo01 (accessed October 19, 2012).

6. John Tudor, quoted in Costello, "John Tudor," www.sabr.org/bioproj/person/b7e0addd.

7. Tudor, quoted in Costello, "John Tudor," www.sabr.org/bioproj/person/b7e0addd.

8. Mike Roarke, quoted in Costello, "John Tudor," www.sabr.org/bioproj/person/b7e0addd.

9. Peter Gammons, quoted in Costello, "John Tudor," www.sabr.org/bioproj/person/b7e0addd.

10. Herzog, quoted in Costello, "John Tudor," www.sabr.org/bioproj/person/b7e0addd.

33

RAY LANKFORD

A solid outfielder, productive hitter, and excellent base stealer, Ray Lankford spent parts of thirteen seasons in St. Louis, establishing himself during that time as one of the most complete players ever to don a Cardinals uniform. Lankford's combination of speed and power enabled him to surpass twenty home runs and twenty stolen bases in the same season five times for the Cardinals, making him the only player in franchise history to accomplish the feat more than once. His offensive versatility also afforded him the opportunity to assume both the leadoff and cleanup spots in the St. Louis batting order at different times during his career. Meanwhile, Lankford's speed and range made him an outstanding ball hawk who led all National League outfielders with 438 putouts in 1992. An extremely loyal individual as well, Lankford invariably chose to remain a Cardinal at contract negotiation time, even though his varied skillset likely would have allowed him to earn more money elsewhere.

Born in Modesto, California, on June 5, 1967, Raymond Lewis Lankford attended Grace Davis High School in Modesto, where he starred in both football and baseball. After continuing his athletic career for two years at Modesto Junior College, Lankford signed with the Cardinals when they selected him in the third round of the 1987 amateur draft. He spent the next three years in the minors, earning 1989 Texas League Most Valuable Player honors by hitting 11 home runs, driving in 89 runs, batting .317, and stealing 38 bases for the Arkansas Travelers.

Lankford's outstanding performance at the minor-league level caught the attention of the Cardinals, who finally promoted him to the big club in August 1990. Taking over in center field for the departed Willie McGee, Lankford batted .286 and stole eight bases in the final six weeks of the campaign. The twenty-three-year-old outfielder assumed a prominent role in the St. Louis offense the following year, when, serving as leadoff hitter much of the time, he finished the season with 9 homers, 69 RBIs, 83 runs scored, a .251 batting average, 44 stolen bases, and a league-leading 15 triples, en route to earning a third-place finish in the NL Rookie of the Year voting. Lankford followed that up by batting .293, scoring 87 runs, stealing 42 bases, and establishing career highs with 175 hits and 40 doubles in 1992. By also hitting twenty home runs and driving in eighty-six runs, he evolved into more of a power threat, prompting the Cardinals to move him down a few notches in the batting order.

After posting slightly subpar numbers in each of the next two seasons, Lankford began an outstanding four-year run in 1995 in which he surpassed 20 home runs, 80 RBIs, 80 runs scored, 30 doubles, and 20 stolen bases each season. He also never batted any lower than .275 in any of those years. Lankford established a new record for Cardinals center fielders in 1995 by hitting twenty-five home runs, nearly equaling the club record by homering in four straight games at one point during the season. He followed that up by scoring a career-high 100 runs in 1996, even though he severely injured his shoulder in September while making a diving catch in the outfield. Subsequently forced to sit out several postseason contests, Lankford later told the *Sporting News*, "That was the part that really hurt. You're there cheering for your team, but you can't be a part of it physically. You can't go out there and produce, and be a part of the glory on the field."[1]

Although Lankford began the 1997 season on the disabled list while recovering from surgery to repair his injured shoulder, he ended up coming back stronger than ever, earning the only All-Star selection of his career by hitting 31 home runs, driving in 98 runs, scoring 94 others, stealing 21 bases, and batting .295. Named to start the annual Midsummer Classic for the senior circuit, Lankford drew praise from NL manager Bobby Cox, who told the *St. Louis Post-Dispatch*, "He's a great center fielder. I know he's hurt, but he's having a great year with the bat, he can steal bases, and he can go get the ball. When Joe Torre was managing St. Louis, he said Ray Lankford could be a MVP, and he's getting close to that now."[2]

Having signed a five-year contract extension worth $34 million during the subsequent off-season, Lankford professed his love for the Cardinals and their fans, telling the *Evansville Courier and Press*, "A lot of guys go other places. But I don't think I could play for a better organization, for a better crowd. Why leave?"[3]

Lankford had another outstanding year in 1998, when, serving as the primary protection in the Cardinals' batting order for Mark McGwire as the slugging first baseman continued his pursuit of the all-time single-season home run record, he hit 31 homers, knocked in a career-high 105 runs, scored 94 others, stole 26 bases, and batted .293. Lankford's thirty-one long balls made him just the third Cardinals player to reach the thirty-homer plateau more than once, enabling him to join Stan Musial and Rogers Hornsby in an extremely exclusive club (Musial accomplished the feat six times, while Hornsby did it twice).

Lankford's aching knees forced him to have surgery at the conclusion of the 1998 campaign, prompting the Cardinals to move him to left field. Appearing in only 122 games in 1999, Lankford hit just fifteen homers and drove in only sixty-three runs, although he also batted a career-high .306. He spent one more full season in St. Louis, hitting 26 home runs, knocking in 65 runs, and batting .253 for the Cardinals in 2000, before being dealt to San Diego in August 2001. Lankford remained with the Padres through the end of 2002, seeing his playing time and offensive production severely limited by injuries. After taking off all of 2003 to give his body time to heal, Lankford returned to St. Louis as a free agent in 2004. He spent the final year of his career there, announcing his retirement at the conclusion of the 2004 campaign. He ended his career with 238 home runs, 874 RBIs, 968 runs scored, 1,561 hits, 356 doubles, 258 stolen bases, a .272 batting average, a .364 on-base percentage, and a .477 slugging percentage. Lankford's Cardinals numbers include 228 homers, 829 RBIs, 928 runs scored, 1,479 hits, 339 doubles, 250 stolen bases, a .273 batting average, a .365 on-base percentage, and a .481 slugging percentage. He ranks among the team's all-time leaders in eight different offensive categories, including home runs (fifth), RBIs (ninth), runs scored (ninth), and stolen bases (eighth). Lankford hit more home runs at Busch Stadium (123) than any other player.

CARDINAL CAREER HIGHLIGHTS

Best Season

An extremely consistent player through the years, Lankford had many solid seasons for the Cardinals; however, the 1997 and 1998 campaigns would have to be considered the finest of his career. Lankford hit 31 homers in the first of those years, drove in 98 runs, scored 94 others, stole 21 bases, batted .295, and compiled the highest on-base and slugging percentages of his career, with marks of .411 and .585, respectively. He posted comparable numbers in most offensive categories the following year, when he again hit 31 home runs, scored 94 times, knocked in 105 runs, stole 26 bases, batted .293, and compiled on-base and slugging percentages of .391 and .540, respectively. Lankford's 1997 on-base plus slugging percentage of .996 would seem to suggest that he produced at a slightly higher rate than he did in the ensuing campaign, when he posted a mark of .932, but injuries limited him to only 133 games in 1997. Meanwhile, Lankford appeared in 154 contests in 1998, enabling him to accumulate more RBIs, total bases, hits, and stolen bases, en route to establishing career highs in the first two categories. His outstanding performance that year also allowed him to provide reasonable protection in the St. Louis batting order for Mark McGwire, as the latter moved inexorably toward shattering the existing single-season home run record. All things considered, Lankford had his best year for the Cardinals in 1998.

Memorable Moments and Greatest Performances

Lankford had one of his greatest days at the plate for the Cardinals as a rookie, hitting for the cycle in a 7–2 win over the Mets on September 15, 1991. He put on a power display in Cincinnati six years later, hitting two upper-deck homers during a 7–4 Cardinals win over the Reds on July 15, 1997. Lankford's two upper-deck blasts represented a first for Cinergy Field. Lankford also homered in four straight games in 1995, nearly equaling the club record of five.

Lankford hit one of the most satisfying home runs of his career in a May 1999 game against the Dodgers. After Los Angeles intentionally walked Mark McGwire in the bottom of the ninth inning, Lankford delivered a game-winning, two-run homer for the Cardinals—his second round-tripper of the contest. He later told the *St. Louis Post-Dispatch*, "I've gotten used to seeing him (McGwire) walked in front of me. It's still motivation. I want to go out there and earn some respect."[4]

Lankford hit an even more memorable home run for the Cardinals in his second tour of duty with the club, hitting a pinch homer at Busch Stadium in his final major-league at bat on October 3, 2004.

Notable Achievements

Hit more than twenty home runs six times, surpassing thirty homers twice.
Knocked in more than 100 runs once (105 in 1998).
Scored more than 100 runs once (100 in 1996).
Batted over .300 once (.306 in 1999).
Finished in double digits in triples once (15 in 1991).
Topped forty doubles once (forty in 1992).
Compiled on-base percentage in excess of .400 once (.411 in 1997).
Posted slugging percentage in excess of .500 four times.
Stole more than twenty bases six times, topping forty steals twice.
Led NL with fifteen triples in 1991.
Led NL outfielders in putouts and fielding percentage once each.
Ranks among Cardinals all-time leaders in home runs (fifth), RBIs (ninth), runs scored (ninth), doubles (ninth), total bases (tenth), stolen bases (eighth), walks (fifth), and games played (tenth).
1997 NL All-Star.

NOTES

1. Ray Lankford, quoted in "Ray Lankford," *Answers*, www.answers.com/topic/ray-lankford (accessed October 22, 2012).
2. Bobby Cox, quoted in "Ray Lankford," www.answers.com/topic/ray-lankford.
3. Lankford, quoted in "Ray Lankford," www.answers.com/topic/ray-lankford.
4. Lankford, quoted in "Ray Lankford," www.answers.com/topic/ray-lankford.

34

PEPPER MARTIN

Nicknamed "The Wild Horse of the Osage" for the reckless abandon with which he played the game, Pepper Martin came to symbolize more than any other player the aggressive style of play employed by the Cardinals' "Gas House Gang" of the 1930s. Whether making a headfirst slide on the base paths, diving after a ball in the field, or swearing at opposing players from the bench, Martin displayed tremendous passion on the ball field, approaching each contest as if it were the seventh game of the World Series. Described in *The National League Story* by author and baseball historian Lee Allen as a "chunky, unshaven hobo who ran the bases like a berserk locomotive, slept in the raw, and swore at pitchers in his sleep,"[1] Martin wore a perpetually dirty uniform that revealed the lack of restraint he displayed on the field. A pretty fair player as well, he helped the Cardinals capture four pennants and three world championships during the course of his career, which he spent entirely in St. Louis.

Particularly dominant in the 1931 World Series, Martin led the Cardinals to victory over a powerful Philadelphia Athletics team that featured future Hall of Famers Jimmie Foxx, Al Simmons, Lefty Grove, and Mickey Cochrane. He also performed extremely well in the Fall Classic three years later, when his team defeated the Detroit Tigers in seven games. Martin accomplished all he did even though he failed to become a regular member of the St. Louis starting lineup until after he celebrated his twenty-seventh birthday.

Born in Temple, Oklahoma, on February 29, 1904, Johnny Leonard Roosevelt Martin followed a long and arduous road to the major leagues. After spending most of his youth in Oklahoma City, Martin began his professional playing career at the age of nineteen, when he signed to play shortstop for a team in the Oklahoma State League. When the league folded in 1924, he spent the next few seasons playing in the East Texas League, before the Cardinals signed him in 1927 and assigned him to their affiliate in Houston. Finally, after five long years in the minor leagues, Martin made his debut with the Cardinals on April 16, 1928, at the age of twenty-four. Serving the eventual National League champions primarily as a backup outfielder and pinch runner, Martin appeared in thirty-nine games during the season, hitting .308 in only thirteen official at bats. Returned to the minor leagues at the end of the year, he spent virtually all of the next two seasons there, before returning to the Cardinals for good at the beginning of the 1931 campaign.

Initially considered to be a fourth outfielder at the start of the year, Martin eventually claimed the starting center-field job by batting .300, driving in 75 runs, and placing third in the league with 16 stolen bases for a Cardinals team that finished first in the senior circuit, a full 13 games ahead of the runner-up New York Giants. Although the Cardinals posted 101 victories themselves during the regular season, most people gave them little chance of defeating in the World Series a Philadelphia Athletics team that concluded the campaign with a record of 107–45. But the A's, who beat the Cardinals in six games in the previous year's Fall Classic, found themselves unable to contend with Martin, who proved to be a one-man wrecking crew. In addition to compiling a batting average of .500 during the Cardinals' seven-game victory, Martin knocked in 5 runs, scored 5 others, and stole 5 bases. The outfielder's tremendous all-around performance made him wildly popular with baseball fans everywhere, prompting baseball commissioner Kenesaw Mountain Landis to remark to him at the end of the Series, "I wish I could change places with you."[2] Meanwhile, A's catcher Mickey Cochrane, who Martin victimized with his thievery on the base paths, told the star of the Fall Classic, "Well, kid, you are sitting on top of the world now, and you deserve it."[3]

After establishing himself as a household name with his extraordinary performance in the World Series, Martin suffered through an injury-plagued 1932 campaign that saw him miss a significant amount of playing time with a dislocated shoulder and broken finger. Appearing in only 85 games throughout the course of the season, he batted just .238, scored only 47 runs, and stole just 9 bases.

Shifted to third base prior to the start of the 1933 season, Martin proved to be anything but a natural at the hot corner. Often fielding balls after having stopped them with his chest, he finished second among NL third sackers with twenty-five errors; however, he returned to top form at the plate. He batted a career-high .316; finished among the league leaders with 189 hits, 36 doubles, and 12 triples; and topped the circuit with 122 runs scored and 26 stolen bases. This was en route to earning a fifth-place finish in the Most Valuable Player voting and the starting assignment at third base for the NL in the inaugural All-Star Game.

Playing under new Cardinals player-manager Frankie Frisch very much agreed with Martin, who brought with him to the field the same intense attitude his skipper carried with him throughout his career. In addition to always hustling and playing the game aggressively, Martin exhibited disdain for his opponent, often throwing at batters who bunted in lopsided games, instead of throwing them out at first base. Emerging as one of Frisch's favorites, Martin eventually became captain of the team, assuming that role from Leo Durocher after the Cardinals traded the shortstop prior to the start of the 1939 campaign.

Although injuries limited Martin to 110 games in 1934, he once again posted solid numbers, concluding the season with a .289 batting average, 76 runs scored, 11 triples, and a league-leading 23 stolen bases. He subsequently helped lead the Cardinals to victory in the World Series for the second time in four years by batting .355, driving in 4 runs, scoring 8 others, and stealing 2 bases against Detroit.

Martin followed that up with two of his finest seasons, posting batting averages of .299 and .309 in 1935 and 1936, respectively, while scoring 121 runs each year. He also led the league with twenty-three steals in 1936, a season in which he returned to the outfield for the first time in four years.

Despite playing well for the Cardinals in each of the next four seasons, Martin found himself relegated to a part-time role by the toll his aggressive style of play took on his body, along with the emergence of young outfield stars Enos Slaughter and Terry Moore. Appearing in fewer than 100 games each year from 1937 to 1940, Martin batted over

.300 three more times, before the Cardinals named him player-manager of their Sacramento affiliate in the Pacific Coast League prior to the start of the 1941 campaign. He spent the next three seasons serving in that capacity, before a shortage of players at the major-league level during World War II prompted him to make a brief comeback with the Cardinals in 1944. After batting .279 in forty games with the pennant-winning Cardinals that year, Martin retired as an active player for good. He left the game with career totals of 59 home runs, 501 RBIs, 756 runs scored, 1,227 hits, 146 stolen bases, a .298 batting average, a .358 on-base percentage, and a .443 slugging percentage.

Upon his retirement, the forty-one-year-old Martin returned to the minor leagues, where he spent the next ten years managing several different teams. Displaying the same passion for the game he had as a player, Martin often exhibited his fiery temperament, once punching one of his players for not performing up to his standards. On another occasion, he found himself fined and suspended for the remainder of the season for choking an umpire.

After serving briefly as a coach with the Chicago Cubs, Martin resumed his minor-league managerial career in 1957, taking his final field assignment as the manager of the Miami Marlins in 1959. He subsequently served for a short period of time as the athletic director of the Oklahoma State Penitentiary at McAlester, Oklahoma. He passed away on March 5, 1965, at the age of sixty-one, after suffering a heart attack.

CAREER HIGHLIGHTS

Best Season

Although Martin earned his only *Sporting News* All-Star selection in 1935, he actually performed somewhat better in both 1933 and 1936. Certainly, the .299 batting average, 121 runs scored, and 41 doubles he compiled in 1935 were nothing to scoff at, but he posted better overall numbers the following season, when he established career highs with 11 homers and 76 RBIs, scored 121 times, batted .309, led the league with 23 stolen bases, and compiled an on-base plus slugging percentage (OPS) of .842, which exceeded his previous year's mark by 53 percentage points. Martin posted extremely comparable numbers in

1933, when he topped the senior circuit with 122 runs scored and 26 steals, while also establishing career highs with 189 hits, a .316 batting average, and an OPS of .843. I ultimately decided to go with Martin's 1933 campaign, since he led the league in two offensive categories, posted his highest marks in seven different departments, and earned his only top-five finish in the NL MVP voting.

Memorable Moments and Greatest Performances

Martin had arguably his greatest day at the plate on May 5, 1933, when he hit for the cycle and scored four of the Cardinals' five runs during a 5–3 victory over the Phillies in Philadelphia; however, he will always be remembered most for his extraordinary performance in the 1931 World Series. Facing a powerful Philadelphia Athletics team that captured each of the two previous world championships, Martin led the Cardinals to a seven-game upset win by excelling at the plate and on the base paths. After collecting three hits against Hall of Fame pitcher Lefty Grove during a losing effort in the opening contest, Martin stole two bases and tallied the only two runs scored by either team in Game 2. With the Series tied at two games apiece, he won Game 5 almost singlehandedly, collecting 3 hits, homering once, and driving in 4 runs, in leading the Cardinals to a 5–1 victory. After Philadelphia evened the Fall Classic by taking Game 6, Martin protected a 4–2 St. Louis lead in the ninth inning of the Series finale by making a game-saving catch with two men out and the tying runs on base.

Martin concluded the Series with twelve hits in twenty-four official at bats, for a batting average of .500. He homered once, doubled 4 times, knocked in 5 runs, scored 5 others, stole 5 bases, and compiled on-base and slugging percentages of .538 and .792, respectively. Long-time New York Giants manager John McGraw described Martin's effort as the "greatest individual performance in the history of the World Series."[4]

Notable Achievements

Scored more than 100 runs three times.
Batted over .300 seven times.

Finished in double digits in triples three times.
Surpassed forty doubles once (forty-one in 1935).
Topped twenty stolen bases four times.
Led NL in stolen bases three times and runs scored once.
Ranks among Cardinals all-time leaders in triples (ninth).
1935 *Sporting News* All-Star selection.
Four-time NL All-Star (1933, 1934, 1935, 1937).
Four-time NL champion (1930, 1931, 1934, 1944).
Three-time world champion (1931, 1934, 1944).

NOTES

1. Lee Allen, quoted in "Pepper Martin Stats," *Baseball Almanac*, www.baseball-almanac.com/players/player.php?p=martipe01 (accessed October 24, 2012).
2. Kenesaw Mountain Landis, quoted in "Johnny Leonard Roosevelt 'Pepper' Martin," *Find a Grave*, www.findagrave.com/cgi-bin/fg.cgi?page=gr&GRid=9769 (accessed October 24, 2012).
3. Mickey Cochrane, quoted in "Frankie Frisch," *Baseball-Reference*, www.baseball-reference.com/bullpen/Pepper_Martin (accessed October 24, 2012).
4. John McGraw, quoted in "Johnny Leonard Roosevelt 'Pepper' Martin," *Find a Grave*, www.findagrave.com/cgi-bin/fg.cgi?page=gr&GRid=9769 (accessed October 24, 2012).

35

SCOTT ROLEN

By the time he joined the Cardinals in 2002, Scott Rolen had already established himself as arguably the National League's finest all-around third baseman. A productive middle-of-the-order hitter with outstanding home-run power, Rolen surpassed twenty homers five times and 100 RBIs twice in his five full seasons in Philadelphia, before requesting a trade to another team when the Phillies seemed unwilling to meet his contract demands. An exceptional fielder as well, Rolen won multiple Gold Gloves during his time in Philadelphia, developing a reputation as the senior circuit's top defensive player at his position. The powerfully built third sacker continued to add to his list of accomplishments after he arrived in St. Louis, posting three of his finest offensive seasons and winning four more Gold Gloves as a member of the Cardinals from 2002 to 2007. Along the way, Rolen helped lead the Redbirds to two pennants and one world championship.

Born in Evansville, Indiana, on April 4, 1975, Scott Bruce Rolen attended Indiana's Jasper High School, where he starred in both baseball and basketball. Although he subsequently received numerous scholarship offers to play basketball in college, Rolen elected to pursue a career in baseball when the Philadelphia Phillies selected him in the second round of the 1993 amateur draft. Advancing rapidly through the Phillies' farm system, Rolen arrived in Philadelphia in August 1996, batting .254, hitting 4 home runs, and driving in 18 runs in the final two months of the campaign. After winning the team's starting third base job in spring training the following year, Rolen went on to capture NL Rookie of the Year honors by hitting 21 homers, knocking in 92 runs, scoring 93 others, and batting .283.

Rolen had his best year in Philadelphia in 1998, when he batted .290, hit 31 home runs, drove in 110 runs, scored 120 others, collected 45 doubles, and led all NL third basemen in putouts for the second straight time, en route to winning his first Gold Glove. He followed that up with three more solid seasons, before growing concerns over Philadelphia's continued lack of success and the team's unwillingness to meet his salary demands prompted him to request a trade to another team. With Rolen having informed the Phillies that he had no intention of resigning with them when his contract expired at the conclusion of the 2002 campaign, Philadelphia dealt him to the Cardinals for three players on July 29 of that year. Rolen played well for the Cardinals during the season's final two months, helping them capture the Central Division title by hitting fourteen homers and driving in forty-four runs in his fifty-five games with the club. Throughout the course of the entire season, he ended up hitting 31 home runs, knocking in 110 runs, and batting .266, en route to earning All-Star honors for the first time in his career. He also claimed his fourth Gold Glove.

After receiving an eight-year, $90 million deal from the Cardinals during the subsequent off-season, Rolen established himself as one of the team's leaders in 2003. Joining fellow sluggers Albert Pujols and Jim Edmonds in the middle of the St. Louis batting order, Rolen hit 28 homers, drove in 104 runs, scored 98 others, batted .286, and finished second in the league with 49 doubles. Rolen helped lead the Cardinals to their second NL Central Division title in three years the following season, when he earned a fourth-place finish in the league Most Valuable Player voting by hitting 34 home runs, knocking in 124 runs, scoring 109 times, batting .314, compiling an on-base percentage of .409, and posting a slugging percentage of .598. The third baseman's numbers would have been even more impressive had he not missed most of the final three weeks of the season with an injury. Yet, he returned in time for the playoffs, helping the Cardinals advance to the World Series by driving in six runs and hitting three home runs, including the game-winning blast in Game 7, against Houston in the National League Championship Series.

As he grew increasingly comfortable in the city of St. Louis, Rolen put on display for all to see his wide array of skills that made him one of the senior circuit's best all-around players. At six feet, four inches tall and 245 pounds, he had good size, outstanding power at the plate, and a powerful throwing arm; he also had excellent quickness in the field and surprising speed on the base paths.

Speaking of his former teammate, current Cardinals manager Mike Matheny proclaimed, "He's as well-rounded a player as I've ever seen."[1] Former Phillies manager Larry Bowa stated, "He (Rolen) does a lot of things that other guys don't. He gets from first to third. He hustles every time he hits the ball. He probably saves 75 to 100 runs a year."[2]

Former Cardinals manager Tony La Russa, who often butted heads with Rolen during his time in St. Louis, suggested, "He's as good as anyone who ever played the position."[3] Shortstop Edgar Renteria, who shared the left side of the Cardinals infield with Rolen for three seasons, said, "He could cover third base AND shortstop."[4]

Jim Edmonds, a pretty fair defender himself in his day, once marveled at his teammate's defensive prowess, stating, "There have been times where he'll make one of those great plays and I'll just be standing there staring. Then I'll see the other guys running off the field because there are three outs."[5] Former teammate Jason Isringhausen stated simply, "When Mike Schmidt says you're the best third baseman he's ever seen, that's pretty good."[6]

Rolen also drew praise for the manner with which he carried himself on the field. Former teammate Matt Clement once noted, "You respect him because he plays the game the right way."[7] Meanwhile, former All-Star Dick Allen, who got to know Rolen during the latter's seven-year stay in Philadelphia, suggested, "He's not caught up in individual stuff. He's a team guy, and that's what baseball is all about."[8]

Unfortunately, Rolen found himself unable to contribute much to the team in 2005, after he injured his shoulder in a collision with Dodgers first baseman Hee-Seop Choe early in the year. He subsequently underwent two different surgeries to repair a torn labrum, limiting him to a total of only fifty-six games. Rolen finished the year with just 5 homers, 8 RBIs, and a .235 batting average. Although he continued to experience problems with the shoulder the following year, he ended up appearing in 142 games for the Cardinals, helping them capture their third consecutive Central Division title by hitting 22 home runs, driving in 95 runs, scoring 94 others, and batting .296.

After struggling at the plate during the first two rounds of the playoffs, Rolen contributed mightily to the Cardinals' five-game World Series triumph over the Detroit Tigers by batting .421, with a homer and two RBIs.

Recurring shoulder problems forced Rolen to undergo a third surgery in late 2007, bringing his season to a premature end after he hit only eight homers and knocked in just fifty-eight runs during the first five months of the campaign. Concerns over his health, combined with a series of arguments he engaged in with St. Louis manager Tony La Russa, prompted the Cardinals to part ways with the All-Star third baseman prior to the start of the 2008 season. Traded to the Toronto Blue Jays for fellow oft-injured slugger Troy Glaus, Rolen ended up missing the first month of the season after he broke his right middle finger during fielding drills at spring training. After he experienced a precipitous drop-off in offensive production in his year and a half in Toronto, the Blue Jays traded him to the Reds for three players just prior to the July 2009 trade deadline. Rolen has since spent three and a half injury-marred years in Cincinnati, experiencing his greatest success in 2010, when he hit 20 homers, knocked in 83 runs, batted .285, earned his sixth All-Star selection, and won his eighth Gold Glove. He concluded the 2012 campaign with 316 career home runs, 1,287 RBIs, 1,211 runs scored, 2,077 hits, 517 doubles, a .281 batting average, a .364 on-base percentage, and a .490 slugging percentage. In parts of six seasons in St. Louis, Rolen hit 111 homers, drove in 453 runs, scored 421 others, collected 678 hits and 173 doubles, batted .286, compiled a .370 on-base percentage, and posted a .510 slugging percentage.

CARDINAL CAREER HIGHLIGHTS

Best Season

Rolen had a big first season with the Cardinals in 2003, hitting 28 home runs, driving in 104 runs, scoring 98 others, batting .286, and finishing second in the NL with a career-high 49 doubles. He also performed extremely well in 2006, hitting 22 homers, knocking in 95 runs, scoring 94 times, batting .296, and amassing 48 doubles.

Nevertheless, there can be no doubting that Rolen had his best year for the Cardinals in 2004, when he helped lead them to the pennant by scoring 109 runs and establishing career highs with 34 home runs, 124 RBIs, a .314 batting average, a .409 on-base percentage, and a .598 slugging percentage. He also won the sixth Gold Glove of his career, en route to earning a fourth-place finish in the NL MVP voting.

Memorable Moments and Greatest Performances

Rolen had perhaps his best day at the plate as a member of the Cardinals on September 15, 2006, when he keyed a 14–4 victory over the San Francisco Giants with a double, 2 home runs, and 7 RBIs. Rolen also came up big against the Detroit Tigers in the 2006 World Series, collecting 8 hits in 19 official at bats, for a .421 batting average, with a homer, 3 doubles, 2 RBIs, and 5 runs scored.

Yet, even though the Cardinals ended up being swept by the Boston Red Sox in the 2004 World Series, Rolen got his most important hit as a member of the team in the decisive seventh game of that year's NLCS. After homering twice in Game 2, Rolen stepped to the plate to face Roger Clemens in the bottom of the sixth inning of Game 7, with Albert Pujols on at second base and Houston clinging to a 2–1 lead. Rolen subsequently deposited a Clemens offering over the outfield wall, giving the Cardinals a 3–2 lead. St. Louis scored twice more, while Houston failed to cross the plate again, giving the Cardinals a berth in the World Series with a 5–2 win. Rolen concluded the NLCS with 3 home runs, 6 RBIs, 6 runs scored, and a .310 batting average.

Notable Achievements

Hit more than twenty home runs three times, topping thirty homers once.
Knocked in more than 100 runs twice.
Scored more than 100 runs once (109 in 2004).
Batted over .300 once (.314 in 2004).
Surpassed forty doubles twice.
Compiled on-base percentage in excess of .400 once (.409 in 2004).
Posted slugging percentage in excess of .500 four times.

Finished second in NL with 49 doubles in 2003.

Finished second in NL with 124 RBIs in 2004.

Led NL third basemen in assists twice.

Finished fourth in 2004 NL MVP voting.

2002 Silver Slugger winner.

Four-time Gold Glove winner (2002, 2003, 2004, 2006).

Three-time *Sporting News* All-Star selection (2002, 2003, 2004).

Five-time NL All-Star (2002, 2003, 2004, 2005, 2006).

Two-time NL champion (2004, 2006).

2006 world champion.

NOTES

1. Mike Matheny, quoted in "Scott Rolen: What They Say," *JockBio.com*, www.jockbio.com/Bios/Rolen/Rolen_they-say.html (accessed October 25, 2012).

2. Larry Bowa, quoted in "Scott Rolen: What They Say," www.jockbio.com/Bios/Rolen/Rolen_they-say.html.

3. Tony La Russa, quoted in "Scott Rolen: What They Say," www.jockbio.com/Bios/Rolen/Rolen_they-say.html.

4. Edgar Renteria, quoted in "Scott Rolen: What They Say," www.jockbio.com/Bios/Rolen/Rolen_they-say.html.

5. Jim Edmonds, quoted in "Scott Rolen: What They Say," www.jockbio.com/Bios/Rolen/Rolen_they-say.html.

6. Jason Isringhausen, quoted in "Scott Rolen: What They Say," www.jockbio.com/Bios/Rolen/Rolen_they-say.html.

7. Matt Clement, quoted in "Scott Rolen: What They Say," www.jockbio.com/Bios/Rolen/Rolen_they-say.html.

8. Dick Allen, quoted in "Scott Rolen: What They Say," www.jockbio.com/Bios/Rolen/Rolen_they-say.html.

36

GEORGE HENDRICK

George Hendrick arrived in St. Louis in 1978 with a reputation as being someone who played the game without passion, frequently failed to hustle, and never spoke to the media. Although Hendrick continued his policy of not dealing with the press, he proved to be a consummate team player in his seven seasons with the Cardinals, sacrificing his personal statistics for the betterment of the ball club and interacting well with teammates and fans alike. En route to establishing himself as one of the Cardinals' most popular players of the early 1980s, he batted over .300 three times and knocked in more than 100 runs twice, earning in the process two National League All-Star selections, two Silver Slugger Awards, and one top-ten finish in the league Most Valuable Player voting. He also helped the Cardinals defeat the Milwaukee Brewers in the 1982 World Series by driving in what proved to be the game-winning run in the decisive seventh contest.

Born in Los Angeles, California, on October 18, 1949, George Andrew Hendrick attended Fremont High School in Los Angeles, where he starred in both baseball and basketball. Although basketball remained Hendrick's first love, he signed with Oakland after the Athletics selected him with the first overall pick of the 1968 Major League Baseball Draft. Displaying the talent that prompted the A's to pick him ahead of every other player in the nation, Hendrick ascended quickly through Oakland's farm system, making his major-league debut with the club at only twenty-one years of age in June 1971. Appearing in forty-two games for the A's the remainder of the season, he batted only .237 and drove in just eight runs. Splitting the ensuing campaign between Oakland and the minors, Hendrick batted just .182 in his fifty-eight games with the A's. Nevertheless, he learned a great deal from starting left fielder Joe Rudi, whom he later credited with helping him become a complete player.

With the A's having acquired center fielder Bill North from the Chicago Cubs shortly after the 1972 season ended, they elected to trade Hendrick to the Cleveland Indians prior to the start of the ensuing campaign. While the speedy North ended up leading the American League in stolen bases in his first year with his new team, Hendrick won the starting center-field job in Cleveland, batting .268 and hitting twenty-one homers in his first full season. He posted solid numbers for the Indians in each of the next three seasons as well, averaging twenty-three home runs and seventy-eight RBIs from 1974 to 1976, while earning two All-Star nominations.

Yet, Cleveland remained somewhat disappointed in his overall performance, since the six-foot, three-inch, 195-pound right-handed-hitting outfielder failed to live up to his enormous potential. Furthermore, Hendrick's smooth and easy style seemed too casual to some, who chose to nickname him "Jogging George" and "Captain Easy," since they felt he played lackadaisically at times and often failed to put forth his full effort. He also acquired the nickname "Silent George" after he adopted the policy of not speaking to the press when the contents of two conversations he considered to be "off the record" ended up appearing in the newspaper.

Finally, after four tumultuous seasons in Cleveland, Hendrick went to San Diego when the Indians traded him to the Padres at the conclusion of the 1976 campaign. He played well in his one full season in San Diego, hitting 23 homers, driving in 81 runs, and batting .311. Nevertheless, the Padres elected to trade him to the Cardinals for young right-hander Eric Rasmussen in May 1978 when Hendrick started off the season slowly.

Hendrick found the city of St. Louis very much to his liking, having the best years of his career playing right field (and later first base) for the Cardinals. After batting .288, hitting 17 home runs, and driving in 67 runs in the final four months of the 1978 season, he batted an even .300 in 1979, while also hitting 16 homers and knocking in 75 runs. Hendrick subsequently led the Cardinals in home runs in each of the next four seasons, averaging twenty homers a year from 1980 to 1983. He had his two most productive seasons in 1980 and 1982, topping 100 RBIs for the only two times in his career. He also drove in ninety-seven runs in 1983, a season in which he posted a career-high .318 batting average.

In addition to blossoming as a player during his time in St. Louis, Hendrick evolved into an exceptional teammate, altering to some degree the inaccurate image the media previously created of him. Gene Tenace, who served as the Cardinals' backup catcher in 1981 and 1982 after previously playing with Hendrick in Oakland and San Diego, commented on one occasion, "George likes to talk about basketball and cars; he loves the Lakers, and he has a Porsche and Mercedes-Benz; but, as a ballplayer, he can do it all—run, throw, hit, and hit with power. As a person, he's one of the nicest guys on our club; easygoing, level-headed."[1] Tenace added, "He's a leader by example. With a runner on second base and none out, he'll hit to the right side and move that runner to third. Lots of fourth-place hitters won't do that."[2]

Meanwhile, Cardinals manager Whitey Herzog liked to talk about Hendrick in terms of "what an excellent defensive player he is." He added, "Once you tell him where you want him to play for a certain hitter, he never forgets. You never have to wave him. And he's an outstanding person . . . a leader in the clubhouse."[3]

As a former center fielder, Hendrick even took it upon himself to tutor youngster Willie McGee on the art of playing the position when the latter arrived in St. Louis in 1982. And, even though Silent George continued his practice of not speaking to the press, he remained polite at all times, typically excusing himself as he eased his way past reporters in the Cardinals clubhouse.

Hendrick remained with the Cardinals through the end of the 1984 campaign, after which a desperate need for starting pitching prompted the team to trade him to the Pittsburgh Pirates for John Tudor. Hendrick spent less than one full season in Pittsburgh, being included as part of a six-player trade the Pirates completed with the California Angels on August 2, 1985. He spent the remainder of his career as a part-time player with the Angels, announcing his retirement at the conclusion of the 1988 campaign. Hendrick ended his career with 267 home runs, 1,111 RBIs, 941 runs scored, 1,980 hits, a

.278 batting average, a .329 on-base percentage, and a .446 slugging percentage. In his seven seasons with the Cardinals, he hit 122 home runs, knocked in 582 runs, scored 457 others, collected 978 hits, batted .294, compiled a .345 on-base percentage, and posted a .470 slugging percentage.

Hendrick returned to St. Louis after his playing career ended, serving as the Cardinals' roving hitting/outfield instructor at the minor-league level from 1993 to 1995, before coaching for the major-league club in 1996 and 1997. He subsequently spent two years coaching for the Angels, before serving as the San Diego Padres' minor-league hitting instructor in 2000 and 2001. After assuming a similar role in the Los Angeles Dodgers' organization in 2005, Hendrick moved on to Tampa Bay, where he continues to serve as the Rays' first base and outfield coach.

CARDINAL CAREER HIGHLIGHTS

Best Season

Although Hendrick hit nineteen home runs and knocked in 104 runs for the Cardinals in 1982, he compiled better overall numbers in 1980 and 1983. In the first of those years, he batted .302 and established career highs with 25 homers, 109 RBIs, 173 hits, 285 total bases, and a .498 slugging percentage. Three seasons later, Hendrick batted a career-high .318, hit 18 home runs, drove in 97 runs, and posted a slugging percentage of .393. He earned a spot on the NL and *Sporting News* All-Star teams both years, making the squads as an outfielder in 1980, and as a first baseman in 1983. Either season would have made a good choice, but I ultimately settled on 1980 since Hendrick compiled the best numbers of his career in five different offensive categories.

Memorable Moments and Greatest Performances

Hendrick had arguably his biggest day at the plate for the Cardinals on August 25, 1978, when he keyed an 11–10 Cardinals victory over Atlanta by driving in a career-high seven runs. Hendrick went 4-for-5 on the day, with 2 home runs, a double, and 3 runs scored.

Hendrick hit one of his most memorable home runs for the Cardinals on July 4, 1980, when he gave them a 1–0 win over Philadelphia by delivering a tenth-inning solo shot against Kevin Saucier. He hit another big homer on May 12, 1984, breaking up a no-hitter by Cincinnati's Mario Soto with a game-tying blast with two men out in the top of the ninth inning. Unfortunately, the Reds rallied for a run in the bottom of the frame, giving Soto a one-hit, 2–1 victory.

However, Hendrick never got a bigger hit than the go-ahead single he delivered in Game 7 of the 1982 World Series. After making a key defensive play earlier in the contest by throwing out from right field a runner attempting to advance from first to third base on a single, Hendrick followed a game-tying bases-loaded single by Keith Hernandez in the bottom of the sixth inning with a RBI single of his own. The hit, which gave the Cardinals a 4–3 lead over the Milwaukee Brewers, proved to be the game winner, since neither team scored the rest of the way.

Notable Achievements

Hit more than twenty home runs once (twenty-five in 1980).
Knocked in more than 100 runs twice.
Batted over .300 three times.
Finished second in NL with 109 RBIs in 1980.
Led NL with fourteen sacrifice flies in 1982.
Led NL outfielders with twenty assists in 1979.
Led NL right fielders with .992 fielding percentage in 1979.
Two-time Silver Slugger winner (1980, 1983).
Two-time *Sporting News* All-Star selection (1980, 1983).
Two-time NL All-Star (1980, 1983).
1982 NL champion.
1982 world champion.

NOTES

1. Gene Tenace, quoted in "Silent George Hendrick Leads Cards by Example," *Google News*, http://news.google.com/newspapers?nid=1320&dat=19821020&id=3WtWAAAAIBAJ&sjid=x-kDAAAAIBAJ&pg=7024,1506955 (accessed October 26, 2012). Originally published in the *Gainesville Sun*, Gainesville, Florida (October 20, 1982), 3C.

2. Tenace, quoted in "Silent George Hendrick Leads Cards by Example," http://news.google.com/newspapers?nid=1320&dat=19821020&id=3WtWAAAAIBAJ&sjid=x-kDAAAAIBAJ&pg=7024,1506955.

3. Whitey Herzog, quoted in "Silent George Hendrick Leads Cards by Example," http://news.google.com/newspapers?nid=1320&dat=19821020&id=3WtWAAAAIBAJ&sjid=x-kDAAAAIBAJ&pg=7024,1506955.

37

WHITEY KUROWSKI

Overcoming numerous obstacles that included a childhood bout with osteomyelitis and the death of both his father and older brother, Whitey Kurowski eventually established himself as arguably the National League's top third baseman of the 1940s. Even though he usually found himself playing in the shadow of Hall of Fame teammates Stan Musial and Enos Slaughter, Kurowski proved to be a key contributor to four pennant-winning teams and three world championship ball clubs during his time in St. Louis, earning All-Star honors on four separate occasions and two top-ten finishes in the league Most Valuable Player voting during his career, which he spent entirely with the Cardinals. A stocky, thick-legged infielder with good power and surprising speed, he hit more than twenty home runs and batted over .300 three times each, while also topping 100 RBIs twice. A solid fielder as well, Kurowski led all NL third basemen in putouts three times, and once each in assists, double plays, and fielding percentage. He accomplished all he did despite playing his entire career with a physical abnormality.

Born in Reading, Pennsylvania, on April 19, 1918, George John "Whitey" Kurowski suffered a serious injury at the age of seven that would have discouraged someone with less resolve from even considering a career in professional baseball. Falling off a fence and landing in a pile of broken glass, he severely cut his right arm, causing blood poisoning and, later, an infection of the bone known as osteomyelitis to develop. After initially fearing that they might have to amputate the youngster's arm, doctors instead chose to perform a surgical procedure in which they removed almost four inches of infected bone and tissue above his wrist, leaving him with a weakened and misshapen limb that remained shorter than his left arm when he grew to adulthood.

In spite of his physical defect, Kurowski set his sights on eventually playing in the major leagues. Not wishing to follow in his father's footsteps of being a coal miner, especially after his older brother lost his life in a mine cave-in in 1937, Kurowski played softball and baseball constantly. He also made a concerted effort to build up the muscles in his wounded arm as a way of compensating for the missing bone. Unfortunately, concerns over his physical condition prevented him from getting any offers when he graduated from high school in 1936. But fellow Reading native Harrison Wickel gave him a chance to play with the Class D team he managed in the Northeast Arkansas League one year later. Making the most of his opportunity, the nineteen-year-old Kurowski ended up batting .339 in his first year of professional ball, before posting a mark of .386 for Portsmouth in the Mid-Atlantic League the following season.

Kurowski spent the next three years playing third base for the Cardinals' Triple-A affiliate in Rochester of the International League, compiling solid numbers each season. Finally called up to St. Louis in late 1941, he appeared in just five games, collecting three hits in nine official at bats, for a .333 batting average.

The twenty-four-year-old Kurowski arrived in spring training the following year prepared to battle veteran Jimmy Brown for the starting third-base job. Although he eventually earned the starting assignment, Kurowski again had to overcome a considerable amount of emotional trauma when his father died of a heart attack shortly before the regular season got underway. Doing his best to put aside his personal woes, Kurowski had a solid rookie campaign, helping the Cardinals capture the NL pennant by batting .254, hitting 9 home runs, and driving in 42 runs. He subsequently came up big for St. Louis in the World Series, knocking in five runs and hitting a home run in the decisive fifth contest that gave the Cardinals their first world championship in eight years.

Kurowski's earlier bout with osteomyelitis made him ineligible for military service, enabling him to spend the next three years developing into the senior circuit's finest all-around third baseman. After batting .287 and knocking in 70 runs in 1943, he batted .270, hit 20 homers, drove in 87 runs, and scored 95 others in 1944. He followed that up with one of his finest seasons, hitting 21 home runs, knocking in 102 runs, scoring 84 others, and batting a career-high .323 in 1945, en route to earning a fifth-place finish in the NL MVP voting.

Kurowski proved that the success he experienced during the wartime years of 1943 to 1945 could not be attributed solely to the absence of many of the game's top players when he batted .301 and drove in eighty-nine runs in 1946. A consummate team player, he contributed greatly to the championship the Cardinals won that year, not only on the field, but off it as well. After engaging in a bitter salary dispute with tightfisted St. Louis owner Sam Breadon prior to the start of the campaign, Kurowski took it upon himself to hold a clubhouse meeting to clear the air when rumors surfaced that he, Stan Musial, and other Cardinal stars might be on the verge of accepting lucrative offers made to them by the outlaw Mexican League. Informing his teammates that he had indeed talked to Mexican League representatives, Kurowski also let them know that he intended to fulfill his St. Louis contract. He urged them to put the Mexican League business behind them and concentrate on winning the pennant, which they did, edging out the Brooklyn Dodgers by just two games, before defeating the Boston Red Sox in the World Series.

Although the Cardinals failed to repeat as NL champions in 1947, Kurowski had arguably his finest all-around season. He batted .310 and established career highs with 27 home runs, 104 RBIs, and 108 runs scored in 1947.

Kurowski managed to become one of the NL's better hitters, even though he invariably found himself compensating for his physical limitations. Due to the fact that the right-handed-hitting Kurowski's right arm was shorter than his left, he had a difficult time reaching pitches on the outer half of the plate. As a result, he crowded the plate and turned over his right wrist when he swung the bat, causing him to become a dead-pull hitter.

Kurowski's outstanding 1947 campaign ended up being his final season as a full-time player. After undergoing thirteen different operations throughout the years to ease the pain in his mended throwing arm, Kurowski found himself limited to only seventy-seven games and a batting average of just .214 in 1948. He spent most of the ensuing campaign trying to rehabilitate his arm with Houston in the Texas League, appearing in only ten games with the Cardinals. No longer able to will his way past the pain and physical restrictions his injured limb placed on him, Kurowski announced his retirement at the end of the 1949 season. Only 31 years of age when he played his last game, Kurowski ended his career with 106 home runs, 529 RBIs, 518 runs scored, 925 hits, a .286 batting average, a .366 on-base percentage, and a .455 slugging percentage. The Cardinals never finished any lower than second in the nine seasons Kurowski wore a Redbirds uniform.

Following his playing days, Kurowski began a long and successful career as a minor-league manager and coach, managing in the Cardinals' organization for more than a decade, before joining the newly formed New York Mets franchise in 1962. He finally left baseball in 1972, after which he worked for Berks County as a sealer of weights and measures until retiring from that post in 1980. Kurowski subsequently spent his retirement living in Shillington, a suburb of Reading, where he passed away on December 9, 1999, at the age of eighty-one. He had been in poor health since suffering a stroke after undergoing heart bypass surgery a few months earlier.

CAREER HIGHLIGHTS

Best Season

Kurowski compiled outstanding numbers for the Cardinals in 1945, when he hit 21 home runs, drove in 102 runs, scored 84 others, batted a career-high .323, and posted on-base and slugging percentages of .383 and .511, respectively. But he put up better overall numbers two years later, when he batted .310 and established career highs with 27 homers, 104 RBIs, 108 runs scored, a .420 on-base percentage, and a .544 slugging percentage. Considering that the game's best players had returned to their respective teams by 1947, Kurowski clearly had his best season for the Cardinals that year.

Memorable Moments and Greatest Performances

Kurowski had a big day at the plate in Game 4 of the 1946 World Series, helping the Cardinals even the Fall Classic at two games apiece by going 4-for-5, with 2 doubles, 1 RBI, and 2 runs scored during a 12–3 St. Louis victory over the Boston Red Sox. However, Kurowski unquestionably delivered the biggest hit of his career four years earlier, when his ninth-inning home run in Game 5 of the 1942 World Series enabled the Cardinals to defeat the Yankees, four games to one. Stepping to the plate with one man on base, one man out, and the score tied at 2–2 in the top of the ninth inning, Kurowski slammed a Red Ruffing offering over Yankee Stadium's left-field wall, giving the Cardinals a 4–2 lead they protected in the bottom of the inning. The blast gave the Cardinals their first world championship in eight years and brought an to end an extraordinary run of World Series success experienced by the Yankees, who had emerged victorious in eight straight trips to the Fall Classic since the Cardinals last defeated them in 1926.

Notable Achievements

Hit more than twenty home runs three times.
Knocked in more than 100 runs twice.
Scored more than 100 runs once (108 in 1947).
Batted over .300 three times.
Compiled on-base percentage in excess of .400 once (.420 in 1947).
Posted slugging percentage in excess of .500 twice.
Led NL third basemen in putouts three times, assists once, and fielding percentage once.
1945 *Sporting News* All-Star selection.
Four-time NL All-Star (1943, 1944, 1946, 1947).
Four-time NL champion (1942, 1943, 1944, 1946).
Three-time world champion (1942, 1944, 1946).

38

BOB FORSCH

Most Cardinals fans probably don't think of utter pitching dominance when they hear Bob Forsch's name mentioned. Such high esteem is generally reserved only for such legendary hurlers as Bob Gibson and Dizzy Dean. And younger St. Louis fans are more likely to associate the names of Chris Carpenter and Adam Wainwright with pitching excellence. Nevertheless, Forsch accomplished something that no other hurler in the rich history of the Cardinals managed to achieve, establishing himself as the only pitcher in franchise history to throw two no-hitters during his time in St. Louis. Although the workmanlike right-hander surpassed twenty victories just once in his career, he also won more games than any other Cardinals pitcher, with the exception of Bob Gibson and Jesse Haines. A regular member of the Cardinals starting rotation in thirteen of the fifteen seasons he spent in St. Louis, Forsch posted double-digit wins a total of ten times, winning at least fifteen games on three separate occasions and leading the Cardinals staff in wins six times. An usually good-hitting pitcher as well, Forsch compiled a lifetime batting average of .213, hitting twelve home runs and driving in seventy-nine runs, in 862 total at bats as a member of the team. Yet, those closest to Forsch during his time in St. Louis remember him more than anything for his toughness, competitive spirit, and high level of professionalism.

Born in Sacramento, California, on January 13, 1950, Robert Herbert Forsch originally signed with the Cardinals as a third baseman after being selected by them in the twenty-sixth round of the 1968 Major League Baseball Draft, eight rounds after the Houston Astros selected his older brother, Ken. With Forsch struggling at the plate his first two minor-league seasons, the Cardinals elected to convert him into a pitcher in 1970. He subsequently compiled an overall record of 41–37 throughout the course of the next four and a half seasons, as he continued to work his way up through the team's farm system.

Finally called up to St. Louis midway through the 1974 campaign, Forsch pitched well for the Cardinals the remainder of the year, compiling a record of 7–4 and an ERA of 2.97, throwing 5 complete games, and tossing 2 shutouts. He followed that up with an outstanding sophomore campaign in which he went 15–10, with a 2.86 ERA and four shutouts; however, Forsch experienced a considerable amount of difficulty his third year in the league, winning only eight of his eighteen decisions, and seeing his ERA increase by more than one run per game, to 3.94. He rebounded in 1977, however, finishing the year with a record of 20–7 and an ERA of 3.48.

Forsch began the following year in style, fashioning a 3–0 record and a 0.71 ERA after his first three starts. He made one of those wins a memorable one, throwing the first of his two no-hitters on April 16, against the Philadelphia Phillies; however, after Forsch improved his record to 6–2 by tossing a three-hit shutout against the Dodgers on May 11, things began to unravel for him. He went just 5–15, with a 4.07 ERA, the rest of the year, concluding the campaign with a record of 11–17 and an ERA of 3.70.

Although Forsch remained an effective starter the rest of his career, even displaying occasional flashes of brilliance, he never regained his earlier form. A power pitcher his first few years in the league, he later found himself relying on a deliberate delivery, pinpoint control, and a changeup, mixed in with a sinker and an occasional fastball.

After compiling an overall record of 32–26 from 1979 to 1981, Forsch reached fifteen victories for the final time in his career in 1982, finishing the campaign with a record of 15–9 and an ERA of 3.48. He made his first postseason appearance that year, helping the Cardinals advance to the World Series by shutting out the Braves on just three hits in Game 1 of the National League Championship Series (NLCS).

After a subpar 1983 season, Forsch missed most of the ensuing campaign when he needed to undergo surgery to relieve pressure on a nerve in his lower back. Fully healthy again by the start of the 1986 season, he had the last big year of his career, going 14–10, with a 3.25 ERA. He spent his final full season in St. Louis the following year, compiling a record of 11–7 and an ERA of 4.32. Although relegated to a spot in the Cardinals bull pen during the ensuing postseason, Forsch helped change the momentum of the 1987 NLCS by delivering a huge pitch in Game 3 to San Francisco Giants outfielder Jeffrey Leonard, who had homered in each of the first two contests, which the teams had split.

The Giants appeared to be well on their way to taking a 2–1 lead in the series when they came up to bat in the bottom of the fifth inning, already leading by a score of 4–0. Coming in to relieve Cardinals starter Joe Magrane, Forsch soon found himself facing Leonard, who he hit squarely in the back with a fastball. Leonard, who hit his third home run of the series earlier in the contest, had agitated Cardinals players and fans alike with the "Cadillac" home-run trot and "one-flap down" running style he had used each time he circled the bases. Forsch, however, put an end to his antics by delivering a clear and resounding message that prompted the St. Louis press to begin calling Leonard "both flaps down." Asked later about the incident, Forsch responded unconvincingly, "Just trying to come inside."[1]

Although the NLCS ended up going the full seven games, the Forsch–Leonard confrontation proved to be a huge momentum shifter. Not only did the Cardinals come from behind to win Game 3 by a score of 6–5, but Leonard, who had previously gone 6-for-10 in the series, with three home runs, went just 4-for-14 the rest of the way.

Looking back on the episode, Cardinals manager Whitey Herzog remembered saying to Forsch a day before Game 3, "You're pitching tomorrow, big boy."[2] He then looked at Forsch, who, in Herzog's words, returned to him a look that seemed to say, "I'll take care of it."[3] Continuing to reflect back on the events surrounding the incident, Herzog commented, "That completely changed the series. He was the thinking man's pitcher. He understood the game and did it his own way. And he never said anything about it."[4]

Forsch remained with the Cardinals just one more year, spending most of the 1988 campaign in St. Louis, before being traded to Houston late in the season. After compiling a record of 4–5 with the Astros in 1989, Forsch elected to call it quits, announcing his retirement with a career record of 168–136, an ERA of 3.76, 67 complete games, and 19 shutouts. His Cardinal numbers include a record of 163–127, an ERA of 3.67, 67 complete games, and 19 shutouts. In addition to ranking third in team history in wins, he ranks third in innings pitched (2,659), fifth in strikeouts (1,079), second in games started (401), and ninth in shutouts (19).

After retiring as an active player, Forsch eventually assumed the role of pitching coach for the Billings Mustangs in the Cincinnati Reds organization. He served in that capacity until 2011, when he died of a chest aneurysm at his home in Florida, just one week after throwing out the first pitch before Game 7 of the 2011 World Series in St. Louis. He was sixty-one.

Remembered fondly by his former Cardinals teammates, Forsch was referred to as one of the "quintessential Cardinals" by Ricky Horton.[5] Horton added, "Most people don't realize how much of a professional Bob was, and how much of a mentor he was to me and a number of other young players. Bob had a wonderful blend of being an absolutely nice human being, but also knowing what was right, and being stern when he had to be."[6]

Former Cardinals right-hander Danny Cox once said of his one-time teammate, "He's an icon in Cardinals history. I'm always going to remember Forschie, not only for being a great pitcher, but that he was a great pitcher who respected the game."[7] Meanwhile, Whitey Herzog said, "Bob Forsch had class not only on the field, but off."[8]

CARDINAL CAREER HIGHLIGHTS

Best Season

Even though Forsch compiled a lower ERA, threw more innings, and allowed fewer base runners per inning pitched in two or three other seasons, he had easily his best all-around year in 1977, when he won twenty games for the only time in his career. In addition to finishing 20–7, with a 3.48 ERA, Forsch made a career-high thirty-five starts and tied his personal high with eight complete games.

Memorable Moments and Greatest Performances

An outstanding hitting pitcher throughout his career, Forsch led the Cardinals to a 5–4 win over the Pirates on August 10, 1986, by hitting a grand slam home run; however, he experienced most of his greatest moments on the mound, putting himself in the record books by becoming the only Cardinals pitcher ever to throw two no-hitters. He accomplished the feat for the first time on April 16, 1978, when he defeated the Phillies by a score of 5–0. Forsch allowed only two base runners during the contest, walking two and striking out three, en route to tossing the first no-hitter in St. Louis by a Cardinals pitcher since Jesse Haines in 1924. He threw his second no-hitter some five years later, on September 26, 1983, once again permitting only two men to reach base during a 3–0 shutout of the Montreal Expos. Forsch may well have pitched his biggest game, however, in Game 1 of the 1982 NLCS, shutting out the Braves, 7–0, on only three hits.

Notable Achievements

Won twenty games in 1977.
Surpassed fifteen victories two other times.
Compiled ERA below 3.00 twice.
Threw more than 200 innings seven times, topping the 230 mark four times.
Threw two no-hitters.
Led NL pitchers in fielding percentage four times.
Ranks among Cardinals all-time leaders in wins (third), strikeouts (fifth), games started (second), innings pitched (third), and shutouts (ninth).
Won two Silver Sluggers (1980, 1987).
Three-time NL champion (1982, 1985, 1987).
1982 world champion.

NOTES

1. Bob Forsch, quoted in Rick Hummel, "Forsch Was 'Icon in Cards' History,'" *STLtoday.com*, www.stltoday.com/sports/baseball/professional/cardinal-beat/forsch-was-icon-in-cards-history/article_bdfb18cc-06f5-11e1-a7f4-001a4bcf6878.html (accessed November 5, 2012).

2. Whitey Herzog, quoted in Hummel, "Forsch Was 'Icon in Cards' History,'" www.stltoday.com/sports/baseball/professional/cardinal-beat/forsch-was-icon-in-cards-history/article_bdfb18cc-06f5-11e1-a7f4-001a4bcf6878.html.

3. Herzog, quoted in Hummel, "Forsch Was 'Icon in Cards' History,'" www.stltoday.com/sports/baseball/professional/cardinal-beat/forsch-was-icon-in-cards-history/article_bdfb18cc-06f5-11e1-a7f4-001a4bcf6878.html.

4. Herzog, quoted in Hummel, "Forsch Was 'Icon in Cards' History,'" www.stltoday.com/sports/baseball/professional/cardinal-beat/forsch-was-icon-in-cards-history/article_bdfb18cc-06f5-11e1-a7f4-001a4bcf6878.html.

5. Ricky Horton, quoted in Hummel, "Forsch Was 'Icon in Cards' History,'" www.stltoday.com/sports/baseball/professional/cardinal-beat/forsch-was-icon-in-cards-history/article_bdfb18cc-06f5-11e1-a7f4-001a4bcf6878.html.

6. Horton, quoted in Hummel, "Forsch Was 'Icon in Cards' History,'" www.stltoday.com/sports/baseball/professional/cardinal-beat/forsch-was-icon-in-cards-history/article_bdfb18cc-06f5-11e1-a7f4-001a4bcf6878.html.

7. Danny Cox, quoted in Hummel, "Forsch Was 'Icon in Cards' History,'" www.stltoday.com/sports/baseball/professional/cardinal-beat/forsch-was-icon-in-cards-history/article_bdfb18cc-06f5-11e1-a7f4-001a4bcf6878.html.

8. Herzog, quoted in Hummel, "Forsch Was 'Icon in Cards' History,'" www.stltoday.com/sports/baseball/professional/cardinal-beat/forsch-was-icon-in-cards-history/article_bdfb18cc-06f5-11e1-a7f4-001a4bcf6878.html.

39

STEVE CARLTON

While many people consider the Ernie Broglio for Lou Brock trade to be the greatest one the Cardinals ever made, the deal team management completed nearly eight years later that sent Steve Carlton to the Philadelphia Phillies for Rick Wise is generally considered to be one of their worst. It isn't that Wise wasn't a good pitcher. In fact, there were those who viewed him as being nearly Carlton's equal when the two teams consummated the deal on February 25, 1972. But while Wise spent only two seasons in St. Louis, compiling an overall record of 32–28, Carlton ended up winning 241 games in his fifteen years in Philadelphia, establishing himself in the process as one of the greatest left-handed pitchers in baseball history. A four-time Cy Young Award winner, "Lefty," as he came to be known, ended his career with 329 victories—the most ever by a southpaw, with the exception of Warren Spahn. He also ranks fourth all-time with 4,136 strikeouts.

Yet, even though Carlton pitched most of his best ball for the Phillies, he also experienced a considerable amount of success with the Cardinals, winning a total of seventy-seven games in parts of seven seasons with them. During his time in St. Louis, he won 20 games once, surpassed 14 victories two other times, earned 3 National League All-Star nominations and 2 *Sporting News* All-Star selections, and contributed to 2 pennant-winning ball clubs and 1 world championship team; therefore, it would be difficult for anyone to question his place on this list.

Born in Miami, Florida, on December 22, 1944, Steven Norman Carlton developed his pitching skills while playing Little League and American Legion baseball in his home state. After graduating from

North Miami High School, he signed with the Cardinals as an amateur free agent in 1963, while still attending Miami-Dade Community College.

Although scouts initially expressed concerns about whether Carlton had the ability to throw hard enough to succeed at the major-league level, the six-foot, four-inch left-hander advanced quickly through the St. Louis farm system after instituting a rigorous workout regimen that enabled him to build himself up through the use of weights. Having developed a decent curveball, an above-average fastball, and a sneaky pickoff move that tested the limits of the balk rule, Carlton joined the Cardinals at the start of the 1965 campaign, appearing in a total of fifteen games for them during the course of the season without recording a decision. He received a more extensive look from the club the following year, compiling a record of 3–3 in his nine starts.

Carlton became a regular member of the St. Louis starting rotation in 1967, helping the Cardinals win the first of two consecutive NL pennants by going 14–9, with a 2.98 ERA, while striking out 168 batters in 193 innings of work. Although Carlton lost his only World Series start to Boston, he allowed the Red Sox just one unearned run and three hits in six innings of work. He followed that up with another solid performance in 1968, earning his first NL All-Star selection by posting a record of 13–11 for the NL champions, along with a 2.99 ERA and five shutouts.

Carlton subsequently developed into one of the NL's dominant pitchers in 1969, rivaling Cardinals staff ace Bob Gibson as the top hurler on his own team. Experimenting for the first time with a slider, which eventually became his signature pitch, Carlton finished 17–11, with an ERA of 2.17 and 210 strikeouts, en route to earning a spot on the *Sporting News* All-Star Team and the starting assignment for the NL in the annual All-Star Game. The big left-hander's 2.17 ERA placed him second in the NL rankings. He also finished among the league leaders in strikeouts, establishing a new major-league record on September 15 by recording nineteen strikeouts against the eventual world champion New York Mets.

Tim McCarver, who served as Carlton's primary receiver in St. Louis (and later in Philadelphia), described the left-hander's pitching style, saying, "Carlton does not pitch to the hitter, he pitches through him. The batter hardly exists for Steve. He's playing an elevated game of catch."[1]

Unfortunately, Carlton's outstanding performance in 1969 caused him to reach an impasse with Cardinals management in contract negotiations at the end of the year. A no-show at spring training in 1970, the twenty-five-year-old southpaw eventually reached an agreement on a new deal with the team; however, difficulties controlling his breaking pitches throughout the year caused Carlton to suffer through a horrendous 1970 campaign that saw him finish just 10–19, with a 3.73 ERA. Relying more heavily on his fastball in 1971, Carlton returned to top form, compiling a record of 20–9, tossing 18 complete games, and throwing 273 innings, en route to earning his third NL All-Star nomination and a spot on the *Sporting News* All-Star Team for the second time.

Carlton subsequently asked the Cardinals to raise his salary from $55,000 to $65,000 during the off-season, raising the ire of team management. Instead of granting the pitcher's request, St. Louis traded him to the Philadelphia Phillies for right-hander Rick Wise. Bing Devine, the St. Louis general manager who dealt Carlton to Philadelphia at the behest of Cardinals owner Auggie Busch, later explained his thinking at the time, saying the following:

> We hadn't been able to sign Carlton. There was no free agency, so he didn't have the freedom to say, 'Sign me or else.' He was being very difficult to sign for the ridiculous amount of $10,000 between what he wanted and what we'd give him. Many times Mr. Busch gave me a little leeway in the budget, but in the case of Carlton, Mr. Busch developed the feeling that Carlton was a 'smart-aleck' young guy, and I'm not used to having young smart-alecks tell me what to do.[2]

Carlton later shared his recollections of the trade that made him a member of the Phillies, saying,

> Auggie Busch traded me to the last-place Phillies over a salary dispute. I was mentally committed to winning twenty-five

> games with the Cardinals, and now I had to rethink my goals. I decided to stay with the twenty-five-win goal and won twenty-seven of the Phillies' fifty-nine victories. I consider that season my finest individual achievement.[3]

Indeed, Carlton's 1972 performance has to be considered one of the finest efforts ever turned in by a pitcher. By going 27–10 for the last-place Phillies, the left-hander established a major-league record by compiling 46 percent of his team's victories. In addition to leading all NL pitchers in wins, he finished first with a 1.97 ERA, 310 strikeouts, 30 complete games, and 346 innings pitched, en route to winning the pitcher's version of the Triple Crown, his first Cy Young Award, as well as the Hickok Belt as the top professional athlete of the year. Carlton performed so magnificently that he also placed fifth in the league Most Valuable Player voting, despite Philadelphia's distant last-place finish.

Carlton attributed much of his success in 1972 to his grueling training regimen, which included Eastern martial arts techniques, the most famous of which involved twisting his fist to the bottom of a five-gallon bucket of rice. His brilliant campaign also resulted from the further development of his three primary pitches. These included a rising fastball; a long, looping curveball; and a legendary slider that he relied on more heavily than ever before. The last offering typically broke down and in to right-handed batters, making it virtually impossible for them to make solid contact with the ball. Tim McCarver, who made a career out of catching Carlton, first with the Cardinals and, later, as a member of the Phillies, once noted, "When I played for other teams against Steve, I could hear the right-handed hitters saying, 'He may have gotten me out, but at least he didn't throw me the slider.'"[4]

Although Carlton led the NL with eighteen complete games and 293 innings pitched the following year, he also topped the circuit with twenty losses, while seeing his ERA almost double, to 3.90. While at least some of Carlton's relative ineffectiveness could be attributed to occasional soreness in his left elbow, articles began appearing in the Philadelphia newspapers questioning his somewhat unusual training techniques, as well as his fondness for fine wine. Growing increasingly indignant about his treatment by the members of the press corps, he severed all ties with the media at the conclusion of the 1973 campaign, vowing to never again answer their questions. Looking back at his acrimonious relationship with the media, Carlton later suggested, "It (not talking to the media from 1974 through the end of his career) was perfect for me at the time. It took me two years to make up my mind. I was tired of getting slammed. To me it was a slap in the face. But it (his silence) made me concentrate better."[5]

Carlton's performance did indeed improve after he stopped talking to the press. After sporadic pain in his pitching elbow limited him to a combined record of 31–27 from 1974 to 1975, he won at least twenty games in four of the next seven seasons, capturing three more Cy Young Awards during that time. Particularly effective in 1977, 1980, and 1982, Carlton led all NL pitchers in wins all three years. In the first of those campaigns, he finished 23–10, with a 2.64 ERA, 198 strikeouts, 17 complete games, and 283 innings pitched. He helped the Phillies capture their first world championship in 1980 by going 24–9, with a 2.34 ERA and a league-leading 286 strikeouts and 304 innings pitched. Two years later, he finished 23–11, with a 3.10 ERA and a league-leading 286 strikeouts, 6 shutouts, 19 complete games, and 296 innings pitched.

Although Carlton pitched fairly well for the Phillies in each of the next two seasons, the 1982 campaign turned out to be his last big year. After going a combined 28–23 in 1983 and 1984, the forty-year-old left-hander went just 1–8 in his first sixteen starts in 1985, before being placed on the disabled list for the remainder of the year. After he began the 1986 season just 4–8, with a 6.18 ERA, the Phillies asked him to retire. Carlton, however, refused to do so, forcing the team to finally release him. He then broke more than a decade of silence in the media to voice his reasons and thank the Philadelphia fans for their support. The left-hander split the remainder of the 1986 campaign between the San Francisco Giants and Chicago White Sox, experiencing little in the way of success, before failing again the following year in both Cleveland and Minnesota. He ended his career in early 1988, after being released by Minnesota.

Upon his retirement, Carlton ranked second only to Nolan Ryan in career strikeouts, with 4,136 (he has since slipped to fourth). In 24 major-league seasons, he compiled a record of 329–244, an ERA of 3.22, and 254 complete games. During his time in St. Louis, he posted a record of 77–62, compiled an ERA of 3.10, struck out 951 batters, tossed 16 shutouts, and threw 66 complete games. He ranks eighth in team history in strikeouts. Although Carlton spent most of his career not speaking to them, the members of the Baseball Writers' Association of America (BBWAA) acknowledged his greatness by electing him to the Baseball Hall of Fame in 1994, the first time his name appeared on the ballot.

Former Phillies outfielder Richie Ashburn served as a broadcaster for the team throughout Carlton's tenure in Philadelphia. Ashburn expressed his admiration for the left-hander by saying, "Lefty was a craftsman, an artist. He was a perfectionist. He painted a ballgame. Stroke, stroke, stroke, and when he got through (pitching a game) it was a masterpiece."[6]

Author Peter Golenbock writes the following in *The Spirit of St. Louis* (2000):

> Carlton was not your normal guy. Communicating with him was not always easy. On the mound, he would tune out all distractions. Off the mound, he did the same. If he considered you the distraction, he'd direct at you an icy stare. Teammates considered him to be a recluse. He hated to sign autographs. He refused to talk to reporters for long stretches at a time. He was devoted to the martial arts. He studied Far East religions. He was a wine connoisseur. He pissed people off with his standoffishness and arrogance. Carlton was also the finest left-handed pitcher of his generation. In a career that would last twenty-four years, he would win 329 games, ninth all-time, with an ERA of 3.22. His 4,136 strikeouts were second all-time only to Nolan Ryan. Unfortunately, most of his career was not spent in St. Louis, but rather in Philadelphia.[7]

After retiring from the game, Carlton waxed philosophical about his career, saying, "Everything I was, physically and mentally, that's what I put on that field. . . . So what I did on the field was the essence of what I am. Remember me like that."[8]

CARDINAL CAREER HIGHLIGHTS

Best Season

Carlton won more games in 1971 than he did in any other season with the Cardinals, finishing the campaign with a record of 20–9. He also made more starts (36), completed more games (18), and threw more innings (273) than he did in any other year he spent in St. Louis. But Carlton pitched more effectively two years earlier. He posted a record of 17–11; threw 12 complete games and 236 innings; struck out 210 batters; and compiled an ERA of 2.17, which bettered his 1971 mark of 3.56 by a considerable margin. Furthermore, while Carlton surrendered 275 hits to the opposition in 1971, he allowed only 185 safeties in 1969, giving him a WHIP (walks plus hits allowed per innings pitched) of 1.176, which far surpassed the figure of 1.365 he posted in 1971.

Memorable Moments and Greatest Performances

Carlton pitched arguably his finest game for the Cardinals on June 19, 1968, allowing just a single to Glenn Beckert in shutting out the Chicago Cubs, 4–0, at Busch Stadium. He struck out nine and walked none during his brilliant one-hit effort.

Yet, ironically, three of Carlton's most dominating performances as a member of the Cardinals resulted in defeat. On September 20, 1967, he worked eight innings against the Philadelphia Phillies, striking out sixteen batters, including seven in a row at one point, but ended up losing to Chris Short by a score of 3–1.

Almost exactly two years later, on September 15, 1969, Carlton established a new major-league record (since broken) by striking out nineteen New York Mets; however, a pair of two-run homers by Ron Swoboda made a loser out of the Cardinals left-hander.

Carlton struck out sixteen Phillies batters for the second time in his career on May 21, 1970, leaving the contest after eight innings with the score tied at 3–3. But Philadelphia pushed across a run in the ninth to defeat the Cardinals by a score of 4–3.

Notable Achievements

Won twenty games in 1971.
Surpassed fourteen wins two other times.
Compiled ERA below 3.00 four times.
Struck out more than 200 batters once (210 in 1969).
Threw eighteen complete games in 1971.
Threw more than 230 innings four times.
Ranks eighth all-time among Cardinals pitchers in strikeouts (951).
Two-time *Sporting News* All-Star selection (1969, 1971).
Three-time NL All-Star (1968, 1969, 1971).
Two-time NL champion (1967, 1968).
1967 world champion.
Elected to Baseball Hall of Fame by members of BBWAA in 1994.

NOTES

1. Tim McCarver, quoted in "Steve Carlton," *Baseball-Reference.com*, www.baseball-reference.com/bullpen/Steve_Carlton (accessed November 6, 2012).
2. Bing Devine, quoted in "Steve Carlton Quotes," *Baseball Almanac*, www.baseball-almanac.com/quotes/steve_carlton_quotes.shtml (accessed November 6, 2012).
3. Steve Carlton, quoted in "Steve Carlton Quotes," www.baseball-almanac.com/quotes/steve_carlton_quotes.shtml.
4. Tim McCarver, quoted in "Steve Carlton Quotes," www.baseball-almanac.com/quotes/steve_carlton_quotes.shtml.
5. Steve Carlton, quoted in "Steve Carlton Quotes," www.baseball-almanac.com/quotes/steve_carlton_quotes.shtml.
6. Richie Ashburn, quoted in "Steve Carlton Quotes," www.baseball-almanac.com/quotes/steve_carlton_quotes.shtml.
7. Peter Golenbock, quoted in "Steve Carlton Quotes," www.baseball-almanac.com/quotes/steve_carlton_quotes.shtml.
8. Steve Carlton, quoted in "Steve Carlton Quotes," www.baseball-almanac.com/quotes/steve_carlton_quotes.shtml.

40

YADIER MOLINA

Although he has excelled behind the plate since he first joined the Cardinals in 2004, Yadier Molina provided little in the way of offense his first few years in St. Louis, failing to hit more than 8 home runs, drive in more than 49 runs, or score more than 36 runs in any of his first four seasons. Molina also batted over .270 and compiled an on-base percentage in excess of .330 just once during that period. However, the youngest of the "catching Molina Brothers" has since developed into a solid offensive performer, establishing himself in the process as one of the finest all-around receivers in the game. In addition to winning seven straight Gold Gloves, Molina has batted over .300 in four of the last seven seasons. He has also finished in double digits in homers three times and knocked in more than sixty runs on four separate occasions, en route to earning six National League All-Star nominations and two top-five finishes in the league Most Valuable Player voting. In so doing, Molina has helped lead the Cardinals to eight playoff appearances, four NL pennants, and two world championships in his eleven years with the club.

Born in Bayamon, Puerto Rico, on July 13, 1982, Yadier Benjamin Molina followed in the footsteps of his older brothers Bengie and Jose when he became the third member of his family to sign a professional contract shortly after the Cardinals selected him in the fourth round of the 2000 amateur draft. Entering the St. Louis farm system just months after he graduated from Puerto Rico's Vega Alta High School, Yadier spent the next three and a half years in the minor leagues before finally earning a call-up to the majors. After making his major-league debut with the Cardinals on June 3, 2004, Molina assumed a part-time role with the club the remainder of the year, serving primarily as the backup for former Gold Glove winner and current St. Louis manager Mike Matheny. In 51 games and 135 official at bats, Molina ended up hitting 2 home runs, driving in 15 runs, and batting .267.

Matheny joined the San Francisco Giants as a free agent during the subsequent off-season, clearing the path for Molina to become the starter in St. Louis. Although the 23-year-old receiver posted modest offensive numbers in his first full season, hitting only 8 homers, knocking in just 49 runs, scoring only 36 others, and batting just .252, he excelled behind the plate, throwing out 64 percent of attempted base stealers, en route to finishing first in that category among all NL catchers. Molina proved to be even less productive on offense in 2006, batting just .216 and scoring only twenty-nine runs. Nevertheless, he led all NL receivers in assists and helped the Cardinals advance to the World Series by batting .348, hitting 2 homers, and driving in 6 runs against the Mets in the National League Championship Series (NLCS). His two-run blast in the ninth inning of Game 7 of that series enabled the Cardinals to clinch their second World Series berth in three years. Molina continued his hot hitting against Detroit in the Fall Classic, collecting seven hits in seventeen official at bats against Tiger pitching, for a batting average of .412.

After increasing his offensive output somewhat in 2007, Molina further improved upon his performance the following season, beginning an extremely successful seven-year run during which he has batted over .300 four times and knocked in more than fifty runs all but once. He had his finest all-around season in 2012, earning a fourth-place finish in the NL MVP voting by hitting 22 home runs, driving in 76 runs, posting a slugging percentage of .501, and finishing among the league leaders with a .315 batting average.

As Molina has gradually evolved into a solid hitter, he has continued to display the exceptional defensive skills behind home plate that make him one of the most respected receivers in the game. In addition to leading all NL catchers in assists three times, he has thrown out the highest percentage of attempted base stealers on four separate occasions, compiling an overall mark of 44.8 percent during the course of his career. Blessed with exceptional quickness and a strong throwing arm, Molina often discourages opposing runners from taking liberties on the base paths. Yet, the thirty-two-year-old receiver also possesses a number of extremely subtle qualities that remain undetectable to the casual observer.

Commenting on Molina's work behind the plate, San Francisco Giants catcher Buster Posey once noted the following:

> The first thing I always see is how quiet he is as far as his set-up. He's very still. Still's not even the right word. But he looks so relaxed, and I think he steals a lot of pitches for his pitchers, and I think that goes unnoticed a lot of times for catchers. And the job he does framing pitches is second to none.[1]

Molina also takes ownership of his team's pitching staff. On one occasion, Adam Wainwright followed up a poor mound performance with an extremely effective one. After Wainwright suggested at the conclusion of the second contest that he had been eagerly awaiting an opportunity to redeem himself, a reporter asked Molina how impatient Wainwright had seemed to him. The Cardinals receiver responded, "No more than me, I guarantee you. I was expecting this game for him."[2] Meanwhile, former Cardinals manager Tony La Russa and pitching coach Dave Duncan once estimated that Molina is responsible for calling more than 75 percent of all pitches thrown during a game.

Molina followed up his exceptional 2012 campaign with another big year in 2013, hitting 12 home runs and establishing new career highs with 80 RBIs, 68 runs scored, 161 hits, 44 doubles, and a .319 batting average, which placed him fourth in the league rankings for the second consecutive season. In addition to winning his sixth straight Gold Glove and being named to the NL All-Star Team for the fifth straight time, Molina earned his first Silver Slugger and a third-place finish in the league MVP voting.

Forced to miss nearly a third of the 2014 season with a torn thumb ligament that required surgery, Molina ended up compiling fairly modest offensive numbers, concluding the campaign with 7 homers, 38 RBIs, 40 runs scored, and a .282 batting average. Nevertheless, he made his sixth consecutive All-Star Team and won his seventh straight Gold Glove.

At thirty-two years of age heading into the 2015 season, Molina figures to have at least two or three more good years left in him before the daily rigors of catching begin to take their toll on him. That being the case, he should be able to advance several places in these rankings before his playing days come to an end. Molina's current career totals stand at 96 home runs, 584 runs batted in, 451 runs scored, 1,297 hits, and 247 doubles. He also has compiled a lifetime batting average of .284, posted a career on-base percentage of .339, and compiled a lifetime slugging percentage of .402.

CAREER HIGHLIGHTS

Best Season

Although he has always been a standout receiver, Molina had easily his two best offensive seasons in 2012 and 2013, earning a top-five finish in the NL MVP balloting both years. After knocking in 76 runs, scoring 65 times, batting .315, and establishing career-high marks in home runs (22), stolen bases (12), and OPS (.874) in the first of those campaigns, Molina reached new career highs in RBIs (80), runs scored (68), hits (161), doubles (44), and batting average (.319) in 2013. Thus, a strong case could be made for either of those years. I ultimately settled on 2012, though, because Molina collected 25 more assists behind the plate (88 to 63) and compiled a higher caught-stealing percentage (47.9 to 43.5).

Memorable Moments and Greatest Performances

While he is better known for his defense, Molina has had a number of big days at the plate for the Cardinals. On August 16, 2007, he keyed an 8–0 win over the Milwaukee Brewers by posting the first two-homer game of his career. On April 5, 2010, he became just the third Cardinals player in history to hit a grand slam home run on Opening Day, doing so during an 11–6 victory over the Cincinnati Reds.

Yet, Molina unquestionably hit the most important home run of his career against the New York Mets in the 2006 NLCS, delivering one of the biggest hits by any Cardinals player in recent memory when his two-run homer in the top of the ninth inning of Game 7 put the Cardinals in the World Series. With the Cardinals barely having sneaked into the playoffs with a regular-season record of just 83–78, in the NLCS they faced a heavily favored New York Mets squad that finished with a league-best 97–65 during the course of the campaign. But St. Louis played New York dead even through the first six contests, forcing a decisive Game 7 to be played at Shea Stadium. The two teams entered the ninth inning with the score tied at 1–1, when Molina stepped to the plate to face reliever Aaron Heilman with one man out and one on base. The light-hitting catcher, who hit only six home runs in more than 400 official at bats during the regular season, turned on Heilman's first offering, driving it over the left-field wall to give the Cardinals a 3–1 lead. Although the Mets ended up loading the bases in the bottom of the frame, they failed to score, giving the Cardinals their second pennant in three seasons. The Cardinals subsequently defeated the Detroit Tigers in the World Series, giving them their first world championship in twenty-four years.

Notable Achievements

Hit more than twenty home runs once (twenty-two in 2012).
Batted over .300 four times.
Surpassed 40 doubles once (44 in 2013).
Posted slugging percentage in excess of .500 once (.501 in 2012).
Led NL catchers in assists three times.
Seven-time Gold Glove winner (2008, 2009, 2010, 2011, 2012, 2013, 2014).
2013 Silver Slugger winner.
Six-time NL All-Star (2009, 2010, 2011, 2012, 2013, 2014).
Three-time NL champion (2004, 2006, 2011).
Four-time world champion (2004, 2006, 2011, 2013).

NOTES

1. Buster Posey, quoted in Gwen Knapp, "Catch as Catch Can," *Sports on Earth*, www.sportsonearth.com/article/39924664 (accessed November 26, 2012).

2. Yadier Molina, quoted in Knapp, "Catch as Catch Can," www.sportsonearth.com/article/39924664.

41

RIPPER COLLINS

One of the most popular members of the Cardinals' famed "Gas House Gang" teams of the early 1930s, James "Ripper" Collins spent eight long years in the minor leagues before he finally arrived in St. Louis in 1931. Once he did, however, Collins quickly established himself as one of the team's most potent batsmen, rivaling Joe Medwick during his time in St. Louis as the ball club's primary power threat. In his six seasons in St. Louis, the switch-hitting Collins batted over .300 four times, led the Cardinals in home runs three times, and topped them in RBIs twice. In helping St. Louis win two world championships, Collins also earned All-Star honors twice and one top-ten finish in the National League Most Valuable Player voting.

Born in Altoona, Pennsylvania, on March 30, 1904, James Anthony Collins acquired the nickname "Ripper" as a boy when he once hit his team's only ball so hard that he snagged it on a fence, ripping its cover. After starring in sandlot baseball as a youth, Collins began his professional career in 1923, at the age of nineteen. He subsequently spent the next eight years playing in various minor leagues, excelling at whatever level at which he performed. Collins began to make a name for himself in 1928, when he won the Triple Crown in the Three-I League by hitting 19 home runs, driving in 101 runs, and batting .388. He followed that up by leading the Rochester Red Wings to the International League (IL) pennant in 1929, topping the circuit with thirty-eight homers and 134 RBIs. Collins finally earned a call-up to the majors with another exceptional performance for the Red Wings in 1930, a year that saw him hit 40 home runs, score 165 runs, and compile a slugging percentage of .684. He led the IL with a .376 batting average, 234 hits, 19 triples, and an all-time IL record 180 RBIs.

Summoned to St. Louis prior to the start of the 1931 campaign, Collins spent his rookie season splitting time at first base with future Hall of Famer Jim Bottomley. Accumulating almost 300 official at bats his first year in the league, Collins ended up batting .301 and driving in fifty-nine runs. He became a full-time member of the St. Louis starting lineup the following season, assuming a spot in the outfield on those days he didn't play first base. He led the team with twenty-one homers and ninety-one RBIs in his first full season, while also batting .279 and scoring eighty-two runs. Impressed with Collins's performance, the Cardinals turned over first base duties to him at the end of the year, dealing Bottomley to the Cincinnati Reds in December 1932.

Although Collins failed to reach the same level of production in 1933, hitting only 10 home runs and driving in just 68 runs, he posted solid overall numbers, batting .310, compiling a .363 on-base percentage, and posting a .452 slugging percentage. He improved upon those figures significantly the following year, helping the Cardinals capture the NL pennant by finishing among the league leaders with 128 RBIs, 116 runs scored, 200 hits, a .333 batting average, and a .393 on-base percentage, while topping the circuit with 35 homers, 369 total bases, and a .615 slugging percentage. His 369 total bases remain a NL record for switch-hitters. Collins also led all NL first basemen with 110 assists, en route to earning a sixth-place finish in the league MVP balloting. He continued to excel during the postseason, batting .367 in the Cardinals' seven-game triumph over the Detroit Tigers in the World Series.

Collins had another big year in 1935, batting .313 and placing among the league leaders in eight different offensive categories, including home runs (23), RBIs (122), runs scored (109), on-base percentage (.385), and slugging percentage (.529). His outstanding performance earned him the first of his three straight NL All-Star selections.

Collins developed into one of the NL's top sluggers during his time in St. Louis, even though he stood only five feet, nine inches tall and weighed just 165 pounds. Usually batting fifth in the Cardinals' lineup, right after Joe Medwick, Collins proved to be a versatile middle-of-the-order hitter, excelling as a bunter, in addition to providing protection for Medwick as the team's other primary long-ball threat. Described in the book *The Gashouse Gang* (1976) by author Robert E. Hood as a "chunky, powerful man who hit long home runs even though he choked up on the bat,"[1] Collins also served as one of the team's leading mischief-makers. The instigator behind many of teammate Pepper Martin's legendary pranks, Collins soon became one of manager Frankie Frisch's favorites due to his sly, engaging personality, which fit in well with the rest of the team, as well as his ability to handle a bat. Author Rob Rains writes in his book *The St. Louis Cardinals: The 100th Anniversary History* (1992) that, "One Cardinal who knew how to play and when to be serious, Frisch's type of guy, was the versatile Collins."[2]

Yet, Collins, too, found himself being reproached by the fiery Frisch from time to time, as can be evidenced by the following passage from *The Gashouse Gang*:

> Rip Collins was clever. Although he had little formal education, he started out the 1934 season writing daily news stories for the *East St. Louis (Ill.) Journal* and the *Rochester (N.Y.) Times Union*. Part way through the season, he suspended his writing career when, after he struck out one day, manager Frisch shouted at him, "Next time, swing your typewriter."[3]

In spite of his tremendous popularity, Collins eventually fell prey to Branch Rickey's policy of trading away players as they began approaching the latter stages of their careers. With the slugging Johnny Mize arriving in St. Louis in 1936, and with Collins experiencing a significant drop-off in virtually every offensive category, Rickey dealt the thirty-two-year-old first baseman/outfielder to the Chicago Cubs at the end of the year for standout right-hander Lon Warneke. Collins spent two seasons in Chicago, helping the Cubs capture the NL pennant in 1938, before he took the next two seasons off. After being purchased from Chicago by the Pittsburgh Pirates prior to the start of the 1941 campaign, he returned to the majors for one more year, before being released by the Pirates at season's end. He concluded his career with 135 home runs, 659 RBIs, 615 runs scored, 1,121 hits, a .296 lifetime batting average, a .360 on-base percentage, and a .492 slugging percentage. In his six years with the Cardinals, Collins hit 106 homers, drove in 516 runs, scored 455 others, collected 852 hits, batted .307, compiled a .370 on-base percentage, and posted a .517 slugging percentage.

After his major-league career ended, Collins returned to the minors, spending the next few seasons playing in the Pacific Coast League and Eastern League. Named Minor League Player of the Year while with Albany of the Eastern League in 1944, he managed to lead the league with 40 doubles, a .396 batting average, a .485 on-base percentage, and a .598 slugging percentage at the age of 40. After finally retiring as an active player, Collins managed in the minor leagues for more than a decade, before making a brief return to the majors as a coach with the Chicago Cubs from 1961 to 1963. He passed away on April 15, 1970, just two weeks after celebrating his sixty-sixth birthday.

CARDINAL CAREER HIGHLIGHTS

Best Season

Collins had an outstanding year for the Cardinals in 1935, when he hit 23 home runs, knocked in 122 runs, scored 109 others, and batted .313. But he posted better numbers in every offensive category one year earlier, when he established career highs with 128 RBIs, 116 runs scored, 200 hits, 12 triples, 40 doubles, a .333 batting average, and a .393 on-base percentage. He added a league-leading 35 homers, 369 total bases, and a .615 slugging percentage, en route to earning a sixth-place finish in the NL MVP voting.

Memorable Moments and Greatest Performances

Putting an exclamation point on his exceptional 1934 campaign, Collins performed brilliantly for the Cardinals in the 1934 World Series, helping them register a seven-game victory over the Detroit Tigers by collecting eleven hits in thirty times at bat, for a batting average of .367. The switch-hitting first baseman also drove in three runs and scored four others.

Notable Achievements

Hit more than twenty home runs three times, topping thirty homers once (thirty-five in 1934).
Knocked in more than 100 runs twice.
Scored more than 100 runs twice.
Batted over .300 four times.
Surpassed 200 hits once (200 in 1934).
Finished in double digits in triples three times.
Topped forty doubles once (forty in 1934).
Posted slugging percentage in excess of .500 three times, topping the .600 mark once.
Led NL in home runs once, slugging percentage once, and total bases once.
Finished second in NL with 128 RBIs in 1934.
Led NL first basemen in assists and fielding percentage once each.
Two-time NL All-Star (1935, 1936).
Two-time NL champion (1931, 1934).
Two-time world champion (1931, 1934).

NOTES

1. Robert E. Hood, quoted in "Rip Collins Was a One-of-a-Kind Hitter for the Cardinals," *Retrosimba*, June 21, 2011, www.retrosimba.com/2011/06/21/rip-collins-was-one-of-a-kind-hitter-for-cardinals (accessed November 7, 2012).

2. Rob Rains, quoted in "Rip Collins Was a One-of-a-Kind Hitter for the Cardinals," www.retrosimba.com/2011/06/21/rip-collins-was-one-of-a-kind-hitter-for-cardinals.

3. Hood, quoted in "Rip Collins Was a One-of-a-Kind Hitter for the Cardinals," www.retrosimba.com/2011/06/21/rip-collins-was-one-of-a-kind-hitter-for-cardinals.

42

EDGAR RENTERIA

Even though he is remembered most for driving home the winning run of the 1997 World Series in sudden-death fashion as a member of the Florida Marlins, Edgar Renteria had most of his finest seasons with the Cardinals. Starting at shortstop in St. Louis for six years, Renteria batted over .300 twice, knocked in 100 runs once, stole more than 30 bases twice, appeared in three All-Star Games, earned two Gold Gloves, and won three Silver Sluggers. Along the way, he helped lead the Cardinals to three division titles, three National League Championship Series berths, and one World Series appearance.

Born in Barranquilla, Colombia, on August 7, 1976, Edgar Renteria signed with the Florida Marlins as an amateur free agent in 1992, while still attending Barranquilla High School. Still nearly three months shy of his twentieth birthday when the Marlins called him up from Triple-A Charlotte in May1996, the rangy shortstop played well the final five months of the season, earning a second-place finish in the National League Rookie of the Year voting by batting .309, scoring 68 runs, and stealing 16 bases in the 106 games in which he appeared.

Renteria followed up his solid rookie campaign by batting .277, scoring 90 runs, stealing 32 bases, and leading all NL shortstops with 242 putouts in 1997. His strong performance helped the Marlins advance to the playoffs for the first time in their young history, earning a postseason berth as the league's wild-card entry. After winning Game 1 of the National League Division Series by singling off San Francisco closer Roberto Hernandez with two outs in the ninth inning, Renteria continued to display his penchant for delivering clutch hits when, stepping to the plate with the score tied at 2–2 in the bottom of the eleventh inning of Game 7 of the World Series, he lined a sharp single up the middle off Cleveland's Charles Nagy that drove home Craig Counsell with the winning run that gave the Marlins their first world championship.

Unfortunately for the fans in Florida, the Marlins subsequently elected to dismantle their team, trading away virtually all of their high-priced talent for young prospects in an effort to lower their payroll. Remaining behind in Florida, Renteria later noted, "I was a twenty-two-year-old veteran."[1]

After the Marlins posted only fifty-four victories in 1998, they decided to part ways with Renteria as well, dealing him to the Cardinals for a trio of prospects that included Armando Almanza, Braden Looper, and Pablo Ozuna. Upon learning of the trade that forced him to leave the heavily Latino-influenced city of Miami, a disappointed Renteria commented, "I'm going to miss Miami. The fans in Miami there love me. I think I might have a little problem in St. Louis because I think they don't have Latin food over there. Colombia is close to Miami."[2]

In spite of the initial sadness he felt about leaving Miami, Renteria proved to be a perfect fit in St. Louis. Still only twenty-three years old when he joined the Cardinals in 1999, he soon developed into the senior circuit's finest all-around shortstop. Generally hitting either first or second in the St. Louis lineup, Renteria batted .275, knocked in 63 runs, scored 92 others, and stole 37 bases in his first year with his new team. He subsequently helped the Cardinals capture the NL Central Division title in 2000 by hitting a career-high 16 home runs, driving in 76 runs, scoring 94 times, and batting .278, en route to earning a spot on the NL All-Star team and his first Silver Slugger.

Although Renteria's offensive numbers fell off somewhat the following season, he rebounded in 2002 to bat .305 and establish a new career high with eighty-three RBIs. He also won his first Gold Glove and his second Silver Slugger that year. Renteria followed up his outstanding 2002 campaign with an even better 2003 season in which he drove in 100 runs, scored 96 others, and placed among the league leaders with 194 hits, 47 doubles, 34 stolen bases, and a .330 batting average, en route to earning All-Star honors and his second straight Silver Slugger. His 100 RBIs made him the first NL shortstop in eighteen years to knock in as many as 100 runs in a season. Renteria also won his second consecutive Gold Glove.

Renteria spent only one more year in St. Louis, helping the Cardinals capture their third division title in five seasons by batting .287, driving in 72 runs, and scoring 84 others in 2004. He then led them to a four-game victory over Los Angeles in the NLDS by batting .455, knocking in 4 runs, and scoring 4 times himself. After subsequently struggling against Houston in the NLCS, Renteria played well against Boston in the World Series, batting .333, even though the Red Sox swept the Cardinals in four straight games.

A free agent at the conclusion of the campaign, Renteria elected to sign with Boston, ending his six-year tenure in St. Louis. He remained with the Red Sox for just one year, batting .276 and scoring 100 runs for the first time in his career, before returning to the NL when Boston traded him to the Atlanta Braves. After two solid years in Atlanta, Renteria joined the Tigers, who acquired him for two prospects shortly after the 2007 season ended. He then split the next four years between the Tigers, Giants, and Reds, experiencing one more moment of glory with the Giants in 2010, when he earned World Series Most Valuable Player honors by hitting game-winning home runs in Game 2 and Game 5. He subsequently signed with Cincinnati as a free agent at the end of the year, batting just .251 and scoring only thirty-four runs in ninety-six games with the Reds in 2011, before announcing his retirement at season's end. Renteria concluded his career with 140 home runs, 923 RBIs, 1,200 runs scored, 2,327 hits, 436 doubles, 294 stolen bases, a .286 batting average, a .343 on-base percentage, and a .398 slugging percentage. In his six years with the Cardinals, he hit 71 homers, drove in 451 runs, scored 497 others, collected 973 hits, accumulated 207 doubles, stole 148 bases, batted .290, compiled a .347 on-base percentage, and posted a .420 slugging percentage. Although Renteria received interest and offers from several teams during the course of the 2012 campaign, he informed them that he intends to remain retired.

CARDINAL CAREER HIGHLIGHTS

Best Season

Although Renteria compiled outstanding numbers for the Cardinals the previous year as well, he had easily his most productive season for them in 2003, hitting 13 homers, batting .330, scoring 96 runs, stealing 34 bases, and establishing career highs with 100 RBIs, 194 hits, 47 doubles, 282 total bases, a .394 on-base percentage, and a .480 slugging percentage. He placed among the league leaders in four different offensive categories, en route to earning Silver Slugger honors for one of three times. He also earned one of his two Gold Gloves.

Memorable Moments/Greatest Performances

Although not known as a home-run hitter, Renteria flexed his muscles for the Cardinals on numerous occasions. He hit two homers in a 5–2 win over Florida on May 31, 1999. The following season, Renteria homered in three straight games from April 9 to April 11, setting a new career high on the last of those days by driving in four runs during a 10–6 victory over the Houston Astros. Later in the year, on August 29, he hit his sixteenth homer of the campaign, breaking in the process Solly Hemus's single-season record for most home runs by a Cardinals' shortstop.

Renteria also experienced a brief power surge in July 2002, hitting a game-winning, three-run homer on July 28 that capped off a six-run, ninth-inning rally that gave the Cardinals a 10–9 victory over the Chicago Cubs. Two nights later, he hit two home runs during a 5–0 win over the Florida Marlins. Renteria also hit a grand slam homer and drove in a career-high five runs during a 10–5 victory over Cincinnati on September 4. He later matched that effort by hitting two home runs and knocking in five runs during an 11–8 win over Houston on April 13, 2003.

In addition, Renteria had huge games against the Boston Red Sox on June 12, 2003 and the New York Mets on August 8, 2004. He collected five hits on both occasions.

Notable Achievements

Knocked in 100 runs once (2003).
Batted over .300 twice, topping the .330 mark once.
Surpassed forty doubles once (forty-seven in 2003).
Stole more than thirty bases twice.
Won three Silver Sluggers (2000, 2002, 2003).
Won two Gold Gloves (2002, 2003).
Four-time *Sporting News* All-Star selection.
Three-time NL All-Star (2000, 2003, 2004).
2004 NL champion.

NOTES

1. Edgar Renteria, quoted in "Edgar Renteria," *BaseballLibrary.com*, http://dev.baseballlibrary.com/ballplayers/player.php?name=Edgar_Renteria_1975 (accessed November 9, 2012).

2. Renteria, quoted in "Edgar Renteria," http://dev.baseballlibrary.com/ballplayers/player.php?name=Edgar_Renteria_1975.

43

GARRY TEMPLETON

The fact that Garry Templeton finished just forty-third in these rankings serves as a testament to the tumultuous nature of the six seasons he spent in St. Louis. Leaving behind him a legacy of unfulfilled potential, "Jump Steady," as he came to be known, proved to be a huge disappointment to so many people within the Cardinals organization who believed he possessed the all-around skills to become one of the greatest shortstops in National League history.

Whitey Herzog, who managed Templeton during the latter's six years in St. Louis, spent his formative years in professional baseball playing alongside Mickey Mantle in the New York Yankees farm system. Herzog also later managed George Brett in Kansas City and Ozzie Smith in St. Louis. Yet, Herzog maintains that Templeton took a backseat to no one in terms of his all-around ability, referring to him as the "most talented"[1] player he ever saw. Speaking of his onetime shortstop, Herzog noted, "He had great running speed, a great arm, he was a switch-hitter. . . . He had everything but power; that was the only thing he didn't have that Mantle had."[2] Herzog added, "When I came here in 1980, I had three of the top ten salaries in baseball. Ted Simmons, Keith Hernandez, and Garry—they were all making $667,000. And, at the end of the year, I said the one guy I wouldn't trade would be Garry."[3]

Unfortunately, Templeton's volatile personality and erratic behavior forced Herzog to reevaluate his position, prompting the manager to deal his star shortstop to San Diego for Ozzie Smith at the conclusion of the 1981 campaign. Yet, even though Templeton's time in St. Louis ended prematurely, he managed to accomplish quite a bit in his six seasons with the Cardinals. After becoming the youngest shortstop (twenty-three) in modern history to reach the 200-hit plateau in 1977, he established himself two years later as the first switch-hitter ever to accumulate 100 hits from each side of the plate in the same season. That same year, Templeton became the first NL player to top the circuit in triples three straight times. Templeton made two NL All-Star teams as a member of the Cardinals, won one Silver Slugger, and earned three *Sporting News* All-Star selections. Still, due to the transient nature of his status as an elite player, the trade that sent him to the Padres for Ozzie Smith will always be viewed as a coup for the Cardinals.

Born in Lockney, Texas, on March 24, 1956, Garry Lewis Templeton grew up in Santa Ana, California, where he starred in baseball while attending Santa Ana Valley High School. After being selected by the Cardinals in the first round of the 1974 amateur draft with the thirteenth overall pick, Templeton advanced quickly through the St. Louis farm system, making his major-league debut with the team in August 1976. Although the twenty-year-old shortstop played erratically in the field in the season's final two months, committing twenty-four errors in only fifty-three games, he batted .291 and displayed tremendous range and an outstanding arm, which earned him the starting shortstop job heading into the ensuing campaign.

Continuing to display his exceptional natural skillset, Templeton performed brilliantly in his first full season, batting .322, driving in 79 runs, scoring 94 others, collecting 200 hits, stealing 28 bases, and leading the NL with 18 triples. And even though he finished third among NL shortstops with 32 errors, he also placed second in putouts. Templeton's outstanding all-around performance earned him his first All-Star selection, a spot on the *Sporting News* All-Star Team, and a thirteenth-place finish in the league Most Valuable Player voting. He followed that up with a somewhat less productive 1978 season in which he batted .280, accumulated 181 hits, knocked in only 47 runs, and scored just 82 others. Nevertheless, he still managed to steal thirty-four bases and top the senior circuit with thirteen triples.

Rebounding from his slightly subpar 1978 campaign, Templeton had a sensational year for the Cardinals in 1979. In addition to batting .314, driving in 62 runs, stealing 26 bases, and hitting a career-high 9 home runs, the 23-year-old shortstop scored 105 runs, accumulated 32 doubles, and led the NL with 211 hits and 19 triples. Although Templeton led all senior circuit shortstops with thirty-four errors, he also finished second in assists (525) and first in putouts (292). Perhaps most significant is the fact that he established himself as the first switch-hitter in major-league history to amass 100 hits from both sides of the plate in the same season. To do so, he got his last six hits batting right-handed against right-handed pitching.

Commenting on his onetime teammate's extraordinary accomplishment, Ted Simmons later marveled, "That was one of the most amazing things I've ever seen. He needed more hits than he had games left, so he batted right-handed against right-handed pitchers to get them. And they weren't dinks; he hit the ball hard. I've never seen anyone in the game do that."[4] Templeton's exceptional season earned him his second All-Star nomination and his second *Sporting News* All-Star selection.

Templeton continued his outstanding play in 1980, batting .319, scoring 83 runs, and stealing 31 bases, even though injuries limited him to only 118 games. At season's end, he was presented with his first Silver Slugger and was named to his third *Sporting News* All-Star team.

Unfortunately, everything began to unravel for the star shortstop shortly thereafter. Never particularly popular with the fans to begin with due to a laid-back demeanor that many felt revealed a lack of interest on his part, Templeton began to incur the wrath of Cardinals fans by voicing his displeasure about his situation in St. Louis. During a 1981 season that included a players' strike, Templeton made public his dissatisfaction about not batting leadoff, his disenchantment with his salary, and his desire to be traded to a California team. After requesting a trade to the San Diego Padres earlier in the season, Templeton reached his nadir in St. Louis in late August, when he responded to a heckling "Ladies Day" crowd at Busch Stadium with a one-finger salute. Subsequently fined $5,000 and suspended for three weeks, he ended up agreeing to undergo psychiatric evaluation.

After the Cardinals and Padres agreed in principle to a deal that off-season that ended up sending Templeton to San Diego for Ozzie Smith, Whitey Herzog expressed his feelings at a speaking engagement, saying, "I have an owner who's the greatest man in the world, and I want to win a world championship for him. I feel I might do it if I get a shortstop who goes out there every day and hounds the ball."[5] Herzog added, "Templeton doesn't want to play in St. Louis. He doesn't want to play on (artificial) turf. He doesn't want to play when we go to Montreal. He doesn't want to play in the Astrodome. He doesn't want to play in the rain. The other eighty games, he's all right."[6]

Although Herzog didn't broach the subject at the time, he later revealed that most of Templeton's behavioral issues were drug-related. Herzog noted, "When Garry came to spring training (in 1981), he was messed up. I told Gussie (Busch) we really got a problem. Garry had been in a car wreck and was running around with the wrong people."[7]

After Templeton batted .288 in only eighty games in St. Louis in 1981, he found himself headed for San Diego when the Cardinals and Padres completed a six-player trade in early December that netted the Cards Ozzie Smith in return. Templeton remained in San Diego nine full seasons, never regaining his earlier form. Hampered by knee and back problems, he batted over .260 just twice in his nine years with the Padres, scored more than 70 runs only once, and stole more than 20 bases just once. Templeton also made the NL All-Star team only one more time. Meanwhile, Smith carved out a Hall of Fame career for himself in St. Louis, establishing himself as the greatest defensive shortstop in baseball history, en route to helping the Cardinals win three NL pennants and one world championship.

But Templeton got his life back together in San Diego, eventually becoming one of the most popular players in Padres history. Considered to be one of the emotional leaders of San Diego's 1984 NL championship team, Templeton served as captain of the Padres from 1987 to May 1991, when the New York Mets acquired him for infielder Tim Teufel. After spending the final four months of the 1991 campaign in New York, the thirty-five-year-old Templeton decided to announce his retirement at season's end. He ended his career with 70 home runs, 728 RBIs, 893 runs scored, 2,096 hits, 106 triples, 242 stolen bases, a .271 batting average, a .304 on-base percentage, and a .369 slugging percentage. In his six years with the Cardinals, Templeton hit 25 homers, drove in 281 runs, scored 443 others, collected 911 hits, accumulated 69 triples, stole 138 bases, batted .305, compiled a .325

on-base percentage, and posted a .418 slugging percentage. He ranks eleventh all-time on the team in triples.

Since retiring as an active player, Templeton has spent the past two decades coaching and managing at the minor-league level. He has served as manager for seven different teams during that time.

CARDINAL CAREER HIGHLIGHTS

Best Season

Templeton performed exceptionally well for the Cardinals in both 1977 and 1979, and either one of those seasons would have made a good choice. In the first of those years, the enigmatic shortstop established career highs with seventy-nine RBIs and a .322 batting average. He also collected 200 hits, scored 94 runs, stole 28 bases, and led the NL with 18 triples. Yet, while Templeton knocked in seventeen fewer runs in 1979, he posted better numbers in virtually every other offensive category. In addition to compiling a .314 batting average that nearly equaled his mark from two years earlier, he established career highs with 105 runs scored, 9 home runs, 32 doubles, 308 total bases, and a league-leading 211 hits and 19 triples. In amassing 100 hits from each side of the plate, Templeton became the first switch-hitter in major-league history to accomplish the feat. Meanwhile, his total of 19 triples represented the highest number compiled by any player since 1957. And even though Templeton's total of twenty-six steals fell just short of the figure he posted in 1977, he compiled a much higher success rate on his stolen base attempts (72 percent to 54 percent). Furthermore, Templeton accumulated a career-high 525 assists in the field in 1979, en route to finishing second among all NL shortstops. He also led all players at his position with 292 putouts. All things considered, Templeton had his greatest season in 1979.

Memorable Moments and Greatest Performances

Templeton had a number of big offensive days for the Cardinals, not the least of which ended up being his April 27, 1977 performance against Chicago in which helped lead his team to a 21–3 thrashing of the Cubs by scoring five times. Templeton put his name in the record books two years later, when, on September 28, 1979, he collected three hits against the New York Mets to become the first player in major-league history to accumulate 100 hits from each side of the plate in a season.

Nevertheless, Templeton's name will always be most closely associated with two unfortunate incidents that took place during his time in St. Louis. The first episode occurred shortly after the NL announced its starting team for the 1979 All-Star Game. Despite posting better numbers than either Dave Concepcion or Larry Bowa, Templeton finished behind both players in the fan balloting at shortstop. Subsequently named to the NL squad as a reserve, Templeton reportedly uttered the now-infamous words, "If I ain't startin', I ain't departin'!" Although it later surfaced that legendary Cardinals broadcaster Jack Buck actually coined the colorful phrase to summarize Templeton's feelings about being snubbed for the starting squad, the expression has been universally credited to Templeton.

Templeton's legacy with the Cardinals has been tainted even more by the erratic behavior he displayed on the field late in his final year with the team. Already having raised the ire of Cardinals fans by constantly complaining about his salary, the manager's refusal to bat him leadoff, and wanting to be traded to a California team, Templeton further antagonized the Busch Stadium faithful by making several obscene gestures toward them during an August 26, 1981 home game.

Striking out in the first inning on a pitch that momentarily eluded San Francisco catcher Milt May, Templeton failed to run down to first base, prompting the vast majority of the 7,766 fans in attendance at Busch Stadium to shower him with a chorus of boos. Angered by the lack of respect shown to him by the fans, he responded by giving them the finger. Jeered loudly once more as he trotted in from the field after the top of the second and third innings, Templeton made another obscene gesture toward the fans, prompting home-plate umpire Bruce Froemming to eject him from the contest. Booed again as he exited, Templeton showed his disdain for those in attendance by grabbing his crotch. Angered by his shortstop's vulgar actions, Cardinals manager Whitey Herzog grabbed Templeton by the arm as he approached the dugout, pulled him down the steps, and backed him against the wall. After players on the team separated the two men, Herzog ordered Templeton to wait in the dugout; however, the latter instead elected to leave the stadium ten minutes later with a suitcase full of clothes, leading to a $5,000 fine, a three-week suspension, and, ultimately, a psychiatric evaluation that resulted in a diagnosis of depression.

Watching the events as they unfolded from the opposing dugout, San Francisco manager Frank Robinson later said, "I've never seen it happen, and I hope I never do again. There's no place for it."[8] Meanwhile, Cardinals backup catcher Gene Tenace expressed the sentiments of most of his teammates when he stated after the game, "I don't think Templeton has the guts to apologize to the rest of us. He's a loser. We're better off without him. I don't think he'll even be playing two or three years from now."[9]

Notable Achievements

Scored more than 100 runs once (105 in 1979).
Batted over .300 three times.
Surpassed 200 hits twice.
Finished in double digits in triples three times.
Stole more than thirty bases twice, surpassing twenty steals two other times.
Led NL in triples three times and hits once.
Led NL shortstops in putouts twice.
1980 NL Silver Slugger winner at shortstop.
Three-time *Sporting News* All-Star selection (1977, 1979, 1980).
Two-time NL All-Star (1977, 1979).

NOTES

1. Whitey Herzog, quoted in Dan O'Neill, "Herzog and Templeton: No Grudges, No Regrets," *STLtoday.com*, www.stltoday.com/sports/baseball/professional/herzog-and-templeton-no-grudges-no-regrets/article_e2ebeb70-ce60-592f-a506-99c938347842.html (accessed November 12, 2012).

2. Herzog, quoted in O'Neill, "Herzog and Templeton: No Grudges, No Regrets," www.stltoday.com/sports/baseball/professional/herzog-and-templeton-no-grudges-no-regrets/article_e2ebeb70-ce60-592f-a506-99c938347842.html.

3. Herzog, quoted in O'Neill, "Herzog and Templeton: No Grudges, No Regrets," www.stltoday.com/sports/baseball/professional/herzog-and-templeton-no-grudges-no-regrets/article_e2ebeb70-ce60-592f-a506-99c938347842.html.

4. Ted Simmons, quoted in O'Neill, "Herzog and Templeton: No Grudges, No Regrets," www.stltoday.com/sports/baseball/professional/herzog-and-templeton-no-grudges-no-regrets/article_e2ebeb70-ce60-592f-a506-99c938347842.html.

5. Herzog, quoted in O'Neill, "Herzog and Templeton: No Grudges, No Regrets," www.stltoday.com/sports/baseball/professional/herzog-and-templeton-no-grudges-no-regrets/article_e2ebeb70-ce60-592f-a506-99c938347842.html.

6. Herzog, quoted in O'Neill, "Herzog and Templeton: No Grudges, No Regrets," www.stltoday.com/sports/baseball/professional/herzog-and-templeton-no-grudges-no-regrets/article_e2ebeb70-ce60-592f-a506-99c938347842.html.

7. Herzog, quoted in O'Neill, "Herzog and Templeton: No Grudges, No Regrets," www.stltoday.com/sports/baseball/professional/herzog-and-templeton-no-grudges-no-regrets/article_e2ebeb70-ce60-592f-a506-99c938347842.html.

8. Frank Robinson, quoted in O'Neill, "Herzog and Templeton: No Grudges, No Regrets," www.stltoday.com/sports/baseball/professional/herzog-and-templeton-no-grudges-no-regrets/article_e2ebeb70-ce60-592f-a506-99c938347842.html.

9. Gene Tenace, quoted in O'Neill, "Herzog and Templeton: No Grudges, No Regrets," www.stltoday.com/sports/baseball/professional/herzog-and-templeton-no-grudges-no-regrets/article_e2ebeb70-ce60-592f-a506-99c938347842.html.

44

TERRY MOORE

Terry Moore never came close to leading the National League in any major offensive statistical category. He batted over .300 just once in his eleven years in St. Louis. He never hit as many as twenty homers in a season. He also never collected 200 hits, drove in 100 runs, or scored 100 times. Nevertheless, the fleet-footed center fielder earned a place in these rankings with his extraordinary defensive skills and exceptional leadership ability. An acrobatic outfielder with outstanding speed, a strong throwing arm, and marvelous instincts, Moore drew favorable comparisons as a defender to legendary center fielders Tris Speaker and Joe DiMaggio during his playing days. A superb leader as well, Moore served as captain on the Cardinals' world championship ball clubs of 1942 and 1946, leading St. Louis to World Series victories over powerful New York Yankee and Boston Red Sox teams. And even though Moore failed to post the gaudy offensive numbers compiled by many other players on this list, he proved to be a solid offensive performer for the Cardinals throughout the years, batting over .290 three times, scoring more than 80 runs four times, surpassing 30 doubles on three occasions, and hitting as many as 17 home runs twice, en route to earning four NL All-Star selections and five top-20 finishes in the league Most Valuable Player voting.

Born in Vernon, Alabama, on May 27, 1912, Terry Bluford Moore began his professional baseball career in 1932, earning a roster spot with the Cardinals three years later after posting a batting average of .328 in the American Association in 1934. A right-handed batter and thrower, Moore claimed the Cardinals' starting center-field job almost as soon as he arrived in St. Louis in 1935. Replacing Ernie

Orsatti as the team's starter at the position shortly after the regular season got underway, the 23-year-old rookie had a solid first season, batting .287, scoring 63 runs, and stealing 13 bases in 119 games, even though a fractured foot forced him to sit out the final two weeks of the campaign. Moore also finished third among NL center fielders with eleven assists and placed fourth with 354 putouts. Although his batting average slipped to .264 the following year, he played well during the course of the 1936 campaign, scoring 85 runs, finishing fourth in the league with a career-high 39 doubles, leading all NL center fielders with 14 assists, and topping all senior circuit outfielders with 418 putouts.

After posting solid numbers again in 1937, Moore sustained a concussion in June 1938, when he crashed into the outfield wall at Sportsman's Park. The injury put him out of action for more than a month, limiting him to only ninety-four games and significantly reducing his offensive production the remainder of the year; however, Moore bounced back in 1939 to begin a four-year stretch during which he compiled the best offensive numbers of his career.

Moore earned All-Star honors for the first of four straight times in 1939 by batting .295, establishing career highs with 17 home runs and 77 RBIs, and leading all NL center fielders with 16 assists. He again hit 17 homers in 1940, while also batting .304, scoring 92 runs, finishing third in the league with 18 stolen bases, topping all NL center fielders with 11 assists, and leading all league outfielders with 383 putouts. Moore continued his outstanding play in each of the next two seasons, scoring in excess of eighty runs both years, while posting batting averages of .294 and .288, despite missing nearly a month of the 1941 campaign after being carried off the field on a stretcher following a beaning by Boston Braves pitcher Art Johnson.

Arriving in St. Louis as he did in 1935, Moore joined the Cardinals the year after the "Gas House Gang" won the 1934 World Series. That being the case, he spent his first few seasons playing alongside such legendary figures as Dizzy Dean, Frankie Frisch, and Joe Medwick. He subsequently spent the next several years teaming up with the likes of Johnny Mize, Enos Slaughter, and Stan Musial. Yet, even though Moore often found himself being overshadowed by several of his more famous teammates, he eventually established himself as the Cardinals' leader, serving as captain of the team for much of the 1940s.

Cardinals manager Eddie Dyer described the impact Moore made on his team when he said, "I don't like to think of the day when Terry Moore won't be able to take his place in our outfield. Terry just does something for our team, and we aren't the same ball club without him."[1] Meanwhile, in *Branch Rickey's Little Blue Book: Wit and Strategy from Baseball's Last Wise Man*, John J. Monteleone quotes Rickey as saying, "Terry Moore was a real Gashouser. In him burned the fire and determination of a crusader; a warrior. He asked no quarter and gave none."[2]

Still at the top of his game at the age of thirty, Moore entered the military at the conclusion of the 1942 campaign, forcing him to miss the next three seasons. An old knee injury limited him to only ninety-one games when he returned to the Cardinals in 1946—a season in which he posted a batting average of just .263. Nevertheless, Moore retained his exceptional ball hawking skills, helping the Cardinals defeat the Red Sox in the 1946 World Series by making two outstanding catches in Game 7—one against Ted Williams, the other against Pinky Higgins. Following the contest, Boston manager Joe Cronin gushed, "What an outfielder! They told us Moore had bad knees. I hate to think of what he does to you when he's running on a good pair of knees."[3]

Moore spent two more years in St. Louis, retiring at the end of the 1948 campaign with 80 career homers, 513 RBIs, 719 runs scored, 1,318 hits, a .280 lifetime batting average, a .340 on-base percentage, and a .399 slugging percentage. In addition to leading all NL outfielders in putouts twice, he topped all league center fielders in assists on four separate occasions.

Following his retirement, Moore served the Cardinals as a coach from 1949 to 1952, before becoming a scout for the Philadelphia Phillies in 1953. He also managed the Phillies for the second half of the 1954 season, replacing Steve O'Neill at the helm after Philadelphia fired him seventy-seven games into the campaign. Moore returned to St. Louis in 1956, once again assuming a position on the Cardinals coaching staff from 1956 to 1958. After leaving the game at the conclusion of the 1958 season, he retired to Collinsville, Illinois, where he lived until March 29, 1995, when he passed away at the age of eighty-two.

CAREER HIGHLIGHTS

Best Season

Although Moore compiled a slightly higher on-base plus slugging percentage, hit the same number of home runs, and knocked in a career-high seventy-seven runs one year earlier, he had his best all-around season for the Cardinals in 1940. In addition to driving in 64 runs and matching his career high with 17 homers, the fleet-footed center fielder posted the best marks of his career in runs scored (92), base hits (163), stolen bases (18), total bases (255), and batting average (.304). He also led all NL outfielders with 383 putouts and topped all senior circuit center fielders with eleven assists.

Memorable Moments and Greatest Performances

Known more for his exceptional defense than for his ability as a hitter, Moore made a number of extraordinary catches for the Cardinals throughout the years, perhaps the most memorable of which took place in Game 3 of the 1942 World Series. With the Fall Classic tied at a game apiece and the Cardinals trying to protect a 1–0 lead in the sixth inning of the third contest, Joe DiMaggio hit a drive to deep left-center field that appeared headed for the bleachers; however, Moore raced over and made a leaping, one-handed catch that one writer called "one of the finest exhibitions of defensive play in the history of postseason games."[4]

Still, Moore proved to be anything but a liability at the plate, contributing greatly to the Cardinals on offense as well. He had a couple of big offensive days in August of his rookie campaign, hitting two doubles and two homers in one contest, before collecting three doubles and a home run in a doubleheader sweep of the Phillies on August 28. Just one week later, on September 5, 1935, Moore had arguably his best day ever at the plate, going 6-for-6 during a 15–3 St. Louis victory over Boston.

After suffering a concussion one month earlier, Moore made a triumphant return to the Cardinals lineup on July 15, 1938. He recovered to collect three hits and score three runs during a 10–6 St. Louis win over Boston.

Moore had another memorable day at the plate on August 16, 1939, when he keyed a Cardinals doubleheader sweep of the Pirates at Forbes Field with a pair of inside-the-park home runs. Only one NL player (Hank Thompson in 1950) ended up hitting two inside-the-park homers in one game in the next fifty years.

Although Moore hit only eighty home runs in the course of eleven major-league seasons, he reached the seats twice in one contest on May 18, 1940. This feat helped the Cardinals defeat the Dodgers by a score of 6–2.

Moore also put together a pair of impressive streaks during his time in St. Louis, hitting successfully in twenty consecutive games at one point during the 1942 season, and collecting nine straight hits during the course of two games in 1947. The Cardinals' captain also collected five hits against the Dodgers in a two-game playoff that gave St. Louis the 1946 NL pennant.

Notable Achievements

Batted over .300 once (.304 in 1940).
Led NL outfielders in putouts twice and fielding percentage once.
Led NL center fielders in assists four times.
Four-time NL All-Star (1939, 1940, 1941, 1942).
Two-time NL champion (1942, 1946).
Two-time world champion (1942, 1946).

NOTES

1. Eddie Dyer, quoted in Mike Shalin and Neil Shalin, *Out by a Step: The 100 Best Players Not in the Baseball Hall of Fame* (Lanham, MD: Diamond Communications, 2002), 289.
2. Branch Rickey, quoted by John J. Monteleone in "Terry Moore Stats," *Baseball Almanac*, www.baseball-almanac.com/players/player.php?p=moorete01 (accessed November 13, 2012).
3. Joe Cronin, quoted in Shalin and Shalin, *Out by a Step*, 289.
4. Quoted in Shalin and Shalin, *Out by a Step*, 288.

45

TIM MCCARVER

Although he has since gone on to even greater fame as one of the most respected baseball analysts of his time, Tim McCarver initially made a name for himself as the starting catcher in St. Louis for nearly a decade. After seeing an extremely limited amount of duty in his first three seasons with the Cardinals, McCarver eventually established himself as one of the National League's top receivers, holding down the starting job in St. Louis from 1963 to 1969. An excellent handler of pitchers, he served as the primary backstop for Hall of Fame hurlers Bob Gibson and Steve Carlton during most of their peak seasons, assuming that role for Carlton in Philadelphia after both men left St. Louis during the early 1970s. A solid hitter as well, McCarver batted over .280 for the Cardinals three times, peaking at .295 in 1967, when he finished second in the NL Most Valuable Player voting. In his seven seasons as their full-time starting catcher, McCarver helped the Cardinals win three NL pennants and two world championships, contributing to their success with his bat, glove, leadership skills, and tremendous baseball acumen.

Born in Memphis, Tennessee, on October 16, 1941, James Timothy McCarver signed with the Cardinals in 1959, shortly after he graduated from Christian Brothers High School, where he starred in both football and baseball. Accumulating a total of only 345 minor-league at bats before earning his first call-up to the majors, McCarver made his first appearance in a Cardinals uniform one month shy of his eighteenth birthday, in September 1959. After going just 4-for-24 in the eight games in which he appeared, he spent virtually all of the next three seasons in the minor leagues, before joining the Cardinals for good in 1963.

Still only twenty-one years of age at the start of the 1963 campaign, McCarver impressed St. Louis management to such an extent that the Cardinals traded away their starting catcher from the previous year, Gene Oliver, shortly after the regular season got underway. Rewarding team management for the faith it placed in him, McCarver posted a batting average of .289 in his first full season in the big leagues. He followed that up by hitting 9 home runs, driving in 52 runs, and batting .288 in 1964, in helping the Cardinals capture the NL pennant. McCarver subsequently starred in the World Series, contributing to his team's seven-game victory over the New York Yankees by batting .478, homering once, and knocking in 5 runs.

After being limited by injuries to only 113 games the following year, McCarver earned the first of two straight NL All-Star selections in 1966 by batting .274, hitting 12 home runs, driving in 68 runs, and leading the league with 13 triples. His thirteen three-baggers tied him with Johnny Kling (1903) for the post–1900 record for most triples by a catcher. Blessed with outstanding running speed for a catcher, McCarver also stole a career-high nine bases. He had his finest all-around season, however, in 1967, contributing mightily to the Cardinals' pennant-winning campaign by hitting 14 homers, knocking in 69 runs, batting .295, and leading all NL receivers with 67 assists and a .997 fielding percentage. His strong performance earned him his only *Sporting News* All-Star selection and a second-place finish to teammate Orlando Cepeda in the league MVP balloting. It also made him the focal point of a July 22, 1967, *Sporting News* article that summarized some rather high praise McCarver inspired in his rookie season. Former major-league catcher Wally Schang, who starred for championship teams in Philadelphia, Boston, and New York nearly fifty years earlier, said of the young receiver, "The kid reminds me of Mickey Cochrane. I don't know if McCarver will hit with Cochrane, but he's got Mickey's same aggressiveness and speed. And, as a kid, McCarver's a pretty good hitter right now."[1]

The same piece quotes Branch Rickey as comparing McCarver to Bill DeLancey, who started behind the plate for the Cardinals' 1934 "Gas House Gang" squad: "DeLancey had the stronger throwing arm, but Tim's arm is strong enough. McCarver's a solid .280 hitter. He could hit .300, and he can run faster than DeLancey could. He has the same aggressiveness and baseball intelligence."[2]

The 1967 campaign proved to be the highpoint of McCarver's career. Although the Cardinals repeated as NL champions in 1968, they ended up losing to Detroit in the World Series, with McCarver hitting only 5 homers, driving in just 48 runs, scoring only 35 others, and batting just .253 during the regular season. He posted slightly better offensive numbers the following year, but, with Ted Simmons waiting in the wings, the Cardinals elected to include McCarver in a seven-player trade they completed with the Phillies on October 7, 1969. The deal netted them slugging first baseman Dick Allen in return.

McCarver spent two and a half years in Philadelphia, before he began a somewhat nomadic existence that saw him split the final eight and a half years of his career between the Expos, Red Sox, Cardinals, and Phillies. Returning to the Cardinals for a second tour of duty in 1973, he spent the next season and a half mostly at first base, although he also found himself catching and pinch-hitting from time to time. After returning to the Phillies in 1975, McCarver spent most of the next three seasons serving as Steve Carlton's personal catcher, while also developing into a solid pinch hitter. Performing in that dual role in 1977, McCarver posted a career-high .320 batting average, hit 6 homers, and drove in 30 runs in only 169 official at bats. He ended his career with the Phillies in 1980, becoming in the process one of the few players in baseball history to play in four decades.

During the course of 21 major-league seasons, McCarver hit 97 home runs, knocked in 645 runs, scored 590 others, collected 1,501 hits, batted .271, compiled a .337 on-base percentage, and posted a .388 slugging percentage. In parts of 12 seasons in St. Louis, he hit 66 homers, drove in 453 runs, scored 393 others, accumulated 1,029 hits, batted .272, compiled an on-base percentage of .329, and posted a slugging percentage of .388.

Having been hired into the broadcast booth by the Phillies at the end of the 1979 season, before he even played his final game, McCarver subsequently began a long and distinguished career as one of baseball's top analysts. Known during his playing days for his quick wit, keen sense of humor, and cerebral approach to the game, he brought those same qualities with him into the booth. Candid, opinionated, and extremely knowledgeable, he soon developed a reputation second to none in the field. After serving as a Phillies broadcaster for three years, McCarver joined the New York Mets broadcasting crew in 1983, remaining there for sixteen years, before finally becoming a member of the team that broadcasts games nationally for FOX sports. Having served as a broadcaster for more than three decades, McCarver has now spent more time in the booth than he did on the playing field. In so doing, he has broadcast more World Series telecasts than any other announcer in baseball history.

CARDINAL CAREER HIGHLIGHTS

Best Season

Although McCarver collected more hits, knocked in virtually the same number of runs, and led the NL with 13 triples one year earlier, he had easily his best all-around season for the Cardinals in 1967, when he batted .295 and established career highs with 14 home runs, 69 RBIs, 68 runs scored, and a .452 slugging percentage. He also led all NL receivers in assists and fielding percentage. McCarver's solid performance earned him his second consecutive All-Star selection, his only *Sporting News* All-Star nomination, and a runner-up finish in the league MVP voting.

Memorable Moments and Greatest Performances

On June 9, 1963, McCarver accomplished the rare feat of hitting an inside-the-park grand slam home run during an 8–7 Cardinals victory over the New York Mets. A solid postseason performer for the Cardinals, McCarver batted .333, with a homer and four RBIs against the Tigers in the 1968 World Series, helping his team post a 7–3 win in Game 3 by hitting a three-run home run against Detroit starter Earl Wilson.

McCarver performed even better against the Yankees in the 1964 World Series, homering once, driving in 5 runs, scoring 4 others, and leading both teams with a .478 batting average. He got the biggest hit of his career in Game 5, hitting a three-run home run off New York reliever Pete Mikkelsen in the top of the tenth inning that gave the Cardinals a 5–2 victory and a 3–2 lead in the Fall Classic. McCarver ended up tying a Series record by hitting safely in all seven contests, helping the Cardinals capture their first world championship in eighteen years in the process.

Notable Achievements

Finished in double digits in triples once.
Led NL with thirteen triples in 1966.
Led NL catchers in assists once and fielding percentage twice.
Finished second in 1967 NL MVP voting.
1967 *Sporting News* All-Star selection.
Two-time NL All-Star (1966, 1967).
Three-time NL champion (1964, 1967, 1968).
Two-time world champion (1964, 1967).

NOTES

1. Wally Schang, quoted in Dave Williams, "Tim McCarver," *Society for American Baseball Research*, http://sabr.org/bioproj/person/b34583db (accessed November 13, 2012).
2. Branch Rickey, quoted in Dave Williams, "Tim McCarver," http://sabr.org/bioproj/person/b34583db.

46

JACK CLARK

Spending only three of his eighteen major-league seasons in a Cardinals uniform, Jack Clark actually had most of his best years earlier in his career as a member of the San Francisco Giants. Nevertheless, the hard-hitting first baseman/outfielder earned a spot in these rankings by helping the Cardinals capture two pennants in his three years in St. Louis. Supplying most of the power to a ball club that predicated much of its success on its outstanding speed, excellent pitching, and solid defense, Clark managed to lead the Cardinals in home runs in two of his three seasons with them, even though injuries plagued him throughout his tenure with the club. Particularly impressive in 1987, he smashed thirty-five of the ninety-four homers the Cardinals hit as a team, en route to earning a third-place finish in the National League Most Valuable Player voting.

Born in New Brighton, Pennsylvania, on November 10, 1955, Jack Anthony Clark signed with the San Francisco Giants shortly after he graduated from Gladstone High School in Covina, California, when the Giants selected him in the thirteenth round of the 1973 amateur draft. After making brief appearances with the Giants toward the end of both the 1975 and 1976 campaigns, Clark earned the club's starting right-field job in spring training of 1977. Although he played well as a rookie, hitting 13 homers, driving in 51 runs, and accumulating 11 outfield assists, Clark really came into his own in his second season, concluding the 1978 campaign with 25 home runs, 98 RBIs, 90 runs scored, 46 doubles, and a .306 batting average, en route to earning All-Star honors for the first time and a fifth-place finish in the league MVP balloting.

Clark continued to excel as a member of the Giants, topping 20 homers in four of the next six seasons, while also knocking in more than 100 runs, scoring 90 times, and batting over .300 once each. An excellent clutch hitter, he led the NL with eighteen game-winning RBIs in 1980. He also tied for the league lead with twenty-one game-winners in 1982. Although Clark lacked outstanding speed, he also developed into an above-average outfielder, leading all NL right fielders in putouts three times and assists twice; however, unhappy with the Giants and the prospect of spending the remainder of his career playing in windy Candlestick Park, he eventually expressed an interest in leaving San Francisco. As a result, the power-starved Cardinals proved to be an excellent trading partner when they offered the Giants a package of four players that included David Green, Dave LaPoint, Gary Rajsich, and Jose Uribe for the right-handed-hitting slugger on February 1, 1985.

Moved to first base after he joined the Cardinals, Clark had a big first year in St. Louis, finishing near the top of the league rankings with a .393 on-base percentage and a .502 slugging percentage, batting .281, hitting 22 home runs, and driving in 87 runs, despite being limited by injuries to only 126 games and 442 official at bats. His strong performance earned him his third All-Star selection, his first Silver Slugger, and a tenth-place finish in the NL MVP voting. He subsequently helped lead the Cardinals to victory over the Dodgers in the National League Championship Series (NLCS) by batting .381, homering once, and driving in 4 runs, with his game-winning, three-run shot in the ninth inning of Game 6 putting the Cardinals in the World Series.

After suffering through an injury-plagued 1986 campaign, Clark returned to top form in 1987, placing among the league leaders in numerous statistical categories. In addition to batting .286 and establishing career highs with 35 home runs, 106 RBIs, and 93 runs scored, he topped the senior circuit with 136 walks, a .459 on-base percentage, and a .597 slugging percentage. His dominant performance earned him his final NL All-Star selection, a spot on the *Sporting News* All-Star Team, and a third-place finish in the league MVP balloting. Clark likely would have finished even higher in the voting had an ankle injury not forced him to miss the final three weeks of the regular season. His inactivity for virtually all of the postseason likely cost the Cardinals the world championship as well.

Although Clark had always presented an imposing figure at the plate to opposing pitchers, he clearly established himself as the league's most intimidating hitter during his time in St. Louis. Possessing a lean, but muscular, six-foot, two-inch, 195-pound frame, jet black hair, and a vicious swing that earned him the nickname "Jack the Ripper," Clark caused the knees of many an opposing pitcher to weaken when he stepped into the batter's box. Since the right-handed-hitting slugger represented the only real power threat in the Cardinals lineup, he drew an inordinate amount of walks, as can be evidenced by his league-leading total of 136 bases on balls in 1987. Even Willie McGee's immediate presence behind him in the batting order could not deter opposing hurlers from pitching around Clark in most pressure situations (McGee knocked in a career-high 105 runs in 1987).

Yet, in spite of the tremendous impact Clark made in the middle of the Cardinals batting order, he eventually wore out his welcome in St. Louis as well. After developing a somewhat contentious relationship with star shortstop Ozzie Smith throughout the course of the three previous seasons, Clark got into a contract squabble with Cardinals management at the conclusion of the 1987 campaign. Displeased with his situation in St. Louis, he elected to sign a free-agent deal with the Yankees.

Despite hitting 27 home runs, driving in 93 runs, and walking 113 times in 1988, Clark's .242 batting average and 141 strikeouts made him a huge disappointment in New York. Seeking to rid themselves of his exorbitant contract, the Yankees traded him to the San Diego Padres for three players in October 1988. Always one to speak his mind, Clark expressed his feelings about the time he spent in the American League when he stated, "I hate that damn league. Every game lasts three and a half to four hours. No wonder the fans are bored over there."[1]

Clark remained in San Diego for two years, hitting a total of 51 home runs for the Padres during that time. After his production fell off considerably in 1990, the Padres grew increasingly weary of his caustic personality, which caused him to feud with teammate Tony Gwynn. The San Diego icon, who had previously developed a reputation as one of the hardest-working and most dedicated players in baseball, found himself being criticized by Clark, who called him selfish and stated that he put his batting average ahead of winning. Clark proclaimed, "No one bothers Tony Gwynn because he wins batting titles, but the Padres finish fourth or fifth every year."[2] Meanwhile, Gwynn responded to Clark's allegations by saying, "I've been doing the same things my whole career, playing the same way. Now, why is it an issue? Because Jack Clark says it is."[3]

The rift between the two men contributed to Clark's decision to sign with the Boston Red Sox when he became a free agent at the end of 1990; however, he had some strong parting words before he left San Diego, calling Padres manager Greg Riddoch a "bad, bad man . . . and he's sneaky. He's a snake. Well, not just a snake, but a s-s-s-n-n-n-a-ke."[4]

Clark also didn't spare the fans of San Diego, suggesting, "Everything that they should cheer for, they'd boo for, and everything they should boo for, they'd cheer for. . . . Tony (Gwynn), he's perfect for them. He just plays the whole thing up, and the town is so stupid that they can't see."[5]

Gwynn once again offered a response to Clark's assertions, saying, "Let's talk about him (Clark) walking 104 times, being a number 4 hitter. Let's talk about his not flying on team flights. Let's talk about him getting booted out of games on a called strike three."[6]

Clark ended up spending two years in Boston, hitting 28 home runs, driving in 87 runs, and batting .249 in the first of those seasons, before assuming a part-time role with the Red Sox the following year. He elected to call it quits at the conclusion of the 1992 campaign, ending his career with 340 home runs, 1,180 RBIs, 1,118 runs scored, 1,826 hits, a .267 batting average, a .379 on-base percentage, and a .476 slugging percentage. In his three seasons with the Cardinals, Clark hit 66 homers, drove in 216 runs, scored 198 times, collected 299 hits, batted .274, compiled a .413 on-base percentage, and posted a .522 slugging percentage.

Following his playing career, Clark ended up being driven into bankruptcy by his appetite for luxury cars. Yet, he eventually got back on his feet, returning to baseball, first as a coach for the Los Angeles Dodgers and, later, as a minor-league manager.

CARDINAL CAREER HIGHLIGHTS

Best Season

Clark posted solid numbers for the Cardinals in 1985, helping them finish first in the NL East by hitting 22 homers, driving in 87 runs, and batting .281. He had a much bigger year in 1987, when he led the Redbirds to the division title by hitting 35 home runs, knocking in 106 runs, scoring 93 others, batting .286, and leading the league with 136 bases on balls, a .459 on-base percentage, and a .597 slugging percentage. With no one else on the team hitting more than twelve home runs, Clark represented the Cardinals' only real power threat (they hit only ninety-four homers as a team), making him absolutely essential to the success of the ball club. Although the writers recognized the contributions Clark made to the Cardinals during the course of the season by awarding him a third-place finish in the NL MVP voting, they could just as easily have presented him with the award, instead of giving it to Andre Dawson, who claimed the honor even though he played for the last-place Chicago Cubs.

Memorable Moments and Greatest Performances

Clark's status as arguably the most feared hitter in the senior circuit enabled him to establish a new NL record in 1987 by drawing a walk in sixteen consecutive games at one point. Nevertheless, he will always be remembered most fondly by Cardinals fans for the game-winning, three-run homer he hit against the Dodgers in the top of the ninth inning of Game 6 of the 1985 NLCS that put St. Louis in the World Series. Voted by Cardinals fans as one of the twenty greatest moments in team history, Clark's blast culminated a comeback by the Cardinals that saw them overcome a two-games-to-none deficit in the series.

After the Cardinals lost the first two contests played in Los Angeles, they won the next three games in St. Louis, with Ozzie Smith's memorable ninth-inning homer ending Game 5. Returning to Los Angeles needing to win just once more, the Cardinals entered the top of the ninth inning of Game 6 trailing the Dodgers by a score of 5–4. Stepping to the plate with two men out and runners on second and third, Clark faced Los Angeles ace reliever Tom Niedenfuer with first base open. Swinging at Niedenfuer's first offering, Clark made Dodger manager Tommy Lasorda regret his decision not to walk the slugging first baseman by smashing the ball well over the left-field wall for a three-run homer that gave the Cardinals a 7–5 lead they protected in the bottom of the inning. Perhaps the most indelible image of Clark's pennant-winning blast is that of Dodgers' left fielder Pedro Guerrero throwing his glove down in disgust as the ball sailed into the outfield stands. Another is that of Clark staring into the Los Angeles dugout to remind Lasorda of his mistake as he began circling the bases.

Notable Achievements

Hit more than twenty home runs twice, topping thirty homers once.
Knocked in more than 100 runs once.
Walked more than 100 times once (136 in 1987).
Compiled on-base percentage in excess of .400 once (.459 in 1987).
Posted slugging percentage in excess of .500 twice.
Led NL in walks once, on-base percentage once, and slugging percentage once.
Holds second-highest single-season walks total in Cardinals history (136 in 1987).
Finished third in the 1987 NL MVP voting.
Won two Silver Sluggers (1985, 1987).
1987 *Sporting News* All-Star selection.
Two-time N.L. All-Star (1985, 1987).
Two-time N.L. champion (1985, 1987).

NOTES

1. Jack Clark, quoted in Rick Reilly, "This Is the Life That Jack Built: Red Sox Slugger Jack Clark Looks Back in Anger," *SI Vault*, July 22, 1991, http://sportsillustrated.cnn.com/vault/article/magazine/MAG1140020 (accessed November 15, 2012).

2. Clark, quoted in Reilly, "This Is the Life That Jack Built," http://sportsillustrated.cnn.com/vault/article/magazine/MAG1140020.

3. Tony Gwynn, quoted in Reilly, "This Is the Life That Jack Built," http://sportsillustrated.cnn.com/vault/article/magazine/MAG1140020.

4. Clark, quoted in Reilly, "This Is the Life That Jack Built," http://sportsillustrated.cnn.com/vault/article/magazine/MAG1140020.

5. Clark, quoted in Reilly, "This Is the Life That Jack Built," http://sportsillustrated.cnn.com/vault/article/magazine/MAG1140020.

6. Gwynn, quoted in Reilly, "This Is the Life That Jack Built," http://sportsillustrated.cnn.com/vault/article/magazine/MAG1140020.

47

ORLANDO CEPEDA

Another powerful right-handed batter who spent only three years in St. Louis after having most of his finest seasons for the San Francisco Giants, Orlando Cepeda posed an even more serious threat to opposing pitchers than did Jack Clark in the course of his Hall of Fame career. A slugger in the truest sense of the word, the six-foot, two-inch, 220-pound Cepeda possessed tremendous physical strength that enabled him to drive a ball out of any part of the park. Nicknamed "The Baby Bull," Cepeda hit 379 home runs and knocked in 1,365 runs during his career, surpassing 30 homers and 100 RBIs five times each. Yet, Cepeda proved to be more than just a home-run hitter, posting a batting average in excess of .300 in nine of his seventeen big-league seasons, while also finishing in double digits in stolen bases in each of his first five campaigns, before knee problems severely limited his effectiveness on the base paths. A difference-maker both on the field and in the clubhouse, he helped improve the fortunes of three different teams, leading the Cardinals to the world championship in 1967, when he captured National League Most Valuable Player honors. He also helped the Cardinals win the pennant the following year.

Born in the southern seaport city of Ponce, Puerto Rico, on September 17, 1937, Orlando Manuel (Pennes) Cepeda grew up idolizing his father, Perucho, who reached legendary status in the Caribbean as a big, power-hitting shortstop. Sometimes referred to as the "Babe Ruth of the Caribbean," the elder Cepeda was more commonly known as "The Bull." Young Orlando learned to play the game of baseball from his father, who often took his son with him when he traveled throughout Latin America during his playing days. The younger Cepeda soon developed a strong desire to pursue a career in baseball as well, although he briefly lost interest after failing to make a local team. He refocused his attention on the sport he grew up playing after injuring his right knee playing basketball around the age of thirteen. Cepeda's injury eventually required corrective surgery that included the removal of knee cartilage. Although the healing process proved to be a lengthy one that kept Cepeda in bed for two months and on crutches for almost half a year, it ended up benefiting the fifteen-year-old, since he added some forty pounds of bulk during his recuperation period that he eventually converted into muscle. The added weight transformed the teenager from a skinny singles hitter into a powerful slugger.

After watching Cepeda compete as an amateur, Pedro Zorilla, owner of the Santurce Crabbers, convinced the seventeen-year-old's family to allow the youngster to travel to Florida to participate in a tryout for the New York Giants. Cepeda's combination of power and speed impressed the Giants, prompting them to offer him a contract; however, after being assigned by the Giants to the Salem Rebels, a Class D team in the southern Appalachian League, Cepeda seriously considered quitting baseball and returning to his homeland when he learned that his father had succumbed to a stomach disorder.

Choosing in the end to remain in the United States, Cepeda spent three years advancing through the Giants' farm system, before earning the team's starting first-base job in spring training of 1958, which marked the year the ball club moved to San Francisco. Excelling in his first major-league season, Cepeda earned NL Rookie of the Year honors by hitting 25 homers, driving in 96 runs, batting .312, and topping the circuit with 38 doubles. The twenty-one-year-old first baseman so impressed Giants manager Bill Rigney that the latter later called him the " best young right-handed power hitter I'd seen."[1]

Building on the success he experienced as a rookie, Cepeda compiled outstanding numbers in each of the next two seasons as well, even after the Giants moved from Seals Stadium to windy Candlestick Park in 1960. The swirling winds at Candlestick made it extremely difficult for right-handed hitters to drive the ball over the left-field fence; therefore, Cepeda, who previously pulled almost everything from a closed batting stance, changed his style of hitting. Adopting a more open stance in the batter's box, he began driving the ball more to right and right-center, hitting many of his home runs to the opposite field.

After totaling 51 homers and 201 RBIs in his second and third seasons, Cepeda had his finest statistical year in 1961, leading the NL with 46 home runs and 142 RBIs, while also placing among the leaders with 105 runs scored, a .311 batting average, and a .609 slugging percentage. Cepeda's outstanding performance earned him a spot on the NL All-Star team for the third straight year and a second-place finish to Cincinnati's Frank Robinson in the league MVP voting.

The 1961 campaign marked the final season in which Cepeda played entirely pain free. After reinjuring his right knee in a home-plate collision with Dodger catcher John Roseboro, he aggravated the knee again while working out with weights during the subsequent off-season. Nevertheless, Cepeda continued to compile outstanding numbers for the Giants each year, averaging 33 home runs and 103 RBIs from 1962 to 1964, while posting batting averages of .306, .316, and .304; however, after playing first base almost exclusively in each of those seasons, he moved to left field at the start of the 1965 campaign to create a full-time spot at first for Willie McCovey.

The switch in positions proved to be disastrous for Cepeda, whose season ended prematurely when he injured his right knee again early in the year while diving for a ball in the outfield. After appearing in a total of only thirty-three games during the course of the campaign, he had to undergo surgery during the off-season to repair his injured knee, which severely limited his mobility the remainder of his career.

After subsequently performing various types of manual labor to strengthen the joint and stay in shape, Cepeda returned to the Giants in the spring asking to play first base; however, San Francisco manager Herman Franks informed him that he intended to use McCovey at first instead. Despite asking to be traded, Cepeda began the 1966 campaign in left field for the Giants, until the team finally dealt him to the Cardinals in early May for veteran left-handed starter Ray Sadecki.

Upon his arrival in St. Louis, Cepeda gave the Cardinals the power threat in the middle of their lineup that they sorely needed. Playing first base and batting cleanup the remainder of the year, Cepeda ended up leading the Redbirds with 17 home runs, 24 doubles, a .303

batting average, and a .469 slugging percentage, despite appearing in only 123 games with them. The slugging first baseman's strong performance earned him NL Comeback Player of the Year honors.

Having finished sixth in the senior circuit in 1966, with a record of 83–79, the Cardinals entered the ensuing campaign as 12–1 longshots to win the NL pennant; with Cepeda leading the way, they ran away with the league championship, finishing the year with a record of 101–60, ten and a half games ahead of the second-place Giants. Serving as the team's primary power threat and inspirational leader in the clubhouse, Cepeda brought together a talented group of players that needed to learn how to win. Playing in spacious Busch Stadium, Cepeda hit 25 home runs, batted .325, scored 91 runs, amassed 37 doubles, and led the league with 111 RBIs and 21 game-winning hits; however, his contributions to the team could not be measured by numbers alone. In addition to supplying the Cardinals with much of their offensive firepower, he provided his teammates with outstanding leadership, proving to be particularly helpful to second baseman Julian Javier—the ball club's only other Latino player. Cepeda's presence alongside him on the right side of the infield enabled Javier to flourish as never before. After batting just .228, hitting only 7 homers, and driving in just 31 runs the previous season, Javier posted a batting average of .281, hit 14 home runs, and knocked in 64 runs in 1967. The baseball writers rewarded Cepeda for his overall contributions by making him their unanimous selection for NL MVP at season's end.

The Cardinals repeated as NL champions in 1968, this time finishing nine games ahead of the runner-up Giants, with a record of 97–65. But with Cepeda hitting only 16 home runs, driving in just 73 runs, and batting only .248, the Cardinals elected to trade him to Atlanta at the end of the year for Joe Torre.

Cepeda had two productive years in Atlanta, faring particularly well in 1970, when he hit 34 homers, knocked in 111 runs, and batted .305. But his days as a full-time player all but ended in 1971, when he freakishly injured his left knee in early May as he rose from a chair in his living room to answer the telephone. Feeling his knee give out, Cepeda subsequently chose to play in pain the next few weeks, before he finally elected to have season-ending surgery.

Finding it increasingly difficult to play on his aching knees, Cepeda split the 1972 campaign between Atlanta and Oakland, appearing in a total of only thirty-one games. After being released by Oakland at the end of the year, he signed with the Boston Red Sox as a free agent when the American League announced its intention to begin using a designated hitter in its games beginning in 1973. Despite limping noticeably whenever he stepped onto the field, Cepeda hit 20 home runs, drove in 86 runs, and batted .289 for the Red Sox in 142 games, en route to earning Designated Hitter of the Year honors.

A subsequent youth movement in Boston marked the end of the thirty-six-year-old Cepeda's days in a Red Sox uniform. Signing with Kansas City after being released by Boston at season's end, Cepeda appeared in only thirty-three games with the Royals throughout the course of the 1974 campaign, before announcing his retirement at the end of the year. He concluded his career with 379 home runs, 1,365 RBIs, 1,131 runs scored, 2,351 hits, a .297 batting average, a .350 on-base percentage, and a .499 slugging percentage. In his three years with the Cardinals, Cepeda hit 58 homers, drove in 242 runs, scored 227 others, collected 469 hits, batted .290, compiled a .355 on-base percentage, and posted a .454 slugging percentage.

Following his playing career, Cepeda ran afoul of the law, serving time in prison for attempting to smuggle marijuana into his native Puerto Rico; however, after eventually returning to the United States, he received an offer to work for the Chicago White Sox, first as a hitting instructor and, later, as a scout. Shortly after he moved back to northern California in 1986, the Giants hired him for a community relations position. Cepeda moved into scouting and player development for the club and eventually became a sort of goodwill ambassador for the organization.

CARDINAL CAREER HIGHLIGHTS

Best Season

This wasn't even close. After having a solid first season in St. Louis the previous year, Cepeda led the Cardinals to the NL pennant in 1967 by posting easily his best numbers as a member of the team, en route to capturing league MVP honors. Cepeda hit 25 home runs, topped the senior circuit with 111 RBIs, scored 91 runs, collected 183 hits, finished second in the league with 37 doubles, and also placed among the leaders with a .325 batting average, a .399 on-base percentage, and a .524 slugging percentage.

Memorable Moments and Greatest Performances

Cepeda had a number of big games during the course of his 1967 MVP campaign. He led the Cardinals to an 11–9 win over the Mets on May 20 of that year by going 3-for-5, with a homer, 2 doubles, 4 RBIs, and 2 runs scored. Cepeda again went 3-for-5 on July 28, when he helped the Cardinals defeat the Braves, 9–1, by homering twice, knocking in 3 runs, and scoring 3 others. He had another extremely productive day at the plate on September 3, when he went 4-for-4, with 2 doubles, 3 RBIs, and 4 runs scored during a 13–1 win over the Astros in St. Louis.

After struggling at the plate in the previous year's World Series, Cepeda performed well in the 1968 Fall Classic, hitting two home runs and driving in six runs. He got arguably his biggest hit as a member of the Cardinals in Game 3, helping St. Louis take a 2–1 lead in the Series by reaching veteran Detroit right-hander Don McMahon for a three-run homer during a 7–3 St. Louis victory.

Notable Achievements

Hit more than twenty home runs once.
Knocked in more than 100 runs once.
Batted over .300 twice.
Posted slugging percentage in excess of .500 once.
Led NL with 111 RBIs in 1967.
1966 NL Comeback Player of the Year.
1967 NL MVP.
1967 *Sporting News* All-Star selection.
1967 NL All-Star.
Two-time NL champion (1967, 1968).
1967 world champion.

Elected to Baseball Hall of Fame by members of Veterans Committee in 1999.

NOTE

1. Bill Rigney, quoted in "Orlando Cepeda," *Baseball Library.com*. www.baseballlibrary.com/ballplayers/player.php?name=Orlando_Cepeda_1937 (accessed November 16, 2012).

48

BRUCE SUTTER

Already the National League's premier closer by the time he joined the Cardinals in 1981, Bruce Sutter subsequently added to his legacy of greatness in his four years in St. Louis. Referred to as "The Sandy Koufax of relievers"[1] by Cardinals manager Whitey Herzog, Sutter perfected and popularized the split-fingered fastball, establishing himself in the process as one of the greatest relief pitchers in baseball history. During the course of his Hall of Fame career, Sutter became the only pitcher to lead the NL in saves five times, retiring from the game in 1988 with 300 saves—the third-highest total in history, at the time. The first pitcher to gain admittance to Cooperstown without starting a single game in the major leagues, Sutter earned NL All-Star honors six times, five top-ten finishes in the league MVP voting, and four top-five finishes in the Cy Young balloting, winning the award in 1979 as a member of the Chicago Cubs. He also earned Fireman of the Year honors four times. Sutter compiled an ERA of less than 2.00 in two different seasons, doing so for the Cardinals in 1984, when his 45 saves established a new NL record. He also helped the Cardinals capture the world championship in 1982, figuring in three of their four victories over the Milwaukee Brewers in the World Series.

Born on January 8, 1953, in Lancaster, Pennsylvania, Howard Bruce Sutter first signed with the Chicago Cubs as an amateur free agent in 1971, after initially electing not to sign with the Washington Senators when they selected him in the twenty-first round of the 1970 amateur draft. The young right-hander's career appeared to be in jeopardy when an injury to his pitching arm forced him to undergo surgery in 1973; however, after struggling upon his return, Cubs minor-league pitching coach Fred Martin suggested that he try throwing a forkball—an off-speed pitch in which the pitcher holds the ball with the index and third fingers split far apart. Sutter, however, had such huge hands that he turned the forkball into something else: a fastball with a devastating late sink.

After spending the next three years perfecting the pitch in the minor leagues, Sutter finally arrived in Chicago in 1976. Armed with his new weapon, he began an extraordinary run of success, continuing to fine-tune the pitch he relied on most heavily with the help of Cubs pitching coach Mike Roarke. Working exclusively out of the Chicago bullpen, Sutter had a solid rookie season, compiling a record of 6–3, with ten saves and an ERA of 2.70. He followed that up with a brilliant sophomore campaign in which he earned his first of five straight All-Star selections by going 7–3, with a 1.34 ERA and thirty-one saves. After saving 27 games for the Cubs in 1978, Sutter earned NL Cy Young honors the following year by posting 6 victories, compiling an ERA of 2.22, leading the league with 37 saves, and striking out 110 batters in 101 innings of work, while allowing the opposition just 67 hits. He again topped the circuit in saves in 1980, prompting the bullpen–needy Cardinals to acquire his services at the end of the year by offering the Cubs a package of three players that included top prospect Leon Durham and slick-fielding third baseman Ken Reitz.

Sutter continued to excel in St. Louis, compiling an ERA of 2.62 and leading the NL with twenty-five saves in the strike-shortened 1981 campaign. He posted nine victories for the Cardinals the following year, along with a 2.90 ERA and a league-leading thirty-six saves, en route to earning a third-place finish in the Cy Young voting and a fifth-place finish in the league MVP balloting. Sutter subsequently helped the Cardinals capture the world championship by saving a game and working four and a third perfect innings against Atlanta in the National League Championship Series (NLCS), before posting one win and two saves against Milwaukee in the World Series.

After a subpar 1983 season, Sutter returned to top form in 1984. He compiled a brilliant 1.54 ERA and established career highs with 123 innings pitched and a league-leading forty-five saves, tying in the process the single-season major-league record in the last category.

Sutter's dominance of NL hitters made a strong impression on teammates and opponents alike. Larry Bowa, who spent much of his career trying to hit against Sutter as a member of the Phillies and Cubs, once stated, "I've never seen anybody, for a guy who didn't throw in the 90s . . . I've never seen anybody embarrass the big hitters like he (Sutter) did. He'd make them swing and miss at pitches that just disappeared out of the zone."[2]

In discussing Sutter's split-finger fastball, longtime manager Dick Williams proclaimed, "It's unhittable, unless he hangs it, and he never does. It's worse than trying to hit a knuckleball."[3] Meanwhile, former Cardinals teammate Tom Herr noted, "I don't think people grasp how impressive it was for him to go two or three innings for a save. When you have to get six, seven, or eight outs, so many things can go wrong for a closer."[4]

A free agent at the conclusion of the 1984 campaign, Sutter signed with the Atlanta Braves, with whom he spent the remainder of his career, never experiencing the same level of success. After saving only twenty-three games and compiling an inordinately high ERA of 4.48 in 1985, Sutter experienced arm problems that limited him to just sixteen games the following year and forced him to miss the entire 1987 season. After saving only fourteen games and posting an ERA of 4.76 upon his return in 1988, he elected to call it quits at the end of the year. In addition to totaling 300 saves, he ended his career with a record of 68–71 and an ERA of 2.83. His numbers as a member of the Cardinals include 26 wins and 30 losses, a 2.72 ERA, and 127 saves. Sutter ranks fourth on the team's all-time saves list, with his 45 saves in 1984 representing the third-highest single-season total in franchise history.

Looking back on his place in history and the manner in which the role of the closer has changed throughout the years, Sutter told *USA Today* the following in 2005:

> It's not good or bad, but closers have changed things. I don't think you are going to win a World Series without one. Where would the Yankees be without Mariano Rivera? Pitching two innings and coming back the next day—that's the stuff we did all season. Saves are not easy, but I think they are

easier now. I warmed up in the seventh and maybe pitched. Then, in the eighth and maybe pitched. Lee Smith, Goose Gossage, and I got a lot of seven-out saves.[5]

CARDINAL CAREER HIGHLIGHTS

Best Season

Sutter pitched extremely well for the Cardinals in three of his four years in St. Louis, compiling an ERA below 3.00, leading all NL relievers in saves, and allowing far fewer hits than innings pitched in each of those three campaigns. He also posted nine wins on two separate occasions. Nevertheless, Sutter unquestionably had his best season for the Cardinals in 1984, when he compiled a career-high forty-five saves and posted an extraordinary 1.54 ERA. His exceptional performance earned him a third-place finish in the NL Cy Young voting and a sixth-place finish in the league MVP balloting.

Memorable Moments and Greatest Performances

Sutter excelled throughout the 1982 postseason, helping the Cardinals sweep the Braves in the NLCS by winning Game 2 and saving Game 3. Appearing in two of the three contests, he worked four and a third perfect innings. He followed that up by posting a win and two saves against the Milwaukee Brewers in the World Series, protecting a one-run lead in the Series finale by retiring all six batters he faced.

Sutter also reached a pair of milestones during his time in St. Louis. On September 3, 1984, he established a new NL record by recording his thirty-eighth save of the season during a 7–3 win over the Mets. Later in the month, on September 28, he tied the major-league record (since broken) by registering his forty-fifth save during a 4–1 win over the Cubs.

Yet, ironically, the seminal moment of Sutter's time in St. Louis may well have been one in which he failed. On June 23, 1984, in a game played at Chicago's Wrigley Field that came to be known as the "Sandberg game," he surrendered game-tying home runs to Ryne Sandberg in both the ninth and tenth innings during an eleven-inning,

12–11 loss to the Cubs. In homering twice against Sutter during the contest, Sandberg became the first player ever to take the reliever deep twice in the same game.

Commenting years later on how television replays shown during the 2005 Hall of Fame induction ceremony of Sandberg recounted for viewers the second baseman's memorable performance against him on that fateful day, Sutter noted, "You never think that giving up two home runs to the same guy helped you get in the Hall of Fame. But . . . that's what might have happened."[6]

Notable Achievements

Saved more than thirty games twice, topping the forty mark once.
Set record (since broken) with forty-five saves in 1984.
Compiled ERA below 3.00 three times, finishing with mark below 2.00 once (1.54 in 1984).
Threw more than 100 innings twice.
Led NL in saves three times.
Ranks fourth in Cardinals history with 127 saves.
Holds third-best single-season marks in Cardinals history with forty-five saves and 1.54 ERA in 1984.
Finished third in NL Cy Young voting twice.
Finished fifth in 1982 NL MVP voting.
Three-time *Sporting News* Fireman of the Year Award winner.
Two-time NL All-Star (1981, 1984).
1982 NL champion.
1982 world champion.
Elected to Baseball Hall of Fame by members of Baseball Writers' Association of America in 2006.

NOTES

1. Whitey Herzog, quoted in "Bruce Sutter," *Baseball-Reference.com*, www.baseball-reference.com/bullpen/Bruce_Sutter (accessed November 17, 2012).

2. Larry Bowa, quoted in Mike Shalin and Neil Shalin, *Out by a Step: The 100 Best Players Not in the Baseball Hall of Fame* (Lanham, MD: Diamond Communications, 2002), 14.

3. Dick Williams, quoted in "Sutter, Bruce," *National Baseball Hall of Fame and Museum*, http://baseballhall.org/hof/sutter-bruce (accessed November 17, 2012).

4. Tom Herr, quoted in "Bruce Sutter," www.baseball-reference.com/bullpen/Bruce_Sutter.

5. Bruce Sutter, quoted in "Bruce Sutter Stats," *Baseball Almanac*, www.baseball-almanac.com/players/player.php?p=suttebr01 (accessed November 17, 2012).

6. Bruce Sutter, quoted in "Bruce Sutter," www.baseball-reference.com/bullpen/Bruce_Sutter.

49

JOAQUIN ANDUJAR

Although he is perhaps remembered most for his mental meltdown in Game 7 of the 1985 World Series, Joaquin Andujar excelled on the mound in four of the five seasons he spent in St. Louis. After being acquired from the Houston Astros midway through the 1981 campaign, the Dominican-born right-hander established himself as the workhorse of the Cardinals' starting rotation, throwing more than 250 innings in three of his four full seasons with the club. Along the way, he posted at least twenty victories on two separate occasions, winning fifteen games another time. Particularly effective during the 1982 postseason, Andujar helped lead the Cardinals to the world championship by winning all three of his starts, while posting a composite ERA of 1.80 against Atlanta and Milwaukee. Nevertheless, his quirky personality and volatile disposition often tend to obscure just how well he pitched during his time in St. Louis.

Born in San Pedro de Macoris, in the Dominican Republic, on December 21, 1952, Joaquin Andujar originally signed with the Cincinnati Reds as an amateur free agent in 1969, one month shy of his seventeenth birthday. He spent the next six years in Cincinnati's farm system, posting an overall record of 33–41 and an ERA of 4.33, before being traded to the Houston Astros following the conclusion of the 1975 campaign for two players to be named later. Making his major-league debut with the Astros in 1976 at the age of twenty-three, Andujar performed well as a rookie, compiling an ERA of 3.60 and completing nine of his twenty-five starts, even though he finished the year with a record of only 9–10. He had a solid second season as well, earning National League All-Star honors for the first of four times by going 11–8, with a 3.69 ERA.

Even though Andujar pitched well in each of his first two years in Houston, the Astros elected to minimize the number of starts he made for them in subsequent seasons, gradually turning him into a spot starter/long reliever. Unhappy with his reduced role, Andujar welcomed the trade Houston completed with the Cardinals on June 7, 1981, which sent him to St. Louis for outfielder Tony Scott.

After posting a record of 6–1 during the remainder of the strike-shortened 1981 campaign, Andujar established himself as the ace of the Cardinals' starting rotation the following year. In addition to finishing 15–10, the hard-throwing right-hander placed among the league leaders with 266 innings pitched, 9 complete games, 5 shutouts, and a 2.47 ERA. He subsequently proved to be invaluable to the Cardinals during their successful postseason run, winning his lone start against Atlanta in the National League Championship Series, before defeating Milwaukee twice in the World Series.

After suffering through a dismal 1983 campaign in which he finished just 6–16, with a 4.16 ERA, Andujar had the two most successful seasons of his career with the Cardinals. In addition to concluding the 1984 campaign with an ERA of 3.34 and 12 complete games, he led all NL hurlers with 20 wins, 261 innings pitched, and 4 shutouts. He followed that up by going 21–12 in 1985, with a 3.40 ERA, 10 complete games, and 270 innings pitched. Andujar earned All-Star honors and a fourth-place finish in the Cy Young balloting both years. He also won the only Gold Glove of his career in 1984.

Yet, in spite of his twenty-one victories, Andujar's 1985 season ended badly, with the temperamental right-hander struggling down the stretch and embarrassing himself in the World Series. After posting a record of 20–7 in the season's first four months, he went just 1–5, with a 5.76 ERA, after August. He continued to struggle in the postseason, losing his only NLCS decision to the Dodgers and getting hit hard in both his starts. The Royals subsequently knocked him out in the fifth inning of Game 3 of the World Series, before Andujar suffered the indignity of being ejected from Game 7 for arguing balls and strikes a bit too vociferously with home-plate umpire Don Denkinger.

Although the entire nation witnessed firsthand Andujar's unpredictable nature during his Game 7 meltdown, those more familiar with the temperamental right-hander were already keenly aware of the many unique qualities that made him one of the sport's more eccentric figures. Often referring to himself as "one tough Dominican," Andujar provided a number of memorable quotes to the members of the media during his time in St. Louis. In addition to uttering the phrase, "There is one word in America that says it all, and that word is 'You never know,'"[1] Andujar provided the following other gems:

> I throw the ball ninety-two miles an hour, but they hit it back just as hard.[2]

> That's why I don't talk. Because I talk too much.[3]

> You can't worry if it's cold; you can't worry if it's hot; you only worry if you get sick. Because then, if you don't get well, you die.[4]

Andujar's poor performance during the latter stages of the 1985 campaign, as well as his admission to cocaine abuse during the Pittsburgh drug trials, prompted the Cardinals to trade him to Oakland for two players prior to the start of the ensuing season. After missing his first start while serving a five-game suspension for his World Series altercation with Denkinger, Andujar went on to post decent numbers in his first year in Oakland, finishing the campaign with a record of 12–7 and an ERA of 3.82; however, injuries limited him to only thirteen starts in 1987, and, when he became a free agent at the end of the year, he elected to return to Houston. Plagued by injuries again in 1988, he found himself playing in the Senior Professional Baseball Association the following year, before attempting a comeback with the Montreal Expos in 1990. After being released by the Expos before the season began, Andujar announced his retirement, claiming that much of his downfall could be attributed to a conspiracy against him, although he never offered any specifics. Andujar ended his career with a record of 127–118 and an ERA of 3.58. In parts of five seasons with the Cardinals, he went 68–53, with a 3.33 ERA.

CARDINAL CAREER HIGHLIGHTS

Best Season

Although Andujar won in excess of twenty games in both 1984 and 1985, it could be argued that he actually pitched his best ball for the Cardinals in 1982, when he posted only fifteen victories. Finishing the campaign with a record of 15–10, he compiled a career-best 2.47 ERA, which proved to be nearly a run per game better than the marks he posted in the other two years. He also threw 9 complete games, 266 innings, and a career-high 5 shutouts, en route to compiling a WHIP (walks plus hits allowed per innings pitched) of 1.080, which represented the best mark of his career. Andujar finished second in the league in shutouts and games started (thirty-seven). He also placed third in ERA.

Still, it is difficult to overlook the fact that Andujar won several more games in both 1984 and 1985. In the second of those years, he finished 21–12, with a 3.40 ERA, 10 complete games, 2 shutouts, and a career-high 270 innings pitched. He allowed many more hits and walked many more batters than he did three years earlier, giving him a significantly higher WHIP of 1.287. However, Andujar pitched more effectively in 1984, concluding the campaign with a record of 20–14, an ERA of 3.34, 12 complete games, and a league-leading 4 shutouts and 261 innings pitched. He also struck out a career-high 147 batters and surrendered only 218 hits to the opposition, en route to compiling a WHIP of 1.102, which nearly equaled the mark he posted in 1982. All things considered, Andujar had his best season for the Cardinals in 1984.

Memorable Moments and Greatest Performances

Andujar, a notoriously weak hitter, provided Cardinals fans with a memorable moment on May 15, 1984, when he hit a grand slam home run during a 9–1 win over the Braves. Far more comfortable on the mound, he pitched exceptionally well during the latter stages of the 1982 campaign, compiling a 1.64 ERA, en route to winning his last seven decisions. He pitched one of his best games on September 15, throwing a three-hit shutout against the Philadelphia Phillies that put the Cardinals in first place to stay. Andujar continued to excel during the postseason, helping St. Louis capture the world championship by winning all three of his starts. After allowing the Braves just two runs in six and two-thirds innings in Game 3 of the NLCS, he started and won Game 3 and Game 7 of the World Series, compiling an outstanding 1.35 ERA against the hard-hitting Milwaukee Brewers. Andujar, however, may have pitched his best game for the Cardinals on September 28, 1984, allowing just two hits in nine innings during a 4–1, ten-inning win over the Cubs.

Nevertheless, Andujar is perhaps remembered most for an incident that took place during the final game of the 1985 World Series. After lasting only four innings in his Game 3 start, he entered the Series finale in the fifth inning, with the Cardinals already trailing by a score of 10–0. With the entire St. Louis team harboring a considerable amount of resentment toward the umpiring crew for missing an obvious call late in Game 6, the volatile Andujar entered the fray with a huge chip on his shoulder. Displaying anger and frustration on the mound as he surrendered a hit and a walk to the first two batters he faced, he soon found himself being ejected for arguing vehemently with home-plate umpire Don Denkinger about balls and strikes. Denkinger, whose blown call at first base in the ninth inning of Game 6 extended the Series to a seventh contest, was bumped twice by Andujar, who had to be restrained by his teammates. Meanwhile, Cardinals manager Whitey Herzog also earned an early exit from the contest by telling Denkinger, "We wouldn't even be here if you hadn't missed the f***ing call last night!"[5] After leaving the playing field, Andujar took out his anger on a toilet in the visitor's clubhouse bathroom in Kansas City's Royals Stadium by demolishing it with a baseball bat. He ended up being suspended for the first five games of the ensuing campaign.

Notable Achievements

Surpassed twenty victories twice.
Compiled ERA below 3.00 once (2.47 in 1982).
Threw more than 250 innings three times.
Led NL pitchers in wins once, shutouts once, and innings pitched once.

1984 Gold Glove winner.
1984 NL Comeback Player of the Year.
Two-time NL All-Star (1984, 1985).
Two-time NL champion (1982, 1985).
1982 world champion.

NOTES

1. Joaquin Andujar, quoted in "Classic Joaquin Andujar Quotes," *Baseball Fever*, www.baseball-fever.com/showthread.php?57101-Classic-Joaquin-Andujar-quotes (accessed November 19, 2012).

2. Andujar, quoted in "Classic Joaquin Andujar Quotes," www.baseball-fever.com/showthread.php?57101-Classic-Joaquin-Andujar-quotes.

3. Andujar, quoted in "Classic Joaquin Andujar Quotes," www.baseball-fever.com/showthread.php?57101-Classic-Joaquin-Andujar-quotes.

4. Andujar, quoted in "Classic Joaquin Andujar Quotes," www.baseball-fever.com/showthread.php?57101-Classic-Joaquin-Andujar-quotes.

5. Whitey Herzog, quoted in "Classic Joaquin Andujar Quotes," www.baseball-fever.com/showthread.php?57101-Classic-Joaquin-Andujar-quotes.

50

TERRY PENDLETON

Although Terry Pendleton played his best ball as a member of the Braves in his first two years in Atlanta, he had several solid seasons for the Cardinals before he left St. Louis via free agency at the conclusion of the 1990 campaign. The slick-fielding third baseman led all National League third sackers in assists in three of his six full seasons with the Cardinals, en route to winning two Gold Gloves. He also topped all players at his position in putouts and fielding percentage once each. A solid offensive performer as well, Pendleton batted over .280 twice, knocked in more than 90 runs once, and scored in excess of 80 runs twice during his time in St. Louis. Pendleton's strong all-around play helped the Cardinals capture two division titles and two NL pennants.

Born in Los Angeles, California, on July 16, 1960, Terry Lee Pendleton began his baseball career as an Eastside Little League player, before moving on to play for his Channel Islands High School team in Oxnard, California. After graduating from Channel Islands, he attended Fresno State University, where he earned All-American honors as a second baseman. Selected by the Cardinals in the seventh round of the 1982 amateur draft, Pendleton spent the next two years in the St. Louis farm system, during which time he gradually shifted to third base. The young infielder developed so rapidly at his new position that the Cardinals ended up trading their starting third baseman, Ken Oberkfell, to the Atlanta Braves and temporarily moved outfielder Andy Van Slyke to third to allow Pendleton to gain a bit more experience at the hot corner; however, when Van Slyke committed seven errors in thirty games, the Cardinals promoted Pendleton to the major leagues, immediately making him their starting third baseman.

Pendleton made his debut with the Cardinals on July 18, 1984, getting three hits in five times at bat during an 8–4 victory over the San Francisco Giants. He stayed hot the remainder of the year, batting .324 in 67 games for St. Louis, while also driving in 33 runs, stealing 20 bases, and hitting his first major-league home run. Pendleton struggled somewhat at the plate during his sophomore season, however, batting only .240, although he managed to knock in sixty-nine runs and steal seventeen bases. Nevertheless, the twenty-five-year-old switch-hitter's outstanding glove work at the hot corner proved to be invaluable to the pennant-winning Cardinals, who benefited greatly from the fact that Pendleton placed second among NL third sackers in both putouts and assists.

Pendleton's offensive struggles continued in 1986, when he batted just .239, hit only 1 home run, and knocked in just 59 runs, hitting mostly out of the sixth spot in the Cardinals batting order. Pendleton's disappointing performance at the plate prompted the members of the St. Louis front office to seriously consider trading him away during the subsequent off-season; manager Whitey Herzog eventually changed their minds by emphasizing to them that Pendleton's great range, quick reflexes, and powerful arm at third made him vital to the success of the team (he led all league third basemen in putouts and assists). Pendleton's savvy baserunning also helped him contribute to the Cardinals' offensive attack (he stole twenty-four bases in thirty attempts).

Pendleton answered his critics in the St. Louis front office by having his finest offensive season for the Cardinals in 1987. In addition to finishing second on the team with 12 home runs, he batted .286, raised his on-base percentage from .279 to .360, scored 82 runs, drove in 96 runs, and stole 19 bases. Pendleton also led all NL third basemen in assists for the second straight year, earning in the process his first Gold Glove; however, his strong campaign ended on a sour note, with a rib injury limiting him to only nine plate appearances against the Minnesota Twins in the World Series, after the Cardinals defeated the Giants in six games in the National League Championship Series. He collected three hits in his seven official at bats against Minnesota in the losing effort, compiling in the process a batting average of .429.

Pendleton's offensive production fell off considerably the next three years, although he put up decent numbers in 1989, when he hit

13 homers, knocked in 74 runs, scored 83 others, and batted .264. He also won his second Gold Glove that year, after leading all NL third basemen in assists for the third time, while also topping all players at his position in fielding percentage. Pendleton spent a considerable amount of time on the disabled list in both 1988 and 1990, limiting him to a total of only 231 games during the course of those two seasons. His various physical ailments also adversely affected his performance whenever he appeared in the St. Louis lineup, enabling him to compile a total of only twelve home runs and 111 RBIs those two years. He also posted batting averages of just .253 and .230. Relegated to sharing playing time with Todd Zeile and Denny Walling by 1990, Pendleton chose to sign with the Atlanta Braves when he became a free agent at season's end.

Pendleton blossomed into a star in the city of Atlanta, serving as the Braves' offensive catalyst, while leading them to the NL pennant just one year after they finished last in their division. In addition to leading the league with a .319 batting average, he topped the circuit with 187 hits and 303 total bases. He also drove in 86 runs and established new career highs with 22 home runs, 94 runs scored, 8 triples, 34 doubles, a .363 on-base percentage, and a .517 slugging percentage. Although Pendleton's outstanding performance failed to earn him his first All-Star selection, it enabled him to edge out Barry Bonds for first place in the league Most Valuable Player voting. The Braves eventually lost the World Series to the Minnesota Twins in seven games, but Pendleton batted .367 in the Fall Classic, with 11 hits, 2 homers, and 3 RBIs.

Pendleton followed up his MVP season with another exceptional campaign in 1992. Leading the Braves to their second straight NL pennant, he batted .311, hit 21 homers, and established career highs with 105 RBIs, 98 runs scored, 39 doubles, and a league-leading 199 hits. He also played extremely well in the field, topping all NL third basemen in both putouts and assists, en route to winning the third and final Gold Glove of his career and earning his only trip to the All-Star Game. Pendleton again vied with Barry Bonds for the honor of being named the league's MVP, but this time he finished a distant second in the balloting. Atlanta also came up short in the World Series for the second straight year, losing to the Toronto Blue Jays in six games, with Pendleton batting just .240, with no homers and two RBIs.

Pendleton had one more productive year for the Braves, posting a .272 batting average, with 17 home runs, 84 RBIs, and 81 runs scored in 1993; however, injuries and age began to take their toll on him the following year. Although he attempted to play through the various aches and pains that beset his thirty-four-year-old body, Pendleton appeared in only seventy-seven games during the strike-shortened 1994 campaign, batting just .252 and driving in only thirty runs. Still, he remained a leader in the Atlanta clubhouse, serving as mentor to Chipper Jones, who eventually replaced him at third for the Braves.

Having prepared Jones to take over at third base in Atlanta, Pendleton signed on with the Florida Marlins when he became a free agent at the conclusion of the 1994 season. After posting solid numbers for the Marlins in 1995, he returned to Atlanta late in the ensuing campaign when the Braves acquired him for the stretch run. Although he batted just .204 in his forty-two games with the Braves, he again provided them with veteran leadership, helping them to capture their fourth pennant in six years.

Once again a free agent after Atlanta elected not to resign him at season's end, Pendleton signed with the Cincinnati Reds, with whom he spent most of the 1997 campaign before being released by the club in late July. After signing with the Kansas City Royals during the subsequent off-season, he finished out his career as a part-time player with the Royals, before announcing his retirement at the end of the year. Pendleton ended his career with 140 homers, 946 RBIs, 851 runs scored, 1,897 hits, a .270 batting average, a .316 on-base percentage, and a .391 slugging percentage. In his seven years with the Cardinals, he hit 44 homers, knocked in 442 runs, scored 404 others, collected 888 hits, batted .259, compiled a .308 on-base percentage, and posted a .356 slugging percentage. In addition to surpassing 20 home runs twice, driving in more than 100 runs once, and batting over .300 three times throughout the course of his career, Pendleton led all NL third basemen in putouts and assists five times each.

Following his playing career, Pendleton spent three years enjoying the company of his wife and three children before getting the urge to return to baseball. He received his first coaching opportunity in November 2001, when he began serving as the hitting instructor for the Braves. He remained in that position for nine years, until the team named him first-base coach at the conclusion of the 2010 campaign.

CARDINAL CAREER HIGHLIGHTS

Best Season

Pendleton displayed a lack of consistency at the plate in his seven years with the Cardinals, posting batting averages that ranged anywhere from .230 to .324. He reached his high-water mark in that category as a rookie, batting .324, en route to compiling an on-base plus slugging percentage of .777, which represented the highest figure he posted as a member of the team. But Pendleton appeared in only sixty-seven games and accumulated just 262 official at bats in his first big-league season, quickly eliminating it from consideration. Factoring everything into the equation, he had his best year in St. Louis in 1987, when he hit 12 home runs, drove in 96 runs, scored 82 others, stole 19 bases, batted .286, compiled a .360 on-base percentage, and posted a .412 slugging percentage. He also led all NL third basemen in assists, earning in the process the first of two Gold Gloves he won during his time in St. Louis.

Memorable Moments and Greatest Performances

Pendleton delivered perhaps the biggest hit of the entire 1987 regular season for the Cardinals when he hit a home run against the New York Mets in early September that provided much of the impetus for the Redbirds to eventually win the NL East title. After seeing the Mets gradually whittle down their seemingly safe nine-game divisional lead in the course of the previous few weeks, the Cardinals entered a three-game series at Shea Stadium in early September with their NL East rivals trailing them by only a game and a half. The Mets appeared to be on the verge of closing the gap even more when they took a 4–1 lead in the top of the ninth inning of the opening contest; however, after the Cardinals pushed across a run to make the score 4–2, Pendleton tied the game with a two-out, two-run homer off reliever Roger McDowell. The Cardinals ended up scoring another two runs in the top of the tenth inning, to come away with a stunning 6–4 victory that increased their lead over the Mets to two and a half games. After splitting the next two contests, the Redbirds maintained their lead the rest of the way, finishing the season three games ahead of New York in the standings.

Notable Achievements

Batted over .300 once.
Surpassed twenty stolen bases twice.
Led NL third basemen in assists three times, putouts once, and fielding percentage once.
Two-time Gold Glove winner (1987, 1989).
Two-time NL champion (1985, 1987).

THE ALL-TIME CARDINALS TEAM

Having identified the fifty greatest players in St. Louis Cardinals history, the time has come to select the best of the best. Based solely on the rankings contained in this book, in this section I list my all-time Cardinals team. Our squad includes the top player at each position, along with a pitching staff that features a five-man starting rotation and a closer. I have also selected a second team, with the closer for that squad having fallen just short of making it into the top fifty.

FIRST TEAM

Starting Lineup

Lou Brock CF
Rogers Hornsby 2B
Stan Musial RF
Albert Pujols 1B
Joe Medwick LF
Ted Simmons C
Ken Boyer 3B
Ozzie Smith SS

Pitching Staff

Bob Gibson SP
Dizzy Dean SP
Jessie Haines SP

Chris Carpenter SP
Mort Cooper SP
Bruce Sutter CL

SECOND TEAM

Starting Lineup

Frankie Frisch 2B
Enos Slaughter RF
Chick Hafey LF
Jim Bottomley 1B
Joe Torre 3B
Jim Edmonds CF
Yadier Molina C
Marty Marion SS

Pitching Staff

Harry Brecheen SP
Adam Wainwright SP
John Tudor SP
Bob Forsch SP
Steve Carlton SP
Lee Smith CL

GLOSSARY

1B	First base.
2B	Second base.
3B	Third base.
AVG	Batting average. The number of hits divided by the number of at bats.
C	Catcher.
CF	Center field.
CG	Complete games pitched.
CL	Closer.
ERA	Earned run average. The number of earned runs a pitcher gives up, per nine innings. This does not include runs that scored as a result of errors made in the field and is calculated by dividing the number of runs given up by the number of innings pitched and multiplying the result by nine.
hits	Base hits. Awarded when a runner safely reaches at least first base upon a batted ball, if no error is recorded.
HR	Home runs. A fair ball hit over the fence, or one hit to a spot that allows the batter to circle the bases before the ball is returned to home plate.
IP	Innings pitched.
LF	Left field.
OBP	On-base percentage. Hits plus walks plus hit-by-pitches, divided by plate appearance.
OPS	On-base plus slugging percentage. The sum of a player's on-base percentage and slugging average.

P	Pitcher.
RBI	Runs batted in. Awarded to the batter when a runner scores upon a safely batted ball, a sacrifice, or a walk.
RF	Right field.
runs	Runs scored by a player.
SB	Stolen bases.
SLG PCT	Slugging percentage. The number of total bases earned by all singles, doubles, triples, and home runs, divided by the total number of at bats.
SO	Strikeouts.
SP	Starting pitcher.
SS	Shortstop.
WHIP	Walks plus hits allowed per innings pitched.
WIN PCT	Winning percentage. A pitcher's number of wins divided by his number of total decisions (i.e., wins plus losses).

BIBLIOGRAPHY

BOOKS

Cobb, Ty. "They Don't Play Baseball Any More." *Life*, XXXII (March 17, 1952), 136–38f.

DeMarco, Tony, et al. *The Sporting News Selects 50 Greatest Sluggers*. St. Louis, MO: Sporting News, a division of Times Mirror Magazines, 2000.

Halberstam, David. *October 1964*. New York: Villard Books, 1994.

Shalin, Mike, and Neil Shalin. *Out by a Step: The 100 Best Players Not in the Baseball Hall of Fame*. Lanham, MD: Diamond Communications, 2002.

Thorn, John, and Palmer, Pete, eds., with Michael Gershman. *Total Baseball*. New York: HarperCollins, 1993.

Williams, Ted, with Jim Prime. *Ted Williams' Hit List*. Indianapolis, IN: Masters Press, 1996.

Williams, Ted, with John Underwood. *My Turn at Bat: The Story of My Life*. New York: Simon and Schuster, 1969.

VIDEOS

A Century of Success: 100 Years of Cardinals Glory. Major League Baseball Productions, 1992.

Sports Century: Bob Gibson. ESPN, 2003.

Sports Century: Fifty Greatest Athletes—Stan Musial. ESPN, 1999.

WEBSITES

The Ballplayers, online at BaseballLibrary.com (www.baseballlibrary.com/baseballlibrary/ballplayers)

Biographies, online at Hickoksports.com (www.hickoksports.com/hickoksports/biograph)

Historical Stats, online at MLB.com (www.mlb.com/stats.historical/individual stats player)

MLB Awards, online at MLB.com (www.mlb.com/awards/mlb_awards/mvp_history)

The Players, online at Baseballanswers.com (www.baseballanswers.com/topic/stan-musial)

The Players, online at Baseballink.com (www.baseballink.com/baseballink/players)

The Players, online at Baseball-Almanac.com (www.baseball-almanac.com/players)

The Players, online at Baseball-Reference.com (www.baseball-reference.com/players)
The Teams, online at Baseball-Reference.com (www.baseball-reference.com/teams)
TSN All-Stars, online at BaseballChronology.com (www.baseballchronology.com/Baseball/Awards/TSN-AllStars.asp)

INDEX

ABOUT THE AUTHOR

Robert W. Cohen is a lifelong baseball fan and sports historian whose earliest baseball memories revolve around the 1964 World Series, in which the Cardinals defeated the Yankees in seven games. The author of several historical baseball books, including *A Team for the Ages: Baseball's All-Time All-Star Team* (2004), *The Lean Years of the Yankees: 1965–1975* (2004), *Baseball's Hall of Fame—Or Hall of Shame?* (2009), *MVP* (2010), and *The 50 Greatest Players in New York Yankees History* (2012), Cohen has appeared on numerous sports-talk radio programs across the nation to discuss his previously published works. He also previously wrote for TheBaseballPage.com. Originally from the Bronx, New York, Cohen now lives in northern New Jersey with his wife, Li, and daughter, Katie.

Other books by the author include *My Life with Rusty* (2008), *The 50 Most Dynamic Duos in Sports History* (2012), and *Pro Basketball's All-Time All-Stars: Across the Eras* (2013).